CONSTITUTIONALISM BEYOND LIBERALISM

Constitutionalism Beyond Liberalism bridges the gap between comparative constitutional law and constitutional theory. The volume uses the constitutional experience of countries in the Global South - China, India, South Africa, Pakistan, Indonesia and Malaysia - to transcend the liberal conceptions of constitutionalism that currently dominate contemporary comparative constitutional discourse. The alternative conceptions examined include political constitutionalism, societal constitutionalism, state-based conceptions of constitutionalism, and geopolitical conceptions of constitutionalism. Through these examinations, the volume seeks to expand our appreciation of the human possibilities of constitutionalism, exploring constitutionalism not merely as a restriction on the powers of government, but also as creating collective political and social possibilities in diverse geographical and historical settings.

MICHAEL W. DOWDLE is an Associate Professor of Law at the National University of Singapore. His research interests are in comparative public law - in particular public law and constitutionalism as it manifests outside of the countries of the North Atlantic - and regulatory geography.

MICHAEL A. WILKINSON is an Associate Professor of Law at the London School of Economics and Political Science. His research interests include European integration, constitutional theory, and legal, political and social theory.

CONSTITUTIONALISM BEYOND LIBERALISM

Edited by

MICHAEL W. DOWDLE

and

MICHAEL A. WILKINSON

CAMBRIDGE
UNIVERSITY PRESS

CAMBRIDGE
UNIVERSITY PRESS

University Printing House, Cambridge CB2 8BS, United Kingdom

Cambridge University Press is part of the University of Cambridge.

It furthers the University's mission by disseminating knowledge in the pursuit of education, learning, and research at the highest international levels of excellence.

www.cambridge.org
Information on this title: www.cambridge.org/9781107112759

First published 2017

A catalogue record for this publication is available from the British Library

Library of Congress Cataloguing in Publication data
Names: Dowdle, Michael W., editor. |
Wilkinson, Michael (Barrister-at-law), editor.
Title: Constitutionalism beyond liberalism / edited by Michael W. Dowdle, Michael A. Wilkinson.
Description: Cambridge [UK] ; New York : Cambridge University Press, 2016. |
Includes bibliographical references and index.
Identifiers: LCCN 2016033204 | ISBN 9781107112759 (hardback)
Subjects: LCSH: Constitutional law. | State, The. | Liberalism. |
Constitutional law (Islamic law) | BISAC: LAW / Constitutional.
Classification: LCC K3165 .C6239 2016 | DDC 342/.001–dc23
LC record available at https://lccn.loc.gov/2016033204

ISBN 978-1-107-11275-9 Hardback

CONTENTS

PART III The Political Construction of the State

PART IV Solidarity

CONTRIBUTORS

HUGH CORDER
Professor of Public Law, University of Capetown (South Africa)

MICHAEL W. DOWDLE
Associate Professor of Law, National University of Singapore

MARCO GOLDONI
Lecturer in Legal Theory, University of Glasgow (United Kingdom)

ANDREW HARDING
Professor of Law, National University of Singapore

BAOGANG HE
Professor, Nanyang Technological University (Singapore)

MATHEW JOHN
Associate Professor of Law, Jindal Global Law School (India)

CLARK LOMBARDI
UW Law School Foundation Professor of Law, University of Washington (United States of America)

MARTIN LOUGHLIN
Professor of Public Law, London School of Economics and Political Science (United Kingdom)

GUNTHER TEUBNER
Professor of Private Law and Legal Sociology, J. W. Goethe University of Frankfurt (Germany)

MICHAEL A. WILKINSON
Associate Professor of Law, London School of Economics and Political Science (United Kingdom)

ACKNOWLEDGMENTS

The motivation for this study grew out of a workshop that was held on August 29–30, 2012, at the National University of Singapore (NUS) School of Law on 'Exploring the Role of Ideas in Constitutionalism: Constitutionalism and the Paradox of Constitutional Development'. That workshop was funded by a grant from the NUS Academic Research Fund (AcRF). We are grateful to all the participants at the workshop, as well as for the superlative logistical and managerial support given us by Elizabeth Chua, now the Assistant Dean of Research at NUS Law. Finola O'Sullivan at Cambridge University Press showed us much more patience than we deserved in getting the manuscript handed in. The Singapore Symposium for Legal Theory – and in particular Andrew Halpin – also provided much needed encouragement.

We also acknowledge the patience and enthusiasm of our contributors.

Introduction and Overview

MICHAEL W. DOWDLE AND MICHAEL A. WILKINSON

I Purpose of the Volume

This volume seeks to explore the limits of liberal constitutionalism, the belief that constitutions serve principally to constrain state power for the benefit of the individual. The architectural expression of this belief is a set of accompanying structural features: for example, the rule of law, judicial protection of both legal and fundamental rights, representative democracy, and the separation of powers. For convenience, we will refer to this constitutional belief and its institutional expression as 'structural-liberal'. In the literature it is sometimes referred to simply as 'constitutionalism'.[1]

The purpose of the volume is not to dismiss liberal constitutionalism. The focus is *beyond* liberalism, not *against* liberalism. Liberal analyses of constitutionalism, both inside and outside constitutional systems that are considered indigenously 'liberal', remain important.[2] There is much of value to the liberal constitutional tradition, concerning both its embodiment in 'Western' constitutional culture and as a broader human project. But as the structural-liberal vision of constitutionalism has grown to dominate constitutionalism in comparative and cosmopolitan terms, there is an increasing need to explore not just what it does, but also what it doesn't do and what it is unable to account for. In the following text we will explain why.

All perspectives have their limits. The structural-liberal vision developed in response to a particular set of social and political circumstances (see Dowdle and Wilkinson, Chapter 1). These circumstances and concerns are not unique to a particular time and place; they are ubiquitous companions of the modern human condition. Liberal constitutionalism

[1] See, e.g., J. Roland Pennock and John W. Chapman (eds.), *Nomos XX: Constitutionalism* (New York University Press, 1979); Jon Elster and Rune Slagstaad (eds.), *Constitutionalism and Democracy* (Cambridge University Press, 1993); Larry Alexander (ed.), *Constitutionalis m: Philosophical Foundations* (Cambridge University Press, 1998).

[2] See, e.g., Tom Ginsburg and Alberto Simpser (eds.), *Constitutions in Authoritarian Regimes* (Cambridge University Press, 2014).

therefore transcends its terrain of origin. But circumstances and concerns are not exhaustive of a polity's constitutional problems, nor are they necessarily always the most pressing concerns faced by a constitutional culture at a particular point in time. Liberal-constitutional remedies to social or political problems might become inappropriate or unduly limited even in a constitutional culture that venerates the values of freedom on which liberalism professes to be based. These limits are the subject of this volume.

The limited reach of liberal constitutionalism has, to some extent, been recognised from within Western liberal constitutional tradition itself. The liberal vision of constitutionalism today is quite different from that of the late nineteenth century, which is different still from that of the late eighteenth century. It has evolved as the circumstances that it is called upon to make sense of evolve. This evolution is the product of an internal, *self*-reflexive, phenomenon – what Neil Walker has termed 'reflexive constitutionalism'[3] (see also Dowdle and Wilkinson, Chapter 1). It involves the interlinking of an open constitutional structure with a shared *experience* (see also Teubner, Chapter 3), and experience always develops out of a particular time and place.

But liberal constitutionalism is increasingly becoming not simply a domestic but also a *cosmopolitan* project,[4] by which is meant that, across the globe, 'constitutionalism' is increasingly presented as a shared institutional *teleology*. This 'cosmopolitanisation' of liberal constitutionalism is expressed, for example, in the recently made claim that an Enlightenment faith in written constitutions and constitutional courts has 'swept the world'.[5] It is manifest in the academic practice of analysing and critiquing 'foreign' constitutions by cataloguing the presence or absence of canonical structural-liberal features. More practically, it is manifest in the growing influence of international organizations and international constitutional experts, often educated in North Atlantic law schools, in the drafting or reforming of constitutions in countries of the Global South,

[3] Neil Walker, 'EU Constitutionalism and New Governance', in Grainne de Burca and Joanne Scott (eds.), *Law and New Governance in the EU and the US* (Oxford: Hart Publishing, 2006), 15–37. Cf. Hans Lindahl, 'Constituent Power and Reflexive Identity: Towards an Ontology of Collective Selfhood', in Martin Loughlin and Neil Walker (eds.), *The Paradox of Constitutionalism: Constituent Power and Constitutional Form* (Oxford University Press, 2007), 9–27.

[4] Cf. Alexander Somek, *The Cosmopolitan Constitution* (Oxford University Press, 2014).

[5] Bruce Ackerman, 'The Rise of World Constitutionalism', *Virginia Law Review* 83 (1997): 771–797.

and, relatedly, in the growing interest in institutions of higher education in the North Atlantic in training constitutional activists from the Global South.[6]

And herein lies a problem. As stated at the outset, liberalism has its limits. In the context of a domestic liberal constitutionalism, these limits can be transcended in the dynamic of 'constitutional reflexivity' – constitutional reform prompted by collective self-reflection. But as we suggested, constitutional reflexivity also requires experience and knowledge that is 'local' in nature.[7] Cosmopolitan constitutionalism, by contrast, is free-floating, rather than locally rooted and delineated. Here, the local, experiential knowledge that is critical for the effectiveness of constitutional reflexivity is missing, and the limits of the liberal vision become more significant, both analytically and practically. Cosmopolitan constitutionalism then begins to look more like a new form of imperialism constitutionalism.[8] Hence the growing need to explore 'the limits of liberalism' in the context of the human project of constitutionalism.

Constitutional theory in the European tradition has evolved in large part as an alternative to the structural-liberal vision. European constitutionalism diverges in practice from the American because of the significantly greater influence of the French Revolution of the late eighteenth century, the (failed) continental revolutions of the nineteenth century, Marxism, totalitarianism, and the collapse of liberal constitutionalism in Europe between the two world wars (see Wilkinson, Chapter 2). Various strands of constitutional theory have recently surfaced with the aim of excavating traditions of European (including British) constitutionalism, which are as old (and sometimes older) and as developed and embedded as the US variant.

[6] Cf. Yves Dezalay and Bryant G. Garth (eds.), *Global Prescriptions: The Production, Exportation, and Importation of a New Legal Orthodoxy* (Ann Arbor: University of Michigan Press, 2002).

[7] See Clifford Geertz, 'Local Knowledge: Fact and Law in Comparative Perspective', in *Local Knowledge: Further Essays in Interpretive Anthropology*. 3rd ed. (New York: Basic Books, 2000), 167–233; cf. Peter L. Berger and Thomas Luckmann, *The Social Construction of Reality: A Treatise in the Sociology of Knowledge* (New York: Anchor Books, 1967), 47–92, 147–163.

[8] James Tully, 'The Imperialism of Modern Constitutional Democracy', in Martin Loughlin and Neil Walker (eds.), *The Paradox of Constitutionalism: Constituent Power and Constitutional Form* (Oxford University Press, 2007), 315–337.

Instead of focusing on particular constitutional structures, European constitutional theory thus returns to foundational constitutional concepts such as constituent power,[9] republicanism,[10] political constitutionalism,[11] organic constitutionalism,[12] and common law constitutionalism.[13] It sometimes adapts the ancient conception of the constitutional polity as a *corpus* (body), whose relevant dimensions include 'strength' and 'health'.[14] (Some of these conceptions, in turn or independently, have been rediscovered in the American constitutional landscape, albeit often as a variant of rather than challenge to liberalism.[15] Indeed, there are alternative readings of the North American constitutional tradition that build on the fact that its initial experiences and concerns at the time of its founding were authentically distinct from what might be implied by today's orthodox structural-liberal reading.[16])

The divergences and differences between European and American constitutionalism were partially masked in the aftermath of World War II, due both to Europe's existential uneasiness with the direction that German constitutionalism in particular, but also Continental European constitutionalism in general, had travelled in the inter-war period and to the extensive American involvement in and influence over the economic, political, and legal reconstruction of Western Europe.[17] Constitutional rights increasingly became a common point of reference in transatlantic comparative constitutional discourse.[18] But divergence has recently re-emerged, not

[9] See, e.g., Martin Loughlin, 'Constituent Power', in *The Idea of Public Law* (Oxford University Press, 2004), 99–113.

[10] See, e.g., Adam Tomkins, *Our Republican Constitution* (Oxford: Hart Publishing, 2005).

[11] See, e.g., Richard Bellamy, *Political Constitutionalism: A Republican Defence of the Constitutionality of Democracy* (Cambridge University Press, 2007).

[12] See, e.g., David Ritchie, 'Organic Constitutionalism: Rousseau, Hegel and the Constitution of Society', *Journal of Law and Society* 6 (2005): 36–81.

[13] See, e.g., Thomas Poole, 'Back to the Future: Unearthing the Theory of Common Law Constitutionalism', *Oxford Journal of Legal Studies* 23 (2003): 435–454.

[14] See Charles Howard McIlwain, *Constitutionalism: Ancient and Modern* (Ithaca, NY: Cornell University Press, 1958).

[15] See, e.g., Frank Michelman, 'Law's Republic', *Yale Law Journal* 97 (1988): 1493–1537; Bruce Ackerman, *We, the People, Volume 1: Foundations* (Cambridge, MA: Belknap Press, 1993).

[16] See, e.g., Gordon S. Wood, *The Radicalism of the American Revolution* (New York: Vintage Books, 1993), 229–324; cf. Jack N. Rakove, *Original Meanings: Politics and Ideas in the Making of the Constitution* (New York: Vintage Books, 1996), 339–364.

[17] See Mark Mazower, *Dark Continent: Europe's Twentieth Century* (London: Penguin, 1999); Jan Werner Müller, *Contesting Democracy: Political Ideas in Twentieth Century Europe* (Princeton University Press, 2013).

[18] See, e.g., Charles Epp, *The Rights Revolution: Lawyers, Activists, and Supreme Courts in Comparative Perspective* (University of Chicago Press, 1998); cf. Mitchell Lasser, *Judicial Transformations: The Rights Revolution in the Courts of Europe* (Oxford University Press, 2009).

only due to rediscovery of their different historical or conceptual foci, but also due to European resistance to the neo-liberal turn that American constitutionalism began to take and export in the 1980s. The 'new constitutionalism' that accompanied this neo-liberal turn could be identified not only in US-led international institutional developments,[19] but also in the process of European integration, which now appears to have drifted into a neo-liberal form of economic constitutionalism almost by default (through a judge-led process of 'constitutionalisation') (see also Wilkinson, Chapter 2).[20] As a nominally political constitution began to take shape in the move from 'Economic Community' to 'Political Union' through the Maastricht Treaty in 1992 (culminating, so far, in the [anti-] climax of Brexit and the failed attempt to make a European Constitution), and as Europe opened up after the fall of the Berlin Wall and subsequent collapse of the Soviet Union, foundational questions of constituent power and national constitutional identity were put firmly back on the agenda, not only insofar as more peripheral Central and Eastern Europe are concerned,[21] but also in the core of what is now 'political Europe'[22] (and ironically, even in the place where these concerns had most thought to have been laid to rest: the German Constitutional Court[23]).

Because the structural-liberal vision is associated primarily with US constitutionalism, European constitutional theorists, in exploring the possibility of a distinctly European constitutionalism (or otherwise arguing against it), had to engage with the American vision, even if 'from the outside', as it were. Some, to be sure, simply celebrated its perceived

[19] See David Gill, *Power and Resistance in the New World Order* (New York: Palgrave Macmillan, 2003); Gavin Anderson, 'Beyond Constitutionalism beyond the State', *Journal of Law and Society* 39 (2012): 359–383; cf. Andrew Lang, *World Trade Law after Neo-Liberalism: Re-Imagining the Global Economic Order* (Oxford University Press, 2011).

[20] See Martin Loughlin, 'What Is Constitutionalisation?', in Martin Loughlin and Petra Dobner (eds.), *The Twilight of Constitutionalism* (Oxford University Press, 2012), 47–69; Fritz Scharpf, 'The Asymmetry of European Integration: Or, Why the EU Cannot be a "Social Market Economy"' *Socio-Economic Review* 8 (2010): 211–250.

[21] Cf. Ulrich Preuss, 'Constitution-Making and Nation-Building: Reflections on Political Transformations in East and Western Europe', *European Journal of Philosophy* 1 (1993): 81–92.

[22] See, e.g., 2 BvE 2/08 *Treaty of Lisbon*, Judgment of 30 June 2009 (the so-called Lisbon Decision). See also Matthias Kumm, 'Rebel without a Good Cause: Karlsruhe's Misguided Attempt to Draw the CJEU into a Game of "Chicken" and What the CJEU Might Do about It', *German Law Journal* 15 (2014): 203–216.

[23] See Christoph Möllers, '"We Are (Afraid of) the People": Constituent Power in German Constitutionalism', in Martin Loughlin and Neil Walker (eds.), *The Paradox of Constitutionalism: Constituent Power and Constitutional Form* (Oxford University Press, 2007), 87–107.

triumph.[24] For the most part, however, that vision was embraced tentatively. It was often borrowed from, sometimes extensively, but even then constitutional scholars also had to explore if and why it applied to Europe, and if so, to which parts, to which levels of the European Union in its multi-level constitutional architecture, and to which of the many constitutions of Europe.[25] In seeking to understand European constitutionalism, constitutional scholars implicitly engaged with the question of the limits of the American, structural-liberal vision.

The wider implications of these challenges to structural-liberalism as a cosmopolitan project have been limited, however, because, at least to date, constitutional theory in the European tradition has tended to limit its analytical and critical focus to domestic, transnational, and supranational *European* developments. It has neglected to explore how its alternative constitutional insights might resonate outside of Europe: how European visions might compare and contrast with those in places other than the North Atlantic. In sum, if the problem with the structural-liberal vision is that it is cosmopolitan in intent but parochial in sensibility, the problem with the European tradition of constitutional theory is that it is cosmopolitan in sensibility but parochial in intent.[26]

This volume seeks to bring the cosmopolitanism of structural-liberal constitutionalism into communication with the 'post-liberalism' of (European) constitutional theory. In keeping with constitutional theory in the European tradition, it seeks to identify significant aspects of the human experience of constitutionalism that escape the structural-liberal perspective. Departing from this tradition, however, the volume seeks to explore alternatives to structural-liberal constitutionalism from the perspective of a diversity of constitutional perspectives, extending significantly beyond those of the North Atlantic. And unlike the structural-liberal vision of 'comparative constitutional law', this volume approaches these other visions and experiences, not from the perspective of a particular liberal teleotype, but by allowing them to speak, as much as possible, for themselves. In doing so, it seeks to show how listening to alternative

[24] Cf. Matthias Kumm, 'The Best of Times and the Worst of Times: Between Constitutional Triumphalism and Nostalgia' in Martin Loughlin and Petra Dobner (eds.), *The Twilight of Constitutionalism* (Oxford University Press, 2012), 201–220.

[25] See Kaarlo Tuori, 'The Many Constitutions of Europe', in Karlo Tuori and Suvi Sankari (eds.), *The Many Constitutions of Europe* (Farnham, UK: Ashgate, 2010), 3–30.

[26] But see, e.g., Michael Hardt and Antonio Negri, *Empire* (Cambridge, MA: Harvard University Press, 2001).

constitutional experiences will help us perceive the limits of liberalism while keeping track of the vitality of the constitutional project as a human endeavour.

II Organization of the Volume

Our volume is presented in four parts. Part I explores in more detail the limits of the structural-liberal vision, including not only its blind spots (see Chapter 1), but also its possible excesses (see Chapter 2). The remaining three parts explore in detail particular blind spots in the structural-liberal vision, and their implication for the application of that vision and its limits. These include blind spots regarding functional symbiosis (Part II), political construction (Part III), and solidarity (Part IV). Each part begins with a theoretical chapter framing the structural-liberal blind spot to be examined, which is then followed by two 'case-study' chapters exploring this particular blind spot specifically in the context of the constitutional system outside the North Atlantic – China and Pakistan in the context of political constitutionalism; Indonesia and India in the context of functional constitutionalism; and South Africa and Malaysia in the context of solidarity.

Part I explores the limits and problems with the structural-liberal vision. Chapter 1, 'On the Limits of Constitutional Liberalism: In Search of Constitutional Reflexivity', by Michael W. Dowdle and Michael A. Wilkinson, identifies three significant constitutional dynamics that are concealed by the structural-liberal vision. These include dynamics of state construction (liberalism focuses on constraint); dynamics of (spontaneous) evolutionary change (liberalism presumes that constitutionalism is driven by rationality); and the symbiosis between the formal constitution and other social systems (liberalism presumes that constitutionalism is normatively autonomous). These limits are the product of the particular time and place out of which the structural-liberal vision emerged. In other times and places in Europe, other constitutional visions emerged that addressed different experiences and concerns. Up until World War II, these different visions were cross-pollinating, an important cosmopolitan dynamic that helped compensate for the limited perspectives of each. The chapter concludes by arguing that the best way to get 'beyond liberalism' is to re-vitalise this kind of cross-pollination using a process characterised by a principle of charitable interpretation combined with a constitutional introspection that we term *reflexive constitutionalism*.

The second and concluding chapter in Part I, Michael A. Wilkinson's 'The Reconstitution of Postwar Europe: Liberal Excesses, Democratic Deficiencies', uses the experience of the attempt to forge a (regional) European constitutionalism to explore what we are calling the excesses of liberalism – the problems that arise when its limitations are overlooked. It first explores how several basic presumptions that underlie liberal constitutionalism – the relationship between liberalism and state sovereignty, democracy, and capitalism – were problematised first by the constitutional experience of the failure of liberalism of inter-war Europe, and later by Europe's post-war efforts to avoid another breakdown of liberal constitutionalism by forming first an economic and later a political 'union' among the states of Europe. But particularly since the Euro-crisis, these problematic vectors have combined with a short-sighted adherence to 'liberalism' in unexpected ways – ways that are increasingly reminiscent of a de-democratising constitutionalism that Hermann Heller, in the context of the decline of late Weimar Germany, termed 'authoritarian liberalism'. In this configuration, political and even legal liberalism are sacrificed for the purposes of maintaining a project of economic integration.

Part II then explores the problems that can result from structural-liberalism's inability to account for that fact that a constitutional system is not really autonomous, but is actually linked symbiotically to other regulatory systems within its domain (as described by Dowdle and Wilkinson in Chapter 1). It begins with a framing chapter by Gunther Teubner entitled 'Constitutional Drift: Spontaneous Co-evolution of Social "Ideas" and Legal "Form"' (Chapter 3). This chapter evacuates the systemic nature of this symbiosis. It involves the nesting of three distinct epistemic feedback loops, what the chapter calls 'reflexive' epistemic systems. One of these systems involves interaction between the epistemology and experiences that construct the formal constitutional system; a second involves the interaction between the epistemologies and experiences that inform the construction of society, that is, the social system (which includes the political and economic). These two kinds of epistemic feedback loops are then brought into symbiosis by a third, 'meta' feedback loop in which social and constitutional epistemologies interact to generate a binary coding of social and political phenomenon as being either constitutional or unconstitutional (what Teubner refers to as a 'hybrid binary meta-coding'). The chapter then shows how the hybrid nature of this third form of coding – the coding that links the formal constitutional to the social – is innately inter-dependent and co-evolutionary – showing that the social, economic, and political cannot be removed from the constitutional. All must constantly adjust to change in the others if the constitutional writ large is to maintain coherence and historical persistence.

The next two chapters in Part II explore how this symbiosis, and its problematic relationship with liberal constitutionalism, plays out in the particular constitutional understandings and experience of the Global South, specifically Indonesia and India. In Chapter 4, '"Constitutionalism Beyond Liberalism" in Indonesian Competition Regulation: Recognising the Constitutional Role of Dominium', Michael W. Dowdle explores what a particular disagreement between an American antitrust attorney and Indonesian interlocutors over the proper role of Indonesia's competition agency exposes about the limits of the structural-liberal vision. It shows how competition regulation has a particular kind of constitutional character that Terence Daintith has termed 'dominium' – which describes a state pursuing state ends by distributing resources ('dominium') rather than by direct command ('imperium'). Liberalism's focus on state constraint means it has difficulty accounting for the constitutional character of dominium. Competition regulation involves an exercise of dominium, one that involves setting up a symbiotic interplay between the (public) constitutional system and the (private) economic system.

Consistent with liberalism's difficulty accounting for the constitutional quality of acts of dominium, the position adopted by the American antitrust attorney did not account for how distinctive aspects of Indonesia's economy rendered the North Atlantic form of antitrust regulation constitutionally problematic when applied to Indonesia. Not only was the Indonesian vision better suited for Indonesia's economic constitution, it also was consistent with the regulatory practices found in late nineteenth century America, whose economic structuring was consistent with that of present-day Indonesia.

Chapter 5, 'Social Intuitions in the Shadow of Liberal Constitutionalism: An Indian Perspective' by Mathew John, examines how India's liberal vision of constitutionalism has worked to perpetuate pluralist fragmentation of the polity, by preventing symbiosis developing between the formal constitutional understandings of the nature of that pluralism and autochthonous, civilizational intuitions of social identity. The issue of the relationship between India's distinctive civilizational pluralism and its constitutional and national development extend well back into the colonial period. It is an issue that is very much defined by liberalism – liberal constitutionalism presumes a 'We the People' whose constituent members are juristically equal, and thus juristically uniform in constitutional character. England saw Indian society as being innately unequal, given its caste and religious divisions, and sought to pave the way for ultimate juristic equality and uniformity by using special legal 'minority rights' to induce some degree of greater political equality within India's polity. This practice continued after independence, driven by structural-liberal understanding that political equality, and hence political identity, has to be *juridically* constituted (compare Wilkinson, Chapter 2). But at the same time, such remedial juridical treatment conflicts with Indian civilizational understandings about the social meaning of one's cultural 'identity'. And consistent with the analysis in Chapter 3, the resulting disconnect between what Teubner calls the formal constitutional and the social systems prevents the constitutional system from developing a coherent symbiosis with the social system.

This brings us to Part III, which explores the problems that can result from structural-liberalism's inability to account for the innately political aspects of constitutional coherence. The framing chapter for this part is by Martin Loughlin, entitled 'On Constituent Power' (Chapter 6), which shows how these lacunae in the conceptual reach of structural-liberalism derives from that vision's structural focus on constitutional form. Constituent power – the constitutional 'We the People' – by contrast, ultimately defies formal delineation. Loughlin outlines three historical approaches to the idea of constituent power. The first, which he labels 'normativist', and which corresponds to what we call the 'liberal-structural model', attempts to disarm or even discard the idea of constituent power by associating constitutionalism with juridifiable rights. The second, the 'decisionist' approach, which developed in reaction to the normativist approach, equates the idea of constituent power with the expression of a sovereign will, but one that is utterly unbound by law. Loughlin concludes by advocating a third, 'relational' approach, which both preserves and goes beyond liberalism by conceptualising constituent power as inhering in the active tension between claims of juridical right and expressions of political will, producing a constitutional dynamic driven primarily by contestations over political right (*droit politique*) rather than juridical right. In contrast to both normativism (liberalism) and decisionism, the relational account of the constituent power is able to capture the innately paradoxical relationship between the formal aspect of constitutionalism (i.e., the polity as subject) and constituent power (i.e., the polity as ruler – a.k.a. the 'popular sovereign').

Our two 'case studies' of this aspect of constitutionalism involve efforts to promote constitutional development in China and in Pakistan. In both cases, we see what we might call 'constitutional entrepreneurs' trying to negotiate the inability of liberal constitutionalism by itself to establish a meaningful connection between constitutional form and the distinctive ideational aspects of the constituent power in their respective polities. In Chapter 7, 'Socialist Constitutionalism in Contemporary China', Baogang He recounts recent ongoing debates taking place regarding the possible future trajectories of China's ongoing constitutional evolution. In these debates, we see elements of liberalism, socialism, and another constitutional tradition, Leninism, colliding and jostling to generate new possibilities insofar as China's constitutional future is concerned, very much along the lines of 'reflexive constitutionalism' as described in the preceding text (and which is described in more detail in Chapter 1). Moreover, these debates are also ongoing despite recent political efforts in China to discourage and censor these types of discussions. In this sense, Professor He gives us a fascinating glimpse into what we might call a 'spontaneous' form of constituting power – one that is amorphous, subject to periodic suppression through deployment of party-constitutional regulatory *form*, but that continues to be active and actually does work to propel regime evolution.[27]

Clark Lombardi's chapter on 'Islamic Constitutionalism Beyond Liberalism' (Chapter 8), explores how beginning in the 1960s, A. R. Cornelius – a liberal, Cambridge-educated Christian who sat on the Pakistani Supreme Court from 1951 through 1968, and who continued to be politically active until his death in 1991 – started advocating that Pakistan could better promote and protect liberal legal values, such as those embedded in the principles of natural justice democracy, by developing a constitutionalism founded on precepts of Islamic law rather than through the innately secular constitutionalism of liberalism. This was because the Pakistani population overwhelmingly identified itself in terms of being Islamic: linking the constitution to this identity, he argued, would catalyse the development

[27] See, e.g., Michael W. Dowdle, 'Of Parliaments, Pragmatism and the Dynamics of Constitutional Development: The Curious Case of China', *New York University Journal of International Law and Politics* 35 (2002): 1–200. See, generally, Stéphanie Balme and Michael W. Dowdle (eds.), *Building Constitutionalism in China* (New York: Palgrave Macmillan, 2009).

of what we are calling 'constituent power'. This, in turn, would allow the constitution to develop and maintain persistence and authority even in the face of internal political challenge – particularly from the military, to whom Pakistan's largely secular political-economic elites were consistently turning when they feared they were losing their political control to often-radicalised political–Islamic elements. With this constituent support and newfound intellectual authority, Justifying their judgments in Islamic jurisprudential terms Pakistani judges could begin identifying within that jurisprudence functional parallels to liberalism whose support and effectiveness would be similar to those liberal legal-constitutional articulations enjoyed in Christian polities. Cornelius's counsel went unheeded. But more recent developments in Pakistan suggest the Cornelius 'might have been on to something': today, express judicial appeal to distinctly Islamic legal principles – often smuggled into Pakistan's legal system through judicial activism – is showing itself to be a surprisingly significant vehicle for defending social arrangements associated elsewhere with the values of 'liberalism'.

In Part IV, we explore a related dynamic: solidarity. Solidarity refers to the polity's identification with the state – to the identification of the state as a common endeavor or telos. In Chapter 9, Marco Goldoni helps us locate this particular aspect of constitutionalism, as contrasted to the liberal vision, by looking at the constitutional thought of Jean-Jacques Rousseau, and in particular his explication of the phenomenon he famously called 'the general will'. Through that vision, Rousseau reminds us that a properly functioning state requires not simply constraints on governmental power, but also imposing constraints on individual autonomy. It is through imposing such constraints that the general will is created, in the process transforming individuals into citizens. Such a transformation requires a certain degree of substantive, or material, equality. Here is where the limits of liberalism lie insofar as solidarity is concerned, because liberalism – with its focus on promoting individual autonomy – has a hard time perceiving, much less incorporating, this need for substantive equality into its constitutional framework (cf. Dowdle, Chapter 4, discussing dominium).

Our final two chapters then present case studies of constitutional solidarity, and its uneasy relationship with constitutional liberalism, as it has played out recently in Malaysia and South Africa. In 'Constitutional Trajectory in Malaysia: Constitutionalism without Consensus?' (Chapter 10), Andrew Harding describes a constitutional system that, like that of Pakistan as described by Lombardi in Chapter 8 has oscillated between and continues to be torn between secular-liberal and

Islamic-nationalist visions of itself. Its polity is similarly fragmented into two distinct political solidarities and organised around a historically defined confluence of ethnic, religious, and economic classes (basically a Malay-Muslim, largely agrarian, and urban working class and a Chinese-secular economic elite). One of the ways in which the Malaysian government has sought to preserve some sort of solidarity in the face of such class cleavage has been by implementing supposedly remedial ethnic distributions of certain kinds of employment, educational, and entrepreneurial opportunities in pursuit of better material equality. And although the *actual* remedial effect of these policies (often rhetorically grouped together under the term *New Economic Policy*) is questionable, its social meaning is not: greater material equality, it asserts, is a necessary condition for national solidarity. And along these lines (and consistent with the constitutional thinking of Rousseau), it is quite remarkable how Malaysia's constitutional system has been able to preserve a persistent degree of stability, longevity, and social peace in the face of such pronounced, persistent, and sometimes *politically-legally* intense cleavages.

Our second case study in solidarity, and the final chapter in this volume, is Hugh Corder's exploration of the quest for solidarity in South Africa, entitled 'A Sense of Grievance and the Quest for Freedom: South Africa's Constitution – the Struggle Continues' (Chapter 11). This quest for solidarity, according to Corder, is manifest in the continual weaving and re-weaving of two core imperatives that have driven South African political consciousness since the onset of English colonisation in the early nineteenth century. These imperatives, what Corder calls 'a sense of grievance' and 'a quest for freedom', are often symbiotic with one another, grievance giving rise to demand for freedom that would then give rise to grievances in others. As in Harding's chapter on Malaysia (Chapter 10), Corder see this *common* framing of often intense intergroup political conflict in South Africa as a possible and positive source of constitutional solidarity. But as per Rousseau, it will ultimately have to be a radical-*transformative* solidarity rather than a liberal-contractual solidarity – a solidarity that needs to *transcend* history, rather than one that serves primarily to preserve earlier constitutional bargains from state usurpations.[28]

[28] Compare Stephen Holmes, *Passions and Constraints: On the Theory of Liberal Democracy* (University Press of Chicago, 1995), 135.

III Conclusion

Again, to reiterate, none of these chapters reject the liberal vision. All are sympathetic to it. What they explore are those places and instances in which the liberal vision gives out, and – either through theory or through practical exploration – a way out has to be found without its guidance.

At the end of the day, like 'liberalism', 'beyond liberalism' can be seen as a quest for a particular kind of freedom – what is often termed *positive freedom*. This is the freedom, not from constraints, but the freedom to overcome the constraints that do inevitably and even necessarily encumber us. In the context of the human project of constitutionalism, these constraints include the constraints of the liberal vision itself. In this way, exploring incidents and exercises of 'constitutionalism beyond liberalism' is very much a 'liberal' project.

PART I

Limits of the Structural-Liberal Vision

1

On the Limits of Constitutional Liberalism: In Search of Constitutional Reflexivity

MICHAEL W. DOWDLE AND MICHAEL A. WILKINSON

I. Introduction: The Foundation of Structural Liberalism

The modern, liberal vision of constitutionalism – what we are calling structural-liberalism – has contributed greatly to the human experience of constitutionalism and has come to dominate the 'comparative' constitutional imagination – that is, 'comparative constitutional law'. But, like all regulatory ideas, it is a product of particular circumstances: Its foci reflect the concerns of time and place. These concerns and prescriptions are important, but at the same time, they inevitably overlook – or conceal – other concerns that can shape constitutionalism in other times and places.

This 'structural-liberal' vision brings together two components: a liberal component, which defines the purpose of constitutionalism to be one of limiting state power;[1] and a structural component, which identifies a particular set of institutional devices – for example, judicial review, rule of law, protection of rights, separation of powers, democratic elections – as being necessary to achieve that purpose.[2] It derives primarily from the particular constitutional concerns and experiences that accompanied efforts to construct a 'United States' immediately after achieving independence from the English in the late eighteenth century: These include an ineffectual central-level government, operating in relative safety from a geo-political perspective,[3]

[1] See, e.g., Graham Maddox, 'Constitution', in Terence Ball, James Farr, and Russell L. Handon (eds.), *Political Innovation and Conceptual Change* (Cambridge University Press, 1989), 50–67; Stephen Holmes, *Passions and Constraint: On the Theory of Liberal Democracy* (Chicago: University of Chicago Press, 1995).

[2] See, e.g., Louis Henkin, 'A New Birth of Constitutionalism: Genetic Influences and Genetic Defects', in Michel Rosenfeld (ed.), *Constitutionalism, Identity, Difference, and Legitimacy* (Durham, NC: Duke University Press, 1994), 39–53.

[3] Akhil Reed Amar, 'Some New World Lessons for the Old World', *University of Chicago Law Review* 58 (1991): 483–510.

but facing significant internal dissatisfaction.[4] The principal purpose of the resulting Constitution of 1789 was thus to create a strong central government capable of bringing internal coherence to the country.

In order to do that, however, it would have to reign in a budding 'constituent power' that was increasingly hostile to the conservative economic views of the (pre-) national political elite.[5] This required diluting the powers of then quite autonomous 'states' that would constitute the union. Supporters of the state governments thus expressed their opposition to the proposed constitution by portraying the central government it created as an unnecessary threat to existing liberties. Because the American state was not under even remote military or existential threat, the debate surrounding the ratification of the constitution focused on whether the central government would be internally overbearing, rather than on whether it would be effective at carrying out national policy or in resisting outside interference.[6]

The newness of post-independence America, and its democratic fragility (as evinced, most particularly, by Shays' Rebellion, the direct inspiration for the drafting of the new constitution[7]), discouraged supporters of the new constitution from appealing to national solidarity or to constituent power as the principal device for protecting these liberties. In fact, as noted in the preceding text, the constitution was intended in part to constrain constituent power, as Madison famously acknowledged in his 10th Federalist.[8] Therefore its defenders, using the mechanical political-economic analyses used by the Baron de Montesquieu to explain the success of the English constitution, focused on particularities of the new constitution's institutional design that, they argued, would prevent the dangerous aggrandisements of political power feared by that constitution's political opponents.[9]

And so emerged the particular foci of the structural-liberal vision – a focus on safety rather than efficiency (because the territorial United States would never seriously be threatened by an outside force[10]); and a focus on structure

[4] See Gordon S. Wood, *The Radicalism of the American Revolution* (New York: Vintage Books, 1993), 229–324.

[5] See id. at 234–270.

[6] See, generally, Ralph Ketcham (ed.), *The Anti-Federalist Papers and the Constitutional Debates* (New York: New American Library, 1986).

[7] Michael Lienesche, 'Reinterpreting Rebellion: The Influence of Shays's Rebellion on American Political Thought', in Robert A Gross (ed.), *In Debt to Shays: The Bicentennial of an Agrarian Rebellion* (Charlottesville: University Press of Virginia, 1993), 161–182.

[8] See, generally, Wood, *The Radicalism of the American Revolution*, 234–270.

[9] See id. at XX.

[10] See Amar, 'Some New-World Lessons'.

rather than on constituent power (because constituent power was the danger that the constitution was trying to overcome[11]). Over the succeeding two centuries, elements would be added to and subtracted from the structural pantheon as the United States responded to new regulatory problems – Tocqueville would introduce 'democracy' in the mid-nineteenth century, and progressivism would then convert that democracy from a participatory democracy to an electoral democracy towards the end of that century.[12] The modern, positivist understanding of the 'rule of law'[13] would also emerge in the late nineteenth century as a regulatory response to national industrialisation.[14] At the same time, industrialisation would also cause the pre-eminent status that the 'right to property' had enjoyed in the nineteenth-century constitution to be considerably demoted.[15] In the aftermath of World War II, the increasing pluralisation of American political society would lead to the substitution of equality for liberty as the constitutional telos.[16]

The American structural-liberal vision was not the only constitutionalism to emerge out of the revolutions of the late eighteenth and early nineteenth centuries. Different visions were to emerge out of Revolutionary France;[17] and Tory,[18] Whiggish,[19] and

[11] Wood, *The Radicalism of the American Revolution*, 234–270.

[12] See Michael W. Dowdle, 'Public Accountability in Alien Terrain: Exploring for Constitutional Accountability in the People's Republic of China', in Michael W. Dowdle (ed.), *Public Accountability: Designs, Dilemmas and Experiences* (Cambridge University Press, 2006), 337–342.

[13] See, e.g., Joseph Raz, 'The Rule of Law and Its Virtue', in *The Authority of Law: Essays on Law and Morality*. 2nd ed. (Oxford University Press, 2009), 210–231. Compare A. V. Dicey, 'The Rule of Law: Its Nature and Application', in *Introduction to the Study of the Law of the Constitution*. 10th ed. (ed., E. C. S. Wade) (London: Macmillan, 1982 [1885]), 183–205.

[14] See Dowdle, 'Public Accountability in Alien Terrain', 332–337; cf. Michael J. Piore and Charles F. Sabel, *The Second Industrial Divide: Possibilities for Prosperity* (New York: Basic Books, 1984), 49–54.

[15] See Mary Ann Glendon, 'Rights in Twentieth-Century Constitutions', *University of Chicago Law Review* 59 (1992): 519–538.

[16] See, generally, Joseph Tussman and Jacobus ten Broek, 'The Equal Protection of the Laws', *California Law Review* 37 (1949): 341–381. Cf. United States v. Carolene Products Co., 304 U.S. 144, 152–53 n.4 (1938).

[17] See Keith Michael Baker, *Inventing the French Revolution: Essays on French Political Culture in the Eighteenth Century* (Cambridge University Press, 1990), 252–306.

[18] See, e.g., Edmund Burke, *Reflections on the Revolution in France* (ed. J.G.A. Pocock) (Indianapolis: Hackett Publishing Company, 1987) (originally published 1790). See, generally, A. V. Dicey, *Lectures on the Relation between Law and Public Opinion in England during the Nineteenth Century* (ed., Richard VandeWetering) (Indianapolis: Liberty Fund, 2008). 45–46, 51–90.

[19] See, e.g., A. V. Dicey, *Introduction to the Study of the Law of the Constitution* (1885).

radical[20] England. These visions were also addressed to their own distinct sets of problems, and often interacted with each other and with the structural-liberal vision, changing and being changed as each continually experienced new kinds of concerns.

But after the end of World War II, these other visions would be significantly overshadowed in Western constitutional consciousness by the structural-liberal vision, as American political influence came to dominate the 'Western' (American and Western European) world as a result of the material and psychological destruction of Europe and the political dynamics of the Cold War. Today, the structural-liberal vision currently enjoys a virtually hegemonic preeminence in a number of important international and geo-political settings: including law and development,[21] law and economics,[22] human rights,[23] 'comparative constitutional law,'[24] and the 'global model' of constitutional rights.[25] But as we shall see, such hegemonic dominance is problematic when applied to constitutional situations that differ from those the structural-liberal vision evolved to address. And this counsels that we need to be more aware of the limits of its vision, and of how they can be overcome.

The remainder of this chapter will proceed in three parts. The second part will explore some of the principal blind spots in the structural-liberal vision. These include a relative disinterest in issues of state-building; difficulties identifying dynamics of constitutional evolution; and an inability to account for the interdependences that tie the effectiveness of particular constitutional structures to particular environmental factors that lie outside the structural-liberal field of vision. The third part will then explore how the structural-liberal vision relates to the other European visions of constitutionalism, particularly the Rousseauean vision and the radical vision of early-industrial England. Finally, Part IV will examine how these limitations might be transcended.

[20] See E. P. Thompson, *The Making of the English Working Class*, rev. ed. (London: Penguin Books, 1991), 111–203. Cf. Dicey, *Lectures*, 150–214.

[21] See, e.g., Noah Feldman, 'Imposed Constitutionalism', *Connecticut Law Review* 37 (2005): 857–889.

[22] See, e.g., John Morison, Kieran McEvoy, and Gordon Anthony (eds.), *Judges, Transition, and Human Rights* (Oxford University Press, 2007).

[23] See, e.g., Tom Ginsburg (ed.), *Comparative Constitutional Design* (Cambridge University Press, 2014).

[24] See Günter Frankenberg, 'Constitutional Transfer: The IKEA Theory Revisited', *International Journal of Constitutional Law* 8 (2010): 563–579.

[25] Kai Mollers, *The Global Model of Constitutional Rights* (Oxford University Press, 2012).

II. The Structural-Liberal Vision of Constitutionalism and Its Blind Spots

A. *State Building*

A constitution plays a significant role in the dynamic process of state building.[26] This is missed in a vision of constitutionalism that approaches it solely as a program of limiting public powers through legal norms. Such a model is incapable of exploring how the constitution gains meaningful purchase in an environment in which the driving concern is one of *creating* state power where the state itself is weak or non-existent.

There is thus irony in the fact that the US Constitution of 1789 was a good example of this process of constitutional state-building, given its subsequent influence on the structural-liberal vision of state-limitation. As noted by Hannah Arendt, the self-conception of the American founders speaks in an entirely clear, unambiguous language: Their question "was not how to limit power but how to establish it, not how to limit government but how to found a new one."[27]

Where it does direct its attention to state-building, the structural-liberal vision's focus is on the development of government regulatory capacity – what Martin Loughlin refers to as 'governance' (see also Dowdle, Chapter 4).[28] However, there is another aspect of state-building that is less well recognised, and equally essential to the constitutional project, but which is largely obscured by the structural-liberal vision. This involves the development of a 'We the People' – that is, the development of the state as an organic construct rather than simply a collection of rules. (See, e.g., Wilkinson, Chapter 2; John, Chapter 5.)

However heterogeneous they be, 'We the People' provide the symbolic unity that underlies the authority of the modern constitution.[29] As Ulrich Preuss has noted, in modern terms 'a constitution involves the idea of

[26] See also Hannah Arendt, *On Revolution* (London: Penguin, 2006), 145.

[27] Id. at 148.

[28] Martin Loughlin, *Foundations of Public Law* (Oxford University Press, 2010), 275–466; see especially id. at 407–434.

[29] See Simone Chambers, 'Democracy, Popular Sovereignty, and Constitutional Legitimacy', *Constellations* 11 (2004): 153–173. Cf. Hans Lindahl, 'Sovereignty and Representation in the EU', in Neil Walker (ed.) *Sovereignty in Transition* (Oxford: Hart Publishing, 2003), 87–115.

an authority and an author whose willpower is the ultimate cause of the polity.'[30] But this is a reflexive process. As Sheldon Wolin commented on the occasion of the bicentenary of the US constitution:

> [A] constitution not only constitutes a structure of power and authority, it constitutes a people in a certain way. It proposes a distinctive identity and envisions a form of politicalness for individuals in their new collective capacity.[31]

The true import of the constitutional need to reflect a 'We the People' is neatly illustrated in the recently failed European Constitutional project, a polity-building exercise which calculated – in hindsight *mis*calculated – 'the power of the constitutional word'.[32] This project failed – or has failed so far – because there is no distinctly 'European' constituent political identity to undergird it.[33] And as will be demonstrated later in this volume, this constitutional failure is a product, at least in significant part, of Europe's pursuit of a liberal constitutional vision (see Wilkinson, Chapter 2).

B. *Change*

All constitutional systems evolve. And they often evolve in ways that are not foreseen by their founders; or even perceived by their contemporaries. They even can evolve in ways that run counter to the intentions both of their founders – as was the case with Jacksonian Democracy in the United States, for example[34] – and current political elites – a process that elsewhere has been referred to as 'runaway legitimation', and that Tocqueville described so well in the context of the French Revolution.[35] Indeed, the

[30] Ulrich K. Preuss, 'Constitutional Power-Making for the New Polity: Some Deliberations on the Relations between the Constituent Power and the Constitution', *Cardozo Law Review* 14 (1992–1993): 639–660.

[31] Seldon Wolin, *The Presence of the Past: Essays on the State and the Constitution* (Baltimore: The Johns Hopkins University Press, 1989), 9.

[32] See J. H. H. Weiler, 'On the Power of the Word: Europe's Constitutional Iconography', *International Journal of Constitutional Law* 3 (2005): 173–190.

[33] Michael A. Wilkinson, 'Political Constitutionalism and the European Union', *Modern Law Review* 76 (2013): 191–222.

[34] See Wood, *The Radicalism of the American Revolution*, 347–370.

[35] See Alexis de Tocqueville, *The Old Regime and the Revolution* (ed., François Furet and Françoise Mélonio) (trans., Alan S. Kahan) (University of Chicago Press, 1998), 230–233, 241–248; see also Jon Elster, 'Strategic Uses of Argument', in Kenneth Arrow et al. (eds.), *Barriers to Conflict Resolution* (New York: W. W. Norton, 1995), 250; Michael W. Dowdle, 'Constitutional Listening', *Chicago-Kent Law Review* 88 (2012): 121–125.

ability to spontaneously adapt to broader environmental changes may be a critical element of constitutional survival.

But such evolution subtly contradicts the predicates of the structural-liberal model, which claims to work by legally assigning and locking-in, in some cases indefinitely, particular configurations of state and non-state power.[36] Such a scheme presumes an ability to strategically control state power: to be able to intentionally disaggregate it, assign it, and limit it to some particular constellation of institutional sites. Constitutional evolution, by contrast, involves the release and reconfiguration of state power in ways that exceed the reins of strategic intentionality.[37] The spontaneous character of this evolution suggests that even in the most mature and robust of constitutional systems, public power is able to evade, or circumvent the formal constitutional architecture, extending itself in ways that bypass initial design constraints.

But at the same time, such spontaneous evolution need not be destructive for the project of constitution-building. On the contrary, challenge and disruption might be necessary in order to 'destabilise' dominant but unsustainable constitutional ideas and practices, to provoke an internal response to an external noise.[38] Indeed, the hallmark of a mature constitutional system might be in structurally recognising when spontaneous circumvention is necessary in order to respond to new imperatives, and in nevertheless being able to ensure that this evolution preserves the constitution's foundational spirit. Again, this is problematic for the structural-liberal vision, because that vision regards un-channelled public power as innately corrupting and dangerous.[39]

While such concerns are often justified, liberalism nevertheless ultimately fails to account for the political reality of constitutional survival. The fact that in all successful constitutions, including liberal ones, power always demonstrates capacity to evade strategic control, and yet nevertheless often ends up contributing to rather than corrupting the constitutional project, suggests strongly that the liberal constitutionalists' blanket

[36] See David Sciulli, *Theory of Societal Constitutionalism: Foundations of a Non-Marxist Critical Theory* (Cambridge University Press, 1992), 1–15.

[37] Cf. Colin Scott, 'Spontaneous Accountability', in Michael W. Dowdle (ed.), *Public Accountability: Designs, Dilemmas and Experiences* (Cambridge University Press, 2006), 174–191; Cf. Gunther Teubner, 'Juridification: Concepts, Aspects, Limits, Solutions', in Robert Baldwin, Colin Scott, and Christopher Hood (eds.), *A Reader on Regulation* (Oxford University Press, 1998), 406–414.

[38] See Sciulli, *Societal Constitutionalism*; Roberto Mangabeira Unger, *The Critical Legal Studies Movement* (Cambridge, MA: Harvard University Press, 1986), 23, 31–32.

[39] See, e.g., Holmes, *Passions and Constraints*.

fear of 'unbridled power' is too simplistic. Sometimes, a constitution needs power to free itself at least somewhat from its constitutional constraints – for the sake of that constitution's own survival.[40]

In short, the structural-liberal vision of constitutionalism cannot satisfactorily account for the phenomena of evolutionary change and revolutionary rupture. In fact, it effectively presumes that our knowledge of the possibilities and impossibilities of constitutionalism and its future is already complete,[41] a presumption that David Sciulli has well-termed 'the presupposition of exhausted possibilities' in the context of American constitutional thought.[42] To identify, for example, constitutionalism with judicial supremacy leaves no conceptual purchase for critical reflection on the possibility that in particular environments there are other ways of achieving the ends that judicial supremacy is supposed to achieve; and that in at least some of these environments, these alternative means may represent improvements over the structural-liberal understanding.[43] By linking liberalism to particular institutional structures, and then by identifying constitutionalism primarily by the presence of these structures, structural-liberalism not only fails to explain constitutional evolution, it also fails to leave conceptual room for constitutional innovation and idiosyncrasy.[44]

C. *Structural Symbiosis*

The structural-liberal vision treats the constitution as a normatively autonomous system.[45] It rejects interdependencies with environmental factors that lie outside its normative grasp (although within the liberal tradition, there are different understandings of what territory is included within that grasp – for example, whether the organisation of capital – the particular 'variety of capitalism'[46] – is or is not a part of the constitution's

[40] Cf. Bruce Ackerman, *We the People*, vol. 1: *Foundations* (Cambridge (MA): Belknap Press, 1991).

[41] See, e.g., Francis Fukuyama, *The End of History and the Last Man* (New York: Simon and Schuster, 1992).

[42] See, e.g., Sciulli, *Societal Constitutionalism*, 9–10.

[43] See Olivier Beaud, 'Reframing a Debate among Americans: Contextualising a Moral Philosophy of Law', *International Journal of Constitutional Law* 7 (2009): 53–68. Cf. Michael W. Dowdle, 'On the Public-Law Character of Competition Law: A Lesson from Asian Capitalism', *Fordham International Law Journal* 38 (2015): 303–305.

[44] See also Michael C. Dorf and Charles F. Sabel, 'A Constitution of Democratic Experimentalism', *Columbia Law Review* 98 (1998): 270–291.

[45] See Ronald Dworkin, *Law's Empire* (Cambridge, MA: Harvard University Press, 1986); cf. John Rawls, *A Theory of Justice* (Cambridge, MA: Harvard University Press, 1971).

[46] See Peter A. Hall and David Soskice (eds.), *Varieties of Capitalism: The Institutional Foundations of Comparative Advantage* (Oxford University Press, 2001).

normative universe[47]). Thus, for example, in the context of American constitutionalism, structural-liberalism for the most part perceives no *normative* distinction between the constitution of the agrarian and pre-industrial America of early nineteenth century, and that of the post-industrial America of today.[48]

In fact, constitutions are not normatively autonomous. Their prescriptions are continually shaped and reshaped by aspects of their environment that elude their own cognitive grasp (see Teubner, Chapter 3). For example, American understandings of the normative shapes of democracy, rule of law, and separation of powers were all fundamentally reconfigured by the rapid onset of Fordist industrialisation (what Alfred Chandler has famously called 'managerial capitalism'[49]) during the latter third of the nineteenth century.

Structural-liberalism has no handle with which to conceptualise this. Thus, for example, the structural-liberal tradition often attributes the collapse of the Weimar Republic to its inadequate constitutional institutions, particularly its lack of judicial review.[50] In doing so, however, it ignores the social devastation and corresponding political panic that was caused by the onset of the Great Depression. Could the German judiciary really have halted such a panic during such a crisis? If so, how? The American Supreme Court Justice Sandra Day O'Connor's observation about the limits of judicial power, even in the United States, is worth repeating here:

> [T]he Court cannot buy support for its decisions by spending money and, except to a minor degree, it cannot independently coerce obedience to its decrees. The Court's power lies, rather, in its legitimacy, a product of substance and perception that shows itself in the people's acceptance of the Judiciary as fit to determine what the nation's law means and to declare what it demands.[51]

[47] Compare Ronald Dworkin, *A Matter of Principle* (Cambridge, MA: Harvard University Press, 1986), chs. 12–13, with Milton Friedman, *Capitalism and Freedom* (University of Chicago Press, 1962).

[48] See, e.g., David A. J. Richards, *Foundations of American Constitutionalism* (Oxford University Press, 1989). Cf. Hans Kelsen, *Pure Theory of Law* (trans., Max Knight) (Berkeley: University of California Press, 1967), 193–223.

[49] Alfred D. Chandler, Jr., 'The Emergence of Managerial Capitalism', *The Business History Review* 58 (1984): 473–503

[50] See Christoph Mollers, "The Scope and Legitimacy of Judicial Review in German Constitutional Law – the Court versus the Political Process', in Hermann Punder and Christian Waldhoff (eds.), *Debates in German Public Law* (Oxford: Hart Publishing, 2014).

[51] Planned Parenthood of Southeastern Pa. v. Casey, 505 U.S. 833, 865 (1992).

A polity in significant material need or existential insecurity will not put much stock in the value of the abstract norms articulated by a remote judge.[52] They will not put much value in the abstract norms articulated by a constitutional text regardless of whether they *should* or not.[53] Weimar Germany was not the only European country threatened by constitutional collapse in the 1930s.[54] England was vulnerable too.[55] The English constitutional system survived of course (the Great Depression was not as brutal there as it was in Germany). But at the same time, it was also able to do so without judicial review. Structural-liberalism has no explanation for how it was able to do so, when Germany could not.

When considerations of systemic symbiosis are brought fully into perspective, the structural-liberal model can seem distorting and even dysfunctional. By obscuring systemic interdependencies, the liberal vision shines a far too narrow light on the range of difficulties that can effect constitutional survival.[56] Similarly, it also threatens to misconstrue, by obscuring and mislabelling as ersatz, constitutional structures and dynamics that diverge from those in the structural-liberal pantheon, but which nevertheless may be more promising and/or appropriate in light of that particular constitutional system's larger social environment (see especially Dowdle, Chapter 4).[57]

Another example involves the relationship between the constitution and the socio-economic-industrial structure of the polity, an issue that has recently been revitalised in the wake of the Global Financial

[52] Cf. Ronald Inglehart and Daphna Oyserman, 'Individualism, Autonomy and Self-Expression: The Human Development Syndrome', in Henk Vinken, Joseph Soeters, and Peter Ester (eds.), *Comparing Cultures, Dimensions of Culture in a Comparative Perspective* (Leiden, The Netherlands: Brill, 2004), 74–96.

[53] See Harold James, 'Economic Reasons for the Collapse of the Weimar Republic', in Ian Kershaw (ed.), *Weimar: Why Did German Democracy Fail?* (New York: St. Martin's Press, 1990), 30–57; see also John Maynard Keynes, 'A Short View of Russia', in *The Collected Writings of John Maynard Keynes*, vol. 9 (London: Macmillan, 1971), 253–271.

[54] See Mark Mazower, *Dark Continent: Europe's Twentieth Century* (London: Penguin, 1999), 17–27; Fritz Stern, 'The New Democracies in Crisis in Interwar Europe', in Axel Hadenius (ed.), *Democracy's Victory and Crisis* (Cambridge University Press, 1997), 15–25.

[55] See Mazower, *Dark Continent*, xx; see, e.g., Keynes, 'A Short View of Russia'.

[56] See Pasuk Phongpaicht and Chris Baker, *Thailand's Crisis* (Singapore: Institute of Southeast Asian Studies, 2000), 35–82; Asli U. Bali, 'Justice under Occupation: Rule of Law and the Ethics of Nation-Building in Iraq', *Yale Journal of International Law* 30 (2005): 431–472.

[57] See Phongpaicht and Baker, *Thailand's Crisis*, 97–104; see also, e.g., John Braithwaite, Valerie Braithwaite, Michael Cookson, and Leah Dunn, *Anomie and Violence: Non-truth and Reconciliation in Indonesian Peacebuilding* (Canberra: ANU E Press, 2010); cf. Dorf and Sabel, 'A Constitution of Democratic Experimentalism', 270–291.

Crisis.[58] Structural-liberalism's inability to visualise the constitution's interdependence with its surrounding social environment can lend it to induce dysfunctional economic biases into its normative prescriptions. Structural-liberalism tends to conflate the economic constitution (i.e., the way a constitution should distribute wealth and resources within its polity) with what we might call the constitution of liberty (i.e., the way a constitution should distribute 'liberty', and especially negative liberty, within its polity) (a conflation that sometimes referred to as 'Manchester liberalism').[59] This causes structural-liberalism to privilege demands for procedural or formal equality over demands for material equality; and that, in turn, causes it generally to privilege demands for economic (neo-)liberalism over demands for social democracy (see also Wilkinson, Chapter 2).[60] But as has been re-emphasised since the Global Financial Crisis, material equality is an equally important factor for constitutional success: Issues of material equality cannot be compensated for simply by promoting greater procedural (formal) equality.[61]

III. Interlocking Visions

As described in the introduction to this chapter, other visions of constitutionalism exist – each, like the structural-liberal vision, adapted to address a particular set of concerns and problems, which have their own non-parochial relevance. In France, the Jacobins – inspired by Rousseau – developed a vision of constitutionalism that celebrated *le pouvoir constituent* – constituent power (see Loughlin, Chapter 6; Goldoni, Chapter 9). In England, a 'radical' vision of constitutionalism,[62] was catalysed by the on-set of industrialisation in the late eighteenth and early nineteenth century.[63] At the same time, this

[58] See, e.g., Gunther Teubner, *Financial Crisis in Constitutional Perspective: The Dark Side of Functional Differentiation* (Oxford: Hart Publishing, 2011).

[59] See Peter Evans, 'Collective Capabilities, Culture, and Amartya Sen's *Development as Freedom*', *Studies in Comparative International Development* 37 (2002): 54–60.

[60] Compare Ronald Dworkin, 'What Is Equality? Part 1: Equality of Welfare', *Philosophy and Public Affairs* 10 (1981): 185–246, with Ronald Dworkin, 'What Is Equality? Part 2: Equality of Resources', *Philosophy and Public Affairs* 10 (1981): 283–345.

[61] See also Michael W. Dowdle, 'On the Public-Law Character of Competition Law: A Lesson from Asian Capitalism', *Fordham International Law Journal* 38 (2015): 355–357; cf. Michael I. Norton, 'Unequality: Who Gets What and Why It Matters', *Policy Insights from the Behavioral and Brain Sciences* 1 (2014): 151–155.

[62] See also Martin Loughlin, 'Constituent Power Subverted: From English Constitutional Argument to British Constitutional Practice', in Martin Loughlin and Neil Walker (eds.), *The Paradox of Constitutionalism* (Oxford University Press, 2007), 27–49.

[63] See Thompson, *The Making of the English Working Class*, 111–203.

radical constitutionalism gave rise to two distinct English counter-reactions, both reflecting a profound distrust of the larger demos. These include the intellectual tradition of 'Whiggish' constitutionalism, as best represented by A. V. Dicey, founded on a vision of parliamentary sovereignty and an uncodified but principled 'rule of law';[64] and a more organic and conservative vision, called the 'Tory Constitution' by Dicey and exemplified by Edmund Burke, which presented the constitution through the lens of a privileged national historical teleology.[65]

Like the structural-liberal vision of constitutionalism, these other constitutional visions emerged from particular historical trajectories: a need to constitutionalise the status of the aristocracy in the case of the conservative, 'Tory' constitution;[66] the extreme social and economic disruptions of industrialisation in the case of England's radical constitutionalism; emancipation of the third estate from feudal repression in the case of the French Jacobin model;[67] and the projection of nationalism and imperialism in the case of Dicey's Whiggish model.

Nor were these visions hermetically sealed. Thus, for example, the American structural-liberal vision was itself strongly inspired by the English Tory constitution, particularly as reflected through the writings of Montesquieu.[68] American constitutional thought would then be (re-) introduced into post-Revolutionary France and radical England through the work of Thomas Paine.[69] (Although the Jacobian vision of constitution was to some extent an express rejection of the American vision, which it found too authoritarian.) Both Paine and the Jacobin constitutionalism would be germinal inspirations for the radical constitutionalism of the early industrial English working class.[70]

During the nineteenth century, England's Whiggish and Tory constitutionalisms, as we also saw, were driven to considerable extent by a fear of French constitutionalism. Similarly, as the commercial and agrarian

[64] See, generally, Matthew Zagor, 'England and the Rediscovery of Constitutional Faith,' ANU College of Law Working Paper (Canberra: Australian National University, July 30, 2009).

[65] See, e.g., Burke, *Reflections*; Cf. Dicey, *Lectures*, 51–60.

[66] See, e.g., Burke, *Reflections*.

[67] See Simon Schama, *Citizens: A Chronicle of the French Revolution*. New ed. (London: Penguin, 2004).

[68] See William D. Liddle, '"A Patriot King, or None": Lord Bolingbroke and the American Renunciation of George III,' *The Journal of American History* 65 (1979): 951–970; Gordon S. Wood, *The Creation of the American Republic, 1776–1787* (Chapel Hill: University of North Carolina Press 1998), 150–161.

[69] See Thompson, *The Making of the English Working Class*, 93–113; Schama, *Citizens*, xx.

[70] See, generally, Thompson, *The Making of the English Working Class*, 111–205.

classes in the early-nineteenth-century United States became increasingly dissatisfied by American constitutionalism's innately aristocratic roots (which it inherited from its Tory influences),[71] they were inspired in part by the experiences of the late-eighteenth-century English radicals[72] – a process that ultimately culminated in the establishment of Jacksonian Democracy.[73] The American structural-liberal vision, and in particular its way of regulating democracy, were influential on Dicey.[74] Towards the end of the nineteenth century, the work of the English constitutional scholar Walter Bagehot would inspire the constitutional understandings of a Princeton professor of political science named Woodrow Wilson, who would later become the twenty-eighth president of the United States.[75]

The revolutionary, Jacobin model that emerged in late eighteenth century France may have been short-lived – as Hannah Arendt put it, a model 'built on quicksand'.[76] But the constitutional ideas of its principal source of inspiration, Jean-Jacques Rousseau, would be influential in popularising the idea of constitutionalism beyond the North Atlantic. His influence, and beyond that French influence, would be felt in the diffusion of constitutional discourse into the 'Tazimat' constitutionalisation of the Ottoman Empire, the Persian Constitutional Revolution of 1906, Japan's initial interest in constitutionalism during the early Meiji restoration, and efforts at constitutionalisation in post-imperial China.[77]

And new conceptual strands continued to be added to this interweaving during the nineteenth and twentieth centuries. During the nineteenth century, these would include, for example, the Prussian Historical School (successors to the German camaralists) and through Max Weber

[71] See Wood, *The Radicalism of the American Revolution*, xx.

[72] See Jason Frank, *Constituent Moments: Enacting the People in Postrevolutionary America* (Durham, NC: Duke University Press, 2010).

[73] Wood, *The Radicalism of the American Revolution*, xx.

[74] See Michael Kamman, *A Machine That Would Go of Itself: The Constitution in American Culture* (New York: Alfred A. Knopf, 1986).

[75] See Ray S. Baker, *Woodrow Wilson: Life and Letters, Youth, 1856–1890* (Westport, CT: Greenwood Press, 1968), 213–214.

[76] Arendt, *On Revolution*, 163.

[77] See George Akita, *Foundations of Constitutional Government in Modern Japan, 1868–1900* (Cambridge, MA: Harvard University Press, 1967) (Japan); Robert Devereux, *The First Ottoman Constitutional Period: A Study of the Midhat Constitution and Parliament* (Baltimore: The Johns Hopkins University Press, 1963) (Ottoman Empire); Abdul-Hadi Hairi, 'European and Asian Influences on the Persian Revolution of 1906', *Asian Affairs* 6 (1975): 155–164 (Persia); Leigh K. Jenco, *Making the Political: Founding and Action in the Political Theory of Zhang Shizhao* (Cambridge University Press, 2010) (China).

the intellectual discoverers of rational-bureaucratic modernity.[78] The constitutional development of what has been called 'infrastructural power',[79] combined with the American doctrine of separation of powers, results in a constitutional construction that today is called the 'regulatory state'.[80] The later part of the nineteenth century would also see the emergence of Catholic corporatism (or corporativism), which would eventually morph, first into Italian Fascism, but eventually and more positively into the 'neo-corporatist' welfare states of Christian democratic Europe.[81]

The twentieth century would see not simply the continued expansion of constitutionalist conceptualisations, but the growing introduction to this discourse of non-Anglo-European experiences. These include the incorporation of Islamic strands (see also Lombardi, Chapter 8),[82] 'Confucianist' strands,[83] developmentalist strands,[84] and Chinese and Asian 'state-capitalist' strands.[85]

[78] See Keith Tribe, *Strategies of Economic Order: German Economic Discourse 1750–1950* (Cambridge University Press, 1995).

[79] See Michael Mann, 'The Autonomous Power of the State: Its Origins, Mechanisms and Results', *European Journal of Sociology* 25 (1984): 188–194.

[80] See Tony Prosser, 'Models of Economic and Social Regulation', in Dawn Oliver, Tony Prosser, and Richard Rawlings (eds.), *The Regulatory State: Constitutional Implications* (Oxford University Press, 2010), 34–49. Compare Bernard S. Silberman, *Cages of Reason: The Rise of the Rational State in France, Japan, the United States and Great Britain* (University of Chicago Press, 1993), 250–286.

[81] Robert E. Goodin et al., *The Real Worlds of Welfare Capitalism* (Cambridge University Press, 1999), 51–55. See also Philippe C. Schmitter, 'Still the Century of Corporatism?', *The Review of Politics* 36 (1974): 85–131.

[82] See also Nathan Brown, *Constitutions in a Non-Constitutional World, Arab Basic Laws and the Prospects for Accountable Government* (Albany: State University of New York Press, 2001). See, e.g., Sherman A. Jackson, *Islamic Law and the State: The Constitutional Jurisprudence of Shihāb Al-Dīn Al-Qarāfī* (Leiden, The Netherlands: Brill, 1996).

[83] See, e.g., Jenco, *Making the Political*; Bui Ngoc Son, 'The Introduction of Modern Constitutionalism in East Asian Confucian Context: The Case of Vietnam in the Early Twentieth Century', *National Taiwan University Law Review* 7 (2012): 423–463. See also Jiang Qing, *A Confucian Constitutional Order: How China's Ancient Past Can Shape Its Political Future* (eds., Daniel A. Bell and Ruiping Fan; transl., Edmund Ryden) (Princeton University Press, 2012).

[84] See Kanishka Jayasuriya, 'Introduction: A Framework for the Analysis of Legal Institutions in East Asia', in Kanishka Jayasuriya (ed.), *Law, Capitalism and Power in Asia: The Rule of Law and Legal Institutions* (London: Routledge, 1999), 1–23.

[85] See Michael W. Dowdle, 'China's Present as the World's Future: China and 'Rule of Law' in a Post-Fordist World', in Leigh K. Jenco (ed.), *Chinese Thought as Global Theory: Diversifying Knowledge Production in the Social Sciences and Humanities* (New York: SUNY Press, 2016), 207–230; see also Dowdle, 'Constitutional Listening', 142–156. Cf. Li-Wen Lin and Curtis J. Milhaupt, 'We Are the (National) Champions: Understanding the Mechanisms of State Capitalism in China', *Stanford Law Review* 65 (2013): 697–759.

Constitutionalism is thus a complex, uneven, and ever-changing historical discourse – it is 'bricolage' rather than blueprint, 'layered narrative' rather than grand narrative.[86] The structural-liberal vision is a significant voice in this discourse. But all-in-all, the realisation of constitutionalism is ultimately pluralist and diverse: No single perspective is able to capture its full possibilities as a political phenomenon; each has its own particular wisdom and folly. It is in their consilience that insights might be found into new possibilities for the constitutional project.[87]

A subtext of this narrative of interlocking narratives is that there is no linear, universal path of constitutional progression. Ideas return that were formerly consigned to the history books. And those that persist throughout do not remain in pristine condition. 'Popular constitutionalism', an idea first popularised by early nineteenth century English and American radicals, has been revived in recent years in the form of a much narrower position in US constitutional debates over the final arbiter of constitutional interpretation, defending a position that rejects strict judicial supremacy.[88] A distinct but not unrelated vision of 'civic republicanism', with its focus on political equality and the *status* of the citizen,[89] has 'rediscovered' the older, classic Republicanism of the early modern era.[90]

In UK public law scholarship, a 'political' – sometimes labelled 'republican' – constitutionalism has re-emerged, attempting to reclaim the broader concept of the constitution as meaning the strength and health of the body politic, a concept that has been erased from view in the modernising processes of constitutional reform and liberal discourses of fundamental rights.[91] But it, too, did not emerge in isolation, but as a dialogical response to the 'legal constitutionalism' of the structural-liberal vision,[92]

86 See Günter Frankenberg, 'Comparing Constitutions: Ideas, Ideals and Ideologies – Towards a Layered Narrative', *International Journal of Constitutional Law* 4 (2006): 439–459.

87 Cf. Edward O. Wilson, *Consilience: The Unity of Knowledge* (New York, Alfred A. Knopf, 1998).

88 Compare Larry D. Kramer, *The People Themselves: Popular Constitutionalism and Judicial Review* (Oxford University, 2004), with Frank, *Enacting the People.*

89 See, generally, Iseult Honohan, *Civic Republicanism* (London: Routledge, 2002). See, e.g., Philip Pettit, *Republicanism* (Oxford University Press, 1997); Quentin Skinner, *Liberty before Liberalism* (Cambridge University Press, 1998).

90 Philip Pettit, 'Two Republican Traditions', in Andreas Niederberger and Philipp Schink (eds.), *Republican Democracy: Liberty, Law and Politics* (Edinburgh University Press, 2012), 169–204.

91 See, e.g., Adam Tomkins, *Our Republican Constitution* (Oxford: Hart Publishing, 2005); cf. Gregoire Webber and Grahame Gee, 'What Is a Political Constitution?', *Oxford Journal of Legal Studies* 30 (2010): 273–299.

92 See, e.g., Martin Loughlin, *The British Constitution: A Very Short Introduction* (Oxford University Press, 2013).

and in particular in the need to question that vision's presumption of the presence of an overarching rational consensus among the polity that supposedly allows for the judicialisation of political process and juridification of social relationships.[93]

Thus, constitutionalism has always been both a cosmopolitan and a pluralist idea. As Neil Walker has noted, '[T]he humanist gene in the idea of popular sovereignty' means that even 'the most introverted, culturally monolithic and exclusionary national ideology will develop certain universalist themes.'[94] At the same time, and despite the universalism of constitutional thought, constitutional *discourse* always has to acknowledge its rootedness in a particular polity, to acknowledge some spatial boundary and limit: "[E]ven the most avowedly universalist framework of self-government must draw from and reinvest in its own particular experience."[95] Whatever ideological commitments it makes towards a moral universalism based on the individual, the constitution is always constructed in a specific social setting with a specific political morality and contributes towards the building of a particular state or polity. But this polity is not a given, it is in turn shaped by the particular ideals that inform that state's constitutional development, those that resonate somewhat uniquely in their particular political community and forge – or fail to forge – social solidarity among its members. (See also Wilkinson, Chapter 2.)

Seen in this light, modern constitutionalism is ultimately a balancing act, informed by an incredible diversity of constitutional experiences, but nevertheless uniquely attached to its political circumstances.[96] The problem with liberalism here is thus twofold. On the one hand, it obscures the diversity of sources from which a 'living' constitutional tradition can be constructed. On the other hand, its own inherent universalism leaves a polity no room or reason for feeling any special attachment to its own particular constitutional order. Given the (generally unacknowledged) evolutions in structural-liberalism described in the preceding text, this threatens to reduce constitutionalism simply to a political-cosmopolitan *zeitgeist*, as when the European Union constitutionalisation process is considered 'an important stage along the route to a politically constituted world society'[97] despite its evident fragmentation and conflict. In order

[93] See Loughlin, *Foundations*, 367–372; compare Dworkin, *Law's Empire*.

[94] Neil Walker, 'The Place of European Law', in Gráinne de Búrca and J. H. H. Weiler (eds.), *The Worlds of European Constitutionalism* (Oxford University Press, 2011), 65.

[95] Id.

[96] See Preuss, 'Constitutional Power-Making'.

[97] Jürgen Habermas, *The Crisis of the European Union: A Response* (London: Polity, 2012), 2.

for constitutionalism to continue to develop its myriad possibilities, its diversity of experiences and visions must be recognised, and critically scrutinised. How we might do this is the subject of the next and final part to this chapter.

IV. Looking beyond Liberalism

As noted in the introduction, the lesson in all this is that we need to expand our constitutional imagination in ways that allow us to look beyond liberalism – not rejecting liberalism per se, but realising its limitations and developing conceptual tools that can help us transcend them.

Some argue that such cosmopolitan, cross-cultural explorations of 'law' – including constitutional law – is impossible.[98] The complexities of cultural diversity – the differences in languages, cultural metaphors, social meanings, social experiences – render any attempt at cross-cultural normative or conceptual synthesis ultimately futile. There are at least two responses to this kind of scepticism.

The first is methodological. Even if it is true that we can never really *know* if we accurately understand another culture (or even another individual), it doesn't matter: We can never really know if we *can't* understand another culture (or person) either. Both positions start from a presumption of either ultimate incomprehensibility or ultimate comprehensibly. There is no reason for preferring one to the other. For that reason, we have at least as much justification for pursuing the possibilities inherent in comprehensibly as we do for presuming that such pursuits will be in vain.

The second response to the sceptical assertion is empirical. It is not hard to find demonstration of complex cooperation across cultures, cooperation that simply could not work if cross-cultural understanding were impossible – for example, cross-cultural marriages, cross-cultural friendships, cross-cultural business partnerships, even cross-culture academic conferences. The prevalence of successful endeavours of this sort argues strongly – we would say conclusively – that cross-cultural communication, understanding, and consilience are eminently possible and feasible. This conclusion is supported by a large number of psychological studies. Meta-studies of the cultural psychology studies find that both perceptions of experience and modes of making sense of those perceptions

[98] See, e.g., Pierre Legrand, 'What "Legal Transplants?"', in David Nelken and Johannes Feest (eds.), *Adapting Legal Cultures* (Oxford: Hart Publishing, 2001), 55–68; cf. Rebecca French, *The Golden Yoke: The Legal Cosmology of Buddhist Tibet* (Ithaca, NY: Cornell University Press, 1995), 57.

(e.g., rationalism, sentimentalism, folk knowledge) in fact do not differ significantly across cultures: that both perception and cognition (reason) are human and not cultural phenomena.[99] What differs among cultures is the way perception and cognition are expressed – that is, the symbols and metaphors that we use to locate particular perceptions and cognitions into our larger understanding of the world.[100] The key to our exploration therefore lies in looking beyond expressions and metaphors, and at the rationality and coherence that underlies the statement.

Along these lines, a good starting point for looking 'beyond liberalism' is the interpretive principle that Donald Davidson famously called 'the principle of charity.'[101] The principle of charity starts from the observation that the best heuristic for determining the meaning of a particular statement is simply to assume that the speaker is 'making sense' – that is, to privilege interpretations that maximise the coherence and meaning of the statement. This involves, for example, presuming that the speaker is rational, presuming that she is not intending to be *normatively* deceptive (although she might be wrong on particular factual matters), and that she is trying to be persuasive *to her particular audience*.[102]

The comparative advantage of the principle of charity is not that it gives the most accurate understanding of the intentions of the speaker. It is not to help us understand why somebody said what she did; or if or how that statement benefits her interests. Its purpose is to maximise our ability to learn from the speaker's statement. Consistent with this approach, this volume demonstrates how listening to alternative constitutional experiences allows us to better perceive and account for the limits of liberalism, and at the same time to defend the cosmopolitan vitality of the constitutional project.

At the same time, the principle of charity demands that this listening be reflexive rather than passive. Reflexivity, as Neil Walker notes, 'amounts to

[99] See Dianne van Hemert, *Patterns of Cross-Cultural Differences in Psychology: A Meta-Analytic Approach* (Amsterdam: Dutch University Press, 2003), 132–133, 136–137. Cf. Steven Pinker, *The Blank Slate: The Modern Denial of Human Nature* (London: Penguin, 2002).

[100] See Hemert, *Patterns of Cross-Cultural Differences*, 136–137. Cf. George Lakoff and Mark Johnson, *Metaphors We Live By* (University of Chicago Press, 1980).

[101] See, generally, Donald Davidson, 'Radical Interpretation', in *Inquiries into Truth and Interpretation*. 2nd ed. (Oxford: Clarendon, 2001), 125–140; see also Neil L. Wilson, 'Substances without Substrata', *Review of Metaphysics* 12 (1959): 521–539.

[102] See Michael W. Dowdle, 'Of Parliaments, Pragmatism, and the Dynamics of Constitutional Development: The Curious Case of China', *New York University Journal of International Law and Politics* 35 (2002): 84–47; Dowdle, 'Constitutional Listening', 126–130.

more than providing a reflection.... Rather it is about the quality of *ipseity* – of the capacity for self-reflection and the possibility of self-transformation inherent in that capacity.'[103]

All-in-all, this is more demanding than the orthodox liberal approach permits. First, it is holistic in the sense of perceiving the 'other' polity – not as an institutionally defined corpus (e.g., as an electorate, or as a civil society, or as a set of survey data) comprised of atomistically autonomous individual beings – but as an organic inter-linkage of an 'ideational' *telos* with a 'structural' *nomos* (again, see Teubner, Chapter 3): It is both population and community, both constituted and constituting.[104] It is both abstract structure, and 'the living individuality of a nation.'[105]

Second, rather than see the constitution as the product of an instance of transcendental moment of pure reason, where the 'house' wherein political freedom can dwell is constructed in one go, it recognises that the constitution is an ongoing narrative constantly interweaving a diversity of perspectives, concerns, and imaginations. Relatedly, rather than seeing the constitution in terms of a dualist structure in which meaningful constitutional discoveries only occur during certain extraordinary and punctuated moments of political sobriety, so as to avoid sliding into political excess during the otherwise normal state of political drunkenness,[106] it sees the constitution as *constantly* negotiated and renegotiated in the public realm (and soberly, as per the principle of charity).[107] It thus constantly reminds us, as discussed in the preceding text, how a 'constitution' is always a perpetually, spontaneously, and even invisibly evolving work in progress.

Third, in order to capture the constitution's structural symbiosis with other social systems in its regulatory environment, this approach must recognise law, politics, and society to be dynamically interrelated in the constitutional evolution of the polity (see also Teubner, Chapter 3).

[103] Neil Walker, 'EU Constitutionalism and New Governance', in Grainne de Burca and Joanne Scott (eds.), *Law and New Governance in the EU and the US* (Oxford: Hart Publishing, 2006), 34.

[104] See, generally, Martin Loughlin and Neil Walker (eds.), *The Paradox of Constitutionalism: Constituent Power and Constitutional Form* (Oxford University Press, 2007).

[105] Georg Wilhelm Friedrich Hegel, 'On the Scientific Ways of Treating Natural Law, on Its Place in Practical Philosophy, and Its Relation to the Positive Sciences of Right', in *Hegel: Political Writings* (ed., Laurence Kickey and H. B. Nisbet; trans., H. B. Nisbet) (Cambridge University Press, 1999), 176.

[106] Compare Holmes, *Passions and Constraints*, 135.

[107] Martin Loughlin, *The Idea of Public Law* (Oxford University Press, 2003), 155.

Of course this interrelationship is not necessarily functional, stable, and/or otherwise constructive. There are no constitutional guarantees for the flourishing or even survival of the polity. Insobriety occurs. Constitutional 'charity' is a method with which to analyse the various tensions that both are latent in the pluralist nature of the constitutional project and are necessary for its evolutionary survival. These tensions are sometimes productive, sometimes destructive. But in either case, they define the focus of 'constitutional' – both insofar as an individual polity is concerned, and insofar as our more cosmopolitan understandings are concerned.

Along these lines, constitutional listening requires us to not privilege or essentialise legal judgment and judicial interpretation as the principle sources of a *normative* constitutional order. Such a presumption is both under-inclusive and over-inclusive. While these are significant components of that order, they must not be confused for its whole. Whether and how a legal judgment is translated into action depends on the degree to which a political culture and background social order have internalised a relatively high level of obedience to the law and on the degree of official acceptance of the rules of law-making.[108] At the same time, the rules of law-making are frequently complex and under-determined. This makes the courts active participants in the balance of constitutional powers – in the language of speech-act theory, it makes judicial judgments 'performative' and not simply 'constative'.[109] They are not merely logical or tautologous propositions, but acquire recognition and meaning only through broader constitutional practice. In short, the constitutional effects of a Court's judgment will depend upon the constitutional context in which it is uttered.

This symbiosis is largely concealed in the structural-liberal tradition, where a separation of powers has been established over years, perhaps centuries, of conflict and negotiation, and has thus attained what appears to be some kind of natural constitutional feature. Juridical authority thenceforth *appears* a distinct and autonomous constitutional phenomenon – at least in the abstract analysis of legal scholars concerned with presenting a snapshot of the constitutional order, or what has revealingly been called a 'momentary legal system'.[110] But this appearance is deceptive, because in constitutional practice juridical authority is one player in a larger game.

Lastly, constitutional listening problematises the constitutional nomos. Structural-liberalism conceptualises the constitutional *nomos* largely

[108] Cf. Tom R. Tyler, *Why People Obey the Law* (New Haven, CT: Yale University Press, 1990).

[109] See John L. Austin, *How to Do Things with Words* (Oxford: Clarendon, 1975).

[110] See Joseph Raz, 'The Identify of Legal Systems,' *California Law Review* 59 (1971): 798.

if not exclusively in terms of positive law. The canonical structures that constitute the structural-liberal vision are *defined* legally. Charitable 'listening' is more sensitive to constitutional change and to the diversity of normative influences that comprise the constitutional arena, and thus allows for constitutional *nomoi* to take a wider varieties of political and legal forms. They can take the form of pre-theoretical practices.[111] They can take the form of particular narratives, including fictional or false narratives.[112] They can even take the form of a particular homeostatic political balance that emerges out of the perpetual clashes among the many irresolvable contradictions and conflicts that course through the social and political corpus of the nation (see, e.g., Harding, Chapter 10). Even transparently duplicitous claims can develop an normative force of their own, a dynamic that that results in part from the innate political need to be seen to be keeping one's word.[113]

Also along these lines, constitutional listening does not privilege any particular conception of the *telos*, of the public or political good.[114] It recognises that like constitutionalism itself, conceptions of what constitutes the public good are also pluralist and reflect different experiences, and traumas. Each perspective has value that transcends its instantiation; each is limited in its imagination. It exposes what is otherwise concealed in debates over the relationship between the constitution, the polity, and the public good. It does not offer to determine which institutional arrangements produce optimal outcomes, let alone to offer a constitutional blueprint for the future. Rather, it contributes to a distinct and deeper enquiry into the nature of the constitution as an ongoing exercise of collective self-commitment.

[111] See, e.g., Clifford Geertz, 'Local Knowledge: Fact and Law in Comparative Perspective', in *Local Knowledge: Further Essays in Interpretive Anthropology*. 3rd ed. (New York: Basic Books, 2000), 167–233; see, e.g., Thompson, *The Making of the English Working Class*, 74–79.

[112] See, e.g., Braithwaite et al., *Anomie and Violence*.

[113] See, e.g., Andrzej Rapaczynski, 'Constitutional Politics in Poland: A Report on the Constitutional Committee of the Polish Parliament', *University of Chicago Law Review* 58 (1991): 596–598. See also Elster, 'Strategic Uses of Argument'.

[114] See also Loughlin, *Foundations*, 159.

2

The Reconstitution of Post-war Europe: Liberal Excesses, Democratic Deficiencies

MICHAEL A. WILKINSON

I. Introduction

Constitutional theory traditionally approaches questions of the authority, legitimacy, and durability of constitutions by employing modern concepts such as sovereignty, government, and constitutional rights.[1] These in turn are constructed on the basis of the autonomy – or at least differentiation – of the political domain from other domains such as the religious, economic, and social.[2] The autonomy of the political is underpinned by popular sovereignty: A master concept that signals that the authority of the modern secular constitution is based on the constituent power of the people (see also Loughlin, Chapter 6).[3] If the modern constitutional state is a representation of the diachronic unity of the people, a lens through which to make sense of our constitutional self-government, how is it affected by recent challenges to the modern state system, and in particular by the post-war project of European integration?

The purpose of this chapter is to sketch an answer to that question. It will be argued that European integration, launched as a functionalist project based on a liberal-democratic ethos and a desire to build a 'European Germany', with the aim of preserving the achievements of the modern constitutional state, is transforming into an authoritarian liberal project in the name of a 'German Europe', with the effect of threatening Europe's most basic constitutional achievements. This mutation is attributed to three features of the conjuncture reached at the end of the 'short twentieth century' (1914–1991): the geo-political challenge of German reunification; the failure to forge a democratic European Constitution; and the excessive (and

[1] See Martin Loughlin, *Foundations of Public Law* (Oxford University Press, 2010), 69–73, 375–406, 342–367.

[2] Id. at 7.

[3] Id. at 221–228.

even illiberal) adherence, sometimes to the rules, and sometimes to the ideology, of economic liberalism.

This transformation affects not only constitutionalism but also the master concept of popular sovereignty, and the modern state itself.[4] To explore it therefore requires a return to the 'ancient' understanding – elided in the modern structural-liberal constitutional vision – of the constitution as represented not only in legal texts and juridical pronouncements, but also in the strength and health of the body politic – national as well as supranational. We need, in other words, to capture the transformation of the European constitutional imagination as well as its legal body.[5]

To unfold this narrative requires returning to the roots of the project: the inter-war period. The post-war European constitutional imagination, it will be argued, is configured on the back of the inter-war breakdown of liberal constitutionalism and in particular of the decline of Weimar Germany. Three predominant concerns resulting from this experience shape the post-war dynamics of constitutional change: fears of state sovereignty, of radical constituent power, and of economic democracy (Part II).

European integration is a response to these concerns through a geo-political reconstitution of inter-state, state-society, and economic relations. The geo-political constitution thus develops along three trajectories: a conditioning of sovereign authority, with the narrower aim of preventing German hegemony (*inter-state relations*); a reconditioning of political authority, which aims to displace the idea of constituent power with the new rhetoric of constitutional rights, triggered by concerns to replace politics and avoid political extremism (*state-society* relations); and a restructuring of the economic constitution, first through ordoliberalism and later in the shift towards neo-liberalism, with the aim of de-politicising the economy (*economic relations*) (Part III).

If these three constitutional-evolutionary dynamics – restructuring the state, political, and economic systems of Europe – combined to restore and safeguard the liberal constitutional ideal in the wake of its inter-war breakdown, the post-Maastricht conjuncture (1992) – represented by the reunification of Germany, the failure of the Constitutional Project, and a neo-liberal turn in the project of economic integration – signposts a different path: an increasingly fractious and unsettled European constitutionalism (Part IV).

[4] See Neil Walker (ed.) *Sovereignty in Transition* (Oxford: Hart Publishing, 2003); Chris Bickerton, *European Integration: From Nation-State to Member State* (Oxford University Press, 2013). Cf. Philip Bobbitt, *The Shield of Achilles* (New York: Alfred Knopp, 2002).

[5] See Martin Loughlin, 'The Constitutional Imagination', *Modern Law Review* 78 (2015): 1–25.

Movement along this path has rapidly accelerated since the Euro-crisis, to the point that European integration is unable to maintain its animating constitutional ideal. Instead, it is now beginning to reproduce an *authoritarian liberalism* that was a significant feature of the inter-war constitutional experience that integration was meant to overcome (Part V).

The chapter will conclude by suggesting that a renewal of the legacy of constitutionalism in Europe depends on a recovery of the autonomy of the political over the economic realm. But this is demanded only by radical social movements and marginal political parties; whether it is compatible with the current project of integration is doubtful (Part VI).

II. Inter-war: A Constitutional Prelude

To make sense of the post-war European constitutional imagination requires looking into its pre-history: namely, at the experience of the inter-war period and specifically at what Carl Schmitt perceived as the decline of the *jus publicum Europaeum* – the European 'public law' that governed relations within and between the states of Europe, and which consolidated the sovereign European state from the Peace of Westphalia (1648) to the outbreak of World War I (1914).[6]

If a principal if often unacknowledged component of classical liberal constitutionalism is this idea of state sovereignty, it is because sovereignty represents the external face of the constituent power from which the constitution draws its authority. Through the emergence of the *jus publicum Europeaum*, constitutional authority and sovereignty became inexorably linked. The modern state acquires its internal monopoly of legitimate force and establishes the secular, political foundations of its governing arrangements: 'We, the People'. Externally, the state is recognised as the only legitimate subject of international relations, with the right to decide on matters of war and peace subject only to conventions regarding civilised warfare. Through the consolidation of this double dynamic, a European 'balance of power' is attained from the early modern age of absolutism through to the 'golden age of the classical interstate system'.[7]

This is a crude snapshot of a complex picture. The emergence of the *jus publicum Europaeum* is a long and uneven historical process, but it crystallises a series of conceptual distinctions that are key to

[6] See Benno Teschke, 'Fatal Attraction: A Critique of Carl Schmitt's International Legal and Political Theory', *International Theory* 3 (2011): 179–227.

[7] Id. at 181.

modern constitutional theory: distinctions between the domestic and the international, the public and the private, state and society, and the political and the economic.[8] It reaches its apotheosis in the German nineteenth-century tradition of *Staatslehre*, as typified by Georg Jellinek's formalisation of the constitution, based on a holy trinity of 'state apparatus', 'territory', and 'people'.[9]

If this is the pure meaning of classical state sovereignty in the Euro-centric tradition, Carl Schmitt adds an elemental dichotomy to capture the brute historical reality of its geo-political formation, its stability dependent on the distinction between sea and land, Behemoth and Leviathan, a balance guarded by the maritime power of the British empire until its waning in the inter-war period.[10] In this early-modern through modern period, a *concrete order* (a *nomos*) based on land appropriation and claim to radical title overseas is established by European imperial powers, which underwrites the foundations of the modern liberal constitutional state in its age of colonial expansion and domestic consolidation.[11]

This Euro-centric *nomos* came to a head, and an end, with the consequences of World War I, when it became apparent that Europe was no longer able to maintain a global balance of power, ending the 'long nineteenth century' that began with the French Revolution of 1789.[12]

The geo-political balance is thus thrown into question in an inter-war and immediate post-war period marked not only by the decline of the British Empire and the emergence of first the United States and later the Soviet Union as rival global superpowers, but by the fate of Germany, first weakened after the Treaty of Versailles and the establishment of the League of Nations, but then characterised by its hegemonic rise and domestic descent into National Socialism and finally collapse and defeat in World War II.

But there is internal, domestic constitutional narrative to the collapse of the *jus publicum Europeaum*, which complements this geo-political

[8] See, e.g., Martin Loughlin, 'Ten Tenets of Sovereignty', in Neil Walker (ed.), *Sovereignty in Transition* (Oxford: Hart Publishing, 2003), 55–86.

[9] See Martin Loughlin, 'In Defence of Staatslehre', *Der Staat* 48 (2009): 1–28.

[10] Carl Schmitt, *The Nomos of the Earth in the International Law of the Jus Publicum Europeaum* (trans. G. L. Ulmen) (New York: Telos Press, 2003 [1950]), 49, 352–353.

[11] Martin Loughlin, 'Nomos', in Thomas Poole and David Dyzenhaus (eds.) *Theorists of Constitutional Crisis: Oakeshott, Hayek and Schmitt on Law, Liberty and State* (Cambridge University Press, 2015), 65–95; cf. Hannah Arendt, *The Origins of Totalitarianism* (New York: Harcourt, 1968 [1951]), 123–157.

[12] Cf. Martti Koskenniemi, 'Histories of International Law: Dealing with Eurocentrism', *Rechtsgeschichte* 19 (2011): 152–176.

frame.[13] Because Germany arrives late to the stage of modern political and economic development, following its own '*Sonderweg*', its conceptions of constitutional statehood and popular sovereignty are concretised at a later stage than in France, for example, but are for that reason less substantively entrenched in the constitutional culture when they are placed under severe stress in the inter-war period.[14]

The stress on the Weimar Republic was placed not only by the humiliation at Versailles and the desire for Germany to restore its former imperialist glory, lost as a result of defeat in the Great War. Weimar liberalism broke down, or so liberal constitutionalists in the inter-war period argued, because it was too tolerant and over-valued ideas of liberal equality, misplaced in the political and social turmoil of the time. Weimar constitutionalism was thus charged with complacency towards the political turbulence that democracy could lead to and had led to during the 1920s and 1930s. Democracy needed to become constitutionally tamed – even 'militantly' – in order to protect itself from those at the political extremes who desired its destruction.

The constitutionalist discourse of 'militant democracy' was a direct response to the breakdown of the Weimar Republic and other liberal constitutions in the inter-war years.[15] The term was coined in 1937 by Karl Loewenstein, a German constitutionalist who emigrated to the United States when the Nazi party took power in 1933 and later played a significant role in the American post-war reconstruction of West Germany.[16] Beginning in the 1930s, he had urged liberal democracy to become more aggressive in resisting the spread of fascism as a domestic and universal social movement, in particular by actively resisting the fascist substitution of the romantic and emotional for the rational and constitutionalist in re-conceptualising the methods of constitutional governance.[17]

[13] See Gopal Balakrishnan, *The Enemy: An Intellectual Portrait of Carl Schmitt* (London: Verso, 2000), 101–115.

[14] Cf. Christoph Schönberger, '"L'Etat de la 'Theorie Generale de l'Etat": Remarkes Comparatives sur un Discipline Specifiquement Allemand', in Alain Chatriot und Dieter Gosewinkel (eds.), *Figurationen des Staates in Deutchsland und Frankreich 1870–1945* (Oldenbourg Verlag Munchen, 2006), 257–275.

[15] See Karl Loewenstein, 'Militant Democracy and Fundamental Rights, Part 1', *The American Political Science Review* 3 (1937): 417–432; Karl Loewenstein, 'Autocracy versus Democracy in Contemporary Europe, Part 2', *The American Political Science Review* 29 (1935): 571–593.

[16] See R. W. Kostal, 'The Alchemy of Occupation: Karl Loewenstein and the Legal Reconstruction of Nazi Germany, 1945–1946', *Law and History Review* 29 (2011): 1–52.

[17] Loewenstein, 'Militant Democracy and Fundamental Rights, Part 1', 424.

Constitutionalism, according to Loewenstein (writing in the mid-1930s), was under severe and imminent threat in numerous European states, both from fascism and also, if to a lesser degree, from Communism. It could not be protected by liberal democratic *tolerance*. Rather, it required a '*militant*' – meaning extraordinary – constitutional protection – including the use of emergency powers and the suspension of fundamental rights and other constitutional guarantees if necessary.[18] Instead, the Weimar Republic, Loewenstein insisted, 'foundered on its own concepts of constitutional legality, which opened the way to power for Hitler'.[19]

Fascism, in Loewenstein's view, was neither a cogent political ideology nor a coherent political programme, but rather was 'the most effective political technique in modern history', serving opportunistically the purposes of attaining and maintaining political power. Democracy must fight it on level terms: in Loewenstein's own words, it must 'fight fire with fire'.[20] Otherwise, liberal democracy would be manipulated by undemocratic and illiberal creeds, using it for its own destruction 'under cover of the constitutional protection afforded by fundamental rights and the rule of law',[21] which would be casually discarded once power had been attained.

But 'militant democracy', for Loewenstein, meant 'militant liberalism'. The goal of 'militant democracy' was to serve liberal capitalism as much as to defend liberal civil and political rights. Capitalism thrives, he argued, because of the predictability of the rule of law, and not because of, but actually in spite of democracy and its potential irresponsibility towards the economy. In the same way that militant democracy was supposed to protect *liberalism* from democracy, it was also, and just as importantly, supposed to protect *capitalism* from democracy. In both cases, it meant a replacement of a constitutionalism founded on constituent power with one founded on *legality*.[22]

In this way, liberal constitutionalists re-established a conceptual linkage between liberalism, democratic legitimacy, and capitalism that was well perceived among nineteenth-century liberals, but whose conception of democracy was limited to a politically homogenous group of male property-holders. The spread of universal franchise, in the Weimar

[18] Id. at 432.
[19] Id.
[20] Id.
[21] Id.
[22] Cf. Lon Fuller, 'Positivism and Fidelity to Law – A Reply to Professor Hart', *Harvard Law Review* 71 (1958): 630–672. Cf. Jan-Werner Müller, *Contesting Democracy: Political Ideas in Twentieth Century Thought* (rev. ed., New Haven: Yale University Press, 2012), 129.

Republic and elsewhere, had upset this comfortable linkage. Weimar Germany exposed Europe to a new and tumultuous vision of democracy, one produced when universal suffrage was combined with class consciousness, intense party politics, parliamentary democracy, and increasing local and regional claims to autonomy, including workers' councils and movements of economic democracy.[23] These socialist and democratic movements were not, of course, limited to Weimar Germany, or even to Europe.[24]

But it was in the turbulence of the democracy of the Weimar Republic that liberal-capitalist constitutional stability was threatened in both a political and an ideological manner: politically, with its increasingly fraught class conflict and class consciousness; and ideologically, through the linking of legitimate constitutional authority with democratic responsiveness rather than with legal constraints.

If this fear of radical democracy, and specifically of a democratic transition to socialism (whether reformist or revolutionary), was the fear that motivated the fascist political parties of Germany and Italy, the problem that democratic emancipation and class struggle posed for the conservative liberal constitutionalist was equally apparent: '[I]n a democratic age it was entirely possible that a legislature based on universal suffrage could chip away at the rules of property and contract which regulate the intercourse of bourgeoise society'.[25] The very idea of popular sovereignty based on a General Will was threatening when the politically active population (previously male property-holders) was no longer discreet and homogenous.

The liberal-constitutional reaction to the threat of social democracy would be disparaged by Hermann Heller as 'authoritarian liberalism'.[26] Heller was taking aim not only at Carl Schmitt, one of its principle proponents and until 1933, an 'implacable conservative opponent of the enemies of the Weimar state',[27] but also the centrist and conservative presidential cabinets ruling the late Weimar (and being advised by Schmitt) until the

[23] See Maurice Glasman, *Unnecessary Suffering* (London: Verso, 1995).

[24] See, e.g., John Dewey, *The Public and Its Problems* (New York: Holt Publishing, 1927).

[25] Balakrishnan, *The Enemy*, 98. Cf. William Scheuerman, 'The Unholy Alliance of Carl Schmitt and Friedrich Hayek', *Constellations* 4 (1997): 172–188.

[26] Hermann Heller, 'Autoritärer Liberalismus', *Die Neue Rundschau* 44 (1933): 289–298; Hermann Heller, 'Authoritarian Liberalism?' *European Law Journal* 21 (2015): 295–301 (trans., S. Paulson).

[27] See Keith Tribe, *Strategies of Economic Order: German Economic Discourse 1750–1950* (Cambridge University Press, 1995), 175.

rise to power of the Nazi party. For Schmitt and other conservative liberals and liberal constitutionalists, authoritarianism was seen as a necessary antidote both to the fragmenting processes of democratisation and social pluralisation, and to the relativism of a formal legal positivism that did not have any substance, weakening the German state and endangering its liberal Constitution.[28] In Schmitt's words:

> Now the proletariat becomes the people, because it is the bearer of this negativity (that was Sieyes' 'third estate': which was nothing and shall become everything). It is the part of the population which does not own, which does not have a share in the produced surplus value, and finds no place in the existing order.... Democracy turns into proletarian democracy, and replaces the liberalism of the propertied and educated bourgeoisie.[29]

With notable exceptions in the tradition of Austrian liberalism (especially Friedrich Hayek), neither liberals nor conservatives of the inter-war period envisaged the possibility of any straightforward return to the political laissez-faire of classical liberalism.[30] Restoring liberal economic order required strong state action and even a temporary (or more permanent) suspension of constitutional democracy by either a commissarial or even sovereign dictatorship.[31] The 'sound economy' – the maintenance of the conditions of the Bourgeois *Rechtsstaat* – now required the 'strong state': A motto that would later be taken up and reformulated by the Freiberg ordoliberals.[32]

In this ordoliberal reformulation, the strong state was not a necessarily a democratic one. Rather, it was one that was capable of upholding and enforcing the rules of the liberal market economy, and this would require a strong, juridical constitution as well as strong bureaucratic institutions capable of intervening to create, or at least approximate, the conditions of the liberal market society. Whatever role democracy took in such a state (if any), it would have to be subordinated to these dictates.

[28] See Balakrishnan, *The Enemy*, 155–163.

[29] Carl Schmitt, *Verfassungslehre* (trans. J. Seitzer) (Durham, NC: Duke University Press, 2008), 271–272.

[30] Cf. Tribe, *Strategies of Economic Order*, 207–208.

[31] See, generally, John P. MacCormick, 'The Dilemmas of Dictatorship: Carl Schmitt and Constitutional Emergency Powers', *Canadian Journal of Law and Jurisprudence* 10 (1997): 163–189.

[32] See Renato Cristi, *Carl Schmitt and Authoritarian Liberalism* (Cardiff: University of Wales Press, 1998); Werner Bonefeld, 'Freedom and the Strong State: On German Ordo-Liberalism', *New Political Economy* 17 (2012): 633–656.

The founding members of the Freiberg school – economist Walter Eucken, and lawyers Franz Bohm and Hanns Grossman-Doerth – first met in 1933, the year the Nazis took power in Germany, just as the period characterised by Heller as 'authoritarian liberalism' came to a close. In working to identify the dynamics of the collapse of the Weimar Republic, and to find ways of transcending the failures of classical liberalism, they would find themselves by the end of World War II right at the intellectual centre of German post-war reconstruction.[33] Working with the economists and sociologists Alfred Muller-Armack, Alexander Rustow, and Wilhem Röpke (who developed softer versions of ordoliberalism based on the slogan of a 'social market economy') and with the support of Ludwig Erhard, West Germany's minister of economics from 1949 through 1963 and then its chancellor from 1963 to 1966, ordoliberalism would become the dominant ideology in post-war West Germany through the 1970s.[34]

Ordoliberalism is a powerful rationalisation of the fears of the weakness of a democratic state, but locates that weakness in its incapacity to prevent the erosion of liberty through the accumulation of excessive, monopolistic, *private* power, as much as in the manipulation of the public powers of government. The ordoliberal focus on legal and constitutional means of protecting the liberal economic order from private as well as governmental interference stressed the implementation of strict rules of market competition. Ordoliberals attributed Weimar's decline to cartelisation policies and resulting state capture by private interest groups, which allowed inter-war Germany to degenerate into a corporatist state-industrial nexus that led inexorably to fascism. It was the weakness of constitutionalism in fighting monopoly capitalism as much as the threat of socialism that led to the demise of the Weimer Republic.

Under these new liberal visions of the strong state, the 'sovereign people', if constitutionalised, could be reconstructed less as a threatening insurgent mass of radical constituent power, and more as a 'formless source of legitimising acclamation … leaving the social property relations of old Europe unmolested'.[35] Liberal constitutional theory could then be reintegrated with European capitalism in an early version of the view that, in the jargon of post-war European reconstruction, would be labelled 'restrained

[33] See, e.g., Tribe, *Strategies of Economic Order*; David Gerber, 'Constitutionalizing the Economy: German Neoliberalism, Competition Law and the "New" Europe' *American Journal of Comparative Law* (1994): 25–84.

[34] Id.

[35] Balakrishnan, *The Enemy*, 100.

democracy',[36] encapsulated especially in the story of West German post-war constitutional development (in Christoph Möllers apt terms, 'we are (afraid of) the people'[37]).

To put it crudely, liberal constitutionalism and liberal constitutional theory became preoccupied with the *manner* of Weimar's constitutional decline and transition to fascism, to the neglect of its social and economic causes. Their lesson was that the turn to fascism is preventable if only constitutionalism could be more firmly able to resist extremist politics by reinforcing liberal constitutional norms against democratic change and specifically anti-liberal political parties (often reformulated in US constitutionalism through the rubric of preventing the 'tyranny of the majority').[38]

Ordoliberalism, while deeply concerned with the causes of Weimar's decline, focused only on one side – on the threat of private power in an unfettered market. It neglected the political concerns of social democracy. The ordoliberal question was how to prevent monopoly capitalism from corrupting the liberal market economy.

The apparent success of this liberal constitutional re-imagination (whether ordoliberal or liberal authoritarian) in eroding constituent power and sidelining of political democracy, was such that by 1966 Loewenstein concluded that, 'the task of checking the bureaucracy which [Max] Weber had assigned to parliament was now effectively fulfilled by courts'. Parliamentarism, which in the nineteenth century 'seemed to be the ultimate in political wisdom', had by then suffered from 'widespread devaluation'.[39]

What was the role of European integration in this new constitutional vision? The route to restoring and maintaining the liberal constitutional ideal in the post-war period was directed through three trajectories of constitutional constraint: restraining state sovereignty, displacing radical constituent power, and curtailing economic democracy. European integration, it will now be argued, played a significant part in each of these constitutionalist projects.

[36] See also Müller, *Contesting Democracy*, at 128.

[37] See Christoph Möllers, '"We Are (Afraid) of the People": Constituent Power in German Constitutionalism', in M. Loughlin and N. Walker (eds.), *The Paradox of Constitutionalism: Constituent Power and Constitutional Form* (Oxford University Press, 2007), 87–107.

[38] Cf. Jeremy Waldron, 'Precommitment and Disagreement', in Larry Alexander (ed.), *Consti tutionalism: Philosophical Foundations* (Cambridge University Press, 1998): 271–301.

[39] Müller, *Contesting Democracy*, 148.

III. European Integration and the Geo-Political Constitution of Authority

If the linchpin of the liberal political constitution of the 'long nineteenth century' was the unconditional political authority of the state, this becomes conditioned in post-war European constitutionalism through the construction of international and supranational frameworks of law, politics, and the economy. This construction occurs both concretely and symbolically, formally and informally. The idea of 'geo-political' constitutionalism signifies that the conditioning of political authority through structures and practices *beyond the state* reshapes not only inter-state relations, but also state-society and economic relations *within* states.

In the geo-political reconstitution of Europe after World War II, three key inter-connected questions thus emerge, relating respectively to state sovereignty, constituent power, and economic democracy: how to resolve the 'German question' (to stabilise power relations in central Europe and prevent a return of German hegemony); how to prevent domestic descent into political extremism of both Right and Left; and how to stabilise the world economic system and prevent a repeat of the uncoordinated protectionism that characterised the 1930s and proved so globally catastrophic.

A. *Restraining State Sovereignty: Imagining a 'European Germany'*

The question for post-war Europe was first and foremost how to constrain Germany, to prevent its re-emergence as a militarily or politically hegemonic central European power. This concern was based on a distrust, felt particularly keenly in France for obvious historical reasons, of German state sovereignty.[40]

But the 'German question' largely disappeared from view during the period from the Treaty of Rome (1957) until the Treaty of Maastricht (1992) due to factors beyond the European sphere of influence: the division of Germany into East and West; West Germany turning inward to focus on its *Wirtshaftswunder*, helped by the cancelling and restructuring of large portions of its national debt in the London Agreement of 1953;[41] the broader effects of the US Marshall Plan, serving economic reconstruction and trade, as well as political ends of stabilising European liberal

[40] See, e.g., Mette Eilstrup-Sangiovanni and Daniel Verdier, 'European Integration as a Solution to War', *European Journal of International Relations* 11 (2005): 99–135.

[41] *The London Agreement on German External Debts 1953.*

democracy in the hope of preventing any movement towards socialism in Europe.[42]

The classical European nation-state was no longer fully in control of its own destiny. This was clearly borne out in concrete terms by the American pressure that drove the resolution of the Suez crisis, humbling the pretensions of the United Kingdom and France to foreign policy autonomy.[43] US control over the new and decisive geo-political element after the sea and land, in its dominance of air power,[44] signalled the fading into the background of the 'German question' as a global issue.

Adenauer's West Germany – abdicating any regionally or globally hegemonic ambitions, which in any case would have been blunted by its position sandwiched between the rival superpowers – made the decisive political choice at the beginning of the Cold War to align itself with the US and Western liberalism more generally (even at the expense of forgoing the possibility of early reunification with the East as a 'neutral power').[45]

None of this is to say that European integration was an insignificant part of the equation; it was an important feature of the transatlantic bulwark against the spread of Communism as well as a vehicle for restraining German ambitions, neutralising its power through the dominance of French political influence on the process of integration from the Coal and Steel Community agreed at the Treaty of Paris in 1951.

In post-war Europe, institution-building in the form of the European Union (EU) (as it is now) and the European Court of Human Rights (ECHR) could initially be viewed as an attempt to renew the *jus publicum Europaeum*, by prolonging the durability of the constitutional nation-state within Europe's evolving regional setting.[46] In this view European integration was less about inter-state politics understood as foreign affairs and more about contributing to domestic socio-economic prosperity and internal security, as the best way to avoid backsliding into political authoritarianism and the domestic oppression that accompanied it.

42 See Paul Sweezy, 'Is the Marshall Plan an Instrument of Peace?', *Monthly Review* 1 (1949): 80–83.

43 See, e.g., Perry Anderson, *New Old World* (London: Verso, 2009), 10.

44 Schmitt, *Nomos*, 352–353.

45 See Thomas Risse and Daniela Engelmann-Martin, 'Identity Politics and European Integration: The Case of Germany', in Anthony Pagden (ed.), *The Idea of Europe: From Antiquity to the European Union* (Cambridge University Press, 2002), 296.

46 See, e.g., Alan Milward, *The European Rescue of the Nation-State* (London: Verso, 1992).

And integration would be pushed forward by additional dynamics– of a Europe uniting along teleological (economic) and technocratic (juridical), rather than purely political or pragmatic inter-governmental lines.[47]

Any project for creating a United States of Europe was sidelined early on, despite its strong support in the inter-war period, especially by the German Social Democratic Party.[48] After the failure of efforts to establish a European Political Community and European Defense Community (rejected in the French parliament), plans for political union were superseded by a juristic plan and a technocratic project. The juristic plan to create a federal-legal form of union was associated with the early jurisprudence of the European Court of Justice (ECJ) but encompassed a wider legal community.[49] The technocratic project to create a common market based on functional logic was associated with Jean Monnet, beginning with steps of 'de facto solidarity', in the words of the Schumann Declaration that led to the Coal and Steel Community of 1951.

Accordingly, the EU was supposed to operate functionally as a quasi-federal polity, with an idiosyncratic split between normative-technocratic authority – which became strongly supranationalised through the jurisprudence of the ECJ and the bureaucratic expertise (i.e., 'comitology') of the European Commission (and later the monetary authority of the European Central Bank [ECB]) – and political power, which remains predominantly with the component national units of the member states.[50]

Substantive member state equality was an important feature of this constitutional framework, pushing beyond the merely formal – and in practice illusory – sovereign equality of international law. So, for example, a balance would be achieved between larger and small member states through allocation of voting in the European Council, digressive proportionality of seats in the European Parliament, and strict unanimity in the rules for Treaty Amendment. (Informally, De Gaulle's Luxembourg compromise demanded unanimity even for ordinary law making.)

[47] See Ernst B. Hass, *The Uniting of Europe* (Stanford University Press, 1958).

[48] See Risse and Engelmann-Martin, Identity Politics and European Integration, 298

[49] Van Gend en Loos v Nederlandse Administratie de Belastingen [1963] ECR 1 (26/93); Costa v ENEL [1964] ECR 585 (6/64); see Antoine Vauchez, 'The Transnational Politics of Judicialisation: *Van Gend en Loos* and the Making of the EU Polity', *European Law Journal* 16 (2010): 1–28; Antonin Cohen, 'Constitutionalism without Constitution: Transnational Elites between Mobilisation and Legal Expertise in the Making of a Constitution for Europe (1940s–1960s)', *Law and Social Enquiry* 32 (2007): 109–135.

[50] See Joseph H. H. Weiler, 'The Transformation of Europe', *Yale Law Journal* 100 (1992): 2403–2483.

But European integration was also an exercise in constitutional imagination, playing a real and symbolic role in reframing the constitution of domestic political authority. This is engrained in seminal constitutional texts – as in the case of the Basic Law of the Federal Republic of Germany, which together with a constitutional 'openness' to international law, commits Germany to the establishment of a 'united Europe'.[51] But beyond this, commitments to belong to the EU and be part of the project of European integration are strongly enshrined informally – there is little imagination of any constitutional alternative to membership of the EU (or, since Maastricht, the single currency).[52]

The apparent success of this goal of restraining (German) state sovereignty was such that the distrust of German power came to be reinterpreted from an internal perspective as a collective *self*-limiting device; European integration was the external dimension of a strategy of domestic *self*-prevention. This has been called the 'German interest paradox': that it was in the German interest that German interests were not perceived as German interests.[53]

B. *The Political Constitution: From Constituent Power to Constitutional Rights*

If the inter-war period problematised the vision of constitutionalism underscored by state and popular sovereignty, the post-war liberal constitutional response was to reframe it, not as an expression of the authority of a constituent power, but of the authority, or even 'sovereignty', of *law*.[54] This is consistent with what this volume calls the 'structural-liberal' vision of constitutionalism, which prioritises juridified forms and grounds of authority and what Loughlin (see Chapter 6) calls 'normativism'.

But the displacement of constituent power in the project of European integration is not without moment. It profoundly reshapes the constitutional imagination and restructures national constitutional politics. This dynamic captures the political evolution of state-society relations – specifically the reform of institutions that mediate conflicts of interest between state and society – so that they operate in a manner removed from

[51] Preamble of the Basic Law ('GG') and Article 23(1) GG.

[52] See, e.g., Neil Walker, 'Our Constitutional Unsettlement', *Public Law* (2014): 529–548.

[53] See Jurgen Mayer, 'Rebels without a Cause? A Critical Analysis of the German Constitutional Court's OMT Reference', *German Law Journal* 15 (2014): 111–146.

[54] See, generally, Francis Jacobs, *Sovereignty of Law: The European Way* (Cambridge University Press, 2007).

traditional sources of democratic authority. In constitutional terms, the substitution of the framing idea of constituent power with constitutional rights occurs in the light of national, transnational, and supra-national processes of 'constitutionalisation'.[55] Constitutionalisation aims progressively to de-politicise and de-democratise state-society relations, replacing political and democratic deliberation with juridical and technocratic forms of decision making and norm setting.

The trend within Europe to limit political democracy through the creation of juridified constitutional rights and other entrenched constitutional rules accelerates in the post-war period, even in jurisdictions, such as France, normally resistant to the notion of 'government by judges'.[56] This includes the use of 'eternity clauses' that prohibit constitutional amendment and the outsourcing of political authority to 'counter-majoritarian' institutions – particularly independent regulatory agencies, independent central banks, and strong constitutional courts – whose legitimacy is technocratic or 'expertocratic'. Oversight of these institutions is also removed from the political process, vesting increasingly in administrative and judicial bodies that are insulated from the constituent power that undergirds the modern political-constitutional order.[57]

These constitutional institutions are meant to domesticate democracy, to avoid the perceived danger of it turning towards extremism of the Left or Right. They derive from a fear based, again, on inter-war European history: namely, the historical experience of fascism and the perceived threat of socialism.

In the aftermath of World War II, both European and US political elites attributed the collapse of inter-war European liberalism to over-politicisation, and to too much democracy rather than too little. European integration was thus initially conceived as an important component of de-politicising state-society relations, restraining democracy so as to deter any threat to liberal order.

Just like restrained sovereignty, restrained democracy was pursued externally through the creation of regional human rights agreements, such as the European Convention on Human Rights, and the trade agreements

[55] See Martin Loughlin, 'What is Constitutionalisation?' in Loughlin and Dobner (eds.) *The Twilight of Constitutionalism* (Oxford University Press, 2010), 47–73.

[56] See Mitchel Lasser, *Judicial Transformations: The Rights Revolution in the Courts of Europe* (Oxford University Press, 2009).

[57] See, e.g., Peter Lindseth, *Power and Legitimacy: Reconciling Europe and the Nation-State* (Oxford University Press, 2010).

and community institutions created by the Treaty of Paris in 1951 and then consolidated and extended by the Treaty of Rome in 1957.

There were also internal pressures. Politically, the project of European integration coincided in Continental Europe with the domestic-constitutional 'Christian-Democratic moment', a reaction to the turmoil of the inter-war period that sought, above all, political and economic *stability*.[58] This was to be achieved through political centrism, Christian-socialist thought (in both Catholic and Protestant variations), and restrained capitalism as well as restrained democracy. If this was based partly on national policy formation, it was also characterised by a growing de-politicisation of society: combining class compromise, the de-radicalisation of organised labour, and the rise of (neo-)corporatism.[59] In some countries, this de-radicalisation was even juridified and given a constitutional stamp of approval, the German Constitutional Court, for example, banning the Communist Party of Germany in 1956, setting the benchmark for Germany's 'militant democracy'.[60]

Reinventing the classic legacy of state sovereignty for the modern age was therefore a vision based on the domestic reconciliation of capitalism and democracy rather than any pretension of the European state to reclaiming external sovereignty. In the immediate post-war period, even Leftwing vanguard parties that had previously been officially committed to revolution, including the French and Italian communists, came to support emerging liberal democratic orders in Western Europe.[61] In the Golden Age or '*trentes gloriueses*', socialist parties contributed to the saving of capitalism 'from above' by means of social policies and the construction of the European welfare state, in diverse variants.[62]

The European project would contribute to this movement of de-politicisation by modifying European conceptions of democratic constitutionalism through its institutional structures and in particular its legal system. Both regionally and domestically, 'constitutionalisation', it has been argued, 'came as a masterly and opportune substitute for a real constitution, and law as a convenient expedient for politics' – effectively neutralising political disputes by turning them into mere 'technical matters'.[63]

[58] See Müller, *Contesting Democracy*, 132–150.

[59] See, generally, Philippe C. Schmitter and Gerhard Lehmbruch (eds.), *Trends toward Corporatist Intermediation* (New York: Sage, 1979).

[60] See Donald P. Kommers and Russell A. Miller, *The Constitutional Jurisprudence of the Federal Republic of Germany* (Durham, NC: Duke University Press, 2012), 291.

[61] See Müller, *Contesting Democracy*, 128.

[62] See Tony Judt, *Ill Fares the Land* (London: Penguin, 2010), 47.

[63] Cohen, 'Constitutionalism without Constitution', 109.

In spite of, or perhaps because of, the early failures to establish a European political community based on a constitution authorised by the 'Peoples of Europe', the ECJ and its legal community more generally pursued, at times aggressively, the legal *fiction* of a constitution.[64] It is this fiction that authorised the shift from political constitution making to judicial constitutionalisation, substituting constitutional rights for constituent power.

This European narrative was inter-linked with a number of domestic constitutional projects. A dialogue between European courts and national courts – through the so-called *Solange* jurisprudence – prompted the construction of a set of unwritten principles of human rights law into the ECJ's jurisprudence and Europeanised domestic projects of constitutional reform.[65]

To be sure, in European constitutional scholarship, there was always suspicion that the ECJ's increasing juridification of superior fundamental rights norms was aimed primarily at elevating its own juridical authority over that of national courts, especially constitutional courts. If the 'surface language' of the Court's jurisprudence was the language of human rights, Joseph Weiler noted, the 'deep structure' was all about supremacy.[66] But provided there was no outright conflict between domestic and supranational courts, the system remained functional, giving rise to various theories of constitutional pluralism, pluralist constitutionalism, contrapuntal law, and so on.[67]

Constitutional rights – from being initially cast as liberal 'trumps' on governmental policy prescriptions in Ronald Dworkin's influential narrative[68] – had come to be considered merely as ubiquitous interests to be 'balanced', with rights inflation undermining their rhetorical power and the doctrine of proportionality increasingly dominating discussion of constitutional and administrative review in both domestic and transnational settings.[69]

Substituting constitutional rights for constituent power is not, however, merely a formal exchange of ideas. Once European integration

64 Id.

65 Cf. Brun-Otto Bryde 'The ECJ's Fundamental Rights Jurisprudence – a Milestone in Transnational Constitutionalism', in Miguel Poiares Maduro and Loïc Azoulai (eds.), *The Past and Future of EU Law: The Classics of EU Law Revisited on the 50th Anniversary of the Rome Treaty* (Oxford: Hart Publishing, 2010), 119–130.

66 Weiler, 'The Transformation of Europe', 2403.

67 See, generally, Jan Komarek and Matej Avbelj (eds.), *Constitutional Pluralism in the European Union and Beyond* (Oxford: Hart Publishing, 2012).

68 Ronald Dworkin, *Taking Rights Seriously* (Cambridge, MA: Harvard University Press, 1978).

69 See Jacco Bomhoff, *Balancing Constitutional Rights* (Cambridge University Press 2013); cf. David Beatty, *The Ultimate Rule of Law* (Oxford University Press, 2005).

is placed into focus, juridification of the rules of European law can be seen substantively to impact on domestic constitutional order, elevating laissez-faire economic freedoms (in the form of fundamental freedoms to trade) above social and welfare rights, as well as other non-economic concerns.[70] To understand this transformation in full we have to turn to a third dynamic of constitutional change in the project of European integration: the economic constitution.

C. *Economic Constitutionalism: From Ordoliberalism to Neo-Liberalism*

'Economic constitutionalism' not only means that political authority is increasingly conditioned by particular economic interests and ideas, but that the economy is increasingly viewed as the principal ground of authority for the 'constitution' of the polity as a whole – in the sense of defining and colonising the totality of our social and political relations.[71]

The idea of an 'economic constitution', prefigured by Frankfurt school theorists Franz Neumann and Hugo Sinzheimer, but now associated with the Freiberg ordoliberals,[72] is analogous to the efforts of Karl Loewenstein in the political sphere. Ordoliberalism thus called for the constitutionalisation of the economic sphere, protecting the conditions underlying free market competition, in an attempt to restore and prolong liberal constitutional ideals in the post-war era by insulating the economic domain from political and democratic interference. The ordoliberal idea of the economic constitution and in particular the constitutionalisation of macroeconomic policy choices made monetary stability and open financial markets as constitutionally significant as private property and contractual freedom.[73]

Ordoliberals and defenders of the (related) tradition of 'social market economy' considered the laissez-faire of classical economic liberalism to be socially and politically bankrupt. As against Friedrich Hayek's brand of 'paleo-liberalism', they saw the economic order as constructed

[70] See Fritz Scharpf, 'The Asymmetry of European Integration: Or Why Europe Can't Have a Social Market Economy', *Socio-Economic Review* 8 (2010): 211–250.

[71] See Emilios Christodoulidis, 'The European Court of Justice and "Total Market" Thinking', *German Law Journal* 14 (2013): 2005–2020.

[72] See Franz Neumann, 'On the Preconditions and Legal Concept of an Economic Constitution', in Otto Kirchheimer and Franz Neumann (eds.,) *Social Democracy and the Rule of Law* (ed., Keith Tribe) (London: Allen and Unwin, 1987), 44–65.

[73] See, generally, Karlo Tuori and Klaus Tuori, *The Euro-Crisis: A Constitutional Analysis* (Cambridge University Press, 2014).

and maintained by strong state apparatus and strong constitutional rules, and not by a spontaneous evolution of the market and market relations. The conditions for competition would not simply take care of themselves: Unbridled capitalism would be as self-destructive as unbridled democracy.[74]

Ordoliberalism thus placed its faith in the economic constitution and a technocratic-juridical governance apparatus rather than in the political constitution and democracy to approximate the conditions of the free market and maintain personal freedom.

If to put the law above man, as Rousseau quipped, 'il faudrait des dieux [one actually would need gods]', the ordoliberals answered the call for a new set of elites, who, confounding Rousseau, could, like Gods, finally 'give laws to men'.[75] If democracy, in other words, must be tamed, economic constitutionalism was the means to achieve this aim.

As constitutional theorist Carl Joachim Friedrich noted in 1955, and Foucault would later explore in his lectures on neo-liberal governmentality in 1979, the decisive theoretical turn triggered by ordoliberalism was to replace constituent power (or popular sovereignty) with individual economic freedom – a freedom to participate in the market – as the legitimating device for the whole constitutional order.[76] Or as German Chancellor Ludwig Erhard put it: 'The revolution of our era is marked by the call for freedom rather than for class warfare', as if these must henceforth be strict alternatives.[77] The economic constitution becomes the political form of the free economy.

The ordoliberals adopted and adapted Schmitt's message of 'strong state, sound economy',[78] and gave it a legal-constitutional foundation; technocratic exercises of governance would be subject to constitutional safeguards and constitutionalised goals. This encompassed macroeconomic decision making as much as the protection of property rights and contractual freedom: In the ordoliberal constitutional imagination,

[74] Id.

[75] Cf. Hannah Arendt, *On Revolution* (London: Penguin, 2006), 184.

[76] Carl J. Friedrich, 'The Political Thought of Neo-liberalism', *American Political Science Review* 49 (1955): 509–525; Michel Foucault, *The Birth of Biopolitics: Lectures at the College de France 1978–1979* (trans., Graham Burchell) (New York: Palgrave MacMillan, 2008).

[77] Quoted in Ludwig-Erhard-Stiftung E. V. Bonn, *Standard Texts on the Social Market Economy: Two Centuries of Discussion* (ed., Horst Friedrich Wünsche) (trans., Derek Rutter) (Stuttgart: Gustav Fisher Verlag, 1982), ix.

[78] See Cristi, *Carl Schmitt and Authoritarian Liberalism.*

independence of monetary policy from political influence is as important as the independence of the judiciary.[79]

And if the new role of the state was primarily to ensure the conditions for fair competition and price stability, it was a role in which European integration could play a key part (see also Dowdle, Chapter 4). As Giandomineco Majone, doyen of European integration studies, puts it:

> The possibility of separating economics and politics was a key, if implicit, assumption of the founders of the EEC. It was not a new idea but rather a return to a classical liberal tenet which in the nineteenth century and up to World War I had made it possible for the world economy to develop in such a fashion that 'between national and international economic integration there was only a difference in degree but not in kind'.[80]

The particular constitutional prescriptions of ordoliberalism were never straightforwardly applied or implemented at either the German or European level.[81] But its particular ideological linkage of neo-classical market economics and liberal constitutionalism was to become a key conceptual plank in the process of Europeanisation.[82] Its legacy can be seen, for example, in how the self-understandings of political actors in Europe have been increasingly conditioned by particular socio-economic ideologies and interests that correspond to the pressures of economic rationality and the logic of market competition. The cosmopolitan economic neo-liberalism that is captured in the term *globalisation* can also be understood as a direct descendent of ordoliberalism's economic critique of the dangers of democratic constituent power.[83]

In practice, from 1945 to 1975, a post-war political consensus tempered this economism, as noted in the preceding text, specifically through the national (neo-)corporatist state that sought to tame capitalism as well as democracy, and was founded on a social contract between labour and

[79] See Alan T. Peacock and Hans Willgerodt, *Germany's Social Market Economy* (London: MacMillan for the Trade Policy Research Centre, 1989).

[80] Giandomenico Majone, *Rethinking the Union of Europe Post-Crisis* (Oxford University Press, 2014), 149 (quoting Wilhelm Röpke, 'Economic Order and International Law', *Recuil des Cours, Academie de Droit Internationale* 86 (1954): 219).

[81] See, e.g., Christian Joerges, 'What Is Left of the European Economic Constitution?', European University Institute Working Papers Law 2004/13 (Florence, Italy: European University Institute, 2004).

[82] Steph Dullien and Ulrike Guérot, 'The Long Shadow of Ordoliberalism: Germany's Approach to the Euro-crisis', *European Council of Foreign Relations Policy Brief* (London: European Council on Foreign Relations, 2012), 49.

[83] See Kanishka Jayasuriya, 'Globalisation, Sovereignty and the Rule of Law: From Political to Economic Constitutionalism', *Constellations* 8 (2001): 442–460.

capital.[84] During this period, European integration sought to square the circle of economic modernisation and market competition together with social protection and widespread material prosperity.

The actual contribution of European economic integration to growth during this 'golden age' is disputed.[85] And beginning in the 1970s, integration is redirected, signalled by the renaissance of Friedrich Hayek and ideas that only thirty years previously had been considered defunct.[86] This period presages the new constitutionalism of *neo-liberalism*.[87]

With the turn towards neo-liberalism, the neo-corporatist state was replaced by what Chris Bickerton has termed the 'member state' – which demanded the dismantling of the social contract between labour and capital; the unravelling of class compromise; and the freeing of capitalism from political constraints, including those deriving from concern for conceptions of the public good.[88] In this period, economic privatisation is combined with administrative nationalisation, and the (constitutional) role of the state becomes one of simply correcting for market failures.[89] Under neo-liberal constitutionalism, market liberalisation, economic efficiency, productivity, and corporate interests become constitutional ends in themselves.

In attempting to rewrite the terms of the post-war social contract by inserting a more laissez-faire approach to political economy, two distinct avenues were pursued.[90] The first was to introduce a strict determinacy to political discourse, that of 'There Is No Alternative' (i.e., 'TINA'), which is particularly associated with Margaret Thatcher, but increasingly infected her neo-liberal and third-way successors.

The second involved pleading the necessity of neo-liberal rules and obligations for both domestic and global political and economic stability.[91] In Fritz Scharpf's narrative, the EU's overall structural asymmetry reflects a neo-liberal bias that prioritises liberal over republican readings of the constitution, and economically liberal over social welfare models of the

[84] See Chris Bickerton, *From Nation-States to Member States* (Oxford University Press, 2013), 74–113.

[85] Cf. Barry Eichengreen, *The European Economy since 1945: Co-ordinated Capitalism and Beyond* (Princeton University Press, 2007).

[86] See Dieter Plehwe, 'Introduction', in Philip Mirowski and Dieter Plehwe (eds.) *The Road from Mont Pèlerin: The Making of the Neoliberal Thought Collective* (Cambridge, MA: Harvard University Press, 2009), 1–44.

[87] Cf. Foucault, *The Birth of Bio-Politics*.

[88] See Bickerton, *European Integration*, 123.

[89] Id. at 107.

[90] See id. at 95.

[91] Id.

relationship between state and society. As Scharpf argues, the ECJ played a significant role in this constitutional prioritisation by elevating European rules into directly effective and supreme constitutional law. The effect of substituting 'integration through politics' with 'integration through law' was not normatively neutral, as Scharpf illustrates, but constitutionalised a set of market liberal rules, homogenising an otherwise heterogeneous set of domestic economies.[92]

There are, of course, wider cultural aspects to this neo-liberal transformation, extending far beyond the EU, which cause understandings of the *public good* to become pathologised or elided: 'Gone is the notion of the common good understood on a political register; instead we have optimization of market outcomes'.[93]

The constitutional implications of neo-liberalism are wide-ranging. Political and social identity is fragmented, and increasingly commodified and quantified as merely consisting of a particular collection of individualist tastes and preferences – replacing the citizen with a simple consumer of economic benefits. And in terms of the political responsiveness of the new 'debt state' and its institutions in this period, the constituency that matters is no longer the *statsvolk* but the *marktsvolk*, 'inaugurating a new stage in the relationship between democracy and capitalism'.[94]

IV. Liberal Excesses, Geo-Political Pressures: 'Maastricht and All That'

If the period from 1957 to 1991 demonstrated that European integration was at least compatible with the liberal-democratic constitutional ideal if not necessarily demanded by it, the subsequent Treaty of Maastricht and its surrounding era (i.e., 'Maastricht and all that'[95]) signals a turning point in the path of integration.

Geo-political shifts of seismic proportions had occurred with the fall of the Berlin Wall, the reunification of Germany, and the collapse of the Soviet Union. First, 'the German question' – the question of how to prevent German domination of the European continent – returns to the centre stage of European constitutional politics, where it had lain dormant for forty years.

[92] See, generally, Fritz Scharpf, 'Legitimacy in the Multi-Level European Polity', in Petra Dobner and Martin Loughlin (eds.), *Twilight of Constitutionalism* (Oxford University Press, 2010), 89–120.

[93] Christodoulidis, 'The European Court of Justice', 2017.

[94] See, e.g., Wolfgang Streeck, *Buying Time* (London: Verso, 2014), 79–88.

[95] Cf. Wynn Godley, 'Maastricht and All That', *London Review of Books* 14 (1992): 3–4.

It also inaugurates the future enlargement programme, with membership of the EU opened up to the countries of Central and Eastern Europe, prompting a discourse of constitutional closure, the 'finality' of integration, which foreshadowed the ill-fated constitutional project, and was a factor in its rejection by the French.[96]

Relatedly, with the end of the Cold War announcing the United States as a sole global superpower and the single market project nearing completion after the Single European Act (1986), the sense emerges that Europe needs to find a new vocation, no longer required as a Western liberal bulwark against the threat of Soviet communism or as a facilitating framework of harmonised rules for a single market.

These geo-political reconfigurations, however, symbolised by the fall of the Berlin Wall, represented not only the triumph of liberal democracy but also the unleashing of a 'disorganised' global capitalism that had been in the making since the informal American empire began to establish its global economic dominance in the aftermath of World War II.[97] Neo-liberal capitalism, as a political-economic system, came to be seen as invulnerable and even invincible – as 'the end of history'[98] – because there seemed, literally, to be no longer an alternative to the free market. Thatcher's TINA ideology was thus widely adopted in the aftermath of the collapse of the Soviet Union. 'Since 1989,' the former standard-bearer of Frankfurt School critical theory Jurgen Habermas suggests, 'it has become impossible to break out of the universe of capitalism; the only remaining option is to civilize and tame the capitalist dynamic from within.'[99]

Indeed, a new phase of economic integration in Europe complemented the neo-liberal revolution of the 1980s, facilitating the turn to financialisation of the economy through the dismantling of fetters on capital accumulation.[100] This incorporated a loosening of capital controls, with the free movement of capital eventually becoming a fundamental legal and even

[96] See Joscka Fischer, 'From Confederacy to Federation: Thoughts on the Finality of European Integration', in Yves Mény, Christian Joerges, and Joseph Weiler (eds.), *What Kind of Constitution for What Kind of Polity: Responses to Joschka Fischer* (Cambridge, MA: Harvard Law School, 2001), 19–31.

[97] See Andrew Glyn, *Capitalism Unleashed: Finance Globalisation and Welfare* (Oxford University Press, 2006); Leo Panitch and Sam Gindin, *The Making of Global Capitalism: The Political Economy of American Empire* (London: Verso, 2012).

[98] Francis Fukuyama, *The End of History and the Last Man* (New York: The Free Press, 1992)

[99] Jurgen Habermas, *The Crisis of the European Union: A Response* (London: Polity, 2012), 106, 113.

[100] See, e.g., Agustín José Menendez, 'The Existential Crisis of the European Union', *German Law Journal* 14 (2013): 453–526.

constitutional right in the EU. The political dominance of monetarism, which, already unleashed in the Anglo-American Thatcher-Reagan revolution, then came to provide the foundation for the project of Economic and Monetary Union (EMU), also launched at Maastricht.

With its commitment to a de-politicised monetary policy based exclusively on price stability; and an independent but limited ECB (with restricted monetary tools but without the guidance of any supranational economic policy capable of dealing with uneven development, socio-economic heterogeneity, or exogenous fiscal shocks), the Maastricht Treaty attempted to supranationalise ordoliberal principles designed for domestic constitutional consumption.[101]

In its compromise between Franco-German interests, EMU was a continuation of the usual course of European integration. The French saw it as a further strategy to prevent or contain the hegemony of the Deutsche Mark, the new 'atom bomb' anticipated to detonate in the light of German reunification and the re-emergence of Germany as a central European hegemon.[102] But if the French got the single currency they wanted it was under the conditions the Germans demanded: An ECB loosely modelled on the structure of the *Bundesbank*.[103]

EMU also signalled a departure, initially thought to be temporary, from the idea of European unity, and the launching of what was euphemistically referred to as 'variable geometry' or 'differentiated integration': the ability to pursue different levels of integration through opt-ins and opt-outs (further formalised at the Treaty of Amsterdam in 1997). More generally, Maastricht called an end to the singleness of the Community Method of law making, beginning an era dominated by visions of 'new governance', 'experimentalism', and the 'Open Method of Co-ordination', an era in which integration would no longer necessarily proceed in a constitutional or even legal fashion, but through 'soft law' and other informal processes.[104]

Maastricht therefore also signalled a departure from the previous, functional logic that economic integration would prompt political integration, and that politicisation would then force elites to engage mass

101 See Tuori and Tuori, *The Euro-Crisis*.

102 See Majone, *Rethinking the Union*, 29.

103 See Ellie Cohen, 'The Euro, Economic Federalism, and National Sovereignty', in Anthony Pagden (ed.), *The Idea of Europe: From Antiquity to the European Union* (Cambridge University Press, 2002), 269; Anderson, *Beyond Constituitonalism*, 29.

104 See, e.g., Joanne Scott and David M. Trubek, 'Mind the Gap: Law and New Approaches to Governance in the European Union', *European Law Journal* 8 (2002): 1–18.

publics in European matters, eventually precipitating a process of Euro-democratisation.[105] On the contrary, EMU entrenched the *de-politicisation* of a key aspect of macro-economic policy, removing an important lever of power from the political pillars of the member states, but without reconstructing it at the supranational political level. The new currency – a 'currency without a state' – was not only democratically unaccountable (which would hardly have differentiated it from national variants), but it also lacked the social and political bonds of community to sustain it, offering a symbol of the new 'economic Messianism' of the era to follow.[106]

Finally, despite its fragmentation, with its inter-governmental pillars in the area of Justice and Home Affairs and Common Foreign and Security Policy rendering the EU into a 'Europe of bits and pieces' – Maastricht signalled a move from economic union to possible political union.[107] The most prominent symbol of this move was the creation of Union Citizenship, an apparently dormant creature that the Court of Justice nevertheless breathed life into during the first decade of its existence.[108] But the sign of things to come was the substitution, at the apparent insistence of the British, of any reference in the treaty to the 'F' word (federalism), with the tamer and constitutionally ambiguous 'S' word, 'subsidiarity'.[109]

Effort at 'political union' was half-hearted at best, and after the German Constitutional Court's famous 'Maastricht decision', it was laid to rest — the decision subduing any dreams of a European federal constitutional project.[110] This more ambitious, constructivist, federal and constitutional vision of European integration had always existed alongside – sometimes in conflict with – ideas of re-inventing, preserving, or transcending the sovereign nation-state. From the very beginning of the post-war period,

105 See Gary Marks and Lisbet Hooghe, 'A Postfunctionalist Theory of European Integration: From Permissive Consensus to Constraining Dissensus' *British Journal of Political Science* 39 (2009): 5.

106 See Michael A. Wilkinson, 'Economic Messianism and Constitutional Power in a German Europe: All Courts Are Equal but Some Courts Are More Equal Than Others' (2014), *LSE, Law, Society and Economy Working Papers*, 26/2014, http://papers.ssrn.com/sol3/papers.cfm?abstract_id=2522919.

107 See Deirdre Curtin, 'The Constitutional Structure of the Union: A Europe of Bits and Pieces', *Common Market Law Review* 30 (1993): 17–69.

108 See, e.g., see Ferdinand Wollenschlager, 'A New Fundamental Freedom beyond Market Integration', *European Law Journal* 17 (2011): 1–34.

109 Treaty on the Functioning of the European Union (TFRU), art. 5(3).

110 *Brunner v. European Union* [1994] 1 CMLR 57.

the prospect of a post-national state – or of a European super-state – cast its shadow over the process of integration. The federal vision remained alive, even if only in the minds of scholars.[111]

This shadow was partly drawn, and occasionally erased, by factors external to the EU – by questions of enlargement; geo-political security; and relations with third countries, accession and candidate countries, and other international organisations such as NATO and the WTO. But the notion of European identity as a counterweight – in their view – to the belligerent, imperialist, market-fundamentalist values of the United States was presented by Jurgen Habermas and Jacques Derrida as central to the development of a constitutional programme of closer European union in their February 14th European 'manifesto'.[112]

Since Maastricht, however, the idea of a supranational constitutional state inhabits a political and constitutional 'no-man's land'. On the one hand, there seemed little prospect of political elites pushing forward with a European constitutional state legitimised through a pan-European representative democracy. But this was in any case effectively proscribed by the Lisbon decision of the Federal Constitutional Court of Germany. This most powerful domestic court in the region has consistently held that the demands of Germany's core domestic constitutional identity must trump those of European political integration.[113] The ambiguous 'not yet' for a European state of its Maastricht decision has morphed into a decisive 'never', at least not without a revolutionary constitution on the basis of a new act of German constituent power.[114]

The status of the EU – and indeed of its member states – thus remains in limbo: not a mere international organisation but neither a fully-fledged federal super-state – or as Jacques Delors put it, an 'unidentified political object'.[115]

[111] See Andrew Glencross and Alexander H. Trechsel (eds.) *EU Federalism and Constitutionalism: The Legacy of Altiero Spinelli* (Lanham, MD: Lexington Books, 2010). Cf. Federico Mancini, 'The Case for Statehood', *European Law Journal* 4 (1998): 29–42; Joseph H. H. Weiler, 'The Case against the Case for Statehood', *European Law Journal* 4 (1998): 43–62.

[112] Jurgen Habermas and Jacques Derrida, 'February 15th or What Binds European Together?' *Constellations* (2003): 291–297.

[113] *Lisbon Case*, BverfG, 2 BVE 2/08, 30 June 2009.

[114] See Michael A. Wilkinson, 'Political Constitutionalism in the European Union', *Modern Law Review* 76 (2012): 198–199.

[115] 'Speech by Jacques Delors (Luxembourg, 9 September 1985)', *CVCE.eu*, http://www.cvce.eu/obj/speech_by_jacques_delors_luxembourg_9_september_1985-en-423d6913-b4e2-4395-9157-fe70b3ca8521.html.

Although this has sometimes been celebrated in the literature as Europe's *Sonderweg*,[116] Europe's inability to resolve the question of its own nature or of its consequences for its members – either as an emerging federal polity or in terms of its impact on the concept of the state and projects of state-building and state-repair – renders it exceedingly fragile in critical political and economic moments.[117] Centrifugal and centripetal forces have combined to make the project look increasingly precarious.

An account of Europe's *Sonderweg* now needs to be corrected and updated to include the effects of asymmetric national political power and a single currency and free movement of capital that deprives member states of the eurozone of one of the few levers left to remain competitive or regain competitiveness. The substantive constitutional effects of an economic supranationalism spearheaded by the symbolic unity of a single currency and an (increasingly) asymmetric political inter-governmentalism are captured in the voguish label, a 'German Europe'.[118] Is this Europe's new *Sonderweg*?

Contrary to its intent, the judicialisation of authority and increasing emphasis on liberal 'negative constitutionalism' – on restraints of governmental power, particularly, through economic constitutionalism (symbolised by the case of *Cassis de Dijon* and the ECJ's introduction of the principle of mutual recognition[119]) – has not lead to the perfection of liberalism or the triumph of liberal constitutionalism in Europe. Instead it has led to increasing contestation, and outright conflict: geo-politically, between core and peripheral EU states; politically, between different levels of government (e.g., national and supranational, sub-national and supra-national, and national and sub-national); and ideologically, between different substantive visions of the good life (e.g., neo-liberal, republican, social-democratic).[120] Far from eradicating politics,

[116] See J. H. H. Weiler, 'In Defence of the Status Quo: Europe's Constitutional *Sonderweg*', in J. H. H. Weiler and Marlene Wind (eds.), *European Constitutionalism beyond the State* (Cambridge University Press, 2003), 7–25.

[117] Cf. Neil Walker, 'Europe's Unresolved Constitution', in Michel Rosenfeld and Andras Sajo (eds.) *The Oxford Handbook of Comparative Constitutional Law* (Oxford University Press, 2012), 1185–1208.

[118] See Ulrich Beck, *German Europe* (London: Polity Press, 2013).

[119] Rewe-Zentral AG v Bundesmonopolverwaltung für Branntwein, Case C-120/78 *Cassis de Dijon* (Feb. 20, 1979) [1979] ECR 649.

[120] But see Matthias Kumm, 'How Does European Union Law Fit into the World of Public Law', in Jürgen Neyer and Antje Wiener (eds.), *Political Theory of the European Union* (Oxford University Press, 2010), 125.

judicial constitutionalisation of social and economic conflicts has led to renewed political and constitutional tensions.

A fuller account of the duality between supranational normative structure and national political power (Joseph Weiler's 'dual supranationalism'[121]) must therefore reject any formalistic picture of a balanced bifurcation of legal and political pillars and capture their dysfunctional inter-relation: signified by two decades of doubt, beginning with the political and constitutional challenges to Maastricht in the French and Dutch referenda, and in the German Constitutional Court; continuing through the failed Constitutional experiment and subsequent 'reform' Treaty of Lisbon; and now culminating with the Euro-crisis.

V. Euro-Crisis: The Constitution of Authoritarian Liberalism

The cumulative effect of integration in its neo-liberal phase has been to transform the constitutional state by opposing (rather than uniting) state-society relations: delinking the sovereign power of the state from the constituent power of the people. This is a foundational shift, because central to the constitutional imagination has always been not only that the powers of the state have to be limited (as liberalism recommends), but also that they have to be limited in the name of 'the people' or at least recognisable as a process of collective *self*-limitation. In the neo-liberal constitution, by contrast, the powers of the state are constrained, not by 'the people' – but by the 'the market'.[122] Politically liberal constitutional democracy is increasingly replaced by an economically liberal constitutional oligarchy.

The current conjuncture seems particularly stark. Tensions between European core and periphery and within nations are not resolved by democratic debate and political contestation, but placated, if at all, by a system of managerial control and vague appeals to the obligations in the Treaty on the Functioning of the European Union.[123] Standing above the conflict and tensions are 'the rules of the game', i.e., Europe's 'economic constitution', which are said to prevent, for example, unconditional bailouts or serious debt restructuring for the periphery. These constraints result not only from resistance on the part of the creditor states and the 'Troika'

[121] Joseph H. H. Weiler, 'The Community System: The Dual Character of Supranationalism', *Yearbook of European Law* (1981): 267–306.

[122] Bickerton, *European Integration*, 67. See also Wolfgang Streeck, 'Markets and Peoples: Democratic Capitialism and European Integration', *New Left Review* 73 (2013): 63–71.

[123] Treaty on the Functioning of the European Union [TFRU], art. 125.

(i.e., the ECB, European Commission, and International Monetary Fund) to transnational solidarity, but from constitutional principles such as the 'avoidance of moral hazard' and the rhetoric of 'fiscal discipline'.[124]

Whether the treatment of debtor states is economically rational in any meaningful way is doubtful, certainly in the long term. The Troika's unwillingness to restructure Greek debt, for example, may well frustrate the surest route to growth and to repayment of creditors. But to do so would be to violate a new shibboleth of neo-liberal political-economic rationality – 'austerity' – irrespective of the extent to which that might affect national democracy, let alone domestic economic policy.[125]

But what is remarkable is that alongside this strong insistence on 'playing by the rules' of the economic constitution (anyway self-serving given their initial violation by France and Germany[126]), there has been, since the Euro-crisis, increasing resort to highly discretionary and intrusive managerial governance.[127] This can be seen particularly in the memoranda of understanding negotiated by the Troika with countries in receipt of financial assistance, as well as in the latitude given to the ECB in its unorthodox measures of monetary policy –such as bond-buying on the secondary market; becoming a qualified 'lender of last resort'; and restricting emergency liquidity to national banks facing immediate financial collapse.[128]

This suggests a transformation of the EMU from a rule-based institution to a policy-based one, sidelining the ordoliberal faith in liberal-constitutionalism and raising the spectre of a qualitative transformation of the European constitution into an 'authoritarian liberalism'.[129] Its first, 'authoritarian' element shows in a twin development of de-democratisation and de-legalisation of integration; its second, 'liberal' element points to a liberal market teleology as the over-riding goal of the formal and informal constitution of Europe.

[124] See, e.g., Bundesverfassungsgericht [BVerfG – Federal Constitutional Court], 2 BvR 2728/13 (Jan. 14, 2014).

[125] Cf. Mark Blyth, *Austerity: The History of a Dangerous Idea* (Oxford University Press, 2013).

[126] See Marco Buti and Lucio R. Pench, 'Why Do Large Countries Flout the Stability Pact? And What Can Be Done About It?', *JCMS: Journal of Common Market Studies* 42 (2004): 1025–1032; cf. Commission of the European Communities v. Council of the European Union, Case C-27/04 (July 13, 2004).

[127] Christian Joerges, 'Europe's Economic Constitution in Crisis and the Emergence of a New Constitutional Constellation', ZenTra Working Paper in Transnational Studies No. 06/2012 (Oldenberg and Bremen: ZenTra Centre for Transnational Studies, 2012).

[128] Cf. BVerfG, 2 BvR 2728/13 (Jan. 14, 2014) ('the OMT Decision').

[129] See Michael A. Wilkinson, 'The Spectre of Authoritarian Liberalism: Reflections on the Constitutional Crisis of the European Union', *German Law Journal* 14 (2013): 527–560.

The continuing de-democratisation of European constitutionalism is evident in the manner through which economic crisis measures – such as the conditionality attached to European stability mechanisms, country-specific recommendations in the European semester, and outright monetary transactions (OMT) promised by the ECB – increasingly avoid or evade normal democratic debate and political contestation, whether these measures are enacted by European institutions directly or are rubber-stamped by domestic actors under unusual pressures of urgency or even 'emergency'.[130]

De-democratisation continues, even if now in accelerated form, the ideological currents of ordo- and neo-liberalism discussed in the preceding text: Not only is there 'no alternative' to market capitalism there is specifically no alternative to austerity and neo-liberal structural reforms, meaning privatisation of state assets, pension reforms, increases in regressive taxation such as VAT, and public sector and social welfare cuts. These are the only means to regain competitiveness and avoid the 'moral hazard' that would otherwise be entailed by unconditional aid.

The turn towards de-legalisation is a more complex shift, not least because the move away from the normal community method of law making, as we saw, predates the Eurocrisis.[131] It can be found in the increasing displacement of formal legal instruments and institutions with less formal, non-legal instruments, or with outright coercion, circumventing judicial and constitutional review. These include 'hard-soft law' such as 'recommendations' and 'opinions' in place of legislation, which despite their nomenclature are *imposed* on the recipient (debtor) state, pushed through without normal procedures of democratic deliberation. The new 'union method' (rather than the 'community method') of rule-making bypasses representative institutions, particularly the European Parliament, and does not therefore benefit from democratic input-legitimacy.[132]

A further landmark has been reached with the ECJ's decision in *Pringle v Republic of Ireland* on the validity of the European Stability Mechanism (ESM),[133] in which the court elevates Europe's interest in defending the financial stability of the eurozone as a whole by offering a 'bail-out fund'

[130] See Jonathan White, 'Emergency Europe', *Political Studies* 62 (2015): 300–318.

[131] See also Claire Kilpatrick, 'On the Rule of Law and Economic Emergency: The Degradation of Basic Legal Values in Europe's Bailouts', *Oxford Journal of Legal Studies* 35 (2015): 325–353.

[132] See Menendez, 'Existential Crisis'.

[133] Pringle v. Government of Ireland and the Attorney General, C-370/12 (Nov. 27, 2012).

above the interest in respecting its constitutional framework as set out in the EU treaties.[134]

Crisis response measures include the exercise of institutional authority, most notably of the ECB, that goes far beyond what is permitted by its constitutional or legal mandate, such as its sovereign bond-buying promise (OMT), but which is, unsurprisingly, also waved through by the ECJ – despite the protestations of the German Constitutional Court, and in its first-ever referral to the ECJ.[135]

If legality was a liberal substitute for democratic legitimacy, or a counterbalance to a process of de-democratisation with deeper roots in the project of integration, the turn away from the legal form, while continuing the process of de-democratisation, is a move of truly constitutional significance. Emergency measures are thus able to escape constitutional and administrative review by courts, which in the absence of democratic processes of norm creation represent the only avenue through which the disciplining effect of fundamental rights (whether emanating from the domestic, European, or international levels), such as the right to social security or to basic health care, can be secured. Indeed, de-legalisation can violate fundamental rights, denying access to justice by preventing legal challenges altogether.[136]

There is, of course, nothing new in government resorting to extraordinary measures – formal as well as informal – in times of crisis or emergency in an attempt to restore order, security, or a return to economic normality;[137] nor in a compliant judiciary. What is distinct in the wake of the raft of measures implemented since the Euro-crisis is the way extraordinary measures appear to be becoming the 'new normal', rather than exceptional or temporary.[138] Thus, they are not justified on the basis of needing to respond an 'emergency' that will be over at any identifiable future point. Rather, their justification lies in the need to assuage the markets, to maintain the 'singleness' of the currency. There is nothing distinctly temporary about these needs – they are the products of

[134] See, generally, Jonathan Tomkin, 'Contradiction, Circumvention, and Conceptual Gymnastics: The Impact of the Adoption of the ESM Treaty on the State of European Democracy', *German Law Journal* 14 (2013): 169–189.

[135] Peter Gauweiler and Others v. Deutscher Bundestag, C- 62/14 (June 16, 2015).

[136] Cf. Claire Kilpatrick, 'Are the EU Bail-Outs Immune to Social Challenge Because They Are Not EU Law?', *European Constitutional Law Review* 10 (2014): 393–421.

[137] See, generally, Victor V. Ramraj, 'No Doctrine More Pernicious? Emergencies and the Limits of Legality' in Victor V. Ramraj (ed.) *Emergencies and the Limits of Legality* (Cambridge University Press, 2008), 3–29.

[138] See White, 'Emergency Europe'.

an ideology, not of a particular situation. In true Schmittian fashion, an enemy has even been identified; the 'enemy within' the authoritarian liberal constitutional project are those 'bad Europeans' who disregard the economic stability criteria.[139]

What then is *liberal* about authoritarian liberalism? To be sure, authoritarian liberalism might not appear 'liberal' in an orthodox sense. De-democratisation does not straightforwardly fit in the classical liberal constitutional mind-set; de-legalisation still less so. If democracy has always had an uneasy role in the structural-liberal constitutional imagination, the idea of the rule of law is firmly part of it, albeit a notoriously contested concept in its own right.[140]

The liberal aspect of authoritarian liberalism comes instead from a liberal economic teleology. The measures that are implemented, whether to stabilise (e.g., the ESM) or prevent future crises (e.g., fiscal compact), are aimed at continuing the process of market integration, fostering competitiveness between national economies, and ensuring neo-liberal structural reform in order to respect *economic* freedom.

The presiding symbol of this new teleology of *economic* liberalism is the Euro-currency, the survival of which is said to represent the fate of the Euro-polity. Like the gold standard of the 1920s, the pressure to maintenance the euro now submits politics to an overwhelming economic rationality.[141]

This 'economic Messianism' – a belief that only neo-liberal economics can redeem politics – requires 'liberal interventionism', where even market norms such as sovereign yields are subject to constitutional override in order to generate or replicate economic rationality under conditions of the 'irreversibility' of the euro.

In the new constitutional configuration, the pursuit of a 'militant economics' appears to be replacing the older pursuit of a 'militant democracy'. Projects of capital accumulation, it now seems, no longer need to be protected only from social democracy, or monopoly capitalism, but from the market and its apparent 'irrationality' (which if left to its devices would have resolved unsustainable Greek debt a different way from that imagined by the ECB).

[139] See Udo di Fabio, 'Karlsruhe Makes a Referral', *German Law Journal* 15 (2014): 107–110.

[140] See, e.g., Judith N. Shklar, *Legalism: Law, Morals and Political Trials* (Cambridge, MA: Harvard University Press, 1964).

[141] See Daniel Wilsher, 'Law and the Financial Crisis: Searching for Europe's New Gold Standard', *European Law Journal* 20 (2014): 241–283.

Liberal constitutionalisation of 'integration through law' has been replaced by a liberal-authoritarian 'integration through fear',[142] a process not limited to economic integration: Thus a weakening of usual avenues of political and legal accountability can be found in Europe's 'Area of Freedom, Security and Justice'[143] – and in particular the development of European criminal law through mutual recognition of judgments in the framework of the European Arrest Warrant.[144]

In the absence of strong bonds of supranational community or transnational solidarity, technocratic regulation represents the principal defence in maintaining the European project, and particularly its central symbol, the euro. But now, even this is under threat. With the placing of 'Grexit' on the table by German Finance Minister Wolfgang Schauble we are now firmly playing outside the rules, or playing a different game altogether: there is no legal option of exit from the single currency.

Looking into the future things look grim from a liberal constitutional perspective. Constitutional reflexivity seems in short supply. There are, for example, gestures towards tightening up the rules and maintaining a harsher surveillance model of member state's budgets. The Excessive Imbalance Procedure, however, which stipulates sanctions against member states for failure to conform with these rules, 'is meant to be an entirely discretionary regime whose scope of delegated authority far exceeds the limits of generally allowable delegation in constitutional democracies'.[145]

In the current geo-political constitution of Europe, constitutional authority in one country can condition and even prevent the normal functioning of political authority in another country: with rescue funds viewed in zero-sum terms, a liberal constitutionalism that protects democratic authority in Germany can conflict with one that protects social rights in Greece, as well as with the constitution defended by the ECJ. It is no surprise that conflict between domestic courts and the ECJ, long simmering, has finally spilled over in the OMT reference.

[142] See Joseph H. H. Weiler, 'Editorial: Integration through Fear', *European Journal of International Law* 23 (2012): 1–5.

[143] See Treaty of Amsterdam, art. 1(5).

[144] Cf. Sandra Lavenex, 'Mutual Recognition and the Monopoly of Force: Limits of the Single Market Analogy', *Journal of European Public Policy* 14 (2007): 762–779.

[145] Fritz Scharpf, 'After the Crash: A Perspective on Multi-Level European Democracy', *European Law Journal* 21 (2015): 393; Menendez, 'Existential Crisis'.

Constitutional imbalance is now apparent.[146] Although Germany, for example, was able to exert ordoliberal pressure on the rescue measures through legal complaints against the ESM and Outright Monetary Transactions (OMT) launched by the ECB, on the basis of a violation of the rights of the *Bundestag* to determine its own economic policies, less attention is paid to legal complaints advanced in peripheral countries, such as Greece or Portugal, of violations of the social rights of their citizens through the austerity measures imposed in the same rescue programmes by the Troika.[147]

German ordoliberal constitutional ideology, a dominant reference in European integration, no longer seems compatible with constitutional democracy in *other* parts of the eurozone, particularly when Germany makes having trade surplus a '*de facto* reason of state'. It is not even clear that a 'German Europe', if desirable, is in any way feasible. Germany cannot coherently insist that all other states have a macro-economic policy that looks like its own, 'because such a result is definitionally impossible' – as regards intra-EU trade, in order for some countries to enjoy a trade surplus, others must sport a trade deficit.[148]

VI. Conclusion: Back to the Future?

Each of the three dimensions of post-war European constitutional integration discussed in the preceding text – state sovereignty, political constitutionalism, and economic constitutionalism – are now under considerable pressure, if they are not already dead-letters. German hegemony, anti-systemic social movements, domestic political parties of both far Left and Right, and severe economic crises have returned. The eurozone has seen deflation and even 'secular stagnation', which, combined with severe unemployment rates in the periphery, recalls the era of the Great Depression.[149]

The domestic constitutions of many European states are increasingly shaped by external pressure through what looks like new forms of imperialism and hegemony. 'Receivership', it has been argued, is too mild a term for the suspension of normal democratic process that countries in

[146] See Mark Dawson and Floris De Witte, 'Constitutional Balance after the Euro-Crisis', *Modern Law Review* 76 (2013): 817–844.

[147] See Kilpatrick, 'Are the EU Bail-Outs Immune to Social Challenge'.

[148] Helen Thompson, 'Austerity as Ideology: The Bait and Switch of the Banking Crisis', *Comparative European Politics* 11 (2013): 730.

[149] See Paul Krugman, 'Secular Stagnation in the Euro Area', *New York Times*, May 17, 2014.

the periphery have been reduced to: 'occupation' (by the Troika) is more appropriate, suggesting as it does, analogy to 'the consequences of military defeat'.[150] As Fritz Scharpf puts it:

> Institutionally, agreement to these conditionalites were not defined by European legislation under the Community method or through consensus voting in the Council but through extremely asymmetric bargaining between creditor and debtor governments that resembled conditions of an unconditional surrender.[151]

This extends beyond Europe's imposition of conditionality as a prerequisite for financial aid in the eurozone periphery. Rather, it reflects the broader potential for capitalist imperialism brought about in an age in which the acquisition of territory is no longer considered necessary to exert economic control over another state. A trade surplus is sufficient, as Claus Offe notes with regards to Hungary – an EU member state that is not even inside the eurozone.[152]

This new form of imperialism is bound to elicit strong social and political reaction: Austerity imposed – or self-imposed – on peripheral eurozone states in exchange for short-term economic bailouts, 'risks letting loose the kind of political passions that were so destructive during the inter-war years'.[153]

According to the liberal constitutionalist, Weimar's collapse has taught us that these passions should be fought by using 'militant democracy', that is, by striking against any perceived threat to the established constitutional or economic order. But there is an alternative narrative of Weimar's decline, however, which suggests a different lesson: Hermann Heller attributes that decline not to excessive democratic equality or tolerance or excessive private monopolistic control of government, but to its inability to respond to excessive *social inequality*.[154] Material inequality – always the Achilles heel of liberalism – has returned to prominence as a political problem, in Europe as

[150] Majone, *Rethinking the Union*, 200.

[151] Scharpf, 'After the Crash', 389.

[152] Claus Offe, 'Europe Entrapped: Does the EU Have the Political Capacity to Overcome Its Political Crisis', *European Law Journal* 19 (2013): 595–611. Cf. Claire Kilpatrick, 'Constitutions, Social Rights and Sovereign Debt States in Europe: A Challenging New Area of Constitutional Inquiry', European University Institute Working Papers Law 2015/34 (Florence, Italy: European University Institute, 2004).

[153] Thompson, 'Austerity as Ideology', 730.

[154] See, e.g., Hermann Heller, 'Political Democracy and Social Homogeneity', in Arthur Jacobson and Bernhard Schlink (eds.), *Weimar: A Jurisprudence of Crisis*. New ed. (Berkeley: University of California Press, 2002), 256–264.

well globally,[155] reactivating debates from the Weimar period, and from further back to the French revolutionary foundations of the Rousseauan constitutional tradition (see also Goldoni, Chapter 9).

Heller's narrative depends on a recognition, occluded by liberal constitutionalists, that Weimar did not move directly from liberal democracy to National Socialism, but went through the interregnum of 'authoritarian liberalism'. In this period the liberal state went to great lengths to avoid the de-differentiation of the state and the economy that was threatened by radical social democratic movements. Echoes of Heller's claim are evident today, despite the many differences in the constitutional landscape of contemporary Europe.[156]

And as meticulously recounted by Karl Polanyi, the breakdown of liberalism and turn to fascism in this inter-war interregnum was a global phenomenon, and one directed primarily by the political response to the market system and the submission of politics to economic rationality entailed by slavish adherence to the international gold standard.[157] The extraordinary pressure built up in an effort to maintain the gold standard, compelling monetary contraction, deflation, and severe unemployment in the late 1920s and early 1930s, would eventually be released. The path this unilateral abandonment of international norms would then take varied a great deal: from the New Deal in the United States, to welfarism in Britain, and national socialism in Germany.

Where market liberal ideology was strongly maintained and social democracy repressed in practice, with the market suspended but only in the interests of the ruling class and business elites, the conditions were created for a 'counter-movement' of devastating proportions. As Polanyi noted:

> The stubbornness with which economic liberals, for a critical decade, … had supported authoritarian liberal interventionism, merely resulted in a decisive weakening of the democratic forces which might otherwise have averted the fascist catastrophe.[158]

To repeat a crude assertion: Europe's post-war liberal constitutionalism has focused too much on the manner of Weimar's decline to the neglect of its causes. Not democratic excesses, but liberal excesses need to be

[155] See, especially, Thomas Piketty, *Capital in the 21st Century* (Cambridge, MA: Harvard University Press, 2014).

[156] See Michael A. Wilkinson, 'Authoritarian Liberalism in the European Constitutional Imagination', *European Law Journal* 21 (2015): 313–340.

[157] See Karl Polanyi, *The Great Transformation: The Political and Economic Origins of Our Time*. 2nd ed. (Boston: Beacon Press, 2001 [1944]).

[158] Id. at 242.

examined. It was, in Polanyi's reading, market liberal excesses that led to the democratic deficiencies that paved the way towards fascism.

Eager for ideological reasons to avoid the appearance of undermining democracy, liberal constitutionalists developed myriad devices to justify restricting democracy to 'save democracy from itself' (or what Loewenstein termed 'fight[ing] fire with fire').[159] But dressing up a fear of democracy as itself a kind of democracy – even a *militant* democracy – leads to all sorts of contortions and distortions that confound the field of liberal constitutionalism to this day. 'Militant democracy' was always an odd expression for a philosophy that meant its opposite, that is, that political democracy must be restricted and curtailed in order to serve 'liberal' (and what would today be 'neo-liberal') economic ends. Emasculated by the liberal constitutionalist, 'democracy' becomes indistinguishable from the rule of law. There is little regard for the substantive political or social commitments, or for the requisite social conditions, that are necessary for 'democracy' to remain a functional and stable part of Europe's 'constitutional' order.

European integration can be cast as a partial solution to a multi-faceted problem: How can modern constitutionalism – and the set of ideas on which it is based – survive in the aftermath of the series of devastating shocks suffered in the first half of the twentieth century? How might it repair or rebuild its political foundations in the post-war period? These questions now need to be posed again. The legacy of Europe's liberal constitutionalism has come under extraordinary pressure. But in reaction to further de-democratisation, and even de-legalisation, there has been an extraordinary re-politicisation of Europe's geo-political, societal, and economic constitutions. Resistance to conditionality and austerity for example, is emerging through anti-systemic social and political movements, as 'post-liberal' alternatives to the current configuration of authoritarian liberalism and militant economics are starting to be explored, in both Left and Right variants. Will the attempt to recover the autonomy of the political from liberal-economic militancy, as pursued by more radical social movements such as Occupy and the Indignados, and articulated as a European programme by the political parties Syriza and Podemos, lead to a reclaiming of democratic power over the economic realm? In reaction to the hegemony of ordoliberal and neo-liberal de-politicisation, the basic social and political functions of constitutionalism can, it seems, only be regained from the 'bottom up', through radical reassertion of constituent power.

[159] Loewenstein, 'Militant Democracy and Fundamental Rights, Part 1', 432.

But can this occur within the eurozone or even the EU? The final irony may be that for liberal constitutionalism to have any purchase in the twenty-first century, the issue of the social inequalities – both within and between states – that are structurally reproduced by liberal capitalism can no longer be deferred. It seems, however, that they can be resolved neither by the member states, nor by the union of which they are part.

PART II

Functional Symbiosis

3

Constitutional Drift: Spontaneous Co-evolution of Social 'Ideas' and Legal 'Form'

GUNTHER TEUBNER

I. Introduction

This volume suggests a drastically different concept of a 'constitution' from that with which we are familiar: A constitution, it shows us, should no longer be seen as a monistic normative phenomenon of higher legal rules, but rather as a dualistic normative arrangement, one that connects otherwise epistemically incompatible processes, that is, the development of constitutional forms and the history of constitutional ideas. This conceptualisation destroys the traditional unity of the constitution – be it the political unity of Carl Schmitt or its legal unity à la Hans Kelsen – and dissolves constitutionalism into the tension-ridden duality of two diverse and often-contradictory autonomous evolutionary processes.

As described in the first chapter, this duality explains the differences between the great historical models of constitutionalism – the American legalist-structural model, the French revolutionary-political model, and the English historicist-social model: Each of which represents a different historical configuration of these two inter-related processes. Moreover, it shows how the three constitutional pathologies – juridification, over-socialisation, and mutual indifference – emerge out of an imbalance in the interaction between constitutional form and constitutional ideas.

In this chapter, I will explore a third consequence of such a conceptualisation: that the conceptual move from constitutional monism to constitutional dualism reveals a specific evolutionary dynamic in constitutions – that is, a 'spontaneous' process that produces unforeseen results against the founders' intentions. My thesis is that there is not one uniform evolutionary process through which a constitution reacts to environmental pressures. Rather, constitutions develop through two distinct evolutionary trajectories – one of constitutional form and the other of constitutional ideas. And, moreover, these two trajectories are connected by the dynamics of co-evolution.

My thesis comprises of three arguments. First, I reformulate the interrelation between constitutional ideas and constitutional structures in terms of a double reflexivity of social discourses and legal rules. Second, I show how this double reflexivity occurs under the umbrella of what we can call a 'hybrid constitutional meta-code'. Third, I demonstrate how a variety of co-evolutionary mechanisms link these two trajectories, and are thereby responsible for a variety of constitutional arrangements. I will develop these three arguments not only in the context of state constitutions, but also in the context of various non-state constitutions, drawing especially on what I will call economic constitutions.

II. First Argument: The Double Reflexivity of Social Discourse and Legal Rules

Even if lawyers do not like to admit it, legal rules do not play the principal role in the workings of a constitution – *any* constitution, be it a state constitution, an economic constitution, or some other form of social system. Rather, constitutionalisation is primarily founded on a self-reflexive set of ideas that give meaning to some autonomous set of social practices, be it politics, the economy, or in some other social sphere. Because of its autonomy, we will refer to this as a 'self-constitutionalisation'.[1] As we shall see, legal structures do play an indispensable role in the process of constitutionalisation, but it is more of a supporting role.

A self-constitution, in the first step, is constructed out of the 'double closure' – in the sense described by Heinz von Foerster[2] – of some set of social operations. These operations generate first-order closure by linking a set of self-produced social operations with one another and thereby setting it set apart from its larger environment. This set can then develop a second-order closure by subjecting these social operations reflexively to a second set of operations that tests for validity.

[1] See Riccardo Prandini, 'The Morphogenesis of Constitutionalism', in Petra Dobner and Martin Loughlin (eds.), *The Twilight of Constitutionalism?* (Oxford University Press, 2010), 316; Chris Thornhill, 'Towards a Historical Sociology of Constitutional Legitimacy', *Theory and Society* 37 (2008): 169–197.

[2] See Heinz von Foerster, *Understanding Understanding: Essays on Cybernetics and Cognition* (New York: Springer, 2003), 242–243; Heinz von Foerster, *Observing Systems* (Seaside, CA: Intersystems Publications, 1981), 304 ff.

Thus, for example, the political constitution acquires its autonomy when it first generates decision-making practices involving a closed community of decision makers, and then generates a double closure by subjecting these practices to a second-order set of autonomous legitimating operations – such as elections, consensus from a diversity of independent power bases (e.g., federalism, separation of powers, or a bureaucratic ordering of diverse specialisations), and social and/or judicial understandings of the demands of fundamental rights. The economic constitution acquires its autonomy when, within the money cycle, payment operations are used not only to effect transactions, but also to control the money supply that makes payment operations possible. In the same way, science acquires its autonomy only when it subjects its first-order operations – that is, empirical observations and formulaic constructs – to second-order operations of epistemology, methodology, and theory of science that determine whether or not some particular formulaic observation belongs to the system of science.[3] Such double closure allows a particular social sector to define its external boundaries and thereby establish an internal identity that distinguishes it and its operations from the other social operations that constitute the larger social sphere. It is in this way that these primordial self-constituting processes become autonomous in the strict sense.[4]

Moreover, the status of double-closure requires that the relationship between these two sets of operations be 'reflexive'. This refers to a condition in which radical changes in one of these orders of operations will induce sympathetic evolutions in the other – that is, radical changes in social operations can induce changes in validity operations, and vice versa. Without reflexivity, the two sets of operations will de-couple, and lose their coherence as a system.

Along these lines, of constitutional 'ideas' – that is, an epistemic constitutional construct involving a medial reflexivity of some association of constitutional practices together with associated cognitive and normative reflections on the identity generated by these practices – represent one kind of doubly-closed system. At the first level, a system of constitutional ideas give meaning to some particular set of constitutional practices; at the second level, it tests for the validity of these meanings by subjecting them to a test for mutual coherence. In this way, it serves to *self-constitute* a particular socio-epistemic system.

[3] Niklas Luhmann, *Die Wissenschaft der Gesellschaft* (Frankfurt: Suhrkamp, 1990), 469 ff.

[4] Id. at 117, 144, 209, 289; Niklas Luhmann, *Die Politik der Gesellschaft* (Frankfurt: Suhrkamp, 2000), 64.

By itself, however, it is not sufficient to generate a 'constitution' in the strict or technical sense. We should only speak of 'constitutions' in the strict sense when a self-constituted socio-epistemic system of 'ideas' is supported by another, complementary, self-constitutionalising process – that of the structural-positive system of law. More precisely, true constitutionalisation occurs when a doubly-closed, self-constitutionalised socio-epistemic system of 'ideas' – be it in politics, the economy, or some other sector – becomes structurally coupled with a second kind of doubly-closed, self-constitutionalised system, that of a 'legal system' – that is, 'form'.[5] Like the epistemic social system of ideas, constitutional form is also a reflexive social system, consisting of both primary legal norms that provide first-order closure, and second-order legal norms that provide second-order closure by establishing the validity of these first-order norms.[6] These higher-order legal norms in particular are critical to the constitutionalisation process: the application of primary legal norms to a social sphere leads merely to that sphere's juridification (i.e., Kant's *Rechtsstaat*), not to its constitutionalisation. The situation only really becomes constitutionalised when norms of norms – that is, secondary norms – prescribe how the identification, setting, amendment, and regulation of competences for the issuing and delegating of primary norms are to occur.

In order to generate a constitutional *system*, however, the structural coupling of constitutional ideas and legal form must itself be reflexive, in the sense that radial changes in the system of ideas cause sympathetic changes in the legal system, and vice versa. As mentioned in the preceding text, this reflexivity is necessary to secure the constitution's systemic coherence. But because both ideas and form are themselves reflexive system, this results in a *double* reflexivity – and it is this double reflexivity that is distinctly characteristic of constitutionalism.

In other words, the precondition for a constitution in the strict sense is that a structural coupling takes place between the reflexive mechanisms of legal structures (i.e., secondary legal norm creation in which norms are applied to norms) and the reflexive mechanisms of the ideas that give meaning to those legal structures. This occurs when self-constitutionalising socio-epistemic processes that render some particular environment of societal rationalities both meaningful and autonomous are themselves *juridified*

[5] See also Gunther Teubner, *Constitutional Fragments: Societal Constitutionalism and Globalization* (Oxford University Press, 2012), 102–110.

[6] Cf. H. L. A. Hart, *The Concept of Law*. 2nd ed. (Oxford: Clarendon, 1994), 79–123.

by a separate set of self-constitutionalised legal processes. Only in this way can the developmental dynamic typical of constitutions, as described by the first chapter, emerge – in the form of an institutionalised co-evolution between these two self-reflexive processes (as will be explored further in part IV of this chapter).

It is in this distinctive, *double* reflexivity of constitutionalism that we encounter its curious duality – a duality that is characteristic of a strict structural coupling and that refutes the widespread presumption that a constitution is a unitary phenomenon. The two extremes of this duality, associated with the names of Hans Kelsen and Carl Schmitt, need to enter into a mutual embrace in both political constitutions and social constitutions. In this sense, a constitution can be reduced neither to a legal structure (à la Kelsen) nor to a socio-political practice (à la Schmitt). It is always a dual phenomenon: a linking of these two innately autonomous processes. From the legal perspective, constitutionalisation involves the production of secondary legal norms that are peculiarly interwoven with the fundamental understandings of the social system. From the social perspective, constitutionalisation involves the production of secondary epistemic norms that are themselves critically informed by the legal norms recognised by the system. Only when both these conditions operate together does it make sense, in terms of both legal sociology and legal doctrine, to speak of the 'elements' of a political constitution, an economic constitution, a constitution of the education and science system, or the digital constitution of the Internet.

What is the reason, though, for this doubling of social reflexivity through the use of secondary legal-constitutional norms? Law comes into the self-constitutionalisation processes of social systems when autonomisation cannot be fully accomplished using just the first- and second-order social operations of those social systems. This might occur, for example, when these social operations are unable to stabilise themselves, or when they become indeterminate due to their own internal paradoxes. In such cases, additional closure mechanisms are needed to complete the self-constitution of social autonomy.

The law is one of these additional mechanisms (albeit not the only one). Consider, along these lines, the self-description of the autonomous 'state'. As noted by Niklas Luhmann, 'The political system is only differentiable at all when it describes itself as a state'.[7] But the closure of

[7] Niklas Luhmann, 'Der Staat Als Historischer Begriff', in Marcel Storme (ed.), *Mijmeringen Van Een Jurist bij 1984* (Antwerp: Kluwer, 1984), 144.

institutionalised politics is not accomplished without formal delineations of what constitutes collectively binding state power. The reflexive application of first-order power dynamics (command) to second-order power processes (oversight) cannot be exposed to the constant fluctuations of power. A higher order to legal norms is needed to bring stability to the reflexive interactions that structure acquiring and exercising power. In this sense, it is only through the structural coupling of politics to law that the political system become autonomous in the form of 'the state'.

More important still is the contribution made by the law to defusing the *paradoxes* of political power. As also described by Martin Loughlin in Chapter 6, traditionally the paralysing paradox of the self-binding nature of 'the sovereign' has been normalised – but not resolved – by the establishment of 'rule of law'.[8] Similarly, the self-constitution of social systems necessarily comes up against its own paradoxes relating to its self-reference – for example, the paradox of the legitimacy of its own founding – and one way of dealing with this paradox is to externalise 'the founding' to the law. This is what happens in state constitutions, but it can also be observed in the self-constitutions other social systems. Thus the autonomy of a social constitution is never autonomy in pure form: It always contains elements of heteronomy. The 'self' of the self-constitution must first be defined heteronomously, through legal norms. This is necessary in order to be able to *identify* itself as an autonomous system.[9]

These additional mechanisms of self-constitution vary quite markedly from one social system to another. Science requires only minimal support from stabilising legal norms to achieve autonomy. Methodologically, the epistemology of science is generally capable of hammering in the boundary stakes that mark out the realm of science on its own, especially because science is not subject to any decision-making imperative. Despite all the worrying about corruption in the academic world, it seems superfluous to attach a binding self-description to science as a collective *qua* scientific community, or even for the scientific community to be incorporated into some formal organisation in order to secure the scientific credentials of knowledge. Legal systems therefore play a relatively small role in the constitutionalisation of scientific activity – although even here, a heteronomous stabilisation is still needed

[8] Niklas Luhmann, 'Two Sides of the State Founded on Law', in *Political Theory in the Welfare State* (Berlin: de Gruyter, 1990), 187–202.

[9] See Hans Lindahl, 'A-Legality: Postnationalism and the Question of Legal Boundaries', *Modern Law Review* 73 (2010): 33.

in order to provide guarantees of scientific freedom and to secure the persistence of scientific institutions, the latter being then left to their own self-constitutions.

The economy, by contrast, requires a huge amount of heteronomous stabilisation from the law for its self-constitution (albeit still not to the same extent as politics). As is well known, the institutions of property, contract, competition, and currency form the cornerstones of the economic constitution. All of these institutions are constructed out of secondary *legal* norms that legitimate and validate the practices associated with these institutions. These secondary norms are essential for allowing a double reflexivity to operate within the economic system: a reflexivity in which primarily norms of economic transactions (e.g., exchange) are subject to secondary norms of economic legitimation (e.g., norms of market expectations), that are themselves critically coupled with corresponding primary and secondary norms articulated in the legal system, such as conscionability and good faith, that give needed persistence to these norms of legitimation and expectation (also discussed in part IV of this chapter.)

III. Second Argument: Hybrid Binary Meta-coding

To some extent, the preceding argument recapitulates one of the arguments presented by Martin Loughlin in Chapter 6. But here I want to go further, and show that double reflexivity by itself is not enough. The end point of constitutionalisation – be it in politics, in the economy, or in other social spheres – is not achieved until the reflexive relationship between social ideas and legal structures has developed in such a way that a *hybrid binary meta-coding* emerges.[10] This coding is 'binary' in the sense that it recognises only two possible encoded states – 'constitutional/unconstitutional' – in the situations to which it is applied. It is 'meta' in the sense that it only operates on decisions that have already been encoded as 'legal/illegal' by the self-constituted legal system that is part of the constitutional system. This produces the distinctive hierarchy that is typical of all constitutions: that of a 'constitutional' law – that is, 'the law of laws' – operating above the ordinary law.

But what is really special about this meta-coding is its 'hybridity'. This constitutional code takes precedence not only over the legal system, but also over the binary codes of the other specialised 'function-systems' – such

[10] See also Teubner, *Constitutional Fragments*, 110–113.

as the economic system, the political system, even the health system when access to health care is a state right – that in toto constitute the constitutional order. As it does with regard to law, this meta-coding exposes the operations of these other function-systems to a higher-level binary reflexivity as to whether or not they are behaving in accordance with their larger responsibilities to the constitutional order.

The hybrid nature of this meta-coding can be observed most clearly in the developed political constitutions of the modern nation-states. Here, the 'constitutional/unconstitutional' distinction is used as a meta-code that applies to two similarly binary-coded subsystems – namely those of law and politics (see, e.g., 'juridical constitutions' vs. 'political constitutions')[11] – but without causing these subsystems to lose their autonomy from one another. It allows the constitution to be a *neutral* process of structural coupling: a way of integrating the two social subsystems of politics and law without causing either to lose its autonomy. Similar hybrid meta-codings also crop up – usually implicitly, occasionally explicitly – in the structural couplings of law with other social systems, producing their own constitutional meta-codes.

For example, the constitution of the modern industrial economy has its own kind of hybrid meta-code that provides a seemingly common formula for two quite different types of economic operations. This meta-code assumes hierarchical precedence over both legal and economic binary codings related to the economy, but it actually takes on different meanings depending on whether it is applied to the economic code or the legal code. Applied to the economic code, it subjects exchange procedures to reflexive evaluation in light of their overall social function, and identifies their social and environmental compatibility. Applied to the legal code, it sits hierarchically over ordinary law, judging legal acts according to whether or not they are in line with the high values and principles set down in the economic constitution.

Thus, while the economic-constitutional meta-code presents itself formally as a simple unitary *distinction directrice* of 'constitutional/unconstitutional', what we really have before us here is an interesting special case of 'essentially contested concepts' – a case in which the same term is interpreted in very different ways in a variety of contexts and is implemented in correspondingly different connecting operations.[12] This Janus-faced

[11] John A. G. Griffith, 'The Political Constitution', *The Modern Law Review* 42 (1979): 1–21.

[12] See Walter B. Gallie, 'Essentially Contested Concepts', *Proceedings of the Aristotelian Society* 56 (1956): 167–198.

character of the constitutional meta-code has to do with the fact that, by itself, the economic constitution, as a structural coupling between two mutually closed social systems (the economic system and the legal system), is unable to attain social-systemic autonomy. Rather than merging together into a single system, both the economic and legal systems remain attached to their own independent operational domains – namely, that of market transactions and of legality, respectively. The 'constitutional/unconstitutional' operation provides a common umbrella formula that nevertheless takes on different meanings depending on whether it applies to the economic system, where it expresses *market* validity, or the legal system, where it expresses *legal* validity.

The duel nature of the economic-constitutional code necessarily means that, within its domain, legal 'structures' and economic 'ideas' develop their own programmes for that constitution – programmes that are normatively independent from each other, but still interrelated (perhaps homeostatically, as Dowdle elsewhere proposes).[13] Each of these programmes emerges initially from the reflexive and recursive application of the system's own primary and secondary operations. Yet, their common meta-coding in terms of 'constitutional/unconstitutional' causes constant mutual irritation that binds both systems into a co-evolutionary relationship.[14] The fact that, in law, the meta-code 'constitutional/unconstitutional' is given hierarchical precedence over the legal system's coding of 'legal/illegal' not only allows basic principles of the economic system to be injected into the principles of the legal system, but also allows both these sets of principles (legal and economic) to co-evolve in response to evolutions of their respective social systems.

This is where we find the real justification for a truly material concept of constitutionalism, as contrasted against the formal and the functional concepts of constitutionalism.[15] Constitutionalised law cannot be reduced simply to compliance with certain decision-making processes (forms), but demands substantive justification by means of content-based

[13] See Michael W. Dowdle, 'On the Public-law Character of Competition Law: A Lesson from Asian Capitalism', *Fordham International Law Journal* 38 (2015): 355–360.

[14] See also Gunther Teubner, 'Idiosyncratic Production Regimes: Co-Evolution of Economic and Legal Institutions in the Varieties of Capitalism', in *The Evolution of Cultural Entities: Proceedings of the British Academy* (ed., John Ziman) (Oxford University Press, 2002), 161–181.

[15] See, e.g., Mattias Kumm, 'The Best of Times and the Worst of Times: Between Constitutional Triumphalism and Nostalgia', in Petra Dobner and Martin Loughlin (eds.), *The Twilight of Constitutionalism?* (Oxford University Press, 2010), 214–219.

constitutional principles (ideas). Such law would not be constitutionally comprehensible without the re-entry of the basic material principles of these two self-constituted social system into the constitution's legal system. In the context of the economic constitution, for example, this binding of constitutional law to specific economic ideas is certainly not prescribed by natural law. Rather, it is the result of historically changing processes of reflexivity in which the social self-constitution of the economic system is constantly being reconstructed in law as an ensemble of content-based, constitutional-legal norms. Something comparable also occurs in the opposite direction. Constitutional meta-coding causes the law to become reconstructed in economic terms, such as the law of contract being reconstructed as a particular operationalisation of economic transactions; property as a particular operationalisation of social relationships; competition law as a particular operationalisation of economic efficiency; and company law as a particular operationalisation of collective economic 'rationality'.

The reciprocal re-entry of the material principles of economy and law into the economic constitution thus gives rise to two different 'imaginary spaces' within that constitution: two different constitutional programmes – one aimed at the economy, the other aimed at the law. These programmes are directed, jointly but separately, by their shared constitutional meta-code. The resulting dualisation of that meta-code's meaning becomes especially clear in relation to one of the classic programmes of the economic constitution, namely property. In economic terms, property describes the 'disjunction of the requirement for consensus' that governs socio-economic coordination.[16] In legal terms, property refers to an exclusive subjective right. The economic constitution uses both concepts according to context. It thereby takes the form of a language game in which there is a peculiar double structure to its common *distinction directrice* of 'constitutional/unconstitutional'.[17] But as a language game, it does not develop the strength to become an autonomous, self-reflexive 'language' in its own right. Rather, it forms a peculiar 'binding institution' in which the law and the economy are closely coupled, and thereby mutually irritate one another. In doing so, it produces a bilingualism in that it continually translates law into economics and vice versa.

[16] See Niklas Luhmann, *Law as a Social System* (Oxford University Press, 2004), 392.

[17] See Kaarlo Tuori, 'The Many Constitutions of Europe', in Kaarlo Tuori and Sankari Suvi (eds.), *The Many Constitutions of Europe* (Farnham, UK: Ashgate, 2010), 3–30.

IV. Third Argument: Channels of Co-evolution

Constitutional history shows itself to be co-evolutionary. Under the umbrella of their 'constitutional/unconstitutional' meta-coding, political constitutions 'develop' through a co-evolutionary process that links the development of their political programmes (i.e., their self-constitutionalising systems of constitutional ideas) and the development of their legal programmes (i.e., self-constitutionalising systems legal forms and structures). Societal constitutions co-evolve by linking their social programmes with their legal programmes. And both the political and the social constitutions co-evolve due to the hybrid capacities of this constitutional meta-coding.

Contrary to a unified social evolution in which constitutional evolution comes about simply from external environmental pressure operating on various social systems, each self-constitutionalising system with the constitutional system has own very specific and very distinct evolutionary mechanisms. Each system – legal, economic, social – displays different patterns of variation, selection, and retention. Their autonomous evolutionary processes influence each other using mechanisms of co-evolution. This is the opposite of the usual assumption in constitutional history of a unified evolutional trajectory that is driven purely by forces of economic, moral, or political natural selection. Rather, it involves diverging evolutionary trajectories taking place simultaneously within a single constitutional system. The 'structure' of constitutional law at the one side and the 'ideas' of the focal social sector (e.g., economy, politics, science, education) on the other all operate according to their own idiosyncratic and independent evolutionary mechanisms, while the co-evolutionary process of the constitution system as a whole coordinates these evolutionary dynamics so as maintain sectorial autonomy and identity.

If one wishes to understand the particularities of any single constitution, one must therefore look not merely at the individual evolutionary paths of its respective sectoral social systems, but also more specifically at how their mutual channels of reciprocal influence have developed within and through this process of co-evolution.

Consider, for example, the two different kinds of economic constitutions identified by the varieties of capitalism literature, those of liberal market economies and those of coordinated market economies.[18]

[18] See, generally, Peter A. Hall and David Soskice (eds.) *Varieties of Capitalism: The Institutional Foundations of Comparative Advantage* (Oxford University Press, 2005).

Economic constitutions have always been shaped by specific legal, political, scientific, and educational developments in their region. This is the first source of their differences: They display cultural particularities that can only be explained by reference to the special histories of their various constituent, self-constitutionalised sub-systems. The other source of their differences, that which interests us now, is to be found in the specific co-evolutionary interactions between their legal and the economic sub-systems. These interactions can be arranged along to two dimensions. One dimension concerns the *quality* of the co-evolutionary *influences*, the other concerns the *density* of their co-evolutionary *coordination*.[19]

As regards the quality of their co-evolutionary influence, the interactions between constitution's subordinate social systems can involve:

- *Irritation*: in which external stimuli originating from one social system excite internal evolutionary selection processes in the other system, but do not direct these processes to any particular procedural or substantive ends;
- *Simulation*: in which external stimuli originating from one subordinate social system cause the selections mechanisms of the other social system to reproduce (through *mimesis*) the selection mechanism of the stimulating system, without necessarily reproducing the selection results of the stimulating system; and/or
- *Endogenous symbiosis*: in which external stimuli originating in one social system cause the other system to incorporate into its own stabilisation mechanisms the *results* of the stimulating system's selection processes.

As regards the density of co-evolutionary coordination, co-evolutionary interactions can be classified as follows:

- *Spontaneous* vs. *organised*: the degree to which the interactions are the product of or subject to human intentionality;
- *Simultaneous* vs. *sequential*: whether the mutually co-evolutionary dynamics occur at the same time;
- *Fragmented* vs. *integrated*: the degree to which the evolutionary changes are systematically harmonised; and
- *Antagonistic* vs. *coordinated*: whether the co-evolution takes the form of positive or negative feedback loops.

[19] See also Teubner, *Constitutional Fragments*.

Drawing from the comparative experience of judicial review of standard form contracts in the United States and Germany, I will sketch how the different economic constitutions of these two countries – the liberal market economy of the United States versus the coordinated market economy of Germany – are products of different co-evolutionary channels.[20]

In private law, judicial review of standard contracts in the economic constitutions is the functional equivalent of constitutional review of political legislation in state constitutions. Standard contracts are not voluntary agreements by two contracting parties, but rather market-regulatory mechanisms that are unilaterally imposed on the market by private economic organisations. When courts review standard contracts under the somewhat old-fashioned private-law principles of good faith (as is the case in Germany) or unconscionability (as in the United States), they are engaged in the same general activity as are constitutional courts when reviewing legislative acts according to constitutional principles.

Traditional comparative law sees judicial review of standard contracts in these two countries in terms of similarities, convergences, and/or possibilities for legal harmonisation. Traditional economics sees it in terms of pressures of natural selection driven by competitive dynamics of economic efficiency. The approach developed here, by contrast, identifies the drastic differences in the legal rules of these two regimes, as well as differences in their respective institutional advantages and disadvantages, and traces these differences back to the different mechanisms of constitutional co-evolution particular to their respective constitutional systems.

From a traditional perspective, the two regimes' treatment of standard contracts seems highly convergent. The formal similarities of what we might call 'economic constitutional review' in the two countries are astounding. Standard contracts are subject in both the United States and in Germany to judicial review using very similar sets of economic-constitutional concepts, policies, and principles. Both regimes have recognised standard contracts as being legally enforceable despite their somewhat asymmetric character. Both make the validity of these contracts dependent on certain conditions (good faith, fairness, unconscionability) that clearly differentiate them from ordinary contracts.

[20] See also Steven Casper, 'The Legal Framework for Corporate Governance: The Influence of Contract Law on Company Strategies in Germany and the United States', in Peter A. Hall and David Soskice (eds.), *Varieties of Capitalism: The Institutional Foundations of Comparative Advantage* (Oxford University Press, 2001), 387–416.; Teubner, *Constitutional Fragments*.

Similarities between these two regimes can also be found with regard to the quality of their respective co-evolutionary influences. Both regimes favour leaving the development of the new forms of contracts to the whims of coincidental irritations: economic innovations in standard-form contractual practices irritate the legal system through introducing new kinds of cases into the court system that produce new, idiosyncratic forms of legal evaluation; while new legal doctrines affect changes in the forms of the standardised contracts. At the same time, however, both systems also evince parallel manifestations of both simulation and endogenous symbiosis. In both countries, the principles of judicial review internally reproduce selection criteria used in economic evaluations of these kinds of contracts (simulation). Both also occasionally assimilate the results of economic evaluations establishing the validity of standard contracts into their own findings of legal validity, even without reproducing the selection processes internally (endogenous symbiosis).

But divergences become apparent when one begins to scrutinise the different weights that each constitutional regime gives to processes of simulation versus processes of endogenous symbiosis. In the United States, legal-economic co-evolution places primarily through endogenous symbiosis. In German practice, it is driven much more by simulation.

This is because in the United States, standard-contracts forms are developed independently by individual firms. This decentralised mode of private governance leads to a plethora of standard-contract types. So great is this individuated diversity that it transcends the informational capacity of the reviewing courts. Courts are therefore forced to defer to the evaluative results produced by the economic system, and autonomous judicial control of standard contracts is relatively underdeveloped.

In Germany, by contrast, it is not the individual firm, but sectorial business associations that formulate standard contract regimes. Thus, in principle, each industrial sector has a standardised standard-contract form that is used by all the firms in that sector. This results in much reduced variation in standard-contract forms. Moreover, these contractual regimes are frequently scrutinised by public authorities – in particular the Federal Cartel Office, or *Bundeskartellamt*. As a result, German courts have a relatively good overview of the standard-contract characteristics in each sector. In contrast to the United States, this allows for autonomous and highly detailed judicial review of standard contract regimes, in which German courts incorporate into their own selection mechanisms autonomous legal principles that reproduce the manner in which the economic subsystem pertinent to the relevant industrial sector distributes risks and imparts transparency. The distinct political and legal factors that underlie their particular formulations in turn frees the courts from having to symbiotically defer to the outcomes of economic selection processes that themselves remain external to the legal system.

And divergence between these two regimes becomes even more apparent when we consider the respective densities of their co-evolutionary contacts. In the United States, as we saw, individual firms implement their own contractual regimes, often with the other side of the transaction replying with its own firm-specific standard contract, and it is market competition that decides which one prevails. It is, in this sense, *spontaneous*. American courts, which as has already been noted exercise relatively weak constitutional control over standard contracts, also react *post hoc* when unacceptable risks have materialised. In this way, the American regime also manifests itself *sequentially*. It is also highly *fragmented*: In deciding issues raised by standard contracts, courts do so not by applying uniform standards of contract law, but by examining for highly context-specific incidents of tort-like misconduct rather than for more generalisable problems of the distribution of risks inherent in the standard contract form, as per contract law. Such fragmentation is further catalysed by the intervention of numerous autonomous state and federal agencies and autonomous state and national legislative frameworks.

In sum, in the United States, the density of co-evolutionary coordination between the legal and the economic subsystems of the economic constitution insofar as standard contracts are concerned is *spontaneous*, *fragmented*, and *sequential*. There is a plethora of standard-contractual regimes, and judicial intervention on constitutional grounds is markedly limited. This is in direct contrast to the density of co-evolutionary coordination in Germany, which is *organised* (rather than spontaneous) and *integrated* (rather than fragmented). It is integrated (rather than fragmented) in the sense that – as we have seen – standard contracts are formulated by sectorial business associations rather than by individual firms. It is organised in that the formulation of such contracts is specifically designed (especially by the *Bundeskartellamt*) to strike a balance between a variety of social concerns – not simply those of a particular firm or industrial sector. These include, for example those of the class of actors that are most likely to be on the other side of that standard contract; classes of likely-affected third parties (especially as concerns distribution of liability for risk and insurance); and various political, administrative, and supervisory bodies (and in particular the *Bundeskartellamt*).[21]

Consequently, in contrast to American courts, German courts do heavily intervene in the construction of the standard contract regulatory regime. This is incomprehensible from an economic standpoint, which regards such heavy intervention as just another case of 'Eurosclerosis'. From that standpoint, such intervention seems inefficient and paternalistic. It is paternalistic in that it not only imposes protections on consumers without their consent, but it also second-guesses professional market judgment regarding the correct assignment of risk. It is inefficient in that it discourages the development of new and more efficient contract formulations.

But such heavy judicial intervention nevertheless does make sense from a *constitutional* standpoint, and in particular from the constitutional perspective that derives from Germany's specific variety of capitalism – its coordinated market economy as distinguished from the American liberal market economy. From that perspective, the criterion for judicial intervention is whether or not the contractual form under review represents an authentic innovation – that is, an innovation that increases the productivity of the industry – or simply a spurious innovation – that is, an innovation that simply transfers exposure to risk to the other party without promoting productivity. The policy principle for such review is not just to protect medium-sized companies, but to promote productivity enhancing cooperation between firms by protecting the autonomy of and facilitating cooperation among all the stakeholders affected by the contractual transaction.

V. Conclusion

In this chapter the interrelation between constitutional structures and constitutional ideas has been reformulated in terms of a double reflexivity of social discourses and legal rules. Double reflexivity means the precondition for a constitution is that a structural coupling takes place between the reflexive mechanisms of legal structures (i.e., secondary legal norm creation in which norms are applied to norms) and the reflexivity of ideas in the social sector related to it. This applies to political constitutions as well

[21] See also Steven Casper, 'German Industrial Associations and the Diffusion of Innovative Economic Organization: The Case of JIT Contracting', *WZB Working Paper*, FS I 96–306 (Berlin: Wissenschaftszentrum, 1996), 28.

as to various non-state constitutions, especially to economic constitutions. This interrelation occurs under the umbrella of a 'hybrid constitutional meta-code'. It has been demonstrated how a variety of co-evolutionary mechanisms link these two trajectories, which makes them responsible for a variety of constitutional arrangements.

4

"Constitutionalism Beyond Liberalism" in Indonesian Competition Regulation: Recognising the Constitutional Role of Dominium

MICHAEL W. DOWDLE

I. Introduction

This chapter uses Indonesian experience with market competition regulation to explore an important aspect of constitutionalism that is largely overlooked by the liberal perspective of constitutionalism. This is an aspect of state power that Terence Daintith has recently termed 'dominium' – that is, the state's power to pursue state ends by distributing wealth and resources to and among private parties.[1] Because dominium works through volitional incentives rather than through direct command (what Daintith refers to as the state's power of 'imperium'[2]), it operates largely outside the liberal constitutional focus, which revolves primarily around protecting individual autonomy from usurpative state coercions.

But a state's exercise of dominium can give rise to significant constitutional issues that are invisibilised by the liberal perspective. To demonstrate this, this chapter will show how the perceptive of dominium reveals important and distinctly *constitutional* aspects of competition law that are invisible to orthodox constitutional understandings.

Competition law is not normally associated with constitutional law. Constitutional law regulates the state; competition law, by contrast, regulates private behaviour in private markets. But as we shall see, things look different when viewed from the constitutional perspective of dominium. Such a perspective reveals that, in fact, the regulation of market competition can raise critical constitutional issues: issues involving the political

[1] Terence Daintith, 'The Techniques of Government', in Jeffrey Jowell and Dawn Oliver (eds.), *The Changing Constitution* (Oxford University Press, 1994), 212–213. See also Terence Daintith, 'Regulation', in Richard Buxbaum and Ferenc Mádl (eds.), *International Encyclopedia of Comparative Law*. Vol. 17 (Tubingen, Germany: Mohr Siebeck, 1997), ch. 10.

[2] Daintith, 'The Techniques of Government', 212.

construction of the state, but that nevertheless escape the attention of the more traditional, liberal vision.

This chapter will first explore some of the constitutional dimensions of dominium. These dimensions include citizenship, sovereignty, legitimacy, and accountability. It will then explore the different forms that dominium can take. Daintith's definition focuses primarily on what we will call direct dominium – this is where the state directly distributes resources to private parties in pursuit of its own political goals. But there is also an indirect form, in which the state enlists private actors to engage in such distributions. As we shall see, this indirect dominium causes particular conceptual and analytic difficulties for liberal visions of constitutionalism.

Then, in part IV, we will turn our attention to competition law. We start with a little vignette from an article by an American antitrust attorney, Kenneth Davidson, about his teaching competition regulation in Indonesia, and in particular with his experience with Indonesian 'misunderstandings' about the nature and purpose of market competition regulation. We shall explore how Davidson was approaching competition law simply as a form of private market regulation. Viewed from a constitutional perspective of dominium, however, we can see that competition regulation is actually an exercise of what we have termed *indirect dominium*, and thus has a constitutional character. These constitutional issues are particularly pronounced in Global Southern countries like Indonesia. Thus, the Indonesian 'misunderstandings' he identified were not really misunderstandings at all – they were alternative understandings that rightly, in the context of Indonesia, focused on the constitutional (and not just private law) import of competition regulation. We conclude by looking at what the constitutional perspective of dominium shows us about the limits of the liberal vision of constitutionalism.

II. Constitutional Dimensions of Dominium

'Dominium' describes how a state uses its abilities to distribute wealth and resources so as to pursue state policy objectives through the generation of material incentives. As described by Karen Yeung:

> Terence Daintith observed that most standard textbooks on constitutional and administrative law create the impression that 'normal' government policy implementation in domestic affairs consists of unilateral changes in legal structures, particularly the creation of legal rights and duties of

> citizens, by means of parliamentary or delegated legislation. Yet he argued that this kind of policy implementation was no longer dominant. Quite apart from the government's use of the command of law in aid of its policy objectives ('imperium'), Daintith claimed that other techniques of government had acquired equal practical importance, including the employment of government wealth ('dominium') by offering incentives to comply with government policy. . . .[3]

As implied by Yeung, the structural-liberal vision of constitutionalism pays very little attention to dominium.[4] In the American Constitution, for example, there are really only three clauses that address the government's ability to exercise this power. The most famous and most discussed is the anti-establishment clause of the First Amendment, 'Congress shall make no law respecting an establishment of religion'.[5] Less attention has been paid to the other two clauses: the spending power clause (which authorises Congress 'to pay the Debts and provide for the common defence and general Welfare of the United States'[6]) and the Appropriations Clause, which states that 'No money shall be drawn from the treasury, but in consequence of appropriations made by law; and a regular statement and account of receipts and expenditures of all public money shall be published from time to time'.[7]

This lacuna in liberal constitutional thought it quite evident in the constitutional problem known as 'unconstitutional conditions' – a problem that American constitutional thought has been unable to effectively address. For example, in the United States, government cannot restrict free speech, but it can sometimes deny governmental funding (i.e., dominium) to persons who engage in otherwise constitutionally protected speech that the government does not like.[8] The effect of these unconstitutional conditions is the same as direct prohibition, but in the United States it nevertheless largely escapes constitutional sanction.[9] So does the ubiquitous practice by which elected officials distribute governmental resources to entities and interests who help them get

[3] Karen Yeung, 'Government by Publicity Management: Sunlight or Spin?', *Public Law* 2005: 360.

[4] Cf. Tony Prosser, *The Economic Constitution* (Oxford University Press, 2014), 3–11.

[5] U.S. Const., amend. I.

[6] U.S. Const. art. I, sec. 8, cl. 10.

[7] U.S. Const., art. I, sec. 9, cl. 7.

[8] See, e.g., Rust v. Sullivan, 500 U.S. 173 (1991).

[9] See, e.g., Richard A. Epstein, 'Foreword: Unconstitutional Conditions, State Power, and the Limits of Consent', *Harvard Law Review* 102 (1988): 4–104; cf. Kathleen Sullivan, 'Unconstitutional Conditions', *Harvard Law Review* 102 (1989): 1413–1506.

elected, despite the fact that many viscerally find this to be constitutionally de-legitimating.[10]

I suspect that the reason why liberal constitutionalism pays so little attention to the constitutional implications of dominium is that that particular conceptualization of constitutionalism developed at a time when dominium was a relatively minor tool in the state's regulatory toolkit.[11] Liberalism, and liberal constitutionalism, is concerned primarily with the state's powers of coercion and force. By contrast, individual response to dominium is voluntary, and thus seems relatively consistent with the individual autonomy that liberalism seek to preserve.[12] Of course, there are two problems with this perspective. First, particularly since the Industrial Revolution, dominium has become a principal, if not *the* principal regulatory tool in the state's regulatory toolkit.[13] Second, 'choices' involving access to material welfare are not always 'voluntary' in any meaningful sense of the term.[14]

But as explored below, if liberalism has a hard time incorporating the state's power of dominium into its conceptualisation of 'constitutionalism', at least some of the constitutional implications of the state's power of dominium have been well recognised. The state's power of dominium plays a critical role in the constitutional construction of citizenship and solidarity; it can play a critical role in the construction of state autonomy and coherence, what we might collectively think of as 'sovereignty'. Its use (and more importantly misuse) has important implications for the state's substantive legitimacy. And it is one of the principal subjects of constitutional concerns for 'public accountability'.

A. *Dominium, Citizenship, and Solidarity*

The state's use of its powers of dominium has important implications for citizenship. There are two aspects to this. First, particularly in advanced industrial nations, the state will agree to provide or otherwise guarantee access to certain basic material resources (what are sometimes called

[10] Cf. Richard L. Hall and Frank W. Wayman, 'Buying Time: Moneyed Interests and the Mobilization of Bias in Congressional Committees', *American Political Science Review* 84 (1990): 797–820.

[11] Cf. Daintith, 'The Techniques of Government', 212.

[12] See Epstein, 'Foreword'.

[13] Daintith, 'The Techniques of Government', 212.

[14] See Alan Wertheimer, *Coercion* (Princeton University Press, 1987), 201.

'citizenship goods'[15]) in exchange for citizen loyalty – an exchange the T. H. Marshall famously referred to as 'social citizenship'.[16] But even with regard to other kinds of good, goods that are not citizenship goods, citizens may still expect certain terms of *equitable* distribution even if the state is not required to provide the good as per the terms of social citizenship.

This notion of 'social citizenship' emerged with the onset of industrialisation in the countries of the North Atlantic. Industrialisation introduced new kinds of vulnerabilities and dependencies to a wide portion of the citizenry.[17] In particular, it made significant portions of the working classes increasingly dependent on employers for their livelihood, which in turn made them distinctly vulnerable to social insecurity and political and economic exploitation. As a result, citizens started demanding that the state insure that they have access to levels and kinds of material welfare necessary to allow them to participate in the social and political life of the nation,[18] and correspondingly, to reify their constituent power (see also Chapter 9).[19]

Clearly, such demands crucially invoke the ever-present possibility that the state will need to exercise its powers of dominium to ensure universal distribution of citizenship goods. And just as clearly, meeting such demands raised a number of constitutional issues. These include what kinds of goods and services are or should be included in social citizenship bargain.[20] In the United States, for example, such a concern has been particularly visibly played out with regard to the question of health care.[21]

[15] See, generally, Michael W. Dowdle, 'On the Public-Law Character of Competition Law: A Lesson from Asian Capitalism', *Fordham International Law Journal* 38 (2015): 321–324; Tony Prosser, *The Limits of Competition Law: Markets and Public Services* (Oxford University Press, 2005), 35–38.

[16] See T. H. Marshall, *Citizenship and Social Class, and Other Essays* (Bloomington: University of Illinois Press, 1950).

[17] See Nicholas Xenos, *Scarcity and Modernity* (London: Routledge, 1989). Cf. Marshall Sahlins, *Stone Age Economics* (London: Tavistock, 1974).

[18] See also Mary Ann Glendon, 'Rights in Twentieth-Century Constitutions: The Case of Welfare Rights', *Journal of Policy History* 6 (1994): 140–156.

[19] Cf. Thomas Jefferson, *Notes on the State of Virginia* (New York: Digireads.com Publishing, 2004).

[20] See Dowdle, 'On the Public-Law Character of Competition Law', 321–324. Cf. Ronald Inglehart and Daphna Oyserman, 'Individualism, Autonomy and Self-Expression: The Human Development Syndrome', in Henk Vinken, Joseph Soeters and Peter Ester (eds.), *Comparing Cultures, Dimensions of Culture in a Comparative Perspective* (Leiden: Brill, 2004), 74–96.

[21] See Brian R. Grossman, Erica Solway, Brooke A. Hollister, Carroll L. Estes, and Leah Rogne, 'One Nation, Interdependent: Exploring the Boundaries of Citizenship in the History of Social Security and Medicare', in Leah Rogne, Carroll L. Estes, Brian R. Grossman, Brooke

There is also the issue as to what 'amount' or quality of citizenship goods satisfy the citizenship bargain. Is one's right as a citizen to access to the state's criminal justice system – which involves state deployment of its powers of dominium in the sense that the state must pay to maintain that system's infrastructure – significantly compromised by the practice of plea bargaining (which arguably imposes a unconstitutional conditionality),[22] or if the judicial proceedings offered are rendered in a language she or he is not able to understand?[23]

In addition to having to use dominium as a last resort to provide citizenship goods, the use of dominium to provide wealth or goods that are not conditions of citizenship still can provoke constitutional demands for *equitable* distribution. Thus, for example, Oliver Wendell Holmes Jr., while sitting on the Bench of the Supreme Court of Massachusetts famously wrote in *McAuliffe v. Mayor of New Bedford* (1892): 'The petitioner may have a constitutional right to talk politics, but he has no constitutional right to be a policeman'.[24] This may be true, but what if the petitioner was denied the opportunity to be a policeman simply because he was of Asian ancestry, or because she was Catholic? Obviously, this would nevertheless provoke constitutional concern, even though, as Holmes wrote, he or she had no constitutional right to be a policeman *per se*.

Thus, with regard to many kinds of acts of dominium, the state has a constitutional obligation to not condition receipt of this dominium on factors that violate social understandings of what constitutes *fair* access, regardless of whether the state has an obligation to distribute those goods at all. *Unfair* distributions of access to non-foundational state goods are as corrosive to citizenship loyalty as failure to distribute foundational goods.[25] Thus, for example, most states cannot condition their deployment of dominium – any form of dominium – on the recipient's ethnicity, place of origin, or religion without provoking constitutional concern.

A. Hollister, and Erica Solway (eds.), *Social Insurance and Social Justice: Social Security, Medicare, and the Campaign Against Entitlements* (New York: Springer, 2009), 115–148.

22 See Daniel A. Farber, 'Another View of the Quagmire: Unconstitutional Conditions and Contract Theory', *Florida State University Law Review* 33 (2005): 924–925 [913–952]; Tina Wan, 'Unnecessary Evil of Plea Bargaining: An Unconstitutional Conditions Problem and Not-So-Least Restrictive Alternative', *The Southern California Review of Law and Social Justice* 17 (2007): 33–61.

23 Cf. Williamson B. C. Chang and Manuel U. Araujo, 'Interpreters for the Defense: Due Process for the Non-English-Speaking Defendant', *California Law Review* 63 (1975): 801–823.

24 55 Mass. 216, 220; 29 N.E. 517, 517 (Mass., 1892).

25 See Joseph Tussman and Jacobus tenBroek, 'The Equal Protection of the Laws', *California Law Review* 37 (1949): 341–381.

Constitutional concern over this aspect of a state's exercise of dominium also takes a variety of vectors. For example, there is concern over what kind of distinctions constitute illegitimate denials of equality: For example, can state universities reserve entry spaces for people of historically disadvantaged ethnicities or minorities, what about for people of disadvantaged economic classes?[26] There is concern over what particular kinds of exercises of dominium should or should not be subject to such concerns: Can a state target opportunity to comment on pending regulation only to a representative sampling of selected organisations, or should it extend it to all interested people and parties?[27] There is also concern over what procedures or qualifications satisfy demands of equitable access or opportunity: Are height and weight standard for entry into the police force that statistically discriminate against female applicants discriminatory?[28]

Closely related to the use of dominium to promote citizenship is the use of dominium to promote solidarity. Solidarity refers to the degree to which the national society thinks of itself as a coherent 'us'. It is that perspective that sees membership in the state not simply as the product of an autonomous bargain, but as a shared pursuit of a substantive collective goal or *teleos*.[29] The uses of dominium we explored in the preceding text in the context of the bargain of citizenship are also frequently used to promote the telos of solidarity. States guarantee access to citizenship goods, and equal access to public services and opportunity, not simply as per their responsibility as per the bargain of citizenship, but also as a way of encouraging the population to identify with the state.[30] Similarly, states will often reserve a certain number of places or opportunities for discriminated-against populations in public institution like public universities or the civil service, not simply as egalitarian compensation for past wrongs, but to help encourage the disaffected minority feel itself to be a part of the larger polity (see also

[26] See Grutter v. Bollinger, 539 U.S. 306 (2003).

[27] See Christine B. Harrington and Z. Umut Turem, 'Accounting for Accountability in Neoliberal Regulatory Regimes', in Michael W. Dowdle (ed.), *Public Accountability, Designs, Dilemmas and Experiences* (Cambridge University Press, 2006), 195–219.

[28] Joyce Hogan and Ann M. Quigley, 'Physical Standards for Employment and the Courts', *American Psychologist* 41 (1986): 1193–1217.

[29] See, generally, Kurt Byertz (ed.), *Solidarity* (Dordrecht, The Netherlands: Kluwer Academic Publishers, 1999), 223–292. See also Craig Calhoun, 'Constitutional Patriotism and the Public Sphere: Interests, Identity, and Solidarity in the Integration of Europe', *International Journal of Politics, Culture, and Society* 18 (2005): 257–280.

[30] See, e.g., Andrea Sangiovanni, 'Solidarity in the European Union: Problems and Prospects', in Julie Dickson and Pavlos Eleftheriadis (eds.), *Philosophical Foundations of European Union Law* (Oxford University Press, 2012), 384–411.

Chapter 10 by Andrew Harding in the context of Malaysia and Chapter 5 by Mathew John in the context of India). Even in the United States, such reservations have been recognised as justified in part because of their contribution to solidarity.[31] And in all the countries surveyed above, these particular distributions provoke constitutional issues.

In the European Union, solidarity is expressly recognised as a constitutional-like principle (as much as the European Union has a constitution).[32] Thus, the Preamble to the Treaty on European Union (TEU) requires Europe 'to deepen the solidarity between their peoples while respecting their history, their culture and their traditions'.[33] In the context of dominium, European competition law recognises 'solidary' as a valid reasoning for allowing certain kinds of governmental undertakings to be except from free market forms of resource distribution that otherwise enjoy effectively 'constitutional' status in political Europe (see Chapter 2 of this volume).[34]

B. *Dominium, State Power, and Sovereignty*

As described in Chapter 1, liberalism's preoccupation with limiting state power causes is to overlook the fact that constitutions exist, perhaps first and foremost, to create state power[35] – what, in a constitutional context, we might call sovereignty.[36] Indeed, this was the principal purpose of the American Constitution of 1789. And its creators were rightfully concerned with ensuring that that government, while 'limited', nevertheless has sufficient power and autonomy to maintain and even advance the new country, as Alexander Hamilton cautioned in the first Federalist Paper:

> An enlightened zeal for the energy and efficiency of government will be stigmatized as the offspring of a temper fond of despotic power and hostile to the principles of liberty. . . . It will be forgotten . . . that the vigor of government is essential to the security of liberty; that, in the contemplation of a sound and well-informed judgment, their interest can never be separated;

[31] Compare Grutter v. Bollinger, 539 U.S. 306 (2003), with Regents of the University of California v. Bakke, 438 U.S. 265 (1978).

[32] Sangiovanni, 'Solidarity in the European Union'; Calhoun, 'Constitutional Patriotism'

[33] Treaty on European Union, J C 326, 26.10.2012, at 13.

[34] See Tamara Hervey, 'Social Solidarity: A Buttress against Internal Market Law?', in Jo Shaw (ed.), *Social Law and Policy in an Evolving European Union* 31 (Oxford: Hart Publishing, 2000), 31–48. See also Dowdle, 'On the Public-Law Character of Competition Law', 379–383.

[35] See Charles Sampford, 'Law, Institutions and the Public/Private Divide', *Federal Law Review* 20 (1991): 202–204.

[36] See Martin Loughlin, *Foundations of Public Law* (Oxford University Press, 2010), 183–208.

> and that a dangerous ambition more often lurks behind the specious mask of zeal for the rights of the people than under the forbidden appearance of zeal for the firmness and efficiency of government.[37]

Sovereignty, in this context, includes three aspects. There is internal autonomy, which describes the state's ability to project its policies on possibly resistant locales and classes. In federal and confederal constitutional systems, there are also issues of local autonomy, which involves preserving the limited terrain of policy autonomy enjoyed by the subordinate jurisdictions that constitute the federation. And there is external autonomy, which describes a state's ability to insulate its policies from interference from both strategic and spontaneous transnational pressures.

The demands of internal autonomy and of locale autonomy are naturally in perpetual existential tension. For example, some argue that the constitutional system should emphasise empowering local exercises of dominium, because local distribution schemes are more likely to be effective given their greater familiarity with conditions 'on the ground'.[38] Others, however, argue that a constitution should emphasise central-level distributional schemes, because central-level distributors are less likely to be captured by special interests.[39]

One of the principal responsibilities of a constitutional system is to continually balance and rebalance these kinds of tensions, and this involves regulating acts of central and local dominium that threaten to irritate that tension. Thus, one of the defining constitutional issues during the first forty years of America's constitutional existence involved the question as to whether the central governance could use its power of dominium to establish a central bank.[40] This was a very controversial move, and many – including Thomas Jefferson and James Madison – initially claimed it to be unconstitutional.[41] This constitutional dispute ultimately led to one of the foundational constitutional cases of the early constitutional period, *McCulloch v. Maryland* (1817), in which the Supreme Court held that the establishment of such a bank was consistent with Congress's power

[37] Alexander Hamilton, 'Federalist No. 1', in Alexander Hamilton, James Madison, and John Jay, *The Federalist Papers* (ed., Clinton Rossiter) (New York: Signet Classics, 2003), 29.

[38] See, e.g., Michael C. Dorf and Charles F. Sabel, 'A Constitution of Democratic Experimentalism', *Columbia Law Review* 98 (1998): 267–473.

[39] See James Madison, 'Federalist No. 10', in Alexander Hamilton, James Madison, and John Jay, *The Federalist Papers* (ed., Clinton Rossiter) (New York: Signet Classics, 2003), 71–79.

[40] See, generally, Edward Kaplan, *The Bank of the United States and the American Economy* (Westwood, CT: Greenwood Press, 1999).

[41] See id. at 31–32.

to use whatever means 'necessary and proper' to 'regulate commerce'.[42] Nevertheless, many did not find the argument convincing, and in 1836, President Andrew Jackson ultimately allowed the bank's charter to expire, claiming that regardless of what the Supreme Court said, the bank was unconstitutional. It would not be until 1913 that the federal government would be able use its powers of dominium to permanently establish a central banking system.

Today, President Barak Obama's effort to use federal funds to establish a national health care system in the United States has provoked much political opposition founded on constitutional argument concerning the proper scope of federal versus state powers.[43] In the European Union, the scope of member states' local autonomy to use state resources to set up enterprises providing state services that they then insulate from market competition has been a frequent source of 'constitutional' contestation in the European Court of Justice.[44] On the other hand, European-level capacity to use its powers of dominium to maintain monetary union by providing emergency funds to distressed national economies has provoked constitutional opposition in the national courts of some member nations.[45]

Another constitutional issue that is often provoked by internal exercises of dominium involves the tension between governmental policy autonomy and individual autonomy. We have already encountered this kind of constitutional issue in our examination of 'unconstitutional conditions'.

States also use and regulate their powers of dominium to promote autonomy from external influences. Such influences include strategic actions of transnational actors, and incidental spontaneous external influences, such as in particular those stemming from fluctuations in transnational markets. In so far as the latter are concerned, examples of state regulation of dominium include maintaining a high currency reserve to protect it from

[42] 17 U.S. 316 (1819).

[43] See, generally, Thomas Colby and Peter J. Smith, 'The Return of Lochner', *Cornell Law Review* 100 (2015): 571–580.

[44] See Hervey, 'Social Solidarity'; see, generally, Markus Krajewski, Ulla Neergaard, and Johan van de Gronden (eds.), *The Changing Legal Framework for Services of General Interest in Europe: Between Competition and Solidarity* (The Hague: T. M. C. Asser Press, 2009).

[45] See, e.g., the 'OMT Reference' before the Bundesverfassungsgericht [BVerfG – Federal Constitutional Court of Germany], 2 BvR 2728/13 (January 14, 2014). See, generally, Michael Wilkinson, 'Economic Messianism and Constitutional Power in a German Europe: All Courts Are Equal but Some Courts Are More Equal Than Others' LSE, Law, Society and Economy Working Papers, 26/2014 (London School of Economics, 2014).

global currency shocks (a practice particularly prevalent in the countries of Southeast Asia following the Asian Financial Crisis of the late 1990s); deciding to peg the value of its national currency to that of some other national currency, such as the American dollar or the English pound.; and limiting domestic spending – such as through balanced-budget requirements or 'debt-brake' devices ('*Schuldenbremse*') – in order to better participate in in international financial markets.[46]

All of these represent restrictions of the state's autonomy and its power of dominium. And all raise important constitutional issues. Most significantly, all potentially represent a state's prioritisation of fiscal interests over social and citizenship interests.[47] (See also Chapter 2.)

Of course, the most paradigmatic example of the use of dominium to promote external autonomy involves the state's development and maintenance of its geo-political power. This power manifests itself in military, diplomatic, and economic realms, and all are sustained primarily by the state's power of dominium. And here critical constitutional issues are also raised. We can divide these constitutional issues into two kinds. One involves protecting the domestic population from abuses stemming from the state's geo-political power projections. The tools used to promote geopolitical power – particularly the military, but also transnational espionage, or 'public security' legislation – can easily be used to also project illegitimate control over the domestic population. This is exactly the kind of danger – abuse of state power – that liberalism is principally concerned with, and thus these kinds of constitutional issues are in fact generally well accounted for in liberal constitutionalism.[48]

But there is another, much less recognised constitutional aspect to this. This is an aspect that focuses on the relationship between the exercise of geopolitical power and the polity's constitutional vision of itself as a moral entity. We will examine this in the next subsection, exploring the relationship between dominium and national 'understandings of the good'.

[46] See, e.g., Karl Heinz Hausner and Silvia Simon, 'Experiences with Budget Rules in Switzerland and Germany', *Intereconomics* 50 (2015): 99–107.

[47] See Dani Rodrik, 'The Social Cost of Foreign Exchange Reserves', *International Economic Journal* 20 (2006): 253–266.

[48] See, e.g., Louis Henkin, *Foreign Affairs and the United States Constitution*. 2nd ed. (Oxford: Clarendon Press, 1997); Harold Hongju Koh, *The National Security Constitution: Sharing Power after the Iran-Contra Affair* (New Haven, CT: Yale University Press, 1990).

C. *Dominium and Understandings of the Good*

A foundational principle of every constitution, whether enshrined in its text or not, is that the state must act for the public good. This by itself imposed a fundamental constitutional limit on its powers of dominium, the violation of which is generally thought of in terms of 'corruption' – often defined as 'the use of public office for private gain', or more specific to dominium, 'the sale by government officials of government property for personal gain'.[49] A number of states have anti-corruption provisions in their constitutions.[50] And even where they do not, the problems and issues of corruption often occupy high constitutional concern. Issues of corruption were foundationals concern to the framers of the American constitution, and continue to be an essential, if largely implicit, element of the American constitutional design, what Zephyr Teachout terms 'the anti-corruption principle'.[51]

But even more legitimate pursuit of the public good can easily provoke constitutional concern. For example, constitutions will commonly hold that certain kinds of public goods *should not be* the beneficiaries of the state's powers of dominium. One of the more famous of such prohibitions is found in Article 8 of the Japanese Constitution, which mandates that 'land, sea, and air forces, as well as other war potential, will never be maintained'. Another well-known example is found in the first amendment to the US Constitution, which prohibits uses of dominium that may have the effect of 'respecting an establishment of religion' (even if incidentally).

The polity may also have particular understanding of what it regards as being and not being constitutive of the good.[52] And it may well require, as a condition for solidarity, that the state not use its powers of dominium in ways that are contrary to this good – not because it harms them personally, and not because it violates some provision in the formal constitution, but simply because they cannot or do not wish to identify with an entity that behaves in such a manner. The success of American demands during the 1980s in compelling the American governments to divest from South

[49] See Andrei Shleifer and Robert W. Vishny, 'Corruption', *The Quarterly Journal of Economics* 108 (1993): 599–617.

[50] See, generally, Marie Chêne, 'Anti-Corruption Clauses in Constitutions' (Berlin: Transparency International, 2013), http://www.transparency.org/files/content/corruptionqas/Anti-corruption_constitutional_clauses_2014.pdf.

[51] See Zephyr Teachout, 'The Anti-Corruption Principle', *Cornell Law Review* 94 (2009): 341–413.

[52] Cf. Loughlin, *Foundations of Public Law*, 108–156.

Africa in protest of South African treatment of what it classified as 'black Africans' (cf. Chapter 11) is a good case in point. While in no way mandated by the formal constitution, the divestment debate implicated core conceptual elements of constitutionalism – the demands of fundamental rights, the reach of state sovereignty, and the extent of a government's public responsibilities. (The constitutional dimensions of this debate generally go unrecognized because they played out in the realm of political constitutionalism[53] rather than the juridical constitutionalism that is the primary focus of America's more liberal vision.[54])

(One might also refer, along these lines, also to the arguments advanced by Jurgen Habermas and Jacques Derrida that one of core teleos of an integrated Europe is to advance a much more humane form of capitalism than the Anglo-American model that presently dominates. In this, they are drawing a clear connection between Europe's ongoing constitutionalisation and a demand that Europe deploy its powers of dominium specifically to counterbalance for more alienating and oppressive aspects of global capitalism, in order to realise a particular global-cosmopolitan vision of the good.[55] See also Chapter 2.)

D. Dominium and Public Accountability

The principal means by which liberal constitutionalism systems seek to discipline state powers of dominium is through the device of public accountability.[56] Simply put, public accountability is a device for relegating act of dominium to political regulation within the sphere of the political

[53] See, e.g., See, e.g., J. A. G. Griffith, 'The Political Constitution', *The Modern Law Review* 42 (1979): 1-21; Adam Tomkins, *Our Republican Constitution* (Oxford: Hart Publishing, 2005); Richard Bellamy, *Political Constitutionalism: A Republican Defence of the Constitutionality of Democracy* (Cambridge University Press, 2007); Loughlin, *Foundations of Public Law*, 157-182.

[54] See Audie Klotz, 'Norms Reconstituting Interests: Global Racial Equality and U.S. Sanctions against South Africa', *International Organization* 49 (1995): 451–478.

[55] Jürgen Habermas and Jacques Derrida, 'February 15th or What Binds European Together?', *Constellations* 10 (2003): 291–297. Cf. Bénédicte Fauvarque-Cosson and Anne-Julie Kerhuel 'Is Law an Economic Contest? French Reactions to the *Doing Business* World Bank Reports and Economic Analysis of the Law', *American Journal of Comparative Law* 57 (2009): 822.

[56] See Jeremy Waldron, 'Accountability: Fundamental to Democracy', NYU School of Law, Public Law Research Paper No. 14-13 (New York, 2014), http://papers.ssrn.com/sol3/papers.cfm?abstract_id=2410812. See also John Dunn, 'Situating Democratic Political Accountability', in Adam Przeworski, Susan Stokes, and Bernard Manin (eds.), *Democracy, Accountability, and Representation* (Cambridge University Press, 1999), 330. Cf. Prosser, *The Economic Constitution*.

constitution.[57] But liberal constitutionalism tends to focus its prescriptive attentions on juridification, which effectively removes political constitutionalism from its analytic purview.[58] As a result, liberal constitutionalism tends to regard public accountability as what Jerry Mashaw has termed a 'protean concept, a placeholder for multiple contemporary anxieties'.[59] In other words, in the context of contemporary liberal constitutionalism, public accountability is not so much a concept per se, but an accretional collection of various public-law practices that originally emerged as pragmatic and originally contingent responses to new political-constitutional problems caused by social and economic evolutions in the structure and operations of the society of the state.[60]

Liberal understandings of public accountability focus primarily on the *procedures* by which dominium is distributed, leaving the normative constitutional implications of that distribution per se – with which, as we saw, liberalism has a difficult time grappling – to the political sphere. These procedures work to make the exercise of dominium constitutionally visible, and thus amenable to political-constitutional oversight.[61] They include number of devices, each with its own history and emerging as a contingent response to some social development.[62] Perhaps the first along these lines was simple 'democracy' itself. As noted by James Madison in in *The Federalist* No. 52:

> As it is essential to liberty that the government in general, should have a common interest with the people; so it is particularly essential that [the House of Representatives], should have an immediate dependence on, & an intimate sympathy with the people. Frequent elections are unquestionably

[57] See, generally, Dunn, 'Situating'. See also Tomkins, *Our Republican Constitution.*

[58] See Griffith, 'The Political Constitution'.

[59] See Jerry L. Mashaw, 'Accountability and Institutional Design: Some Thoughts on the Grammar of Governance', in Michael W. Dowdle (ed.), *Public Accountability: Designs, Dilemmas and Experiences* (Cambridge University Press, 2006), 115.

[60] See, generally, Michael W. Dowdle, 'Public Accountability: Conceptual, Historical, and Epistemic Mappings', in Michael W. Dowdle (ed.), *Public Accountability: Designs, Dilemmas and Experiences* (Cambridge University Press, 2006), 1–32; Colin Scott, 'Spontaneous Accountability', in Michael W. Dowdle (ed.), *Public Accountability: Designs, Dilemmas and Experiences* (Cambridge University Press, 2006), 174–191. Cf. Gunther Teubner, 'Juridification: Concepts, Aspects, Limits, Solutions', in Robert Baldwin, Colin Scott and Christopher Hood (eds.), *A Reader on Regulation* (Oxford University Press, 1998), 406–414.

[61] See, generally, Prosser, *The Economic Constitution.*

[62] See, generally, Michael W. Dowdle, 'Public Accountability: Conceptual, Historical, and Epistemic Mappings', in Michael W. Dowdle (ed.), *Public Accountability: Designs, Dilemmas and Experiences* (Cambridge University Press, 2006), 1–32.

> the only policy by which this *dependence* and sympathy can be effectually secured.[63] [emphasis added]

Particularly when combined with other foundational constitutional principles – such as freedom of the press, ministerial responsibility, and public reporting requirements – democracy both catalyses the public visibility of the constitutional issues associated with particular uses of dominium[64] and allows for possible electoral disciplining if the use is seen to be 'contra-constitutional'.[65]

As industrialisation caused democracy to become increasingly radicalised during second half of the nineteenth century, constitutionalists began looking for other ways of ensuring accountability[66] (see also Chapter 2). In the United States, their new solution was bureaucratic rationalisation, specialisation, and professionalisation, as evidenced in the creation of the technocratic 'independent regulatory agency'.[67] In the United Kingdom – where there was greater distrust of bureaucratisation, they focused instead on the use of courts as vehicles for promoting administrative accountability – that is, judicial review.[68] This technique would later be adopted and adapted by the Americans, culminating the passage of the Administrative Procedures Act in in 1946.[69] But come the 1960s, a new set of scandals involving the American executive gave rise to demands for new vehicles for public accountability that focused on direct transparency – that is, open government and 'government in the sunshine' – as a means of restoring

[63] James Madison, 'Federalist No. 52', in *The Federalist Papers* (ed., Clinton Rossiter) (New York: Signet Classics, 2003), 324. See also James Madison, 'Federalist No. 57', in *The Federalist Papers* (ed., Clinton Rossiter) (New York: Signet Classics, 2003), 348–353.

[64] See, e.g., Koh, *The National Security Constitution.*

[65] See, generally, Adam Przeworski, Susan Stokes, and Bernard Manin (eds.), *Democracy Accountability, and Representation* (Cambridge University Press, 1999). Cf. Michael Perry, *The Constitution, the Courts, and Human Rights* (New Haven, CT: Yale University Press, 1982), 17–36.

[66] See David Schneiderman, 'A. V. Dicey, Lord Watson, and the Law of the Canadian Constitution in the Late Nineteenth Century', *Law and History Review* 16 (1998): 501–512; Robert H. Wiebe, *The Search for Order* (New York: Hill and Wang, 1967), 166.

[67] See See Michael W. Dowdle, 'Public Accountability in Alien Terrain: Exploring for Constitutional Accountability in the People's Republic of China', in Michael W. Dowdle (ed.), *Public Accountability: Designs, Dilemmas and Experiences* (Cambridge University Press, 2006), 332–333.

[68] See Dicey, *Introduction to the Study of the Law of the Constitution*, 496, 498–499; see also id. at 389–390, 394–396.

[69] See Morton Horowitz, *The Transformation of American Law, 1870–1960: The Crisis of Legal Orthodoxy* (Oxford University Press, 1992), 225–226.

public accountability to the political system and polity.[70] However, as government exercises of dominium have become increasingly complex, the public-political arena has increasingly lost capacity to make sense of the mass of data exposed by transparency, and still more new responses had to be developed in order to produce accountability.[71] These include the development of the ombudsman system,[72] and a growing use of an increasing diversity of regulatory audits (resulting in what Michael Power has called 'the auditing society').[73] Another response has been to devolve governmental exercises of dominium to markets, where economic competition is thought to provide the accountability and the discipline that the present political system no longer can.[74]

This one-hundred-year evolution in public-accountability mechanisms has been a direct response to the increasing (and evolving) role that dominium plays in government's implementation of state goals and policy – the rise of the administrative state in the case of Diceyian judicial review;[75] the growing demand for public utilities and public welfare provision in the United States in the case of bureaucratisation;[76] the abuse of the president's dominium powers (in particular war powers) in the case of open government;[77] the increasing complexity of what Tony Prosser calls 'the economic constitution' in the case of the audit society;[78] and a belief that government dominium had become too big and too inefficient in the case of marketisation.[79] Indeed, at least some are coming to feel that as governmental deployments of dominium

[70] Michael A. Genovese, *The Watergate Crisis* (Westport, CT: Greenwood, 1999), 86; Frank Anechiarico and James B. Jacobs, *The Pursuit of Absolute Integrity: How Corruption Control Makes Government Ineffective* (University of Chicago Press, 1996), pp. 8, 23–26. See, generally, Harlan Yu and David G. Robinson, 'The New Ambiguity of "Open Government"', *UCLA Law Review Discourse* (2012): 184–187.

[71] See Dunn, 'Situating Democratic Political Accountability', 336.

[72] Ann Abraham, 'The Ombudsman as Part of the UK Constitution: A Contested Role?', *Parliamentary Affairs* 61 (2008): 206–215.

[73] Michael Power, *The Audit Society: Rituals of Verification* (Oxford University Press, 1997).

[74] See Mashaw, 'Accountability and Institutional Design', 122–124; cf. Jody Freeman, 'Extending Public Accountability through Privatization: From Public Law to "Publicization"', Michael W. Dowdle (ed.), *Public Accountability: Designs, Dilemmas and Experiences* (Cambridge University Press, 2006), 90–96.

[75] See Gavin Drewry, 'Public-Private Partnerships: Rethinking the Boundary between Public and Private Law', in Stephen Osborne (ed.), *Public-Private Partnerships: Theory and Practice in International Perspective* (London: Routledge, 2000), 62.

[76] See Dowdle, 'Public Accountability in Alien Terrain', 332–341.

[77] See Anechiarico and Jacobs, *The Pursuit of Absolute Integrity*, 8.

[78] See, generally, Power, *The Audit Society*; cf. Prosser, *The Economic Constitution*.

[79] Freeman, 'Extending Public Accountability', at 84–85.

continue to become ever more complicated, it is becoming increasingly difficult to maintain accountability per se in a modern constitutional democracy.[80] It is to this issue that we now turn.

III. The Special Problems of 'Indirect Dominium'

A. *'Direct' vs. 'Indirect' Dominium*

So far, this chapter has been examining the constitutional implication of direct dominium – where the state directly distributes state resources to the recipient. But state dominium can also take what we might call an 'indirect' form: This happens when the state does not directly distribute the resources, but makes use of resource distributional dynamics of non-state actors.

Perhaps the most common form of indirect dominium makes use of markets. Like states, markets are also devices for distributing resources. The archetypical market of classical economies, for example, works to distribute resources so as to promote productive and allocated efficiency, thereby generating greater material welfare, and because the procurement of greater material welfare for the citizenry is also a goal of the state (as we saw previously), states will often piggyback on this aspect of a private market's distributional capacities to help realise their own goals of welfare maximisation. It will do this, for example, by using state resources to enforce contracts between *private* and parties; or by providing administrative protection against monopolies in order to help markets be more effective in producing such allocations.[81]

But states also use indirect dominium involving private-market distributions to pursue state goals that are *political* as well as economic. A paradigmatic example of this in the context of the American constitution is found in the Commerce Clause, which gives the American Congress 'Power … [t]o regulate Commerce with foreign Nations, and among the several States, and with the Indian tribes'.[82] The Commerce Clause was intended in part to ensure that goods from one state would not be discriminated against in other states' markets – the alleged prevalence of local protectionism under the pre-constitutional Articles of Confederation being

[80] See, generally, Michael W. Dowdle (ed.), *Public Accountability: Designs, Dilemmas and Experiences* (Cambridge University Press, 2006).

[81] Cf. Louis Kaplow and Steven Shavell, *Fairness versus Welfare* (Cambridge, MA: Harvard University Press, 2009).

[82] U.S. Const., art. I, sec. 8.

one of the principal concerns behind the creation of that Constitution.[83] And its intent was primarily political rather than economic. As noted by Laurence Tribe, '[T]he function of the [Commerce] clause is to ensure national solidarity, not economic efficiency'.[84] By insuring fair and uniform competition across the American nation, the Commerce Clause forged for the United States a truly *national* economy – one that bound the desperate regions of the country together in common economic interdependence. The framers believed that such a distinctly *national* economic structuring was critical for securing the national unity – 'solidarity' – necessary for the state to develop a political identity.

Perhaps the first person to theorise about the use of private markets to help realise state goals was the mid-nineteenth-century German economist, Friedrich List. In his book *The National System of Political Economy*, he proposed to examine 'how a given nation can obtain (under the existing conditions of the world) prosperity, civilisation, and power, by means of agriculture, industry, and commerce'.[85] He contrasted this examination against more classical-liberal concern of 'how the entire human race may attain prosperity'.[86] List's field of inquiry would eventually become known – albeit often pejoratively – as 'economic nationalism'. Although often associated as simply another term for state socialism,[87] the ideology of economic nationalism actually is largely coterminous with what we are calling indirect dominium, and its practices are easily found in liberal constitutional democracies. Examples during the middle part of the twentieth century include industrial planning and, to a certain extent Keynesianism. Not only are both common features of liberal economies, both are also paradigmatic examples of the use of indirect dominium: Industrial planning, which was one of the principal foci of Friedrich List's vision of economic nationalism, uses state interventions in the market dynamics of 'core' domestic industries to promote state geo-political

[83] See, e.g., Max Farrand, *The Fathers of the Constitution: A Chronicle of the Establishment of the Union* (Yale University Press, 1921), 29–30, 97, 99; see, generally, Julian N. Eule, 'Laying the Dormant Commerce Clause to Rest', *Yale Law Journal* 91 (1982): 430.

[84] Laurence H. Tribe, *American Constitutional Law*. 2nd ed. (St. Paul, MN: Foundation Press, 1988), 417. See also Richard B. Collins, 'Economic Union as a Constitutional Value', *New York University Law Review* 63 (1988): 53, 63–64.

[85] See Friedrich List, 'The National System of Political Economy' [1841], reprinted in Lars Magnusson (ed.), *Free Trade: 1793–1886*. Vol. 2 (London: Routledge, 1997), 72.

[86] Id.

[87] See Eric Helleiner, 'Economic Nationalism as a Challenge to Economic Liberalism? Lessons from the 19th Century', *International Studies Quarterly* 46 (2002): 308–309.

power and modernity.[88] Keynesianism – Keynes seems to have been quite sympathetic to the goals of economic nationalism[89] – uses the state's power of indirect dominium to help markets promote state goals of internal autonomy and solidarity.[90]

Since the 1980s, a good many other forms of indirect dominium have become increasingly common and popular. These include privatisation and contracting-out, which assigns the distribution of citizenship goods and other public services to private markets in order to reduce state costs and/or provide better services;[91] public-private partnerships, in which states allocate public funds to set up joint collaborations with private market entities, often to promote state developmental goals;[92] state-sponsored schemes of private economic governance, through which the state delegates the governance of particular industrial and social sectors to private associations and other private actors, again to either reduce state costs[93] or more often to use these actors' local knowledge to promote the local effectiveness of the state's larger policy goals;[94] and the use of sovereign wealth funds, in which the state invests state funds in private markets in order to promote economic stability and through that state economic sovereignty.[95]

It should be emphasised the indirect dominium can piggyback on the distributional capacities of non-market actors as well – including civil

[88] See Shaun Breslin, 'The 'China Model' and the Global Crisis: From Friedrich List to a Chinese Mode of Governance?', *International Affairs* 87 (2011): 1323–1343.

[89] See, e.g., John Maynard Keynes, 'National Self-Sufficiency', *The Yale Review* 22 (1933): 755–769; John Maynard Keynes, 'A Short View of Russia', in *The Collected Writings of John Maynard Keynes*, vol. 9 (London: Macmillan, 1971), 253.

[90] See, generally, Takeshi Nakano, 'Theorising Economic Nationalism', *Nations and Nationalism* 10 (2004): 223.

[91] See Graeme A. Hodge, 'Tendering and Contracting Out: Rhetoric or Reality?', *Public Productivity and Management Review* 22 (1999): 455–469.

[92] See Graeme A. Hodge and Carsten Greve, 'Public-Private Partnerships: An International Performance Review', *Public Administration Review* 67 (2007): 545–558.

[93] See Jacco Bomhoff and Anne Meuwese, 'The Meta-Regulation of Transnational Private Regulation', *Journal of Law and Society* 38 (2011): 138–162; cf. Philip J. Harter, 'Negotiating Regulations: A Cure for Malaise', *Georgetown Law Journal* 71 (1986): 2–113.

[94] Cf. Aviation Safety Reporting System [ASRS], 'ASRS: The Case for Confidential Incident Reporting Systems', ASRS Research Papers. No. 60 (2001), http://asrs.arc.nasa.gov/docs/rs/60_Case_for_Confidential_Incident_Reporting.pdf.

[95] See Donghyun Park and Gemma Bolotaulo Estrada, 'Developing Asia's Sovereign Wealth Funds and Outward Foreign Direct Investment', Asian Development Bank Economics Working Paper Series No. 169 (Manila: Asian Development Bank, 2009), 4; Ronald J. Gilson and Curtis J. Milhaupt, 'Sovereign Wealth Funds and Corporate Governance: A Minimalist Response to the New Mercantilism', *Stanford Law Review* 60 (2007): 1349–1350.

society organisations and inter-national non-governmental organisations.[96] States will often give resources to civil society organisation, and direct them to distribute those resources in furtherance of state goals. Examples include block grants (i.e., grants that give the recipient considerable discretion as to how to allocate the grant) to private educational institutions to promote public access to education – a citizenship good; block grants to non-governmental organisations to help provide citizenship goods, public services, or solidarity goods (such as when the state gives block grants to a private orchestra or theatrical group); and block grants to local and international public interest organisations to promote state association with some and support for some particular understanding of the good (like human rights).

B. *Distinctive Constitutional Issues*

Indirect dominium causes problems for liberal constitutionalism, above and beyond those caused by direct dominium. As noted previously, the principal way in which constitutionalism has addressed the exercise of dominium is through the deployment of public accountability. But the standard devices for public accountability are founded on the presence of a clear distinction between the realm of the 'public' and that of the 'private' – that is, the 'public-private divide'.[97]

The public-private divide is the principal way liberal constitutionalism identifies acts of dominium. It delineates both the functionalities of state, and the realm of actors that constitute the state – and through that which acts and actors need to be subject to the demands of public accountability.[98] Indirect dominium – having private actors and institutions act towards state goals – blurs the boundaries between public and private.[99] The private

[96] See Beth Gazley, 'Beyond the Contract: The Scope and Nature of Informal Government–Nonprofit Partnerships', *Public Administration Review* 68 (2008): 141–154; Gordon P. Whitaker, Lydian Altman-Sauer, and Margaret Henderson, 'Mutual Accountability between Governments and Nonprofits: Moving beyond "Surveillance" to "Service"', *American Review of Public Administration* 34 (2004): 115–133.

[97] See Morton J. Horwitz, 'The History of the Public/Private Distinction', *University of Pennsylvania Law Review* 130 (1982): 1423–1428.

[98] See Robert S. Gilmour and Laura S. Jensen, 'Reinventing Government Accountability: Public Functions, Privatization, and the Meaning of "State Action"', *Public Administration Review* 58 (1998): 247–57; cf. Freeman, 'Extending Public Accountability'.

[99] See Norman Lewis, 'Regulating Non-Government Bodies: Privatization, Accountability and the Public-Private Divide', in Jeffrey Jowell and Dawn Oliver (eds.), *The Changing Constitution*. 2nd ed. (Oxford: Clarendon Press, 1989), 219–247. See, e.g., Richard Mulgan,

character of the entities effectuating the dominium distribution removes them from the gaze of public accountability.[100] And thus this makes exercises of what we are calling indirect dominium even more difficult for liberal constitutionalism to evaluate.

In sum, liberal constitutionalism uses the concept of public accountability to assign the constitutional regulation of dominium to the political side of constitutionalism, a side that lies largely outside its own, juridical focus. But, as Jerry Mashaw noted, the liberal understanding of public accountability is a 'protean concept',[101] and as such it does not project well onto new constitutional configurations. One of these configurations is indirect dominium. And what this means, at the end of the day, is that liberal constitutionalism has a particularly difficult time perceiving the political-regulatory needs that attend to state acts of indirect dominium.

IV. Dominium and the Limits of the Liberal Vision: Teaching Competition Law in Indonesia

Of course, liberal constitutionalism has often worked out quite well for those jurisdictions in which it has taken root. It might not track the dynamics of dominium especially well, but one can argue that the 'spontaneous' dynamics of public accountability's historical evolution seem nevertheless to have worked well enough.[102] The liberal-constitutional states' exercises of dominium and indirect dominium do not seem to be producing authoritarian degeneration.

Nevertheless, even if liberalism handling of dominium generally works, there are times when it does not – there are times when it even becomes dysfunctional. And we would do well to at least remember this, and to be better aware of those kinds of situations in which this can become a problem. A demonstration of this can be found analysing one American antitrust attorney's experiences teaching competition regulation to Indonesian regulators and legal professionals. [103]

'Contracting Out and Accountability', *Australian Journal of Public Administration* 56 (1997): 106–116; compare Mashaw, 'Accountability and Institutional Design', 128.

[100] See also Mark Bovens, Thomas Schillemans, and Paul 'T Hart, 'Does Public Accountability Work? An Assessment Tool', *Public Administration* 86 (2008): 240.

[101] Mashaw, 'Accountability and Institutional Design', 115.

[102] See, generally, Scott, 'Spontaneous Accountability'.

[103] See, generally, Kenneth M. Davidson, 'Creating Effective Competition Institutions: Ideas for Transitional Economies', *Asian-Pacific Law and Policy Journal* 6 (2005): 71–129.

A. *Teaching Competition Law in Indonesia*

In August of 2002, Kenneth Davidson, an attorney with the American Federal Trade Commission, was assigned to Jakarta to help the Indonesian Commission for the Supervision of Business Competition develop more effective enforcement of its new competition law regime.[104] He was disheartened, however, by what he found when he got there:

> In furtherance of my goals while in Indonesia, I conducted classes for the Indonesian commission staff on competition concepts. Early in these sessions, I asked the members of the class to raise their hands if they favored free markets and competition. Out of the thirty-five or so individuals who were attending that day, two to three hands were raised.
>
> Initially, I thought perhaps that my question was misunderstood or that the members of the class were shy or unused to volunteering opinions. While both of these reasons proved to be true, further questioning revealed that most of the class did not believe that free markets would benefit Indonesian society or the Indonesian economy. It was their shared belief that free markets would result in higher prices and worse service for Indonesian consumers.
>
> ....
>
> [I felt] troubled by the general lack of insight by these educated and enthusiastic people of how the market mechanism is supposed to work.... In an effort to increase understanding of competition laws and their purpose, I tried to explain the purpose of competition laws and their beneficial intent for consumers to my classes with the Indonesian staff, and in my public speeches.[105]

One of the reasons underlying Indonesian confusion, Davidson discovered, was that they did not seem to understand what competition law was supposed to be about:

> A member of one of these consumer groups provided an example of why he thought his country needed a competition agency. The government, he explained, had recently privatized a previously public agency. He was furious because the private water company had raised rates and service for water problems had declined seriously. He wanted the 'competition' agency to order the private water company to lower its rates and to provide better service.... Our discussion revealed that rather than a competition agency, what was needed in that instance was a regulatory agency.[106]

104 See also Tao Kong and Arief Ramayandi, 'Survey of Recent Developments', *Bulletin of Indonesian Economic Studies* 44 (2008): 25–28.

105 Davidson, 'Creating Effective Competition Institutions', 77.

106 Id. at 76–77.

Davidson's response is understandable. In present-day Euro-American understanding, competition regulation is and should be solely about the need to promote price competition.[107] Price competition increases social welfare, which is what markets do best.[108] Other concerns, while valid, simply are not and should not be part of the competition agencies remit. As Robert Bork so famously stated in his germinal *The Antitrust Paradox*:

> A different line of attack comes from those who observe, quite correctly, that people value things other than consumer welfare, and therefore, quite incorrectly, that antitrust ought not to be confined to advancing that goal. As non sequiturs go, that one is world class.[109]

A competition agency should therefore limit it regulatory focus exclusively to promoting private market competition based on price.[110] Other regulatory concerns should be dealt with elsewhere.[111] For convenience, and given its universal prevalence among the global community of leading competition law scholars,[112] I will refer to this as the 'orthodox' model of competition regulation.

All this sounds well and fine – until we look at competition law through the lens of indirect dominium.

B. Competition Law as an Exercise in Indirect Dominium

We examined in the preceding text how states will often piggyback on market mechanisms for material distribution in order to achieve state ends. One of these ends is the maximisation of social welfare – market forms of distribution, as we have seen, are classically very well suited for that. Competition law serves to facilitate that aspect of markets: It seeks to guarantee that 'the market', as much as possible, is 'efficient', in the sense of getting the most product (material welfare) from a limited set of resource inputs. It does this by ensuring that market competition is based on

107 See Dowdle, 'On the Public-Law Character of Competition Law', 309–313; cf. Barak Orbach, 'How Antitrust Lost Its Goal', *Fordham Law Review* 81 (2013): 2253–2278.

108 See Kaplow and Shavell, *Fairness versus Welfare*.

109 Robert H. Bork, *The Antitrust Paradox: A Policy at War with Itself*. 2nd ed. (New York: Simon and Schuster, 1993), 428.

110 See also Lawrence S. Liu, 'In Fairness We Trust? – Why Fostering Competition Law and Policy Ain't Easy in Asia' (Oct. 19, 2004), *available at* http://ssrn.com/abstract=610822.

111 Cf. Kaplow and Shavell, *Fairness versus Welfare*.

112 See, e.g., Einer Elhauge and Damien Geradin, *Global Competition Law and Economics* (Oxford: Hart Publishing, 2007), v; see, generally, David J. Gerber, *Global Competition: Law, Markets, and Globalization* (Oxford University Press, 2010), 79–120.

price – that is, that markets distribute resources to those entities that are able to sell their product at the lowest cost. This gives evolutionary advantage to those firms that are able to produce most from less, which in turn maximises the market's ability as a whole to drive firms in the aggregate to maximise social welfare.[113]

Because maximising social welfare is also a political concern of the state, this means that competition law can be seen as a form of indirect dominium. Moreover, under this vision of competition regulation, public accountability is not a particularly problematic. The principles governing allocational and productive efficiencies in competitive markets are technocratic, not political. And accountability can be established by assigning competition regulation to politically independent regulatory agencies whose decisions are both public and in conformity with these technocratic principles.[114]

But this vision is too narrow. In particular, it presumes that states piggyback on markets for only one (legitimate) purpose, that of maximising social welfare. This is not correct. For example, many argue that competition law does not merely serve to promote social welfare, but it also is a critical device for promoting the robustness of the democratic system – a claim perhaps most famously associated with the German economic school of ordoliberalism,[115] but which also has enjoyed much support in the United States, particularly during the latter part of the nineteenth century and first half of the twentieth century.[116] This plurality of state goals make the 'indirect dominium' of competition law more complicated. While largely coterminous, pursuit of social welfare and pursuit of democratic robustness do sometimes point in different directions – as evidenced, for example, in the divergences between American antitrust law, which focuses more or less exclusively on welfare maximisation, and European competition law, which pay much more attention to competition regulation's implications for democracy.[117] Legislation can help the

[113] See Dowdle, 'On the Public-Law Character of Competition Law', 311–312.

[114] See also Imelda Maher, 'The Institutional Structure of Competition Law', in Michael W. Dowdle, John Gillespie, and Imelda Maher (eds.), *Asian Capitalism and the Regulation of Competition: Towards a Regulatory Geography of Global Competition Law* (Cambridge University Press, 2013), 61–75.

[115] See, generally, Gerber, 'Constitutionalizing the Economy', 25–84; see especially id. at 37–38.

[116] See Abba P. Lerner, 'The Economics and Politics of Consumer Sovereignty', *American Economic Review* 62 (1972): 258–266; Walter Lippmann, *Drift and Mastery: An Attempt to Diagnose the Current Unrest* (New York: Prentice Hall, 1961 [1914]), 54–55.

[117] See, generally, Gerber, *Global Competition*, 60. Cf. Eleanor M. Fox, 'US and EU Competition Law: A Comparison', in J. David Richardson and Edward M. Graham

regulator negotiate such conflicts somewhat, but it can never eliminate these conflicts from regulatory consideration completely. In some circumstances, the technocratic aspect of 'promoting perfect competition' runs out, and the regulator will herself have to choose which state policy goal – maximising social welfare or promoting democratic robustness – should take precedence, at least for that particular instance. As described by former EU Competition Commissioner Karel Van Miert in the context of Europe:

> The aims of the European Community's competition policy . . . is concerned not only with promoting efficient production but also achieving the aims of the European treaties: establishing a common market, approximating economic policies, promoting harmonious growth, raising living standards, bringing Member States closer together, etc. To this must be added the need to safeguard a pluralistic democracy, which could not survive a strong concentration of economic power. *If competition policy is to reach these various goals, decisions must be made in a pragmatic fashion*, bearing in mind the context in which they are to be made. . . .[118]

And this act of choosing cannot be technocratic, because the competing goals are incommensurate – there is no common metric by which economic losses in social welfare can be objectively weighed against countervailing *political* gains in democratic robustness, or vice versa.[119]

Beyond this, market competition can be, and frequently is, legitimately asked to serve a number of other public ends: each involving a different logic for resource distribution; and each able to assist the state in realising equally valid – but sometime divergent – state goals.[120] Thus, for example, in some markets, producers compete on the basis of design rather than price – producers of mainstream movies in the United States would be an example of this.[121] This type of competition, called product competition as opposed to price competition, allows the producer rather than the consumer to retain a significant share of the value created by product. It does not do so well in

(eds.), *Global Competition Policy* (Washington, DC: Peterson Institute for International Economics, 1997), 343–344, 347–351.

118 Karel Van Miert, 'A Pragmatic Approach to Europe's Competition Policy', Frontier-Free EUROPE Monthly Newsletter (April 5, 1993), as quoted in Brian A. Facey and Dany H. Assaf, 'Monopolization and Abuse of Dominance in Canada, the United States, and the European Union: A Survey', *Antitrust Law Journal* 70 (2002): 527.

119 See Michael Pusey, 'Economic Rationalism, Human Rights and Civil Society', *Australian Journal of Human Rights* 4 (1998): 131–153. Cf. Polanyi, *The Great Transformation.*

120 See, generally, Dowdle, 'On the Public-Law Character of Competition Law', 349–354.

121 See Edward Hastings Chamberlin, *The Theory of Monopolistic Competition: A Re-Orientation of the Theory of Value*. 8th ed. (Cambridge, MA: Harvard University Press, 1965 [1933]).

promoting social welfare, but it does better in promoting innovation and market leadership, which in turn can be important elements of sovereign economic autonomy.[122] These, too, represent important state goals, and as with price competition, states will frequently use their powers of indirect dominium to promote this kind of competition in particular markets – such as through the development and application of intellectual property rights, for example.[123] But at the same time, competition on the basis of product design and competition on the basis of price respond to different and somewhat incompatible sets of institutional structures. Promoting produce competition impedes the allocative and productive efficiencies of the market (and the associated state goals of maximising social welfare); while promoting price competition impedes innovation and industrial leadership (and the state goal of greater economic sovereignty and state geo-political power).[124]

Similarly, as we saw, something states find it convenient to use private markets as the primary distributors of citizenship and solidarity goods. (This might be, for example, because it saves the state the cost of having to construct from scratch new allocative procedures and networks for distributing these goods.) But citizenship and solidarity goods, in order to be politically effective, have to be distributed at least somewhat on the basis of equity. And such a distributional logic impedes a market's capacity both to maximise aggregate social welfare, as per the classic competitive emphasis on price competition.[125]

In all of this, the question of which market or industrial sector is to be subject to which kind of competitive logic so as to serve some particular

[122] See, generally, Cosmo Graham and Fiona Smith, eds., *Competition, Regulation and the New Economy* (Oxford: Hart Publishing, 2004). See also Joseph A. Schumpeter, *Capitalism, Socialism, and Democracy*. 3rd ed. (New York: Harper and Row, 1975), 82–85.

[123] See William E. Kovacic, 'A Regulator's Perspective on Getting the Balance Right', in R. Ian McEwin (ed.), *Intellectual Property, Competition Law and Economics in Asia* (Oxford: Hart Publishing, 2011), 23–34; Katarzyna Czapracka, *Intellectual Property and the Limits of Antitrust: A Comparative Study of US and EU Approaches* (Cheltenham UK: Edward Elgar, 2009), 36–91.

[124] See J. Gregory Sidak and David Teece, 'Favouring Dynamic Competition over Static Competition in Antitrust Law', in R. Ian McEwin (ed.), *Intellectual Property, Competition Law and Economics in Asia* 53 (Oxford: Hart Publishing, 2011), 53; cf. James Crotty, 'Core Industries, Coercive Competition and the Structural Contradiction of Global Neoliberalism', in Nicholas Phelps and Philip Raines (eds.), *The New Competition for Inward Investment: Companies, Institutions and Territorial Development* (Cheltenham, UK: Edward Elgar, 2003), 9–38.

[125] See Prosser, *The Limits of Competition Law*. Cf. Arthur Okun, *Equality and Efficiency: The Big Tradeoff* (Washington, DC: Brookings Institution Press, 1975).

state goal can easily become too complex to be formally delineated. Markets bleed into one another (e.g., through the effects of substitute goods or externalities) – they don't come with jurisdictional boundaries. As with the choice between economic efficiency and democratic robustness, choosing between social welfare, economic sovereignty, and solidarity involves making trade-off between equally valid but incommensurate political and social values. And such trade-offs can often be too complex to be effectively resolved through juridical or technocratic fiat.[126]

So as an exercise of indirect dominium, competition law involves pursuit of not just one but also a number of incommensurate and often structurally competing state goals. It is, in a word, 'pluralist', and this means its needs to be constantly negotiating among these competing state goals with regard to which kinds of market competitions will be given precedence in which markets at any particular point in time.[127] This gives competition law a distinctly and inevitably *political*-regulatory character – one that is not captured by the technocratic perspective of Davidson, and one that cannot be adequately regulated simply using the technocratic forms of public accountability that he, following orthodox understandings, advocates.[128]

C. *Appreciating the Indonesian Perspective*

Once we recognise the constitutional complexity of competition law as an exercise of state dominium, the views expressed by Davidson's Indonesian interlocutors begin to make a great deal more sense. Recall, for example, how one suggested that one of the reasons why Indonesia needed a competition agency was demonstrated by the experience of governmental privatisation of the water industry. Such privatisation – that is, assigning principal responsibility for the distribution of particular citizenship goods, in this case water, to the market rather than the state – had resulted in both higher rates and worse service. A competition agency, she or he concluded, would be useful in preventing this kind of thing from happening.[129]

Davidson dismissed this concern, stating that this kind of problem should properly be the concern of what he called a 'regulatory agency' rather than a competition agency, reflecting the orthodox understanding that competition agencies should focus their regulatory attentions solely

[126] See, generally, Dowdle, 'On the Public-Law Character of Competition Law', 355–366.

[127] See id. at 349–359.

[128] See, generally, id. at 349–366.

[129] Davidson, 'Creating Effective Competition Institutions', 76–77.

on enforcement of price competition in price competitive markets.[130] But as we saw previously, the perspective of dominium shows us that this significantly mischaracterises the social and constitutional complexity of market competition. State regulation of competition does not exist solely to serve one single purpose. As an exercise in indirect dominium, it invariably serves a variety of state purposes. And regulating this diversity of purposes requires constant political negotiation and re-negotiation, it cannot be accomplished technocratically.

This could well have been what Davidson's interlocutor was getting at: here, privatisation – that is, having distributions be subject to competitive market logic – fell into conflict with the need to insure equitable access to water as a foundational citizenship good.[131] The question of whether and to what degree the water industry should be compelled to engage in some form of price competition was ultimately a question as to how it should effectuate the distribution of water and related resources to balance the different political goals that that industry and its markets inevitably serve. Privatisation reduces state costs, it may – even with higher consumer costs and worse service –promote productive efficiency and or innovation, but at a cost to solidarity and citizenship. Such conflicting concerns, and the conflicting distributional patterns they entail, have to be negotiated, they can't be technocratically dictated. Someone needs to step in to make sure that the proper regulatory balance is struck when this happens. And the competition agency would seem like as good a choice as any.

Davidson agrees with the first part of this argument – in the sense that he agrees that this raises an important regulatory matter. Where he disagrees is over the claim that this is best made the job of a competition agency. As per the orthodox model, he believes that a competition agency should focus solely on maintaining price competition in markets that are to be governed by price competition. But here, Davidson overlooks issues of accountability, which as we noted is the weak spot in liberal attempts to account for exercises of dominium – and in particular for exercises of indirect dominium. *Someone* has to regulate the intersection between those state goals that are advanced by price competition and other state goals that are advanced using other forms of competition. But in doing so, someone also *has to be held accountable.*

[130] Id. at 77.

[131] See, e.g., Bronwen Morgan, 'Technocratic v. Convivial Accountability', in Michael W. Dowdle (ed.), *Public Accountability, Designs, Dilemmas and Experiences* (Cambridge University Press, 2006), 243–268.

A competition agency would seem to be the best candidate for effecting this kind of regulation, since given its complexity, dividing such regulation among multiple regulators would create considerable coordination problems. But as we saw, public accountability best issues from the political side of the constitutional system, and as advocated by the orthodox model, competition agencies are supposed to be *independent* regulatory agency, meaning that they are supposed to be *insulated* from politics.[132] This would mean that they cannot be subject to political accountability stemming from an outside political body. How can we solve this apparent conundrum?

One way is by having the competition agency *internalise* the political negotiations involving the different state goals pursued by the state's regulation of competition. Here, the competition agency is still 'independent' in that it is not being affected by outside political influence, but being nevertheless *internally* political, and thus amenable to political accountability.[133]

In fact, this is how competition regulation was structured in the United States during the early years of American competition regulation. For the first twenty-five years after its founding in 1887, the American Interstate Commerce Commission (ICC), America's first 'independent' regulatory agency, and its first agency tasked with regulating market competition, regulated railroad competition primarily by providing a forum in which different social interests involved or affected by railway transportation – railroads, shippers, passengers, workers – to develop, advance, and negotiate ongoing developments in the new regulatory framework.[134] The early ICC would thus have been very comfortable with the kind of competition regulation proposed by Davidson's interlocutors. It was not until the 1910s that the ICC's regulation began to take that more technocratic character presumed by Davidson. And this was only because the earlier period of negotiation gave time and impetus for industrial practices to become stable and standardised. This stability and standardisation was essential to the development of a more technocratic style of regulation

[132] See Kong and Ramayandi, 'Survey of Recent Developments'; compare with Maher, 'The Institutional Structure of Competition Law'.

[133] Examples include Dorf and Sabel, 'A Constitution of Democratic Experimentalism'; Harter, 'Negotiating Regulations'; Dowdle, 'Public Accountability in Alien Terrain', 344–357. Cf. Ian Ayres and John Braithwaite, *Responsive Regulation: Transcending the Deregulation Debate* (Oxford University Press, 1995), 63–71. See also Dowdle, 'On the Public-Law Character of Competition Law', 360–367.

[134] See, generally, Michael W. Dowdle, 'The Peripheral Regulatory State', in Navroz K. Dubash and Bronwen Morgan (eds.), *The Rise of the Regulatory State of the South: Infrastructure and Development in Emerging Economies* (Oxford University Press, 2013), 211–212; see also Dowdle, 'Public Accountability in Alien Terrain', 332–337.

because it alleviated the need for continual constitutional negotiation and renegotiation demanded by the earlier, more dynamic and more developmental regulatory environment.[135]

There is much similarity between the market-regulatory environment of Indonesia today and that of the United States during the last quarter of the nineteenth century. In both cases, you have a new competition regulatory regime being introduced into an environment in which both the constitutional structure and the industrial structure were and are very much in flux. By the 1880s, everyone in American knew that American social, economic, and political society was entering a completely different world; nobody knew what that world was going to look like.[136] The same is true for Indonesia today. In such an environment, the need for a constant negotiation and *renegotiation* of the limits of competition law is going to be much more pronounced than it is in long-stabilised confines of present-day United States. And competition regulation is therefore in much greater need of political and public accountability rather than simply technocratic accountability. In such an environment, it is the regulatory vision of Davidson's interlocutors, rather than that of Davidson, that appears to make the most sense.

V. Conclusion: Dominium and the Limits of the Liberal Vision

The North Atlantic constitutional and economic environments have been remarkably stable over the past century or so. Its present industrial order was basically established at the end of the nineteenth century.[137] The present American political-constitutional order (the principal referent for the structural-liberal model) also dates from around that period, even if the document that symbolically represents that order dates from a century before that.[138]

Such long periods of stability have a tendency to make particular contingencies look like they represent the natural order of things. In

[135] See also Michael J. Piore and Charles F. Sabel, *The Second Industrial Divide: Possibilities for Prosperity* (New York: Basic Books, 1984), 49–54.

[136] See, generally, Stephen Skowronek, *Building a New American State: The Expansion of National Administrative Capacities, 1877–1920* (Cambridge University Press, 1982).

[137] See, generally, Bob Jessop and Ngai-Ling Sum, *Beyond the Regulation Approach: Putting Capitalist Economies in Their Place* (Cheltanham, UK: Edward Elgar, 2006), 58–68; Piore and Sabel, *The Second Industrial Divide*, 21–26; Alfred D. Chandler Jr., 'The Emergence of Managerial Capitalism', *The Business History Review* 58 (1984): 473–503.

[138] See, generally, Skowronek, *Building a New American State*; see also Dowdle, 'Public Accountability in Alien Terrain', 331–341.

the field of governance, it has a tendency to cause political governance to evolve over time into technocratic governance.[139] This seems clearly evidenced in the structural-liberal vision of constitutionalism. Here, emphasis on the juridical replaced our earlier emphasis on the political as socio-economic stability (and in the case of the United States, relative geo-political stability and insularity[140]) increasingly reduced the need for political re-negotiation of bargains struck generations years earlier. As described previously, its constitutional practices of public accountability experienced a similar fate.[141]

This suggests at least two limits on the functionality of the liberal vision: one geographic, the other temporal. Both are well brought out by our analysis of the constitutional dimensions of dominium, and in particular indirect dominium, in the context of Indonesia's competition-regulatory environment.

Lesser industrialised (and other what we might call 'alternatively industrialised'[142]) and lower-income countries seem more prone to resort to indirect dominium. If for no other reason, this is because they frequently lack the resources necessary to develop and maintain the highly complex financial and legal infrastructures necessary to maintain a legally and socially functional public-private divide.[143] It is may also be encouraged by the great volatility and evolutionary dynamism of more peripheral socio-industrial-economic environments. Such volatility demands a more relational form of capitalism, of which indirect dominium is a type.[144] Consistent with our observations regarding indirect dominium, relational capitalism requires a constant negotiation and renegotiation of bargains in response to ever-evolving patterns of contingencies.[145] And as we saw, this pushes the constitutional system strongly to the political side of constitutionalism – a side that the structural-liberal vision has greater difficulty conceptualising.

[139] See, e.g., Dowdle, 'On the Public-Law Character of Competition Law', 325–327.

[140] See Akhil Reed Amar, 'Some New World Lessons for the Old World', *University of Chicago Law Review* 58 (1991): 483–510.

[141] See, generally, Dowdle, 'Public Accountability: Conceptual, Historical, and Epistemic Mappings".

[142] See, e.g., Jessop and Sum, *Beyond the Regulation Approach.*

[143] See, e.g., Pasuk Phongpaicht and Chris Baker, *Thailand's Crisis* (Singapore: Institute of Southeast Asian Studies, 2000), *Thailand's Crisis*, 35–82, 97–104; see also Dowdle, 'Public Accountability in Alien Terrain', 341–344.

[144] See Dowdle, "On the Public-Law Character of Competition Law', 336–341; Cf. Oliver E. Williamson, *The Economic Institutions of Capitalism* (New York: The Free Press, 1985), 71–72.

[145] See Williamson, *Economic Institutions*, 71–72.

But the use of indirect dominium is also increasing rapidly even in the advanced democratic constitutional states of the North Atlantic.[146] And this suggests a possible temporal dimension to the limits of the structural-liberal vision. Socio-industrial-economic environments in 'the West' are becoming increasingly unstable.[147] The industrial-constitutional bargains that were struck generations ago and that once seemed eternal are beginning to unravel (see also Chapter 2). And as was the case in the United States during the last decades of the nineteenth century, we appear yet again to be transiting into a new socio-industrial epoch, the political and hence constitutional outlines of which remain largely unrevealed. It may well be that, as suggest by Daintith, state use of indirect dominium may be becoming 'the new normal'.[148] So here too, the gravitational pull is towards political constitutionalism, and political forms of constitutional accountability. And the structural-liberal vision of constitutionalism that has governed our constitutional imaginations for so long again begins to confront its limits.

This is not to suggest that the structural-liberal constitutionalism will become obsolete, or that it has nothing significant to contribute to the constitutional experiences of the Global South. What it does suggest is that it is going to have to adapt. And perhaps ironically, the keys to such adaptation lie precisely in that aspect of liberal constitutionalism that is giving it so much trouble – that of political accountability.

Accountability is somewhat distinctive insofar as the structural-liberal constitutionalism is concerned in that it is not primarily an exercise in what Daintith termed 'imperium'. At least conceptually, accountability describes a discursive rather than command-driven dynamic.[149] To give account is to invite one's interrogators to see things from one's own perspective. And this includes not simply the unique factual perspectives of local knowledge, but different normative perspectives as well. Sometimes,

[146] See Daintith, 'The Techniques of Government', 212–213.

[147] See, e.g., Piore and Sabel, *The Second Industrial Divide*. See also J. Bradford DeLong and Lawrence H. Summers, 'The "New Economy": Background, Historical Perspective, Questions, and Speculations', *Economic Review* (Federal Reserve Bank of Kansas City) 29.4 (2001), 33–34; see, generally, David Held, Anthony G. McGrew, David Goldblatt, and Jonathan Perraton, *Global Transformations: Politics, Economics and Culture* (Stanford, CA: Stanford University Press, 1999).

[148] Daintith, 'The Techniques of Government', 212–213.

[149] See also Dowdle, 'Public Accountability: Conceptual, Historical, and Epistemic Mappings', 14; cf. John Gardner, 'The Mark of Responsibility (with a Postscript on Accountability)', in Michael W. Dowdle (ed.), *Public Accountability: Designs, Dilemmas and Experiences* (Cambridge University Press, 2006), 237–242.

when one gives account, it can cause us to see our own world in a different normative light.[150] And political forms of accountability are particularly useful in this regard because they are less formalistically constrained in what they are able to look at.

This is an overlooked but extremely important aspect of accountability. Accountability's discursive nature makes it unique in the liberal's pantheon of constitutional structures in that it offers an opportunity for the constitutional system to 'learn'.[151] Thus, somewhat ironically, it is precisely in its pushing accountability into the political sphere of constitutionalism, that sphere that liberal constitutionalism has difficulty envisioning, that indirect dominium might offer liberal constitutionalism its greatest services – for it is precisely in the sphere of political accountability that liberalism may be best able to learn about and re-envision itself in the context of our evolving world.

[150] See, e.g., 'Mr. Fred Rogers: Senate Statement on PBS Funding, delivered 1 May 1969', American Rhetoric Online Speech Bank, http://www.americanrhetoric.com/speeches/fredrogerssenatetestimonypbs.htm. See also Robert A. Levin and Laurie Moses Hines, 'Educational Television, Fred Rogers, and the History of Education', *History of Education Quarterly* 43 (2003): 272.

[151] See Dowdle, 'Public Accountability: Conceptual, Historical, and Epistemic Mappings', 28–29; Mark Bovens, 'Public Accountability: A Framework for the Analysis and Assessment of Accountability Arrangements in the Public Domain', *European Law Journal* 13 (2007): 463–465; see, e.g., Sasha Courville, 'Understanding NGO-Based Social and Environmental Regulatory Systems: Why We Need New Models of Accountability', in Michael W. Dowdle (ed.), *Public Accountability: Designs, Dilemmas and Experiences* (Cambridge University Press, 2006), 271–300. Cf. Dorf and Sabel, 'A Constitutional of Democratic Experimentalism'; John Braithwaite, 'Accountability and Responsibility Through Restorative Justice', in Michael W. Dowdle (ed.), *Public Accountability: Designs, Dilemmas and Experiences* (Cambridge University Press, 2006), 33–51.

5

Social Intuitions in the Shadow of Liberal Constitutionalism: An Indian Perspective

MATHEW JOHN

I. Introduction

The first chapter in this volume suggests that liberal constitutionalism understood as a set of structural restraints on government has reached its limits in the contemporary world. It is argued that this is especially so as constitutionalism founded on structural restraints – such as separation of powers, electoral democracy, and judicial review – is unable to explain state building or satisfactorily to account for constitutional change and evolution. A series of normative analytical and conceptual accounts that demonstrate these problems are duly outlined. In response, the editors to this volume advance a different approach that emphasises the epistemic framework of constitutionalism as the motor of constitutional evolution and development.

This chapter is also concerned with the limits of liberal constitutionalism. It examines these limits by describing Indian constitutionalism as a revolutionary project in state building – one that has been formally founded on the structural architecture of liberal democratic ideas for more than a hundred years, but has been continually faced with the limits of that architecture as it encounters and rubs against India's autochthonous social and cultural traditions and epistemologies. Unable to draw on India's own social understandings, it is argued, the institutional tropes and structures of liberal constitutionalism are operationalised by co-opting autochthonous and organic social categories into constitutionally formalised identities.

The chapter's argument is elaborated in three parts. The first part outlines the Indian constitution's initial emergence out of a halting liberalism stemming from a pedagogical mission in colonial government to steward India towards a unified nation. This liberalism went hand in hand, however, with a deep colonial pessimism about whether the 'factions' of Indian society would permit the realisation of nationhood. The second part shows how even as the post-independence constitution rebutted the colonial account of Indian society as a nation of factions, it did so by merely reproducing the pedagogical agenda of the colonial era. That is, the ideal of a constitutionally unified nation was still conceptualised in a manner that has sidelined autochthonous social intuitions and understandings about politics and community. Finally, it presents the constitutional thinking of Gandhi, and in particular his conception of the '*Hind Swaraj*', as a preliminary foray into notating social identities in ways that surpass the limitations of the liberal constitutional politics of both colonial and post-colonial India.

II. The Vanishing Horizon of Nationalism: Forging Constitutionalism in Colonial and Post-Colonial India

The structure as well as the evolving dynamic of contemporary Indian constitutionalism was designed under conditions of colonialism, when constitutionalisation was conceptualised as a pedagogical project of instructing India in the ways of liberal constitutionalism. This pedagogical frame saw traditional Indian society as being in need of the transformative, modernising leadership of colonial government. Even as there have been different normative orientations in this colonial pedagogy, its goals have remained largely undisturbed during the post-colonial era, and the broad structure of government established in colonial India is preserved into the contemporary moment. Thus, at an institutional level, the entire structural-liberal repertoire of Indian government – including limited government, separation of powers, judicial review, and perhaps ironically, even that of representative government – trace their roots to India's colonial period. In fact, as will be demonstrated, the constitutional nationalism of post-independence has in many ways only deepened the presumptions of colonial government.

From the moment of its introduction by the British, liberal constitutionalism in India has been articulated as a state-led project of education and social transformation. The only question marks surrounding this project were as to whether its liberal values would be internalised by Indian society and, relatedly, whether it would be able to draw on local social epistemologies. As we will see, this has not been the case. Liberal constitutionalism has flattened, bypassed, and largely been unable to tap into or otherwise capture autochthonous social intuitions in demanding acquiescence for its pedagogic reforming claims.

A good perspective from which to examine this unusual case of an ostensibly liberal government being unable to draw upon social epistemologies is through the doctrinal prism of 'minority rights', as it has evolved in Indian constitutional history over the last hundred years. The choice of minority rights to discuss constitutional development in India draws on the observation that colonial government regarded the introduction and institutionalisation of minority rights as a critical component of its pedagogical-constitutionalising mission. That is, minority rights formed the ground on which liberal constitutionalism in India was conceived, and this has continued to be the case even as parts of the intellectual framework of justifying minority rights were altered at independence.

The principal legislative milestones that mark British colonial attempts, as pedagogues, to introduce ordered liberal politics into what they viewed to be the feuding races, classes, and castes of India are the constitutional settlements of 1909, 1919, and 1935.[1] In this regard, it is especially important to note the colonial assumptions regarding the Indian social body that formed the basis for facilitating native participation in British colonial-constitutional government in India. That is, the British saw Indian society as deeply divided by interests of religion, ethnicity, class, and so on. Of these, those of Muslims were initially considered particularly important, and through the Indian Councils Act of 1909, Indian Muslims were granted the privilege of having places reserved to them in colonial legislatures and, eventually, in public employment.[2] Similar representational allotments were then extended to other special groups – or 'minorities' as they came to be called – through the Government of India Acts of 1919 and 1935. Such allotments became the most important gateway to local political participation in British India. In practical terms, they provided the framework for governing the cultural diversity of India and through which Indians came to be drawn into participating in British government, by way of limited representation both in political institutions and government jobs.[3]

[1] See The India Councils Act of 1909; the Government of India Act of 1919; and the Government of India Act of 1935. See also Reginald Coupland, *Report on the Constitutional Problem in India: The Indian Problem, 1833–1935* (Oxford University Press, 1943). Cf. Uday Singh Mehta, 'Constitutionalism', in Niraja Gopal Jayal and Pratap Bhanu Mehta (eds), *The Oxford Companion to Politics in India* (Oxford University Press, 2010).

[2] See *East India (advisory and legislative councils, &c.)*, vol. 1: *Proposals of the Government of India and despatch of the Secretary of State: in continuation of Cd. 3710 of 1907* (London: House of Commons, 2008), at 8. See also Coupland, Report, 25–27.

[3] See also Sufiya Pathan, 'A Historical and Theoretical Investigation into Communalism' (Manipal, India: Manipal University PhD thesis, 2009).

In discussing the social conditions within which the new constitutional scheme sought to draw the groups recognised to be minorities into colonial politics, the *Montagu Chelmsford Report*, which provided the basis for the Government of India Act of 1919, noted cleavages of religion, race, and caste as being a pathological social condition of India, and as being constant threats to social solidarity and eventual political citizenship. Insofar as universal citizenship was a desired goal of colonial constitutionalism, then to the colonial officialdom, these social divisions seemed to represent an overwhelming barrier in the path to such citizenship.[4] In other words, Indian society was viewed as being analogous to a Hobbesian state of nature, unto which history had entrusted to the British the duty of guiding India past its social divisions towards ordered government.

The problem of a divided society was a challenge for the makers of India's post-independence constitution as well. However, they viewed the justification for colonial constitutionalism as a contrivance aimed at dividing and preventing the realisation of what they felt was a nation in waiting. For instance, when in 1947, Govind Ballabh Pant sought to outline the 'minority question' before the Constituent Assembly, which had been established to draft a post-independence constitution for India, he casts the problem in the following manner:

> [T]he question of minorities everywhere looms large in constitutional discussions. Many a constitution has foundered on this rock.... *It has been used so far for creating strife, distrust and cleavage between the different sections of the Indian nation. Imperialism thrives on such strife.* It is interested in fomenting such tendencies. So far, the minorities have been incited and have been influenced in a manner which has hampered the growth of cohesion and unity.[5] [emphasis added]

In Pant's account, social divisions are produced and reproduced by the mischievous designs of imperial government. Despite disagreements regarding the sources of social division, the only real difference between the earlier colonial account of these divisions (such as that articulated in the *Montagu Chelmsford Report*) and the later nationalist account like that of Pant was the latter's belief that the constitutional-pedagogical goals of national unity and universal citizenship were now within reach.

[4] See *Montagu Chelmsford Report on Indian Constitutional Reform* (Superintendent, Government of India Press, 1918), 85.

[5] B. Shiva Rao and others, *The Framing of India's Constitution*. Vol. 2 (Dehli: Indian Institute of Public Administration, 1966), 61.

When deliberating the new constitution, however, the wishes of nationalists like Pant notwithstanding, the framers could not escape the epistemic and practical challenges left behind by the fragmented liberal foundations of British constitutionalism. The Constituent Assembly called to draft India's post-independence constitution had inherited a model of constitutional-liberal government built around the idea that India's social divisions could only be constitutionally negotiated through an entrenched scheme of privileges granted to assorted scheduled minorities. This was a model that was now so embedded in colonial constitutionalism that it seemed unavoidable for any post-independence constitutional framework. Therefore, the nationalist mission to sweep away the framework of differentiated citizenship in post-independence India simply could not easily overcome entrenched native interests.

Thus, in relation to the then-existing framework of minority rights, the question as it initially arose before the Constituent Assembly was not whether the framework of differentiated and fragmented citizenship would continue but what shape it would assume in Independent India. In fact, during the early debates, the Constituent Assembly adopted a report by the Advisory Committee on Fundamental Rights granting minorities a set of minority rights similar to those they had hitherto enjoyed under the colonial state – the only significant difference being the case of separate electorates, which many minorities enjoyed in British India but were not included in the Advisory Committee's report.[6]

But when the partition of India on May 26, 1949 into a largely Hindu India and a predominantly Muslim Pakistan removed the Muslim League as a force in Indian constitutional politics, it allowed the Indian National Congress, the political party that controlled the Constituent Assembly, to push towards a position of universal equal citizenship quite like the position envisioned by Pant and other leading nationalist voices of the Assembly.[7] Accordingly the leadership of the Constituent Assembly was able to get ratified a revised proposal on minority rights, also drafted by the Advisory Committee on Fundamental Rights, which recommended 'that the system of reservation for minorities other than Scheduled Castes in Legislatures

[6] See Part XIV of the Draft Constitution of February 1948.

[7] Cf Rochana Bajpai, *Debating Difference: Group Rights and Liberal Democracy in India* (Oxford University Press 2011). See also Iqbal Ansari, 'Minorities and the Politics of Constitution Making in India', in D. Sheth and Gurpreet Mahajan (eds.), *Minority Identities and the Nation-state* (Oxford University Press, 1999), 111–123.

be abolished.'[8] 'Scheduled Castes' referred to caste groups that had been identified during the colonial era as eligible for reserved allotments in legislatures and jobs due to social discrimination stemming from traditional Hindu caste hierarchies. Other 'minorities' who had enjoyed similar minority rights under colonial India but who were not classified as scheduled castes – Muslims being the most prominent – were now only entitled under the new constitution to a limited set of educational and cultural rights. Importantly, the term *minority* was now used to describe a category that was clearly distinct from that described by the term *Scheduled Castes*.

This new constitutional formulation was clearly set within a nationalist imagination that denied the colonial account of an Indian society that was inexorably divided. Even so, it continued to recognise specific 'minority' identities to which attached a now much more limited band of special rights, and continued to grant to the Scheduled Castes special rights analogous to those enjoyed by the 'minorities' of colonial India. This was, of course, in recognition of the practical needs to politically accommodate different social groups in Indian society. In post-partition India, the overwhelming political dominance of the Indian National Congress permitted the constitution makers to fend off the demands for special rights by groups like the Muslims and the Sikhs. However, as a vehicle of social reform and justice, the new Indian republic could not afford to be as dismissive to the Scheduled Castes, whose political identities were largely defined by the historical injustices of caste society in India, and which had already been recognised by the Poona Pact of 1932.[9] (The constitutional settlement also included special political rights for Scheduled Tribes. But the constitutional import of this classification is not relevant to the focus of this chapter.)

Thus as the Constituent Assembly was able to whittle down the rights of the non-caste minorities, it nevertheless continued to defend special rights for the Scheduled Castes. In the new context of post-colonial independence, this required a new justificatory language. Accordingly, the new framework of special rights, for minorities as well as castes, was now justified in the name of 'social transformation'; or in terms of needing to alleviate the injustices of contemporary Indian society, thus allowing the identities of castes and minorities to be braided together into a common citizenship through a granting of a universal justice, if not through the immediate articulation of universalist articulation of citizenship rights.

[8] *Constituent Assembly Debates: Official Report*. Vol. 4 (New Delhi: Lok Sabha Secretariat 1999), 601.

[9] See S. V. Desika Char (ed.), *Readings in the Constitutional History of India 1757–1947* (Oxford University Press 1983), 561–563.

Commenting on constitutionalism as a project in social transformation, Uday Mehta notes insightfully that it was the assertion of this new transformational form of politics that shed the colonial pessimism about the possibility of a unified national polity.[10] That is, social revolution was framed as an assertion of the supremacy of political claims channelled through the new national-constitutional order over those of an autochthonous social order that it sought to subject to its control. Within this now unified field of politics, different constitutionally recognised identities like castes and minorities could be treated differently from the 'majority' and from each other, as it could be argued that these castes and minorities needed to be differently prepared for the transformations that a unified politics demanded.[11] Furthermore, the special rights granted to castes were seen as temporary.[12] And this meant that these rights did not seriously dent the idea of a universal citizenship, but merely functioned as preconditions for a future society with full freedom and equality for all.

By contrast, the rights granted to minorities by the new constitution were not considered temporary. But these were not political rights and therefore were not regarded as threatening to the idea of national unity as were the rights granted to the Scheduled Castes and Tribes. It was in this manner that the revolutionary or transformative approach to constitutionalism could accommodate the differentiated grant of rights both to Scheduled Castes and Tribes, and to (other) minorities, and yet present this as simply a part of an integrated journey towards universal citizenship.

However, if the nationalist objection to colonial politics was that it misidentified or misrepresented the actual social condition of India as being divided by factions, then it is far from certain that the nationalist reframing of this condition has been any more successful. Evaluating the ability of nationalist politics to legitimately and credibly represent the divisions of Indian society as constituents of a unified nation requires training the spotlight of enquiry onto the particular constitutional practices that have been used to incorporate those distinct social identities into a broader national community. Focussing on the 'minorities' of independent India, we shall see that the constitutional framework of special privileges has also been unable to represent or notate the condition of 'community' in ways that ring true to the social and cultural intuitions and understandings that underlie these distinct identities.[13]

[10] Mehta, 'Constitutionalism'.

[11] See, e.g., Narasu Appa Mali v. State of Bombay AIR, 1952 Bom 84.

[12] See Constitution of India, art. 334.

[13] Mathew John, 'Identity and the Social Revolution: On the Political Sociology of Constitutionalism in Contemporary India', Jawaharlal Nehru University Centre for the

III. The Structure of Minority Rights in the Indian Constitution

A. *The Constitutional Framework*

The Indian Constitution grants 'minorities' special rights, capturing its vision of the distinct composition and needs of these groups as set against those of the broader national community. Vastly reduced in scope in comparison to those of the colonial regime that preceded it, the present-day Constitution grants both 'minorities' and other distinct cultural groupings special rights grouped under the heading 'cultural and educational rights', which are elaborated in Articles 29 and 30 of the Indian Constitution. Article 29 grants '*any section of the citizens* ... having a distinct language, script or culture of its own ... the right to conserve the same'. Article 30 grants '*minorities*, whether based on religion or language, the right to establish and administer educational institutions of their choice' (emphasis added).

It is important to note that only Article 30 mentions the word 'minority', and it grants to a minority a special right to establish and administer educational institutions. Article 29, however, simply refers to any 'section' of citizens having distinct language, script, or culture, and it merely grants to these sections the rights to preserve same. Despite these differences, the rights granted by these two provisions are organised under a common heading, and must therefore be understood as drawing from a common inspiration. Further, to the extent that legislative history is relevant to understanding the structure of these rights, B. R. Ambedkar, the chairman of the drafting committee of India's Constitution and independent India's first minister of law, asserted in the Constituent Assembly when discussing a draft version of Article 29 that the phrase 'any section of citizens' also referred to 'minorities', although in a more loosely defined sense.[14] This raises the question of the definitional framework that constitutional understanding and practice have brought to bear on the term *minority*, whether loosely defined or more firmly tethered to conceptual and definitional parameters. And, in the context of our larger enquiry, it also raises the question of how this definitional framework comports which larger social intuitions and understandings of Indian society.

As to the constitutional identification of a minority under Article 30, the commonsense nationalist opinion would identify its essence in terms

Study of Law and Governance Working Paper No. CSLG/WP/18 (New Delhi: Jawaharlal Nehru University, 2012).

[14] See *Constituent Assembly Debates: Official Report*. Vol. 7, 922–923.

of cultural distinctness from the 'Hindu' majority. Thus, in an archetypically nationalist portrayal of India's constitutional future, the Nehru Report of 1928 identified the idea of political community, and by implication a 'minority', in the following way:

> The communal problem in India is essentially the Hindu-Muslim problem. Other communities have however latterly taken up an aggressive attitude and have demanded special rights and privileges. The Sikhs in the Punjab are an important and well knit community which cannot be ignored. Amongst the Hindus themselves there is occasional friction especially in the south, between non-Brahmans and Brahmans. But essentially the problem is how to adjust the differences between Hindus and Muslims.[15]

The Nehru report exemplified the essence of conceptualising a 'minority' as being something in contradistinction to being 'Hindu', which was regarded as being the majority community of India. This position is also supported by judicial decisions, although these decisions seldom represented this foundational division in Indian political community with such clarity.

At the same time, however, this new conception of political community ran and continues to run against fundamental social intuitions. We examine this mismatch between state-led identification of political community and social intuitions by examining several important cases in which the Supreme Court of India had to address the issue of defining minorities.

B. Two Conceptualisations of 'Minorities'

The challenge of defining minorities within a larger representative framework of Indian nationhood has been posed most sharply by particular 'Hindu' groups with claims to minority status. Within the nationalist framework, these claims possess the least credibility. However, in practice, the claims made by these groups display a conceptual coherence and credibility that has caused considerable problems for courts seeking to defend the nationalist demarcation of political community. The cases involving 'Hindu' groups have brought to a head two very different conceptions of political community in addressing the challenge of identifying minorities. On the one hand, the liberal conception of minority refers to a distinct community that is numerically smaller than that larger community that defines the 'national' culture. This is also how India's constitution makers

[15] *The Nehru Report: An Anti-Separatist Manifesto* (New Delhi: Michiko and Panjathan, 1975), 27.

tried to model political community in Independent India. On the other hand, the court has also had to contend with a conceptualisation of a minority as being distinct along a *civilisational* continuum, and not simply or necessarily in numerical terms. The intersection of these different ways of thinking about community and the Supreme Court's efforts at resolving the challenge they raise, is well outlined in the cases of *Bramchari Sidheswar Bhai & Ors. v. State of West Bengal*,[16] *Sastri Yagnapurshdasji v. Muldas Bhudardas Vaishya*,[17] and *Bal Patil & Anr. v. Union of India*.[18]

In *Bramchari Sidheswar Bhai v. State of West Bengal*,[19] decided in 1995, the Ramakrishna Mission Residential College found itself in conflict with the revised policies of the government of West Bengal regarding the college's management. The college was established by the Ramakrishna Mission in 1960 at the request of the West Bengal state government and was partially funded by both the central and the state governments. The Ramakrishna Mission is a religious organisation devoted to the teachings of Sri Ramakrishna (Ramakrishna Paramahansa) (1836–1886). When the college was established, the state government exempted it from government rules pertaining to academic governance. However, the subsequent government action revoked this exemption, which the college challenged claiming theirs was a minority institution under Article 30, and thus enjoyed special rights to administer the college autonomously and free of government interference.

The Ramakrishna Mission was founded by the Ramakrishna Order of supposedly 'Hindu' monks. But in advancing their claim to be a minority community, the Ramakrishna Mission argued that they constituted a world religion and were not simply a parochial sect within Hinduism. They noted that Ramakrishna Paramhansa, their spiritual founder, 'practiced various religions including Islam and realized the truth underlying these religions.... That all religions are true ... that all religions are only different paths leading to the same goal'.[20] Along these lines, the mission was distinctive in that it allowed members and followers to retain their identity as a Christian, Muslim, Jew, Hindu, and so forth while still being members of the mission. This particular distinction, they argued, differentiated them sufficiently from other religions, particularly Hinduism, and

[16] MANU/SC/0413/1995.
[17] AIR 1966 SC 1119.
[18] MANU/SC/0472/2005.
[19] MANU/SC/0413/1995.
[20] Id., para. 24.

thus made them a religious minority in their own right and not simply a particular philosophical articulation of Hinduism.

Their argument was accepted by the High Court at Kolkata. On appeal, however, the Indian Supreme Court overturned the High Court decision, holding that the Ramakrishna Mission could not credibly claim to place itself apart from the broader Hindu community. And because the Hindu community constituted the majority religion of India, this meant that the Ramakrishna Mission did not enjoy minority status under Article 30.

At the heart of the Supreme Court's reasoning was what it held to be the High Court's incorrect departure, on the question of Hindu identity, from an earlier and widely studied[21] Supreme Court decision in *Sastri Yagnapurshdasji v. Muldas Bhudardas Vaishya*.[22] This case dealt with the followers of Swaminarayan, a nineteenth-century social reformer. The Swaminarayans had built several temples, which they claimed should enjoy immunity on grounds of religious freedom, from the Bombay Hindu Places of Public Worship (Entry-Authorisation) Act 1956, which prohibited *Hindu* temples that were accessible to the general public from refusing entry to persons because they belonged to an untouchable Hindu caste or community.

The Swaminarayans limited rights of entry to their temples solely to members of their sect. They claimed that they were not covered by the Hindu Places of Public Worship Act because they constituted a religious sect that was distinct from that of Hinduism. They argued that even though they might be considered socially and culturally Hindu, they were not part of the Hindu 'religion' because:

> Swaminarayan, the founder of the sect, considered himself as the Supreme God, and as such, the sect that believes in the divinity of Swaminarayan cannot be assimilated with the followers of Hindu religion ... that the temples in suit had been established for the worship of Swaminarayan himself and not for the worship of the traditional Hindu idols.... [T] he sect propagated the ideal that worship of any God other than Swaminarayan would be a betrayal of his faith, and lastly, that the Acharyas who had been appointed by Swaminarayan adopted a procedure of 'Initiation' (*diksha*) which showed that on initiation, the devotee became a Swaminarayan and assumed a distinct and separate character as a follower of the sect.[23]

[21] See also Marc Galanter, 'Hinduism, Secularism, and the Indian Judiciary', in Rajeev Bhargava (ed.), *Secularism and Its Critics* (Oxford University Press, 1999), 233–267.

[22] AIR 1966 SC 1119.

[23] Id. at 1123.

Quite like the Ramakrishna Mission, the Swaminarayans also claimed that their sect was open to all as long they were appropriately initiated. However, also as in the case of the Ramakrishna Mission, it was not clear whether and how this particular description of their religious practices set them apart from the Hindu 'religion' per se. This required inquiry into the essential nature of the Hindu religion, which formed a central part of Chief Justice Gajendragadkar's majority opinion disallowing the Swaminarayan claims and pronouncing them 'Hindus' subject to the demands of the Bombay Act.

However, Justice Gajendragadkar's opinion is ultimately built upon an unresolvable contradiction. On the one hand, he argued that the Hindu religion

> does not claim any one prophet; it does not worship any one God; it does not subscribe to any one dogma; it does not believe in any one philosophic concept; it does not follow any one set of religious rites or performances; in fact, it does not appear to satisfy the narrow traditional features of any religion or creed. It may broadly be described as a way of life and nothing more.[24]

Despite its fuzziness, this is not an uncommon way to describe 'Hindu' religiosity or even a broader traditional sub-continental religiosity.[25] In other words, through this intuitive sociology, Justice Gajendragadkar characterises the term *Hindu* as referring to the *civilisational* bond holding together and binding the traditions of the peoples of the Indian subcontinent.

On the other hand, however, Justice Gajendragadkar's opinion also advanced a much more formalist, reductive definition of Hinduism. Drawing significantly from the writing of Dr. S. Radhakrishnan and other modern commentators on the Hindu tradition, Justice Gajendragadkar went on to note that the wide variety of practices and philosophical reflections found in the Hindu tradition were nevertheless held together by a common philosophy of monistic idealism. That is,

> [b]eneath the diversity of philosophic thoughts, concepts and ideas expressed by Hindu philosophers ... lie certain broad concepts which can

[24] Id. at 1128.

[25] See, e.g., Ashish Nandy, 'The Politics of Secularism and the Recovery of Toleration', in Rajeev Bhargava (ed.), *Secularism and Its Critics* (Oxford University Press, 1999), 321–344; T. N. Madan, *Modern Myths, Locked Minds: Secularism and Fundamentalism in India*. 2nd ed. (Oxford University Press, 2009).

> be treated as basic. The first amongst these basic concepts is the acceptance of the Veda as the highest authority in religious and philosophic matters.[26]

In this way, Justice Gajendragadkar defined *Hinduism*, not in civilisational terms, but in terms of particular religious doctrines such as rebirth and predestination. It is this doctrinal account of Hinduism that he ultimately used to refute the Swaminarayans' claim that they were sufficiently distinct from Hinduism as to constitute a separate religion, which he dismissed as simply a product of 'superstition, ignorance and complete misunderstanding of the *true teachings* of Hindu religion and of the real significance of the tenets and philosophy taught by Swaminarayan himself'[27] (emphasis added).

In other words, Justice Gajendragadkar justified his rejection of the Swaminarayans claims by appealing to, and affirming, an *authoritative* version of Hindu belief and practice. His opinion was thus founded on a dogmatic and doctrinal conception of Hinduism that contradicted his earlier description of Hinduism as a civilisational phenomenon, a product of intuitive social identity. (It could be argued that in moving to this more doctrinal definition, he was not denying a broader 'way of life' or civilisational conception of the Hindu tradition, but only emphasising that communities like the Swaminarayans are denominations within that broader tradition, and in this way are not analogous to more archetypically distinct religions – like, for instance, Islam or Christianity.)

It is here that the Swaminarayan case becomes salient to the case of the Ramakrishna Mission, as both these cases deal with similar tensions between a formal doctrinal account of the Hindu religion and sociological or civilisational accounts of the Hindu traditions that run at parallels to it. And in both cases there is a judicial attempt to incorporate civilisational accounts into the doctrinal as far as might be possible. In doing so, the Supreme Court recognised the enormous diversity of doctrines practices and traditions within what is considered to be the Hindu religion, but nevertheless proceeded to affirm an authoritative doctrinal conception of Hinduism that had little to do with any civilisational way of life.

Moreover, as between these civilisational and doctrinal definitions of Hinduism, the courts clearly find the latter to be dominant simply as a legal doctrinal matter. The courts in these two cases marshalled no argument to actively disarm the intuitive sociological appeal of the alternative civilisational account of Hindu religiosity. They simply assert that

[26] AIR 1966 SC at 1130.
[27] Id. at 1135.

the doctrinal account trumps the civilisational. By contrast, it is useful to examine a later decision of the Court in *Bal Patil & Anr. v. Union of India*,[28] which actively engages with the civilisational conception of Hindu religiosity and the anxieties it produces for the liberal nationalism on which constitutionalism in India has been founded.

In *Bal Patil*, decided in 2005, the Supreme Court dismissed a petition of the Jain community arguing that the central government ought to have declared them a 'minority' under the Minorities Commission Act 1992, a statute providing for the welfare of communities that have been formally classified as 'minorities' by the central government for the purposes of that Act. The government had denoted Muslim, Sikhs, Christians, Parsis, and Buddhists as constituting such 'minorities', but had left the Jains out of this list. The Jains then petitioned the Supreme Court to direct the government to include them in this list.

It must be emphasised that, like *Sastri Yagnapurshdasji*, this case did not directly involve questions about definition of minority identity under Article 30. Even so, as with *Sastri Yagnapurshdasji*, *Bal Patil* offers important heuristic pointers on the judiciary's thinking about the issue of minority identity. In dealing with the Jain petition, the Court ultimately held that the power to declare a 'minority' was vested in the central government and that it was inappropriate for the court to second-guess this exercise of executive discretion. Nevertheless, a significant portion of the Court's opinion looked to justify the government's exclusion of the Jains, and this dictum provides an important lens into examining the tense relationship between civilisational distinctiveness and the liberal nationalism of the Indian Constitution.

(Insofar as their status as 'minorities' is concerned, the Jains have always been a hard case. They have sometimes been identified as being part of the broader Hindu community;[29] at other times, however, they have been identified to be distinct.[30] In fact, despite losing this case, the Jains would eventually succeed in persuading the government to have themselves declared a minority community under the under the Minorities Commission Act in early 2014.)

In writing the opinion of the Court, Justice Dharmadhikari argued that Jains ought not to be declared minorities, not because of the absence of any civilisational or even doctrinal distinction, but simply due to the effect

[28] MANU/SC/0472/2005.

[29] See, e.g., the Hindu Marriage Act of 1955.

[30] See Survepalli Radhakrishnan, *Indian Philosophy*. Vol. 1 (London: George Allen and Unwin Ltd., 1948), 361.

such a declaration would have on India's quest for constitutional unity. According to him. 'Hindu society ... is itself divided into various minority groups.... In a caste-ridden Indian society, no section or distinct group of people can claim to be in a majority. *All are minorities among the Hindus*' (emphasis added). Consequently, he argued, the government should not act in ways that encouraged groups like the Jains to adopt what he called a 'minority sentiment'. Doing so would fragment the conceptualisation of political community on which constitutionalism in India was built.

Of course, Muslim assertion of a distinct 'minority' identity would presumably not trouble Justice Dharmadhikari as much as similar claims made by groups like Ramakrishna Mission, the Swaminarayans, and – in this particular case – the Jains. In the history of Indian nationalism, Muslims and certain other groups have *always* been recognised as distinct from the dominant strands of national culture, without contention. But from Justice Dharmadhikari's vantage point, the Jains form part of that particular social spectrum that constitutes the Hindu-majority foundation on which liberal nationalism is to be built. Consequently, any demand for minority status from these kinds of groups would fracture this foundation and its unifying force.

All in all, in their quest for national unity Indian courts have consistently and decisively crowded out of *civilisational* conceptualisation of minority identity in favour of a *political* identity that comports with liberal nationalism. However, the very fact that civilisational arguments continue to assert themselves in Indian courts suggest that liberal's political aspirations to build a uniform nationalism have not been able to establish the desired conceptual hegemony. In fact, the continuing and widespread social appeal of these civilisational conceptualisations of what distinguishes a 'minority' would suggest that constitutional practice cannot continue to ignore the force of these social intuitions.

This frustration of liberalism has not received much attention in contemporary Indian constitutional thought. However, in early writing on the challenges for what was then the future Indian nation, Mahatma Gandhi's perspicuous insights on the limits of liberal constitutional design throw light on the problem we have identified and how it might be surpassed.

IV. Gandhi on the Alienating Effects of Constitutional Liberalism

As one of the most formidable opponents of colonialism in the twentieth century, Mahatma Gandhi foresaw and clearly diagnosed the limits of constitutional liberalism as arising from the alienating effects of colonial rule.[31] All pivotal institutions of colonial rule – ranging from parliamentary government, modern science and medicine, railways, lawyers, and the political forms of organising community – are seen by Gandhi as producing alienating effects.[32] Accordingly, the location or the site of Gandhian politics was local practice and quotidian social forms interrupted by colonialism. And, the methodological route Gandhi offers for Indian freedom and home rule – *'Hind Swaraj'* – is not found simply in the transfer of state power from the British to Indians, but in the reconnecting of Indians to the autochthonous structures of experience and understandings that had been interrupted by colonial sensibilities, institutions, and forms of knowledge. Regarding the dislocations caused by colonial rule, it is important to note, as does Vivek Dhareshwar, that the target of Gandhi's attack was not the institutions and sensibilities of modernity that colonialism brought with it *per se*, but their occlusion of the autochthonous experiences and understanding in Indian society.[33]

A detailed theoretical discussion of the structures of experience that colonialism occludes, and how Gandhi thought India could best overcome this occlusion, will have to be reserved for another occasion.[34] Nevertheless, Gandhi's observations provide an important perspective from which to view the problem of developing a constitutional definition for 'minorities' in India. Reframed in a Gandhian light, such a project can be seen as a particular example of a now post-colonialist 'occlusion' produced by the operation of constitutional liberalism.

Gandhi's thoughts are rarely organised in neat logical argument, and his reflections on the claims that liberal constitutionalism makes on Hindu practices are not as clearly enunciated as we have just restated them. However, it is altogether obvious that in Gandhi's thinking the category 'Hindu' had very little to do with what he termed 'exclusive nationalism'.[35] To Gandhi, Hinduism was a merely an ethic that constituted individual and collective life in India. That is, he invoked the term primarily to

[31] See Akeel Bilgrami, 'Gandhi (and Marx)', in *Secularism, Identity, and Enchantment* (Cambridge, MA: Harvard University Press 2014), 122–174.

[32] M. K. Gandhi, *Hind Swaraj and Other Writings* (ed., Anthony Parel) (Cambridge University Press, 1997).

[33] Vivek Dhareshwar, 'Politics, Experience and Cognitive Enslavement: Gandhi's *Hind Swaraj*', *Economic and Political Weekly* 45 (2010): 51–58.

[34] See, e.g., Uday Singh Mehta, 'Gandhi on Democracy, Politics and the Ethics of Everyday Life', *Modern Intellectual History* 7 (2010): 355–371.

[35] See Sabyasachi Bhattacharya, *Mahatma and the Poet; Letters and Debates between Gandhi and Tagore 1915–1941*. 1st ed. (New Dehli: National Book Trust, 1997), 30.

identify a 'search after the truth through non-violent means. . . . Hinduism is a relentless pursuit after truth'.[36]

Insofar as he addressed the problem of factional or 'communal' conflict within the nation, Gandhi seemed to grant some credence to the nationalist view that the conflict between Hindus and Muslims was the defining problem for national unity. However, because he saw *swaraj* – freedom – as a process of 'self-transformation' 'to be experienced by each one for himself',[37] his concern about Hindu-Muslim conflict can be described merely as a location where the occlusions of exclusive-nationalist understanding of identity had to be engaged with and resisted. This engagement he hoped would clear false understanding regarding these identities and reconnect Indians to the promise of self-transformation contained in terms like Hinduism, or for that matter in any religious tradition.

Thus recognising the devastating effects of the Hindu-Muslim conflict, he notes that this much-touted socio-political enmity was a British invention and was by no means a defining problem of the Indian nation per se. He goes to say that 'there are as many religions as there are individuals. . . . [I]n no part of the world are one nationality and one religion synonymous terms: nor has it ever been in India'.[38] Most significantly, he also questions why the conflict between Hindus and Muslims should be any more significant for national life in India than those conflicts between other communities, such as the Vaishnavites and Shaivites, or the Vedantins and Jains.

In other words, in thinking about social identity and social conflict, Gandhi made fervent efforts to dislodge socio-cultural traditions from exclusive nationalist identities and relocate them in traditions of ethical self-discovery. It was in this manner he put his faith in India's civilisational or religious traditions and simultaneously sought to loosen the claims that liberalism's universal nationalism made and continues to make on these traditions.

Constitutional practice for over the last half a century has, however, belied the Gandhian hope that Indians would come to think with and reflect on their problems through autochthonous categories and traditions of Indian thought and experience. On the contrary, the very logic of contemporary constitutionalism in India is founded on the need to transform Indian social categories so that they may become serviceable for the particular kind of national political community authorised by the

[36] Mahatma Gandhi, *Hindu Dharma* (New Delhi: Orient Paperbacks, 1978), 18–19.
[37] Gandhi, *Hind Swaraj*, 73.
[38] Id. at 53.

liberal-constitutional imagination. Even so, as we saw, the judicial cases described earlier in this chapter demonstrate that India's autochthonous social imagination continues to interrupt (albeit episodically and unsystematically) or limit the reformist ambitions of Indian constitutionalism. But as we have also seen, constitutional discourse is unable to draw on these social understanding in any meaningful way. It is against this background that both Gandhi's diagnosis of the damaging social transformation that constitutionalism demands from Indian society, as much as his exhortation towards self-discovery through the idioms of autochthonous Indian social traditions, continue to be relevant to India's ongoing efforts to identify its own constitutional identity.

But what prospects does the Gandhian route of charting freedom through self-liberation in the frameworks of everyday life have in the liberal constitutional republic India established at independence? In considering this question, this chapter concludes with some observations on a more forthright constitutional acceptance of India's social diversity.

V. Conclusion: The Space for Diversity in the Independence Constitution

Recapping our discussion, the limits of India's liberal constitutional vision has been shown up for its inability to draw on autochthonous social practices and intuitions in its conceptions of political community. These limits were illustrated through the court cases involving claims by the Ramakrishna Mission and the Swaminarayans that their identity and traditional practices made them significantly distinct from Hinduism – claims that were brushed aside in the courts' pursuit of a constitutional *telos* identified as a liberal political community organised along nationalist lines. Viewed in this manner, even the Gandhian approach, which emphasises social diversity as a distinguishing feature of India's civilisational terrain, seems doomed when faced with the nationalising logic of Indian constitutional law.

However, Indian social identities and practices tenaciously continue to resist and interrupt liberal constitutional visions of political community, even in the face of constitutional non-recognition. Can these diverse social traditions, now largely unrecognised, chart identities that might someday find constitutional recognition on their own terms?

Perhaps we can begin answering this question by drawing on a distinction that Michael Oakeshott makes between different traditions of thinking about state formation in modern Europe – the idea of the state as a *societas*, or social partnership and that of the state as a *universitas*, or corporation. A *societas* specifies a moral condition defined by laws where 'government is a nomocracy whose laws are to be understood as conditions of conduct, not devices instrumental to the satisfaction of preferred wants'.[39] Thus a ruler in a *societas* is merely a 'custodian of the loyalties and the guardian administrator ... his concern is to keep the conversation going',[40] By contrast, a *universitas* is a state imagined on the lines of a corporation to pursue a common end.[41] A universitas is accordingly "telocratic" in its orientation such that it may facilitate the management of its common purposive concerns.[42]

Drawing on this distinction, Martin Loughlin notes that constitutional self-expression in all European states has been constituted through the tension between these different forms of orienting and organising constitutional community, between the state as *universitas* and the state as *societas*.[43] But the Indian constitutional framework, by contrast, both in its colonial and post-colonial avatars, has heretofore been defined as almost exclusively in terms of *universitas*, whose defined purpose is the eventual making a modern, unified nation out of the social diversity of India through processes of social and economic transformation. Clearly, the desire for such a *universitas*, founded on pursuit of a liberal justice and equality that is universal to all Indians, runs deep in India. It cannot be ignored. However, neither can India afford to ignore the deeply diverse forms of life that constitute its society as illustrated in the present discussion of minority. And the maintenance of a unity that recognises and embraces such diversity lies precisely in that realm of *societas* that Indian constitutionalism has heretofore overlooked in its overriding quest for a universal, liberalising modernity.

It is against this background that it is useful to observe that there has been scant attention to an intellectual tradition of constitutional thought, in the West or elsewhere, that has used social diversity as a positive ground on which to fashion the identity of the state (but cf. Chapter 10). Gandhi is an important exception. And, though the prospects for an inquiry inspired by Gandhi are not entirely certain, it would most certainly initiate an important conversation about a liberal constitutionalism in India that has been run aground by its demand for an unyieldingly homogenous liberal universalism.

[39] Michael Oakeshott, *On Human Conduct* (Oxford University Press, 1975), 202–203.
[40] Id.
[41] See id. at 205–206.
[42] See also Martin Loughlin, *Foundations of Public Law*, (Oxford University Press, 2010), 160–161.
[43] See, generally, id. at 157–182.

PART III

The Political Construction of the State

6

On Constituent Power

MARTIN LOUGHLIN

I. Introduction

Constituent power is a modern concept. Its source can certainly be traced to debates in medieval political thought,[1] but it emerges in distinct form only with the establishment of the early-modern institution of the state. The concept is a product of the secularising and rationalising movement of eighteenth-century European thought known as the Enlightenment, and it comes to occupy a central place in constitutional thought only after the late-eighteenth-century American and French revolutions. Its meaning derives from two elementary assumptions of Enlightenment thinking: that the ultimate source of all political authority is located in an entity known as 'the people', and that a 'constitution' is a thing – specifically, a document – that is made. Consequently, the concept of constituent power comes into its own only when the constitution is understood as a juridical instrument that derives its authority from some principle of popular self-determination. The constitution is, in short, an expression of the constituent power of the people to make and re-make the institutional arrangements through which they are governed.

In this distinctively modern understanding, constituent power performs the critical role of a boundary concept. Bolstering the autonomous character of the political domain, it operates to police the boundaries, and to specify the limits, of this singular worldview.[2] It is, for example, by virtue of the workings of this concept that material force is converted into

[1] This chapter is adapted from Martin Loughlin, 'The Concept of Constituent Power', *European Journal of Political Theory* 13 (2014): 218–237. See, e.g., Francis Oakley, 'The Absolute and Ordained Power of God and King in the Sixteenth and Seventeenth Centuries: Philosophy, Science, Politics, and Law', *Journal of the History of Ideas* 59 (1998): 669–690. Cf. Carl Schmitt, *Political Theology: Four Chapters on the Concept of Sovereignty* (trans. G. Schwab) (University of Chicago Press, 2005 [1922]), 36.

[2] See Schmitt, *Political Theology*, 5; Ernst-Wolfgang Böckenförde, 'Die verfassunggebende Gewalt des Volkes. Ein Grenzbegriff des Verfassungsrechts' in *Staat, Verfassung, Demokratie: Studien zur Verfassungstheorie und zum Verfassungsrecht*. 2nd ed. (Frankfurt: Suhrkamp, 1992), 90–112.

'political power', that a 'crowd' is transformed into a 'people', and that a governing regime (i.e., constituted power) is conceived as one that derives its authority from the consent of its subjects. The concept thereby enables us to identify the source and nature of the constitutional authority within modern political regimes.

Given this pivotal function, it should not be surprising to discover that constituent power remains a contested concept. It evidently expresses a democratic aspiration, but this remains an aspiration of uncertain institutional form. Commonly expressed in the language of 'we the people', it authorises the establishment of a constitution founded on some notion of popular consent. The particular question I want to consider in this chapter is whether, and to what extent, this democratic foundation also incorporates adherence to certain liberal values associated with the political theory of constitutionalism.

This is not obviously the case. In 1804, for example, Napoleon notoriously claimed that 'I am the constituent power', a conviction that many authoritarian rulers have subsequently – if only implicitly – embraced.[3] I examine this question by considering three main perspectives on the concept of constituent power. These are emanations of three types of legal thought: normativism, decisionism, and relationalism.

Normativism is the prevailing mode of legal thought today. It fashions itself on the autonomy of legal and constitutional ordering. In its positivist form – the idiom that in this volume is referred to as 'structural-liberalism' – it presents itself as a scientific analysis that eliminates all questions of value from its inquiries. In its anti-positivist variant, which includes the 'moral liberalism' of such scholars as Lon Fuller, Ronald Dworkin, and David Dyzenhaus – it extolls the values of liberal legal ordering. But, significantly, in both cases it renders constituent power a redundant concept. Normativism promotes liberal legal ordering and marginalises the significance of democratic foundation.

By contrast, the second type of legal thought – decisionism – founds itself on a conception of law as will, and especially as an expression of democratic will-formation. Although one strand can be identified in the school of American legal realism and its various instrumentalist offshoots, its most prominent exponent within constitutional thought is Carl Schmitt. Schmitt maintains that, being unable to guarantee the terms of their own existence, modern constitutions must be underwritten by a sovereign will.

[3] Napoleon I, *The Corsican: A Diary of Napoleon's Life in His Own Words* (ed., R. M. Johnston) (Boston: Houghton Mifflin Co, 1910), 182.

This sovereign will is the constituent power. Decisionist legal thought highlights the importance of democratic will and marginalises the significance of liberal constitutionalist values.

The third type of legal thought, relationalism, rejects both the (liberal) normativist assumption that constituent power is redundant and the (democratic) decisionist contention that it expresses the will of a constituent subject. For relationalists, constituent power involves a relationship of right: It is a manifestation of political right (*droit politique*/*jus politicum*), and it expresses the open, provisional, and dynamic dimensions to constitutional ordering. It acknowledges the significance of both democracy and liberalism in the constitution of political authority, while keeping active the tensions between those two aspirations. I suggest, finally, that the relational method provides the key to understanding the nature and function of the concept of constituent power in contemporary constitutional thought.

II. Origins

Before examining these three basic perspectives, I should set the context by briefly sketching an account of the origins of the concept of constituent power. Its main source is to be found in Calvinist reinterpretations of Bodinian sovereignty.[4] Calvinist jurists maintained that within any political regime, there existed what they called a 'double sovereignty', with personal sovereignty (*majestas personalis*) being held by the ruler and real sovereignty (*majestas realis*) vesting in the people. This dualist distinction was then deployed in various conflicts that arose during the sixteenth and seventeenth centuries over the competing claims of 'divine right' and 'popular sovereignty'. Though the details of these historic struggles are local and particular, the trajectory of this line of thought ended in a critical distinction being drawn between the 'constituted power' (the power vested in the prince to rule) and the 'constituent power' (the power through which the prince's power to rule was authorised).[5]

This distinction left its mark on late-eighteenth-century revolutionary thought. Locke's influence over the American colonists is evident, for example, in the words of the Declaration of Independence: 'whenever any form of government becomes destructive of these ends, it is the *right of*

[4] See Martin Loughlin, *Foundations of Public Law*, (Oxford University Press, 2010), 60–73.

[5] See, e.g., Samuel Pufendorf, *On the Law of Nature and Nations*. Vol. 7 (trans. C. H. and W. A. Oldfather) (Oxford: Clarendon Press, 1934 [1672]), 2–3.

the people to alter or to abolish it, and to institute new government'.[6] The constituent power of the people is also invoked to establish the authority of the American Federal Constitution notwithstanding an unlawful break with the Articles of Confederation. But it was most explicitly deployed in French revolutionary discourse, where the Abbé Sieyes pressed home the claim that 'the people' – in his words 'the nation' – possesses the constituent power of political establishment. Government, Sieyes explained, is an office of delegated authority, a form of constituted power. But it is the government, not the nation, that is constituted: 'Not only is the nation not subject to a constitution, but it *cannot* be and *must not* be'.[7]

It has become an orthodox tenet of modern legal thought that constitutional law is fundamental law. The point Sieyes makes is that while the law of the constitution may take effect as fundamental law with respect to the institutions of government, no type of delegated power can alter the conditions of its own delegation. Constituent power remains. The nation is prior in time and prior in authority: 'It is the source of everything. Its will is always legal; indeed, it is the law itself'.[8] By expressing in legal language the idea that 'the nation' is the ultimate source of political authority, Sieyes produced a concise and abiding statement of the concept of constituent power.

As constitutions came to be drafted in the name of 'the people', Sieyes's formulation became a staple of constitutional discourse. But it has its ambiguities, and Joseph de Maistre immediately pounced on one difficulty. 'Over whom', he asked, 'are the people sovereign?' He supplied his own answer: 'over themselves, apparently' – meaning that the sovereign people are also subjects. De Maistre not surprisingly felt that there is 'something equivocal if not erroneous here, for the people which *command* are not the people which *obey*'.[9] Sieyes had already acknowledged this point when arguing that political power originates in representation: He accepted that the people exercise sovereign authority only through the medium of their representatives. But this suggests that the constituent power can be exercised only through the constituted (i.e.,

6 *American Declaration of Independence*, July 4, 1776 (emphasis added). Compare John Locke, *Two Treatises of Government*. Vol. 2 (ed. P. Laslett) (Cambridge University Press, 1998), § 222.

7 Emmanuel-Joseph Sieyès, *What Is the Third Estate?* (trans. M. Blondel) (London: Pall Mall Press, 1963 [1789]), 126.

8 Id. at 124.

9 Joseph de Maistre, 'Study on Sovereignty', in *The Works of Joseph de Maistre* (ed. and transl., J. Lively) (London: Unwin Brothers Ltd., 1965), 93–129.

representative) authorities.[10] Or, as de Maistre put it more caustically, 'the people are the sovereign which cannot exercise their sovereignty'.[11] Some have finessed this problem by contending that 'the people' are not sovereign as such but are merely the source of the sovereign authority of the established regime.[12] But that hardly provides an unambiguous solution.

One further problem with Sieyes's formulation is his use of legal terminology. He believed that without an instituted order of government, the nation exists in a state of nature, governed only by the law of nature. But if constituent power is a modern concept brought into being with the establishment of the state as an expression of self-actualisation, the idea of natural law does not seem to offer an adequate explanation of its source: The world of classical natural law is precisely what is being left behind.[13] Sieyes uses this terminology because once he moves beyond the positive law relationship between sovereign and subject he can conceive only of natural law. But need this be so? Rousseau had already shown that the establishment of the constitution of government is regulated, not by natural law, but by *les principes du droit politique*. Rousseau contended that, by virtue of the political pact, a new entity comes into existence: this 'public person', formed 'by the union of all' is called a *Republic* or *body politic*, or *State* when passive; *Sovereign* when active; and *Power* when compared with others like itself. And 'those who are associated in it take collectively the name of *people*, and severally are called *citizens*'.[14] The relationship 'of the Sovereign [the people] to the State,' he explained, is governed not be natural law but by fundamental laws called 'political laws'.[15] This modern idea of constitution acquires its meaning within the broader frame of the political life of the nation.

In general, the origins of constituent power lie in the concept of real sovereignty – *majestas realis* – that early-modern writers vested in 'the people', and *majestas realis* is a political rather than a natural category. Sieyes, the leading architect of the concept, clearly specifies the hierarchical

[10] Sieyès, *What Is the Third Estate?*, 139.

[11] Id.

[12] Westel Willoughby, *The Fundamental Concepts of Public Law* (New York: Macmillan, 1924), 99–100.

[13] See Richard Tuck, 'The "Modern" School of Natural Law', in Anthony Pagden (ed.), *The Languages of Political Theory in Early-Modern Europe* (Cambridge University Press, 1987), 99–122; Knud Haakonssen, *Natural Law and Moral Philosophy from Grotius to the Scottish Enlightenment* (Cambridge University Press, 1996).

[14] Jean-Jacques Rousseau, *The Social Contract*. In *The Social Contract and Other Later Political Writings* (trans., V. Gourevitch) (Cambridge University Press, 1997), 51.

[15] Id. at 12.

relationship existing between the legislative power, constitutional authority, and the constituent power of the nation. But constituent power is not the expression of the nation operating in accordance with some law of nature; it is a modern concept expressing the evolving precepts of political conduct that breathe life into the constitution. This claim is amplified by examining how the concept is situated within the main categories of legal thought.

III. Normativism

Broadly conceived, public law divides into three main strands: the law concerning the acquisition and generation of political power, the law concerning the institutionalisation of political power, and the law concerning the exercise of political power. The latter two address aspects of 'constituted power', conventionally of constitutional and administrative law respectively, but constituent power relates only to the first strand, the way in which political power is generated.[16]

Many contemporary jurists reject this categorisation. The most prominent illustration concerns the school of legal positivism, which presents itself as a science of positive law that abstains from all forms of value judgment. In early formulations, such as that of John Austin, law is defined entirely in non-normative terms, with the result that even positive constitutional law is merely a type of political morality and not strictly law at all.[17] But this school reaches its apogee in Hans Kelsen's 'pure theory of law', in which Kelsen presents legal theory as a science that is 'purified of all political ideology and every element of the natural sciences'.[18] He is therefore able to portray law as a scheme of interpretation whose reality rests in the sphere of meaning.[19] Law is, in short, a system of norms.[20]

Following Hume's injunction against deriving an 'ought' from an 'is', Kelsen argues that a norm acquires its meaning and status as law only from another norm, a higher norm that authorises its enactment. But if law is a hierarchy of norms, eventually the chain of authorisation runs out.

[16] See Martin Loughlin, *The Idea of Public Law* (Oxford University Press, 2003), ch. 6.

[17] John Austin, *The Province of Jurisprudence Determined* (ed. W. Rumble) (Cambridge University Press, 1996 [1832]). See also Dicey, *Introduction to the Study of the Law of the Constitution*, 70–71.

[18] Hans Kelsen, *Introduction to the Problems of Legal Theory* (trans., B. L. Paulson and S. L. Paulson) (Oxford: Clarendon Press, 1992 [1934]), 1.

[19] Id. at 10.

[20] Id. at 55–58.

We are left with a *Grundnorm* (founding norm) at the apex that authorises the lower norms but is not itself authorised by a higher norm. This *Grundnorm* is the original constitution of the legal order. Who authorises this original constitution? Kelsen answers that, in legal science, this particular question – the question of constituent power – cannot be addressed: The *Grundnorm* can only be presupposed.[21] Constituent power, the will that makes the constitution, is for Kelsen a political and not a legal issue.

In positivist legal science, the concept of constituent power either belongs to the world of myth – a political myth that grounds the authority of the basic norm – or is an expression of raw power. It is a political, metaphysical, or theological concept with no juristic significance.[22] Legal science limits itself to a question of validity: Is this or is this not a valid norm of an extant legal order? The theory thus acquires a scientific status only by eliminating all questions concerning the relationship between legality and legitimacy. The first strand of public law, which concerns establishment and maintenance of authority, is not the subject of legal cognition.

What this volume calls the structural-liberal vision of constitutionalism is ultimately a particular expression of normative positivism, in which the central features of structural-liberalism – separation of powers, judicial review, multiparty elections for national office – take the form of norms whose authority or validity is presupposed. From this perspective, constituent power is indistinguishable from raw power, and it therefore ultimately is anti-constitutional and of no affirmative constitutional significance.

This stance of rejecting the concept of constituent power as being of no juristic or constitutional significance is not confined to the school of legal positivism. It is now being implicitly promoted by a broad range of contemporary normative legal theory founded on the autonomy – or intrinsic morality – of law. This is an alternative version of liberalism that can be called legal-moral liberalism. The argument has been most explicitly presented by David Dyzenhaus, who contends that the concept of constituent power is superfluous for the legal theories of scholars such as Lon Fuller, Ronald Dworkin, Robert Alexy, and their followers. What unites this group is their commitment 'to showing how legal order and law itself are best understood from the inside, from a participant perspective that argues that legal order has intrinsic qualities that help to sustain an

[21] See id. at 61–62, 113–125.

[22] See id. at 105. Cf. Schmitt, *Political Theology*.

attractive and viable conception of political community'.[23] Law acquires its authority from these intrinsic qualities; without these, there is neither law nor authority. And once this essential point is acknowledged, the concept of constituent power (i.e., 'the people' as authorising agent) is redundant.[24]

Dyzenhaus's argument is founded on the claim that legality is basic in a way that 'constitution', let alone constituent power, is not. This claim to legality – to 'the rule of law' – is to a 'higher law behind the law'. Adopting a reconstructive methodology that promotes the integrity of legal ordering, it rejects the concept of constituent power on the ground that it remains tied to the status of an enacted constitution whose author is an entity known as 'the people'. Theorists of constituent power, the argument runs, must hypothesise an event – a decision by 'the people' – that takes effect as the ultimate authority of a legal-constitutional order. And this, they argue, yields a distorted image of the authority of 'government under law'.

This is a prominent theme running through contemporary normative legal theory. Even Kelsen contends that 'positive law is justified less by appeal to a higher law, different from positive law, than by appeal to the concept of law itself'.[25] Anti-positivists make a similar argument, adjusting only to incorporate in their claim an 'intrinsic morality' of law.[26] Either way, public law and private law is undifferentiated. In legal positivism, these are merely conventional categories (or subsets) of positive legal norms and, because law can only be understood in terms of positive law, the 'law' that establishes the authority of government does not exist.[27] In the anti-positivist normativist reformulation of this argument, legality is a moral practice of subjecting official conduct to principles and values that make up an ideal, and entirely liberal, vision of law. Public law and private law remain undifferentiated, but in this case because 'law' is conceived as an overarching structure of principles governing all forms of human conduct. To the extent that this version accepts the first strand of public law (i.e., the acquisition and generation of political power), this is regarded as an intrinsically moral endeavour. In both strands of normativism – which together embrace a very broad swathe of Anglo-American

[23] David Dyzenhaus, 'Constitutionalism in an Old Key: Legality and Constituent Power', *Global Constitutionalism* 1 (2012): 233.

[24] See also David Dyzenhaus, 'The Question of Constituent Power', in Martin Loughlin and Neil Walker (eds.), *The Paradox of Constitutionalism: Constituent Power and Constitutional Form* (Oxford University Press, 2007), 129–145.

[25] Kelsen, *Problems of Legal Theory*, 37.

[26] Lon L. Fuller, *The Morality of Law*. 2nd ed. (New Haven, CT: Yale University Press, 1969), ch. 2.

[27] Kelsen, *Problems of Legal Theory*, 92–96.

jurisprudence – the notion of constituent power simply does not register. Law, it would appear, is a liberal practice whose authority does not ultimately rest on a democratic decision of a majority to promulgate rules.

IV. Decisionism

However sophisticated it may be as legal theory, normativism is a peculiarly inadequate expression of constitutional thought. In its positivist variant (as structural-liberalism), it either assumes the existence of a sovereign (e.g., Austin), or else adopts a conception of law as a system of norms authorised by some founding norm whose authority is pre-supposed (e.g., Kelsen). In its anti-positivist variant (as moral-legal liberalism), this type of legal thought focuses on the moral evolution of legality as a social practice, but avoids any analysis of the political conditions under which constitutional authority is established. In place of a founding norm, the anti-positivist variant postulates a morality of law that promotes certain (intrinsically good) legal values.

Such inquiries avoid reference to the institution of the state (i.e., the state as the political unity of a people) or to the concept of sovereignty.[28] In place of the state, normativists substitute an autonomous concept of 'constitution'. The stance of scholars such as Dyzenhaus, who argue that too much attention is paid to the idea of the constitution and that the concept of legality is more basic, is not far removed. What unites these strands is the abstract and ideal character of the directing idea, whether that of the ideal constitution or of some overarching principles of legality. In either case, the constitution is posited as an idealised representation of legal ordering.

This is constitutional thought in blinkers. Constitutional legality is not self-generating: The practice of legality rests on political conditions it cannot guarantee.[29] For scholars who inquire into these factors – and indeed also for lawyers and judges[30] – the constituent decisions of sovereign actors must remain part of the analysis.

Consideration of the origins of constitutional ordering invariably brings the concept of constituent power into play. Constituent power is sometimes invoked as a formal concept postulated to make sense of the

[28] See Kelsen, *Problems of Legal Theory*, 99.

[29] See Ernst-Wolfgang Böckenförde, 'The Emergence of the State as a Process of Secularization', in *State, Society, Liberty: Studies in Political Theory and Constitutional Law* (Oxford: Berg, 1981), 26–64.

[30] See, e.g., Joel I. Colón-Ríos, *Weak Constitutionalism: Democratic Legitimacy and the Question of Constituent Power* (London: Routledge, 2012), 79–80.

authority of an agent to alter the terms of the constitution.[31] In this context, it is merely a pre-supposition. But once we inquire into the conditions that sustain constitutionality, the question of how legal authority is generated within the political domain becomes critical. This is the inquiry Carl Schmitt undertakes. For Schmitt, the modern written constitution is the circumstantial product of particular historical conditions. It is the result of a specific political decision that is given jural form as constituent power.

Schmitt's argument is derived from his theory of state and constitution. The state is the political unity of a people. Given competing interests within any association, unity is maintained only if some means of overcoming conflict can be devised. This is achieved by a sovereign power imposing its will in response to a threat to political unity. In normal times, the existence of a sovereign will is often masked: Under relatively peaceful conditions, formal constitutional mechanisms will be sufficient to resolve disputes. But because the issues that threaten unity cannot be determined in advance, sovereign will cannot be given up. The sovereign is the agent that identifies the exceptional situation in which unity is threatened and acts to resolve that threat. In this situation, the law may recede but the state remains.[32]

The state as the political unity of a people is not simply a hypothesis. The state comes into existence through a historical process. Unity does not rest on some abstract idea: It is the expression in practice of the relative homogeneity of a people. Just as the concept of the state presupposes the concept of the political,[33] so too does the concept of the constitution presuppose the state. Contrary to those jurists who treat the constitution as a contract, Schmitt argues that at base it is a decision, a decision of the sovereign will. It involves, in other words, an exercise of constituent power. Normativist jurists try in various ways to eliminate all reference to the existence of this sovereign act of will from the sphere of legal thought. Decisionists claim that by severing the norms of legal ordering from the facts of political existence normativism skews understanding of the nature of constitutional arrangements.

Schmitt offers a clear answer to the question, 'what is constituent power?' Constituent power 'is the political will, whose power or authority

[31] See also Raymond Carré de Malberg, *Contribution à la Théorie générale de l'Etat* (Paris: Sirey, 1922), 483–504; Olivier Beaud, *La puissance de l'état* (Paris: Presses Universitaires de France, 1994), 17–19.

[32] Schmitt, *Political Theology*, 12.

[33] Carl Schmitt, *The Concept of the Political* (trans., G. Schwab) (University of Chicago Press, 1996 [1927]), 19.

is capable of making the concrete, comprehensive decision over the type and form of its own political existence'.[34] It is 'concrete political being'.[35] It determines the nature of the institutional arrangement of political unity. It establishes the constitution. And its continuing existence (as sovereign will) bolsters the authority of the constitution.

Schmitt's concept of constitution, it should be emphasised, does not correlate with the modern legal conception: 'A concept of the constitution is only possible when one distinguishes constitution and constitutional law'.[36] The latter, the set of provisions laid down in a text called 'the constitution', is a 'relative concept' that is adopted because of the tendency, under the influence of normativist thinking, to conflate the constitution of a state with a document drafted at a particular moment in time and containing a set of constitutional laws. The relative nature of constitutional law means that 'the concept of *the* constitution is lost in the concept of individual constitutional *law*'.[37] Many provisions in written constitutions relate to matters that do not concern the fundamentals of a state's constitution. These provisions may be fundamental from the perspective of normativism, but this is merely the perspective of positive law. The foundational claim made by normativists for constitutional *law* is a formal condition, whereas for Schmitt the constitution itself is a substantive concept.

Because the provisions of modern constitutions do not always regulate fundamental political matters, constitutional laws should not be confused with fundamental decisions made by the exercise of constituent power.[38] For Schmitt, the constitution in its true meaning is valid only 'because it derives from a constitution-making capacity (power or authority) and is established by the will of this constitution-making power'.[39] Whatever unity one finds in the constitution arises from 'a pre-established, unified will' that is not found in norms but only in 'the political existence of the state'.[40]

Schmitt's concepts of state and constitution now fall into alignment. The state is 'the concrete, collective condition of political unity' and in this sense the state 'does not *have* a constitution'; rather, 'the state *is* constitution'. The

34 Carl Schmitt, *Constitutional Theory* (trans., J. Seitzer) (Durham, NC: Duke University Press, 2008 [1928]), 125.
35 Id.
36 Id. at 75.
37 Id. at 71.
38 Id. at 76–77.
39 Id. at 64.
40 Id. at 65.

state/constitution is 'an actually present condition, a *status* of unity and order'.[41] The constitution equates to the form that the state takes. This is not an expression of legal principle: It is an existential condition.

The key to understanding the significance of constituent power in Schmitt's thought lies in the fact that the state is not a static entity. It continues to evolve, expressing 'the principle of the *dynamic emergence* of political unity, of the process of constantly renewed *formation* and *emergence* of this *unity* from a fundamental or ultimately effective *power* and *energy*'.[42] Constituent power is therefore not entirely encapsulated in the term *sovereign will*; it also expresses the formative process by which that sovereign will exhibits itself through time.[43]

But who exercises constituent power? In *Political Theology* (1922), Schmitt addresses this question by asking: '[W]ho is entitled to decide those actions for which the constitution makes no provision?'[44] Although in the early-modern period that power was held by the prince, Schmitt recognises that since the eighteenth century the decisionist and personalist elements of sovereign will have become submerged in the concept of 'the people' as an organic unity.[45] Following Donoso Cortés, he accepts that 1848 marks the end of the epoch of kingship.[46] But does he also follow Donoso Cortés in arguing that the only solution to this gap in authority is that of dictatorship? In *Constitutional Theory* (1928), Schmitt recognises that the bearer of constituent power varies over time. There are, he suggests, two main types of legitimacy: the dynastic (blending Max Weber's 'charismatic' and 'traditional' categories of authority) and the democratic (an expression of the rational). These correspond to the two main bearers of constituent power: the prince and the people. In this later work, Schmitt accepts the notion that 'the people', or at least some powerful group acting in their name, could qualify as bearers of constituent power.

With respect to Weimar Germany, Schmitt recognises that the sovereign people have defined their mode of political existence by adopting a modern constitution allocating governmental powers to various offices. But he follows de Maistre in maintaining that the concept of 'the people' in this constitution takes an essentially representative form.[47] The people

41 Id. at 60.
42 Id. at 61.
43 Id. at 62.
44 Schmitt, *Political Theology*, 64.
45 Id. at 99–102.
46 Carl Schmitt, *The Crisis of Parliamentary Democracy* (trans., E. Kennedy) (Cambridge, MA: MIT Press, 1985 [1923]), 8.
47 See Schmitt, *Constitutional Theory*, 272–273.

as such cannot deliberate or advise, govern or execute: They are able to act only in plebiscitary mode and in response to a precise question.[48] Political action is therefore undertaken primarily by those who claim to act in the name of the people. The constituent power of the people is, for the most part, delegated to their elected representatives.

For Schmitt, then, the democratic character of the Weimar Constitution remains ambivalent. This is because he follows Aristotle and Rousseau in maintaining that the basic criterion of democracy is not representation but the identity of rulers and ruled.[49] This leads him to re-assess the relative roles of parliament and president. As a deliberative or opinion-forming assembly, parliament expresses a liberal rather than democratic principle. And with the emergence of disciplined political parties, it becomes an unsuitable vehicle for decision making because the essential decisions are in reality made elsewhere. Contrary to normativists, who claim a strict political neutrality for the role of the president, Schmitt argues that the president, being directly elected by the people, has become 'the republican version of the monarch'.[50] The president is the true bearer of constituent power. Schmitt explains this claim using legal analysis, especially of the breadth of the emergency power vested in the president under Article 48 of the Weimar Constitution.[51] But his formal, legal argument is underpinned by the decisionist claim that the bearer of constituent power exists 'alongside and above the constitution'.[52] That is, the president is not merely a creature of the *legal* constitution (i.e., of constitutional 'law'), he also possesses the constituent power to maintain the unity of political will. The president's power exists to safeguard the 'substance' of the constitution.

The significance of Schmitt's claim that the sovereign is he 'who decides on the exception' can now be grasped.[53] The constituent power of the president authorises him to undertake a sovereign act, an act that demonstrates the primacy of the existential over the merely normative.[54] But what type of sovereign power does the president possess? Writing *Dictatorship* (1921)

[48] Carl Schmitt, *Legality and Legitimacy* (trans., J. Seitzer) (Durham, NC: Duke University Press, 2004 [1932]), 89.

[49] Schmitt, *Constitutional Theory*, 264–267; Schmitt, *The Crisis of Parliamentary Democracy*, 1–17.

[50] Id. at 316.

[51] Carl Schmitt, *Dictatorship: From the Origin of the Modern Concept of Sovereignty to Proletarian Class Struggle* (trans., M. Hoelzl and G. Ward) (Cambridge: Polity Press, 2014 [1921]), 180–226.

[52] Schmitt, *Constitutional Theory*, 126.

[53] Schmitt, *Political Theology*, 5.

[54] Schmitt, *Constitutional Theory*, 154.

in the shadow of the Bolshevik Revolution, Schmitt was conscious of the emergence of a new type of constituent power, that of 'sovereign dictatorship': a power not merely to suspend normal legal procedures to preserve the state (and that Schmitt calls 'commissarial dictatorship'), but one that could be used to overturn the old regime and replace it with a new state founded on social revolution.[55] The emergence of this new manifestation of constituent power overshadows his analysis in *Constitutional Theory*. Is the constituent power that underpins the Weimar Constitution, which is of social-democratic form but of uncertain authority, of a commissarial or of a sovereign nature? The power is to be exercised in the name of the people, and it exists to safeguard their political unity. But what type of unity does the Weimar Republic express? Under the constitution, this existential question, of necessity, falls to the president to determine.

Schmitt's analysis in *Dictatorship* reflects the ambivalent political situation in 1921. He concludes that it was unclear whether, under the Weimar Constitution, these powers were of a commissarial or sovereign character.[56] However, in the supplement to the second edition of *Dictatorship*, published in 1928, he changed his position. Explaining that the two types of power (i.e., commissarial or sovereign) are incompatible, he argued that since the regime of the Weimar Republic had now consolidated its authority, the president's emergency powers under Article 48 of the Weimar Constitution take the form of commissarial rather than sovereign powers.[57] Schmitt had undoubtedly been concerned about the radical implications of the rise of mass democracy, and his analysis of the constituent power vested in the president served the purpose of safeguarding the authority of the social-democratic form of governmental ordering under the Weimar Constitution: The extensive decision-making powers needed to protect this order are vested in the president, and they are of a commissarial nature.

This decisionist account has evident advantages over normativism, especially in acknowledging that a constitution-founding power is a political undertaking that, of necessity, has an existential dimension. Constitutions are not purely normative constructions: They are bound up with the historical processes of state-building. Modern constitutions, drafted at particular moments in time, establish their authority only through a political process in which allegiance is forged. Achieving this while simultaneously

[55] Schmitt, *Dictatorship*, ch. 4.
[56] Id. at 177.
[57] Id. at 204.

generating political will is not straightforward. For the purpose of building political unity and overcoming conflict the imposition of will – whether through use of emergency powers or the promotion of a cult of strong (charismatic) leadership – is often required.

V. Relationalism

Valuable though Schmitt's decisionist account is, it appears now to contain limitations or ambiguities. But rather than rejecting his analysis, it might be more productive to rework it. This is what the relational method seeks to do. Relationalism accepts many of Schmitt's contentions about constitutional ordering. It recognises the necessity of relating the normative to the existential: Constitutional claims must always be interpreted in the light of material and cultural conditions. It recognises the political as a domain of indeterminacy and therefore one that cannot be organised in accordance with some grand theory, such as liberalism. It recognises that the constitution is a way of political being and, as a consequence, that there will always be a gulf between the norm (the written constitution) and the actuality (the way of being). And it recognises that that gulf must be filled by the activity of governing. Because conflicts in this domain are inevitable, it also accepts that the activity of governing is a sphere of domination in which decisions must be taken. There is, one might say, an intrinsic tension between sovereignty (the representation of the autonomy of the political domain) and the sovereign (the constituent power that makes decisions about the nature of the political formation). Acknowledging the appeal to universal values, it recognises that we are never in an ideal situation.[58]

But relationalism diverges in significant respects from Schmitt's decisionism. The pivotal issue concerns representation. Sieyes founds his analysis of constituent power on the principle of representation, but this he conceives as a necessary response to the continuing division of labour in modern society. Schmitt, by contrast, argues that representation 'contradicts the democratic principle of self-identity of the people present as a political unity' and, perhaps because of the serious threats to political stability the Weimar regime faced, places great reliance on the presence of a sovereign.[59] Neither gets to the core of the issue, which is that once representation is invoked for the purpose of generating political power,

[58] See Martin Loughlin, *The Idea of Public Law*, ch. 5 ('Sovereignty'), ch. 6 ('Constituent Power'), and ch. 8 ('Method').

[59] Schmitt, *Constitutional Theory*, 289.

'the people' must itself be regarded as a representation. Political power is generated only when 'the people' is differentiated from the existential reality of a mass of particular people (the multitude).[60]

Schmitt seems to recognise this point only implicitly, and he finds a solution in decisionism – that is, in a leader charged either with acting as the authentic will of the multitude (sovereign dictatorship) or as the effective will able to protect the unity of the established order (commissarial dictatorship). But this is not the only way to conceptualise the issue or posit a solution. The transfer of authority from prince to people in modernity also brings about a profound change in the order of symbolic representation. The transcendent belief in divine authority might be effaced but that space remains.[61] The transcendent figure of the sovereign is lost, but the space of sovereignty is retained. This is the space of the political, an autonomous domain that, despite its uncertainties, expresses a distinctive way of being that is revealed in its logic of action and singular conception of power.

This space of the political is what normativist liberalism – whether in its positivist (structural) or anti-positivist (moral) variation – seeks to remove from constitutional discourse. The former does this by equating state with a particular legal construction and designating sovereignty as metaphysical mumbo-jumbo masking naked force. The latter conceives constitutional discourse as a type of moral philosophy, a conviction that rests on 'superficial ideas about morality, the nature of the state, and the state's relation to the moral point of view'.[62] Schmitt accepts the autonomy of the political but cannot conceive the maintenance of the political domain without the constant presence of a determinate sovereign. He seeks closure by way of a sovereign that maintains unity through identity. But this attempt at closure through a materialisation of 'the people-as-one' can lead only to totalitarianism, in which any form of opposition is to be regarded as 'the enemy'.[63] If the democratic potential of this modern shift in the source of authority is to be retained, the political space must be recognised as incorporating an unresolved dialectic of determinacy and

[60] See Loughlin, *The Idea of Public Law*, ch. 4 ('Representation').

[61] Claude Lefort, 'The Permanence of the Theological-Political?', in *Democracy and Political Theory* (trans., D. Macey) (Cambridge: Polity Press, 1988), 213–255. Cf. Paul Ricoeur, 'The Symbol … Food for Thought', *Philosophy Today* 3 (1960): 196–207.

[62] Georg Wilhelm Friedrich Hegel, *Hegel's Philosophy of Right* (trans., T. M. Knox) (Oxford: Clarendon Press, 1952 [1821]), § 337.

[63] Cf. Michael Mann, *The Dark Side of Democracy: Explaining Ethnic Cleansing* (Cambridge University Press, 2005), esp. ch. 3.

indeterminacy, of closure and openness. This is the basis of the relational approach.

A relational analysis begins with the problem of the foundational moment. Rousseau was the first to highlight its paradoxical character: How can a multitude of strangers meet, deliberate, and rationally agree upon a constitution for the common good? For this to happen, he explains, "the effect would have to become the cause," in that humans would have to already be beforehand that which they can only become as a consequence of the foundational pact itself.[64] How, in other words, can 'the people' act as the constituent power to establish the form of the political union if they can be identified as such only by virtue of the pact? Normativism resolves this by treating the foundation as a pure act of representation. Constituent power is entirely absorbed into the constituted power: It is merely a presupposition of legal thought. Decisionism resolves it by pre-supposing some mysterious prior substantive equality of the people. Is it possible to move beyond such an opposition between representation and presence?

The paradox of constituent power can be overcome only by adopting a relational approach. The notion of 'self-constitution' is to be understood by reference to reflexive identity. Building on Paul Ricoeur's distinction between *idem*-identity (sameness) and *ipse*-identity (selfhood, implying ability to initiate),[65] Hans Lindahl illuminates the ambiguous nature of foundational moment. He argues that 'although Schmitt is right to assert that foundational acts elicit a presence that interrupts representational practices, this rupture does not – and cannot – reveal a people immediately present to itself as a collective subject'.[66] This is because constituent power not only involves the exercise of power by a people: It simultaneously constitutes a people. Constituent power expresses the fact that unity is created from disunity, inclusion from exclusion. Constitutional ordering is dynamic, never static. So instead of treating the constituent power of the people as an existential unity preceding the formation of the constitution, this power expresses a dialectical relation between 'the nation'

[64] Jean-Jacques Rousseau, *The Social Contract*, 71. See also Louis Althusser, 'Rousseau: *The Social Contract* (the Discrepancies)', in *Politics and History: Montesquieu, Rousseau, Marx* (trans., Ben Brewster) (London: Verso, 2007), 113–160; Jacques Derrida, 'Declarations of Independence', *New Political Science* 15 (1986): 7–15; See, generally, Bonnie Honig, *Political Theory and the Displacement of Politics* (Ithaca, NY: Cornell University Press, 1993).

[65] Paul Ricoeur, 'Narrative Identity', *Philosophy Today* 35 (1991): 73–81.

[66] Hans Lindahl, 'Constituent Power and Reflexive Identity: Towards an Ontology of Collective Selfhood', in Martin Loughlin and Neil Walker (eds.), *The Paradox of Constitutionalism* (Oxford University Press, 2008), 9.

posited for the purpose of self-constitution and the constitutional form through which it can speak authoritatively.

Schmitt had argued that for the decisionist, 'the sovereign decision is the absolute beginning' that 'springs from the normative nothing and a concrete disorder'.[67] From a relational perspective, this situation can never arise. Action always entails reaction; constituent power always refers back to constituted power. In this sense, the foundation in its ideals (i.e., with respect to its normative form) can only be understood virtually. Yet this virtual event founds actual association. The actuality is always messy. The break often takes place through an act of violence (war, conquest, revolution, etc.) and the territorial dimension of the emerging idea of state is invariably arbitrary, in the sense that no 'natural' community inhabits this political space.[68] These factors explain the necessity for government. The space of the political can be seen as a space of freedom ('the absolute beginning'), but if it is to be maintained, institutionalisation of rule is required. This institutionalisation, needed for power generation, implies domination. This leads to a dialectical engagement between what Ricoeur calls conviction and critique, institutionalisation and its irritation.[69] It forms a dynamic of constitutional development without end.

From a relational perspective, constituent power vests in the people, but this does not mean that political authority is located in the people (*qua* the multitude), as adherents to the principle of popular sovereignty maintain.[70] Constituent power expresses a virtual equality of citizens. This is generated *inter homines* (establishing the principle of unity), but it founds an actual association divided into rulers and ruled in a relation of domination (establishing the principle of hierarchy).[71] It founds constitutional rationality (normativity), but the association evolves through action (decision). This tension between sovereignty (the general will) and the sovereign (the agent with authority to enforce a decision in the name of the general will) ensures that the constituent power is not to be understood merely as power (in the sense of force). It involves a 'dialectic of

[67] Carl Schmitt, *On the Three Types of Juristic Thought* (trans., J. Benderskey) (Westport, CT: Praeger, 2004), 62.

[68] See Michael Oakeshott, *On Human Conduct* (Oxford University Press, 1975), 188.

[69] See, generally, Paul Ricoeur, *Critique and Conviction* (trans., K. Blaney) (New York: Columbia University Press, 1998).

[70] Cf. Hegel, *Philosophy of Right*, § 279.

[71] See Paul Ricoeur, 'The Political Paradox', in *History and Truth* (trans., C. A. Kelbley) (Evanston, IL: Northwestern University Press, 1965), 247–270.

right' – of political right (*droit politique*) – that seeks constantly to irritate the institutionalised form of constituted authority.

Once set in a relational frame and conceived as an elaboration of right, the paradoxical aspects of constituent power can be viewed more constructively. Does the foundational moment begin with 'the constitution *of* a political unity through a legal order' or as 'the constitution of a legal order *by* a political unity'? Lindahl recognises that 'someone must seize the initiative to determine what interests are shared by the collective and who belongs to it' and notes that, notwithstanding Schmitt's explicit denial, 'political unity first arises through the "enactment of a constitution." '[72] But many of these difficulties are removed when it is recognised that 'the constitution of a legal order by a political unity' involves an exercise in positive law making, whereas 'the constitution of a political unity through a legal order' refers not to the positing of a legal order (in a strict sense) but to the continuous construction of political unity through *droit politique*.[73] Once constituent power is conceived to be an expression of *droit politique*, it does not seem correct to say that political unity arises through the 'enactment' of a constitution because this suggests an exercise in positive law making to establish a formal constitution. Political unity is formed through the way in which *droit politique* operates to frame the constitution of the state.

Conceived in this way, Schmitt's argument may not be so far removed from a relational perspective as has so far been presented. Schmitt builds his analysis on a distinction between the constitution and positive constitutional law, and he recognises that the state is constantly in the process of formation. Most significantly, it should be noted that from the late 1920s, in response to criticisms of his decisionism, Schmitt modified his position and adopted an institutionalist method similar to that of the early-twentieth-century French public lawyer, Maurice Hauriou.[74] In *On the Three Types of Juristic Thought* (1934), Schmitt again criticises normativism, but he also argues against decisionism and in favour of what he calls 'concrete-order' thinking.[75] Concrete order thinking is his attempt to finesse the distinction between normativity and facticity. It brings his legal thought much closer to Hegel's legal and political philosophy, in which

72 Lindahl, 'Constituent Power and Reflexive Identity', 22.

73 See Loughlin, *The Idea of Public Law*, ch, 8; Loughlin, *Foundations of Public Law*, see also ch. 6.

74 See Maurice Hauriou, *Précis de Droit Constitutionnel*. 2nd ed. (Paris: Sirey, 1929), 73–74.

75 See also Joseph Bendersky, 'Introduction: The Three Types of Juristic Thought in German Historical and Intellectual Context', in Carl Schmitt, *On the Three Types of Juristic Thought* (Westport, CT: Praeger, 2004), 14.

'the state is a "form (*Gestalt*), which is the complete realization of the spirit in being (*Dasein*)"; an "individual totality", a *Reich* of objective reason and morality'.[76]

Although Schmitt here comes close to adopting a relational method, his concept of concrete-order thought remained under-developed. A clearer illustration of relationalism is found in the work of his contemporary, Herman Heller. Heller follows Hegel in arguing that a concept of law depends on the idea of law, and this, he argues, can be formulated only by 'the relativization of positive law by supra-positive, logical and ethical (*sittliche*) basic principles of law'.[77] These basic principles – *Rechtsgrundsätze* – come from existing practices and their explication requires the deployment of a dialectical method: 'Every theory that begins with the alternatives, law or power, norm or will, objectivity or subjectivity,' Heller contends, 'fails to recognize the dialectical construction of the reality of the state and it goes wrong in its very starting point'.[78] Normativism and decisionism, he is suggesting, are erroneous legal methodologies. Once the 'power-forming quality of law' has been grasped, it is impossible to understand the constitution 'as the decision of a norm-less power'.[79] Because power and law are mutually constitutive and reciprocally dependent, we can never embrace the 'normative nothingness' of decisionism. And by 'law' here, Heller is referring not to positive law but to *droit politique*: 'the fundamental principles of law which are foundational of positive law'.[80] Heller's relationalism points in the right direction, though it still leaves us with a highly abstract account of constituent power.

VI. Conclusion: Constituent Power in Constitutional Thought

Schmitt's concrete-order thought and Heller's dialectical analysis each mark advances, but the former is left under-developed and the latter is both incomplete and highly abstract. It remains, then, to examine how the relational method provides an account of constituent power that is able to enrich understanding of the nature of constitutional ordering.

[76] Schmitt, *Three Types of Juristic Thought*, 78.

[77] Hermann Heller, 'Bermerkungen zur Staats- und Rechtstheoretischen Problematik der Gegenwart', in *Gesammelte Schriften*. Vol. 2 (Leiden, The Netherlands: A. W. Sijthoff, 1971 [1929]), 275 (my translation).

[78] Hermann Heller, 'Staatslehre', in *Gesammelte Schriften*. Vol. 3 (Leiden, The Netherlands: A.W . Sijthoff, 1971 [1934]), 393. See also Hermann Heller, 'The Nature and Structure of the State', *Cardozo Law Review* 18 (1996): 1214 (trans., David Dyzenhaus).

[79] Heller, 'Staatslehre', 393.

[80] Id. at 332. See Loughlin, *Foundations of Public Law*, 234–237.

The key is found in the concept of political power. Political power derives its character from the paradoxical nature of the foundation. It exists by virtue of humans coming together as a group. Power is created through a symbolic act in which a multitude of people recognise themselves as forming a unity – a collective singular: *We the People*. That act cannot exist only in the realm of belief. It must also take effect in reality, and this will often involve the use of force. It follows that, however powerful this transcendent act of symbolic representation, conflict and tension within the group are not eliminated. After all, what some celebrate as liberation others experience as defeat. Political power is maintained and augmented only through institutionalisation. And because political conflict can arise in all aspects of group life, a constitutional framework is needed. The people consequently *do ordain and establish a constitution*.

This constitution vests authority in the constituted authorities to legislate, adjudicate, and govern in the interests of the group. By limiting, channeling, and formalising these competences, the constitution itself becomes an instrument of power generation. This follows from a nostrum bequeathed to us by Bodin, and repeated many times since: '[T]he less the power of the sovereignty is (the true marks of majesty thereunto still reserved), the more it is assured'.[81] But through whatever form the constitution institutionalises power, the constituted authorities inevitably retain an extensive, discretionary authority to determine the best interests of the group. That is, there is always a gulf between the constitutionally prescribed arrangement (an expression of sovereignty) and the decisional capacity of the governing authorities (an expression of sovereign authority). Political power is generated through symbolic representation of foundation and constitutionalisation and is then applied through the action of government. Power thus resides neither in 'the people' nor in the constituted authorities: It exists in the relation established between constitutional imagination and governmental action.

The meaning of constituent power in constitutional thought can now be specified: Constituent power expresses the generative aspect of the political power relationship. Contrary to the decisionist claim, it cannot be equated to the actual material power of a multitude. This is the (democratic) materialist fallacy, entailing the reduction of constituent power to fact.[82] Constituent power exists only when that multitude can project itself,

[81] Jean Bodin, *The Six Bookes of a Commonweale* (trans., R. Knolles) (Cambridge, MA: Harvard University Press, 1962), 517. Cf. Jon Elster, *Ulysses Unbound: Studies in Rationality, Precommitment, and Constraint* (Cambridge University Press, 2000), 1.

[82] See, e.g., Antonio Negri, *Insurgencies: Constituent Power and the Modern State* (trans., M. Boscagli) (Minneapolis: University of Minnesota Press, 1999).

not just as the expression of the many (a majority), but in some senses at least, of the all (unity). Without this dimension of symbolic representation, there is no constituent power. Constituent power, produced by an intrinsic connection between the symbolic and the actual, signifies the dynamic aspect of constitutional discourse.[83]

But constituent power similarly cannot entirely be absorbed into the constituted order and equated with some founding norm. Were this to be the case, then the tension that gives the political domain its open and provisional quality would be eliminated. This is the liberal (normativist) fallacy. Its realisation would not result in the achievement of 'the rule of law', which is an impossible dream, but it would surely lead to the destruction of political freedom.

The relational account also explains why constituent power is not engaged only at the (virtual) founding moment, but continues to function within an established regime as an expression of the open, provisional, and dynamic aspects of constitutional ordering. There are various ways in which this open quality can be formulated. In terms already adopted, it exhibits a tension between sovereignty and the sovereign. This replicates the distinction Rousseau draws between sovereignty (the general will) and government (the institution charged with its actual realisation). Rousseau believed that, owing to the lack of any *institutionalised* will to oppose to the constituted power, this distinction establishes a tension that leads only to the corruption of the constitution.[84] That could be so, although Rousseau's pessimism derives from his postulation of an ideal at the foundation (the general will), while in reality constitutional development is the ongoing struggle to give particular institutional meaning to general democratic ideals.

But Rousseau's pessimism is contestable. Constituent *power* might just as appropriately be termed constituent *right* because this struggle entails the attempt to explicate the meaning of political right (*droit politique*). It follows that constituent power/right does not spring from 'normative nothingness'. Rather, the written constitution formalises precepts of political right that express the political unity of a people. Similarly, Rousseau claims that the constitution is eventually corrupted because 'the people' remains a non-institutionalised entity. But the problem here lies not so much in the fact that 'the people' remains unformed, as it does in the

[83] Cf. Zoran Oklopcic, 'Constitutional (Re)vision: Sovereign Peoples, New Constituent Powers, and the Formation of Constitutional Orders in the Balkans', *Constellations* 19 (2013): 81–101.

[84] Rousseau, 'Social Contract', 106.

claims by constituted authorities to act as the authoritative voice of the people. Noting that the people are institutionalised in various ways within a constitutional framework (e.g., as electors, participants in referendums, or as a voice in the adoption of constitutional amendments), Carl Schmitt, in *Constitutional Theory*, stresses that their potential political role is not exhausted by 'constituted' manifestations. The people 'continue to exist as an entity that is directly and genuinely *present*, not mediated by previously defined normative systems, validations, and fictions'. The people cannot become a mere organ of the state: In a democracy they persist 'as an entity that is unorganized and unformed'.[85] This argument flows from his distinction between constitutional law and the constitution: The people in its non-instituted manifestation irritate the instituted power in a dialectic engagement through which real political will results.

When elaborating this point, Schmitt takes it beyond the idea of the people as a political unity. He states that the people 'are everyone ... *not* honoured and distinguished, everyone *not* privileged'.[86] Now that the bourgeoisie dominates government, he explains, the proletariat has become the people 'because it becomes the bearer of this negativity'.[87] Schmitt here partitions the ideal unity of the people: The concept of the people is now 'the part of the population that does not have property, does not participate in the productive majority, and finds no place in the existing order'.[88]

This double aspect of the people is accentuated in the relational method. The paradoxical nature of the foundation rests on the fact that it both constitutes a unity (a state) and establishes a hierarchy (a governing relationship). In this foundational moment, so too must 'the people' be grasped in a double sense – conceptualised not only as a virtual unity (the nation/state), but also as a non-institutionalised entity established in opposition to the constituted authority (the ordinary people, the people-as-the governed).

In *The Social Contract*, Rousseau elaborates an ideal arrangement that can 'combine what right permits with what interest prescribes'.[89] We might doubt that this ideal can be realised, but the tension between right and interest (the virtual and the actual) throws into relief the double aspect to this concept of 'the people'. From a juristic perspective, the driver of constitutional development is the struggle over the explication of right. But

[85] Schmitt, *Constitutional Theory*, 271.
[86] Id.
[87] Id. at 272.
[88] Id.
[89] Rousseau, 'Social Contract', 41.

from a phenomenological perspective, the driver is interest rather than right, and in particular the interests of ordinary people rather than the virtual entity. Constituent power embraces both right and interest and the relation between them.

One of the greatest challenges of modern republican government has been to maintain the power of 'ordinary people'. In a regime that acquires symbolic authority as 'a government of the people, by the people and for the people', the main danger is that of institutionalised co-optation. There is no shortage of contenders for the job of representing the people as 'a sovereign that cannot exercise sovereignty'. In the British system, for example, Parliament played a pivotal role in constitutional struggles over such a long period that it came to be perceived as the 'nation assembled', acting not merely as a legislative body but also as the constituent power.[90] The growth of presidential power in republican regimes has led many to accept the substance of Schmitt's Weimar claim that the president acts as the bearer of constituent power.[91] With the recent growth in the constitutional jurisdiction of courts, some claim that constitutional courts no longer speak in an adjudicative or even legislative voice: They speak directly in the name of the sovereign people and as the authentic voice of constituent power.[92] And some might even argue that the expression of 'public opinion', which has traditionally been invoked to explain shifts in the meaning of the constitution law, has become the prerogative of the institutionalised mass media.

Constituent power exists only insofar as it resists institutionalised representation. Claude Lefort notes that modern democracy leads to the creation of the 'empty place' of the political.[93] The problem is not that it is empty, but that the space is crowded with the many who claim the authentic voice of constituent power. This is his point: Legitimacy must be claimed in the name of the people, and the question of who represents the people remains the indeterminate question of modern politics. The function of constituent power is to keep that question open, not least because 'the people-as-one' is the hallmark of totalitarianism.[94] In that

[90] See Alexis de Tocqueville, *Democracy in America* (trans., H. Reeve) (New York: Vintage Books, 1990), 100.

[91] See also Woodrow Wilson, *Constitutional Government in the United States* (New York: Columbia University Press, 1908), 68.

[92] Paul Kahn, *Political Theology: Four New Chapters on the Concept of Sovereignty* (New York: Columbia University Press, 2011), 13–17.

[93] Lefort, 'The Permanence of the Theological-Political?', 226.

[94] See, e.g., Carl Schmitt, *State, Movement, People: The Triadic Structure of the Political Unity* (trans., S. Draghici) (Corvallis, OR: Plutarch Press, 2001 [1933]).

struggle, perhaps the most pressing issue today concerns the continuing significance of Machiavelli's thesis that political development is driven by the struggle between two opposing classes: the nobility who rule and the people who desire not to be oppressed.[95] This requires an understanding of constituent power that, unlike liberal normativism, does not seek to erase it and, unlike decisionism, does not reduce it to one particular form of institutionalised action. A relational account, by contrast, recognises the need to conjoin right and interest, the symbolic representation of all with the concerns of the many, and it sets in place an understanding of the concept of particular importance in a world in which government is both ubiquitous and increasingly remote from ordinary people.

[95] See also John McCormick, *Machiavellian Democracy* (Cambridge University Press, 2011).

7

Socialist Constitutionalism in Contemporary China

BAOGANG HE

I. Introduction

This chapter examines the Chinese discourse on a socialist vision of constitutionalism as an alternative to liberal constitutionalism.[1] Chinese scholars have been searching for a new constitutionalism – one which differs from the so-called state-socialism of the Chinese Communist Party (CCP), and at the same time also goes beyond liberal constitutionalism. This 'socialist constitutionalism' can be seen as a subversive vision of socialism, one that Chinese scholars are developing to challenge the state's present political order. Because China's ideological commitment to socialism predates the constitutionalisation of the Chinese state, heterodox constitutional theorists are able to use this new conceptualisation to construct a new constitutionalist discourse that challenges the authoritarian and developmentalist vision of socialism espoused by China's ruling party-state apparatus. This new socialist constitutionalism differs from the Chinese state's authoritarian socialism by focusing on the value of popular sovereignty and civil society. It differs from liberal constitutionalism in its focus on providing effective and responsive governance rather than simply limited and constrained government.

Constitutional reform in China is a top priority in the minds of many Chinese and is sure to rise even further as an increasingly important political agenda over the next two or three decades.[2] Despite current government censorship on public deliberation over constitutionalism, it persists as a subject of great interest to the Chinese both privately and publicly (e.g., in online debates). Despite the claims of many in the CCP to the contrary,

[1] The chapter draws heavily on my own personal involvement with the development of this school of constitutionalism. I have participated in meetings and conferences and since 2012 have served as a member of the editorial committee of the *Constitutional Socialism Series* [Xianzheng Shehui Zhuyi Luncong].

[2] See, generally, Stéphanie Balme and Michael W. Dowdle (eds.), *Building Constitutionalism in China* (New York: Palgrave, 2009).

the question is no longer whether China needs constitutionalism, but what kind of constitutionalism it needs.

As to this latter question, there are three schools of thought as to what China's constitution should look like. The *Liberal* school sees constitutionalism as the institutionalisation of checks and balances on both governmental and CCP power. This includes general elections, bicameralism, multi-party competition, and an independent judicial system. As described in the preceding text, the *Socialist* school wants a constitution that retains China's socialist tradition, albeit in a humanist rather than authoritarian guise. On the one hand, it contests the hegemonic constitutional status of the CCP; but on the other hand, it also challenges the narrow focus of liberal constitutionalism on constraining rather than enabling the state.[3] A third school is the *Confucian* school. It argues that China's constitutionalism should focus on reifying Confucian values. This includes, for example, the establishment of an unelected 'House of Confucian Scholars' as a deliberative and legislative body.[4]

Despite being censored by the CCP, the discourse on American liberal constitutionalism dominates the public discussion among the Chinese. It is the way in which most Chinese have come to understand constitutionalism. Subsequently, within the more conservative ranks of the CCP, many conflate constitutionalism with liberal constitutionalism. One prominent conservative CCP commentator, for example, asserted that constitutionalism only serves capitalism and the bourgeoisie class.[5] Such people therefore regard constitutionalism as a dangerous doctrine that at best would only constrain the effectiveness of the CCP, and at worse would cause its downfall.[6] They consequently reject constitutionalism per se.

Given the scope of the public discourse around liberal constitutionalism, can socialist constitutionalism or Confucian constitutionalism offer possible alternatives? This chapter explores whether Chinese socialist thought can construct an attractive and viable socialist constitutionalism that does indeed go beyond liberal constitutionalism. In part II, it introduces the background in which the socialist constitutional discourse has

3 See Michael Dowdle, 'Of Comparative Constitutional Monocropping: A Reply to Qianfan Zhang', *International Journal of Constitutional Law* 8 (2010): 977–984.

4 Jiang Qing, *A Confucian Constitutional Order: How China's Ancient Past Can Shape Its Political Future* (ed., Daniel A. Bell and Ruiping Fan; trans., Edmund Ryden) (Princeton University Press, 2012).

5 'Yang Xiaoqing', 'A Comparative Study of Constitutionalism and People's Democratic System', *Hongqiwengao* [Red Papers] No. 10 (2013): 4–10.

6 Zhen Zhixue, 'Understanding the Essence of "Constitutionalism"', *Dangjian* [Party Construction] No. 6 (2013): 29–31.

taken place. Part III then examines the various ways in which socialist constitutionalism has been conceptualised, contrasting and comparing 'socialist constitutionalism' to 'constitutional socialism', and societal visions of socialist constitutionalism to institutionalised visions of socialist constitutionalism. It will also look at how Chinese socialist-constitutionalist scholars conceptualise the proper role of the CCP in socialist constitutionalism. Part IV examines how socialist constitutionalism addresses the weaknesses found both in China's current 'party-state constitutionalism' and in liberal constitutionalism as it applies to China.

II. The Origin and Development of 'Constitutional Socialism'

Modern China has had a number of constitutions over its almost seven decades of existence. Its first constitution was promulgated in 1954, but was never really put into practice, due to the political disruptions of the Anti-Rightist movement (1957–1959) and then the Great Proletarian Cultural Revolution (1966–1976). A new 'Cultural Revolution constitution' was promulgated in 1975, but with the death of Mao and the ending of the Cultural Revolution one year later, it was quickly superseded by a more conventional, transitional constitution in 1978. The present constitution was enacted in 1982, with significant amendments in 1988 (legitimating the private economy); 1993 (establishing the 'socialist market economy'); 1999 (establishing 'rule of law' as a constitutional principle); and 2004 (strengthening citizens' rights to private property provisions).

Today, the major challenge faced by China lies in how to build a practice of constitutionalism out of the text of the constitution.[7] This is a common issue throughout socialist Asia: Cambodia, Vietnam, and Laos – in addition to China – have all called for transforming their constitutions into constitutionalism.[8] As latecomers to the constitutional project, all these countries have the advantage of copying and combining the best provisions from constitutions around the world. For this reason, their constitutions are often longer, more detailed, and relatively better written and well-crafted. But there remain significant obstacles to the actual implementation and enforcement of these constitutions. Effectively, they remain merely a piece of good paperwork.

[7] See Qianfan Zhang, 'A Constitution without Constitutionalism? The Paths of Constitutional Development in China', *International Journal of Constitutional Law* 8 (2010): 950–976.

[8] See, generally, Clanspeter Hill and Jors Menzel (eds.), *Constitutionalism in Southeast Asia. Vol. 2: Reports on National Constitutions* (Singapore: Konrad-Adenauer-Stiftung and Time Edge Publishing, 2010).

In China, there is significant popular pressure demanding that the constitution not simply be well written but also well put into actual practice.[9] And China's leaders do fully understand that compliance with constitutional provisions is more likely to create an orderly society. Since the late 1980s, the CCP has stressed the importance of the constitution.[10] This is clearly evident in the speech made by Hu Jintao, then President of the People's Republic of China (PRC) and head of the CCP, on September 15, 2004 to mark the fiftieth anniversary of the founding of the National People's Congress (NPC) (China's national parliament), when he said, 'Governing according to the law first requires governing according to the constitution, ruling according to law first requires ruling according to the constitution'.[11] Some years later, Wen Jiabao, who had been the leader of China's executive branch from 2003 to 2013, said in an interview that '[a]ny party, organisation, or individual cannot be above the constitution or the law; the constitution must be the fundamental criteria for conduct'.[12] The current PRC president and party leader, Xi Jinping, has also stressed that the exercise of political power should be in accord with the constitution in a speech celebrating at the sixtieth anniversary of the NPC.[13]

CCP leaders appear to desire a particular kind of constitutional order, similar to the party-dominated constitutionalism found in Malaysia and Singapore. Yet many Chinese scholars pursue a different path – advancing a distinctly socialist vision of constitutionalism that goes beyond both party-dominated constitutionalism and liberal constitutionalism.

The term *socialist constitutionalism* dates at least to 1993. But the term did not gain much traction until 2003,[14] when Professor Hu Xingdou,

[9] See Michael W. Dowdle, 'Popular Constitutionalism and the Constitutional Meaning of Charter 08', in Jean-Philippe Béja, Fu Hualing, and Eva Pils (eds.), *Liu Xiaobo, Charter 08, and the Challenges of Political Reform in China* (Hong Kong University Press, 2012), 205–228.

[10] See Michael William Dowdle, 'Of Parliaments, Pragmatism and the Dynamics of Constitutional Development: The Curious Case of China', *New York University Journal of International Law and Politics* 35 (2002): 1–200.

[11] Sun Shangwu, 'Rally Marks 50th Anniversary of NPC', *China Daily*, Sept. 15, 2004.

[12] Cited in Guo Daohui, 'Realizing Historical Change from Revolutionary Party to Constitutional Party', *Xianzheng Shehui Zhuyi Luncong* [Constitutional Socialism Forum] 2 (2011): 169–170.

[13] See Hou Ruili, 'Rule of Law Takes Center Stage', *China Today* (English edition), Nov. 11, 2014, at 4.

[14] Cf. Michael Dowdle, 'Of "Socialism" and "Socialist" Legal Transformations in China and Vietnam', in John Gillespie and Pip Nicholson (eds.), *Asian Socialism and Legal Change: The Dynamics of Vietnamese and Chinese Reform* (Canberra: ANU E Press, 2005), 21–44.

from the Beijing Institute of Technology, made explicit reference to 'Constitutional Socialism',[15] and Professor Jiang Ping, the former president of the University of Politics and Law and one of China's most influential constitutional scholars, subsequently expressed his strong approval of the concept.[16] In 2010, Northwest University Press published a 560,000-character monograph by a young scholar, Hua Bingxiao, titled *Beyond Liberalism: A Discourse on Constitutional Socialism* [*Chaoyue Ziyou Zhuyi: Xianzheng Shehui Zhuyi de Sixiang Yanshuo*].[17]

A year later, Hua launched a book series with that same press entitled *Constitutional Socialism* [Xianzheng Shehui Zhuyi]. Notably, the editorial board of this series includes two scholars over the age of seventy and five scholars over the age of eighty. This is quite extraordinary. These older scholars shared a genuine faith in socialism as young students, and subsequently suffered great hardship first during the anti-right movement and then during the Cultural Revolution. Given China's constitutional progress in recent years, they have come to view themselves as having a 'second life' – another chance to inject the socialist ideals of their youth into present-day public debate, policy formation, and political reform. They know the inner workings of both the party censorship apparatus and of the policy-making processes, and they have strong networks of academic and political support. They are both well motivated and well equipped to fight for better social justice in China. It is a measure of their integrity that on reaching what many regard as the twilight years they are willing to take up such a struggle.

This new school of socialist constitutionalism had gained significant support from governmental organisations. These organisations provide funding and conference venues to scholars of socialist constitutionalism, and grant or secure publication licences for their writings. In March 2004, Yang Jingyu, then Chairman of the Law Committee of the NPC, made a public proposal that 'China should build up a socialist constitutional state'.[18] Hu Deping, the son of former CCP leader Hu Yaobang, endorsed a conference on socialist constitutionalism in an open speech on December

[15] See Zhang Zhixin, 'An Overview of the Socialist Constitutionalism Study', *Xianzheng Shehui Zhuyi Luncong* [Constitutional Socialism Forum] 2 (2011): 148–149.

[16] See also Jiang Ping, 'On Constitutional Socialism', *Xianzheng Shehui Zhuyi Luncong* [Constitutional Socialism Forum] 1 (2011): 3–6.

[17] Hua Bingxiao, *Chaoyue Ziyou Zhuyi: Xianzheng Shehui Zhuyi de Sixiang Yanshuo* [Beyond Liberalism: A Discourse on Constitutionalism] (Xian: Northwest University Press, 2011).

[18] Zhao Tao, 'Department of Propaganda and Other Departments Hold a Study Meeting on the Constitution', *Renmin Ribao* [People Daily], March 26, 2004, at 4.

24, 2011.[19] Yu Keping, Director of the Center for Chinese Government Innovations at Beijing University and New World Senior Fellow in the Ash Center for Democratic Governance and Innovation in the John F. Kennedy School of Government at Harvard University, has stated that the debate on socialist constitutionalism is 'a new form of intellectual liberation'.[20]

In May 2013, however, a party publication criticised the socialist constitutionalism school as harbouring a hidden agenda to overthrow CCP rule,[21] and the CCP began strictly censoring any public discussion of constitutionalism, socialist or otherwise. Even this author was requested in October 2015 to delete the word *constitutionalism* from a Chinese article on the status of political studies in China.

III. What Are the Core Values of Socialist Constitutionalism?

The ideal of socialist constitutionalism derives from Chinese practices of popular resistance, citizen engagement, and local self-governing.[22] Influential examples include the united investigative group of local parliamentary representatives and political consultative councillors in Wukan, a village in Guandong Province, where villagers protested against corrupt leadership – a practice that is now known as 'training civil society in plural governance'.[23] The Nanshan District of the Shenzhen Special Economic Zone instituted a similar practice in which local governmental officials, local community representatives, local parliamentary representatives, and local party officials get together to solve local issues.[24] Through such devices, civil society can become included in the organisational structure of the state while at the same time remaining functionally separate from the state. In this way, China is a good example of what Gavin Anderson has recently termed 'incorporating social movements within constitutional discourse'.[25]

19 Hu Deping, 'Study the Urgently Needed Big Topic in Our Time', *Xianzheng Shehui Zhuyi Luncong* [Constitutional Socialism Forum] 3–4 (2012): 1–4.

20 Li Yang, 'The Heated Debate Arising from the Constitutionalist Socialism Study', *Xianzheng Shehui Zhuyi Luncong* [Constitutional Socialism Forum] 2 (2011): 164–169.

21 Zhen, 'Understanding the Essence of "Constitutionalism"', 29–31.

22 See, generally, *Xianzheng Shehui Zhuyi Luncong* [Constitutional Socialism Series] 3–4 (2012).

23 Dai Jietao, 'The Constitutional Meaning of Wukan Event', *Xianzheng Shehui Zhuyi Luncong* [Constitutional Socialism Series] 3–4 (2012): 505–509.

24 Hua Bingxiao, 'Local Governance and the Grassroots of Constitutional Socialism', *Xianzheng Shehui Zhuyi Luncong* [Constitutional Socialism Series] 3–4 (2012): 476–485.

25 Gavin Anderson, 'Societal Constitutionalism, Social Movements, and Constitutionalism from Below', *Indiana Journal of Global Legal Studies* 20 (2013): 881–906.

Beyond this, however, there are many different visions of what socialist constitutionalism looks like. Jiang Ping, mentioned in the preceding text, sees the heart of constitutional socialism as lying in its promotion of rule of law and democracy within a China's party-state system. The great lesson to be learned from the Soviet Union, he argues, is that party-*dominated* constitutionalism (as contrasted against a party-*led* state) is doomed to failure. China needs to change from party-dominated constitutionalism to a people-dominated constitutionalism in which people will have the right to monitor and help the CCP correct its mistakes.[26]

Zhou Shuzhi, by contrast, sees four basic principles as lying at the heart of socialist constitutionalism. These are (1) that the constitution is superior to the CCP; (2) that citizen welfare is fundamental; (3) that common prosperity is ensured (including wealth redistribution so that the whole of society is able to share meaningfully in the means of production); and (4) that the 'reform and opening up' initiative initiated by Deng Xiaoping in the late 1970s be extended to include the reform and opening up of public and political institutions. Like Jiang, Zhou also believes that by incorporating a democratic framework, socialist constitutionalism is the only way to regulate the power of the CCP, and thereby safeguard the rights of citizens, the public interest, and the cause of socialism.[27]

A. 'Socialist Constitutionalism' or 'Constitutional Socialism'?

In the past, many scholars distinguished 'socialist constitutionalism' [Shehui Zhuyi Xianzheng] from 'constitutional socialism' [Xianzheng Shehui Zhuyi]. The former, they claim, puts the emphasis on constitutionalism, and thus too diminishes the ultimately socialist goals of the project. Hua Bingxiao, who as we noted is one of the founders of what I am (in English) calling the 'constitutional socialism school', sees 'socialist constitutionalism' as being too restrictive because it subordinates the socialist aspect of the constitution to the larger demands of constitutionalism per se. Like the 'market economy', he argues, constitutionalism is not necessarily 'capitalist', 'socialist,' or 'liberal'. It is therefore inappropriate to label 'constitutionalism' with a prefix. 'Constitutional socialism' is a more commanding concept precisely because it describes a political-legal system

[26] Jiang Ping, 'On Constitutional Socialism'.

[27] Zhou Shuzhi, 'On the Origin of Constitutional Socialism School in China', *Xianzheng Shehui Zhuyi Luncong* [Constitutional Socialism Forum] 3–4 (2012).

that is *comprehensively* socialist.[28] While he sees the two terms as being inextricably tied together, he favours 'constitutional socialism' because it advocates for a more expansive pursuit of socialism, one that is constitutionalist in means but socialist in ends.

But at the end of the day, Hua Bingxiao regards the concepts of socialist constitutionalism and of constitutional socialism as being inexorably linked together. By contrast, Gao Fang, a law professor at People's University and an expert on the law of the Soviet Union, argues that 'socialist constitutionalism' and 'constitutional socialism' do not have much in common, and ought not be confused or conflated. According to him, the term *socialist constitutionalism* is a far more accurate understanding of the proposed changes to the constitution in China than *constitutional socialism*. In contrast to Hua, Gao believes that the ultimate focus of the constitutional project should be on constitutionalism – and in particular on constitutional control of the CCP – rather than just on socialism.[29]

Similarly, Wang Zhanyang, Director of the Political Science Department at the Central Institute of Socialism, also prefers 'socialist constitutionalism'. Like Gao Fan, he holds that the principal function of constitutionalism lies in its safeguarding of democratic governance, separation of powers, rule of law, human rights and civil rights, and civil society. It is the only way that a state can be made to obey and serve society.[30] For this reason, constitutionalism is a prerequisite for rather than an adjunct to the realisation of socialism, which makes socialist constitutionalism a more accurate description of what China ultimately needs from its constitutional system.

By contrast, Professor Tong Zhiwei, formerly dean of the East China University of Politics and Laws and one of China's most respected constitutional scholars, argues that whether 'socialist constitution' or 'constitutional socialism' is the correct term is simply a matter of opinion. The key is to ensure that China's constitutional system is accurately tailored to the distinct, and distinctly socialist, needs of China's social and political environments. According to him, whether we call it socialist constitutionalism

[28] Hua Bingxiao, 'On the Constructive Reform Path of Constitutional Socialism', paper presented at the 2011 China's Reform Summit: Present and Future (Beijing, 2011).

[29] Gao Fang, 'Party-dominated Constitutionalism Is Not the Essence of Constitutionalism', *Xianzheng Shehui Zhuyi Luncong* [Constitutional Socialism Forum] 3–4 (2012): 627–633.

[30] Wang Zhanyang, 'What Is Constitutional Socialism?', *Xianzheng Shehui Zhuyi Luncong* [Constitutional Socialism Forum] 2 (2011): 470–472.

or constitutional socialism, its principal purpose has to be establishing and protecting rule of law.[31]

Overall, the Chinese scholar community tends to prefer the term *socialist constitutionalism* to *constitutional socialism*. In November 2014, the Chinese Academic Journal Database [Zhongguo Zhiwang] returned 435 listings under a subject search for the term '*socialist constitutionalism*', but only forty-five listings under a subject search for '*constitutional socialism*'. A title search for '*socialist constitutionalism*' returned ninety-one items, whereas a title search for 'constitutional socialism' returned only seven items. And seven PhD dissertations have listed 'socialist constitutionalism' as one of their key words, whereas none have listed 'constitutional socialism'.

B. Societal Constitutionalism or Institutionalised Constitutionalism?

Scholars of socialist constitutionalism also disagree as to what socialist constitutionalism should focus on in restricting state power. Some argue that state power is best restricted by the proper design of political and legal institutions. They argue for what is sometimes called an 'institutional' [zhidu] approach to constitutionalism. Others believe that effective constrains on state power must come more organically, from society itself, what they call 'societal constitutionalism' [shehui de xianzheng zhuyi]. Of course, these different strategies are not mutually exclusive of one another.

Professor Guo Daohui, a former Vice Chairman of NPC Law Committee and editor-in-chief of the journal *China Law* [Zhongguo Faxue], favours societal constitutionalism over its institutionalised version. Doing so, he reinterprets the idea of 'socialism' as a political system in which society reigns supreme, 'counterbalancing the power of the state'.[32] For Guo, this means that the rights and the interests of society need to be core, whereas the needs of the state, government, and institutions should be more peripheral concerns. This comports better with what he sees as the historical processes of societal development, in which society evolved prior to the emergence of the state. The rights of the state in this sense are bestowed by society and the people, not the other way around.

Guo holds that this social power resides in civil society and individual citizens. It exerts external influence on state power, keeping the state free from corruption, in addition to bringing benefit to social

[31] Tong Zhiwei, 'The Core Value of Constitutional Socialism Is to the Rule of Law', *Xianzheng Shehui Zhuyi Luncong* [Constitutional Socialism Forum] 2 (2011): 478–481.

[32] Guo Daohui, 'An Outline of Constitutional Socialism', *Xianzheng Shehui Zhuyi Luncong* [Constitutional Socialism Forum] 2 (2011): 453–459.

groups – especially disadvantaged groups – that the state might otherwise ignore. Social power promotes equality of opportunity, legitimises the government exercise of its coercive powers, and guarantees the political and economic rights of the citizenry and their social organisations, with the aim of achieving common prosperity for all society.

In Guo's opinion, it misses the point if we only focus our attention on implementing the constitution in governmental institutions. Instead we should look at strengthening civil society and social power vis-à-vis the state. Admittedly, he says, we also need to pay attention to the separating and balancing of state power among state bodies (and China still has a long way to go in this area), but without the participation and support of civil society even this will be very difficult to achieve and implement.

Guo also emphasises the need to uphold human rights and protect constitutional equality. China's official policy of 'social management [shehui guanli]' should mainly rely on the input, support, and power of civil society. In light of this, he is highly critical of China's particular regime of criminal law, which puts the interest of the state and its police above that of the people. For instance, it allows police or other security personnel to legally detain people, for up to seven months, without going through standard warrant procedures or without court authorisation.[33] In addition, it allows people accused of being a 'national threat' or of being engaged in 'terrorist activities' to be detained in secret – that is, without informing family members of the detention.[34] He is also critical of the *Decision on Reforming the Identity Law* [Guanyu xiougai shenfenzhenfa de jueding], issued by the NPC Standing Committee on October 29, 2011, because this decision clearly contained at least two rules that diminished citizens' rights to privacy – one holding that all citizens must have their fingerprints recorded on their identity card and the other expanding police powers to investigate the identities of individuals – without going through any process of public consultation.[35]

Of course, societal constitutionalism also needs the help of political institutions to be feasible and workable. Hua Bingxiao, for example, while supporting the key ideas of societal constitutionalism, argues that we should nevertheless focus our attention primarily on the institutional needs of constitutionalism. In particular, he proposes:

- Implementing intra-party rule of law and expanding intra-party democracy, by strengthening the status and capacity of the CCP's plenary body,

[33] Id.

[34] Id.

[35] Guo Daohui, 'The Constitutionality of Social Management and Socialization', *Xianzheng Shehui Zhuyi Luncong* [Constitutional Socialism Forum] 3–4 (2012): 462–466.

the National Party Congress, and by strengthen the status and capacity of the CCP's 'judicial organs', i.e., its Central Discipline Inspection Commission;

- Implementing judicial reforms that uphold and guarantee judicial independence by building an independent judicial-organisation system within the CCP;
- Reforming the People's Congress system by expanding people's democracy; that is, by converting the standing committees of People's Congresses into what he calls 'participatory councils', while nevertheless guaranteeing the leadership role of the CCP;
- Reforming the People's Consultative System by promoting the use of democratic consultation, which involves transforming the People's Consultative Congresses at all levels into what he calls 'political deliberative councils [*yizheng yuan*]', whose councillors are nominated and elected by the people.[36]

Hua Bingxiao's ideas on institutionalised constitutionalism have strong root in local practice. For example, his institutional ideas resemble the ways that Hunan Province has been greatly enhancing 'rule of law' in governmental administration. On April 17, 2008, Hunan Province promulgated the *Hunan Province Administrative Procedure Regulations* [Hunansheng xingzheng chengxu guiding], the first one in China. This was then followed by the *Hunan Province Regulations on Administrative Power* [Hunansheng kuifan xingzheng cailiangquan] and the *Hunan Province Government Service Regulations* [Hunansheng zhengfu fuwu guiding].[37] Collectively, these three legislative instruments represented the first time anywhere in China where all aspects of administrative behaviour – including law enforcement, governmental contracting, the issuing of executive legislation and executive rulings, process of mediation and popular consultations, and demands of openness, monitoring, and accountability – have been integrated into a single, coherent, comprehensive regulatory framework. Collectively, they mandate that administrative decision making must go through a process of investigation and collective research, expert discussion, public participation, and other measures that insure social legitimacy and prevent misuse of governmental power.

[36] Hua Bingxiao, *Chaoyue Ziyou Zhuyi* [Beyond Liberalism], ch. 8.

[37] See, generally, Jiang Haisong and Su Dan, 'The Unique Features of the Rule of Law in Hunan', *Xianzheng Shehui Zhuyi Luncong* [Constitutional Socialism Forum] 3–4 (2012): 495–504.

C. *The Role of Chinese Communist Party*

Hua Bingxiao's analysis of the institutional predicates of socialist constitutionalism brings us to one of the primary distinguishing concerns of that school: What is the role of the party in a *constitutional* party-state? When the United States developed its constitution it did not have competing political parties. In fact, James Madison, often regarded as the 'father' of the American Constitution, famously detested the idea of political parties.[38] As a result, the American framers could focus on constructing long-term political solutions without having to worry as much about their immediate impact on electoral support. As a matter of contrast, Nepal's present prospects for federalism are being undertaking in a political environment in which three major political parties are locked in intense competition.[39] This is making the process of drafting a constitution exceedingly difficult. These parties' competing proposals are directed at securing immediate electoral support, not at the construction of a long-term, sustainable system.

China, in contrast to the political systems of Nepal and the United States, has a single, dominant party – the CCP. All constitutional reform proposals must deal with the role and place of the CCP in the constitutional order, and the nature and role of the CCP therefore is of critical concern in thinking about China's constitutional future. This is a very thorny issue. It is now very difficult for the CCP to return to being a totalitarian party, in the way it was historically conceived. But it is equally problematic for the CCP to introduce pluralist political competitiveness, because of its historical claim to be the best guardian of China's future.[40] Similarly, the CCP has long claimed to operate within the boundaries set by the Constitution and its laws. But at the same time, it often sees these constraints as unnecessarily impeding its quest for a better China. Such constraints are also structurally incompatible with the CCP's organisational reliance on internal self-discipline on the part of its members rather than on the checks and balances of independent and external enforcement. Nevertheless, at some point, for

[38] See, e.g., James Madison, 'Federalist No. 10', in Alexander Hamilton, James Madison, and John Jay, *The Federalist Papers* (ed., Clinton Rossiter) (New York: Signet Classics, 2003), 71–79.

[39] See Manjushree Thapa, 'Nepal's Slippery Fast-Track,' *The Wire*, June 13, 2015, http://thewire.in/2015/06/13/nepals-slippery-fast-track/.

[40] Cf. Zhu Suli '"Judicial Politics" as State-building', in Stéphanie Balme and Michael W. Dowdle (eds.), *Building Constitutionalism in China* (New York: Palgrave Macmillan, 2009), 23–36.

the sake of its legitimacy, the CCP will likely have to yield to the provisions and constraints of constitution.

Within the school of socialist constitutionalism, different people offer different approaches to this dilemma. Some think that the party-dominant state can be made compatible with socialist constitutionalism by installing that constitutionalism within the structure of the party, rather than outside the party as is the case with most Western constitutional systems. According to Larry Catá Backer, a Cuban-American legal scholar and professor of law and international affairs at Pennsylvania State University, China's party-state model of constitutionalism is moving toward a legitimately 'constitutional' governance system by apportioning power between the administrative organs of government and the CCP. There are four features of this party-state constitutionalism: (1) a division of citizenship in which social and economic citizenship is held directly by all, but political citizenship held and exercised through the CCP; (2) the subordination of state power and institutions to political rather than legal authority; (3) the institutionalisation and segmentation of the CCP's political authority so that its exercise is beyond the control of any particular clique of individuals, and will therefore be deployed in the service of constitutional values; and (4) a reliance on internal party discipline for the elaboration of rule-of-law values.[41]

But when this author gave a brief account of Backer's work on China's party-state constitutionalism at a recent academic conference in China, many Chinese scholars immediately rejected Backer's model of party-state constitutionalism because they thought it augments the power of the CCP without taking into account the complexity of the relationship between the party and the state – a complexity that in their minds imposed foundational limits to the utility of a party-led constitutional system.

Gao Fang, for example, argues that a party-led constitution has nothing to do with the essence of socialist constitutionalism. The main reason for the disintegration of the Soviet Union, he claims, was precisely because it had a party-led constitution rather than a society-led constitutionalism. When excessive power is concentrated in the party, especially in the central party secretariat, the people's freedoms and democratic rights will inevitably become limited and constrained. Gao further claims that

[41] See, generally, Larry Catá Backer, 'The Party as Polity, the Communist Party, and the Chinese Constitutional State: A Theory of State-Party Constitutionalism', *Journal of Chinese and Comparative Law* 16 (2009): 101–164; Larry Catá Backer, 'The Rule of Law, the Chinese Communist Party, and Ideological Campaigns: Sange Daibiao (The "Three Represents"), Socialist Rule of Law, and Modern Chinese Constitutionalism', *Journal of Transnational Law and Contemporary Problems* 19 (2006): 29–102.

party-led constitutionalism, such as that which led to the collapse of the Soviet Union, is actually simply a distorted form of constitutional monarchy.[42] His historical analysis of the Soviet Union implies that China's socialist constitutionalism should rid itself of one-party domination. The difficult task facing China's constitutional reform, therefore, lies in the political question of how to change China's Soviet model of party-led constitutionalism into a democratic constitutionalism.

Guo Daohui also questions the wisdom of party-led or party-dominated constitutionalism. In 1994, in the first issue of the journal *Legal Studies* [*Fa Xue*], Guo published an article discussing the legal relationship between the CCP's power and power of the NPC. In it, he questions the whether the CCP could be meaningfully described as representing the interests of the country as a whole, and whether its political power correspondingly should be able to override the parliamentary power of the NPC: 'Our party's rule is not from divine right, nor is it settled once and for all', he wrote. In order to guarantee citizens' freedoms, what is now most urgent is that the citizen's rights and interests are constitutionally protected from interference or encroachment by either the state or the party.[43]

(It should be noted that both Gao Feng and Guo Daohui are more than seventy years old, and are therefore representative of the more radical and much bolder older generation of socialist constitutionalism thinkers discussed.)

As evident from his particular, institutional approach to socialist constitutionalism, Hua Bingxiao, by contrast, defends the necessity of the party leadership of the constitution through his concept of 'new unitary constitutional structure'.[44] This concept acknowledges that national sovereignty belongs to the people, but also claims that the people need the CCP's leadership and support to exercise that sovereignty. Hua also provides historical justifications for this claim. These include the CCP's role in the success of the national revolution; the CCP's success in bringing national stability to China; and the CCP's success in expanding the economy and improving people's lives.

At the same time, however, Hua also discusses the idea of establishing 'a separation of and balance between sovereign power, party power, government power, and public power'. Sovereign power belongs to the people, as exercised through national, regional, and local parliaments;

[42] Gao, 'Party-dominated Constitutionalism Is Not the Essence of Constitutionalism'.

[43] Guo Daohui, 'Authority, Power, or Rights? A Legal Reflection on the Relationship between the Party and People's Congress', *Legal Studies* [Fa Xue] No. 1 (1994): 3–11.

[44] Hua, *Chaoyue Ziyou Zhuyi* [Beyond Liberalism], 383–412.

party power belongs to the CCP; government power belongs to the 'government', which in the Chinese constitutional system includes both the executive (i.e., the State Council) and the judiciary; and public power belongs to civil society.

Under his system, sovereign power works to check party power, party power works to check government power, and public power works to check both sovereign power and party power. For example, the NPC checks the CCP by its power to pass laws and constitutional amendments to which the CCP must conform (what Hua terms 'ruling-party laws'). The CCP checks the government by nominating persons for high-level constitutional and governmental office and by monitoring their performance, and public power checks sovereign power, party power, and government power through interest group activities and public opinion.[45]

Geng Guojie is another who thinks that party-led constitutionalism can be compatible with socialist constitutionalism. This can be done, he argues, by establishing what he calls a public will-based form of party building.[46] Similarly, Xu Yaotong advocates an intra-party constitutionalism based on the following principles:

- Implementing open debate within the party: party members should have the right to criticise the party's path, direction, policies, principles, system and actions; and the work of party leaders – imposing one particular point of view on others or on the party as a whole should not be permitted;
- Developing intra-party elections: the nomination process should be improved so that a nomination system includes nominations not simply by party officials, but also by civil society organisations, and by ordinary party members or their representatives;
- Dealing scientifically with party factions: it is and should be strictly forbidden to organise *personalized* factions within the party (i.e., cliques), but *ideological* factions should be permitted, for two reasons. First, they both promote and help regulate the trend of increasingly open policy debate within the CCP. It is completely natural for ideological factions to form under such conditions, and there is no need or reason to stop this from occurring. Secondly, since reform and opening some thirty years ago, some ideological factions, most notably the 'left' and 'new left', have

[45] See id.

[46] Geng Guojie, 'The Transformation of the Party and the Reconstruction of China's Governance Model', *Xianzheng Shehui Zhuyi Luncong* [Constitutional Socialism Forum] 3–4 (2012): 438–460.

for practical reasons been permitted to exist without impeding party effectiveness.[47]

In closing, it might be noted that while the idea of a party-led constitutionalism might sound odd to contemporary ears, there is a strong affinity between this vision of constitutionalism and that of Jean-Jacques Rousseau. Rousseau's vision of constitutionalism revolved around his claim that representative assemblies could be constructed so as to naturally articulate the 'general will' of the polity. Many of the arguments for party-led constitutionalism make a very similar claim, except that they locate the general will in the CCP rather than in the parliament, and the powers they would give to the CCP parallel those Rousseau gave to his parliament. At the same time, however, these advocates seek to reform the CCP so that it is able to functionally replicate a Rousseauian assembly, thus bringing their vision of party-led constitutionalism into general agreement with Rousseau's constitutional vision.

IV. 'Beyond Liberal Constitutionalism': The Different Views

As detailed in part in this volume, many countries are attempting to find ways of overcoming the limit of liberal constitutionalism. Nepal, for example, has to accommodate a diversity of ethnic groups' demands. Nepal's constitutional design therefore has to go beyond the classical version of liberal constitutionalism that does not take into account ethnic identities in its institutional design.[48] Beyond this, Larry Catá Backer has identified at least three alternatives to liberal constitutionalism: global constitutionalism, Islamic constitutionalism, and party-state constitutionalism.[49]

In China, both the socialist and Confucian schools offer a critique of the dominant liberal constitutionalism. Within socialist constitutionalism, there is a diversity of views as to why and how Chinese constitutional design needs to go beyond liberal constitutionalism.

'Going beyond liberal constitutionalism' refers to a departure from liberalism's straightforward focus on limiting state power, looking in addition

[47] Xu Yaotong, 'The Issues Concerning Intra-Party Democracy Need to Be Explored', *Xianzheng Shehui Zhuyi Luncong* [Constitutional Socialism Forum] 3–4 (2012): 345–349.

[48] D. B. Gurung, Narad Bharadwaj, Khagendra Neupane, and Aparajita Acharya, *Towards a Federalized Democratic Nepal* (Kathmandu: Friends for Peace Publishers, 2009).

[49] Larry Catá Backer, 'Theocratic Constitutionalism: An Introduction to a New Global Legal Ordering', *Indiana Journal of Global Legal Studies* 16 (2008): 85–172; Backer, 'The Party as Polity'.

at developing more 'societal' forms of constitutionalism;[50] at paying more attention to the inevitability of party politics; and at exploring more complex divisions of power (often involving the party as well as the government).[51]

Wang Zhanyang sees socialist constitutionalism as being close to liberal constitutionalism in most aspects: that is, preventing despotism; implementing universal suffrage; placing political power in the hands of the people; implementing separation of powers; placing the constitution first; and implementing and safeguarding the human rights and civil rights of all members of society. He sees socialist constitutionalism as differing from liberal constitutionalism in its concern for providing middle-class income levels for government workers, so that legislative, executive, and judicial powers are not controlled wholly by the bourgeoisie. He argues that although the democratic ideals of classical Marxism surpass those of classical liberalism in some aspects, they do not replace them completely, but rather combine with them to make what he calls a 'universal liberalism'. Contemporary liberal constitutionalism is not fundamentally opposed to socialism, but rather simply needs to be 'socialised' into socialist constitutionalism.[52]

Zhou Shuzhi, by contrast, is very critical of the liberal school and searches for a new constitutionalism with Chinese characteristics. He argues that liberalism in China is a school of politics formed by scholars who have studied in the United States. Its supporters openly advocate American forms of economic privatisation, corporatisation, and laissez-faire capitalism. They excessively idealise the American versions of constitutional democracy, separation of powers, and the multi-party political model. They overlook the problems with the American system: that its elections are controlled by money interests; that its political parties are locked into paralysing and short-sighted competition for money and votes; and that its pursuit of international and transnational hegemony contradict its professed liberal ideals. Along these lines, he cites the American response to the global financial crisis – which was caused by American capitalist interests, but during which the America government nevertheless took to protecting these interests above all others. In light of all this, he writes:

[50] David Sciulli, *Theory of Societal Constitutionalism: Foundations of a Non-Marxist Critical Theory* (Cambridge University Press, 1992), 1–15.

[51] Baogang He, 'Intra-Party Democracy: A Revisionist Perspective from Below', in Kjeld Erik Broedsgaard and Yongnian Zheng (eds.), *The Chinese Communist Party in Reform* (London: Routledge, 2006), 192–209.

[52] Wang Zhanyang, 'Reflections on the Concept of Constitutional Socialism', *Xianzheng Shehui Zhuyi Luncong* [Constitutional Socialism Forum] 3–4 (2012): 590–600.

> How can we study this kind of political model? In my view we cannot pursue comprehensive Westernisation. We must maintain the Chinese people's own road of political system reform and create a new kind of political system suitable for China's national conditions.[53]

Hua Bingxiao also seeks the development of a constitutionalism that goes beyond liberalism. According to him, liberalism treats freedom as the paramount value of constitutionalism and therefore places the individual at the core of constitutional discourse. By contrast, constitutional socialism sees societal development as the paramount value of constitutionalism and therefore focuses its attentions first and foremost on matters of state and social capacity, and on fairness. Instead of focusing on the rights of individuals, it focuses on the rights and capacities of civil society, seeking freedom and democracy in the name of fairness rather than of individual autonomy.[54]

V. Conclusion

Societal constitutionalism has adopted different forms. In Nepal, societal constitutionalism focuses on the constitutional implications of ethnic diversity. In China, it focuses on the constitutional role of civil society.

In this way, the Chinese discourse on socialist constitutionalism opens up a conceptual space in which a variety of constitutional ideals that are not well captured by liberal visions of constitutionalism can be presented and discussed. These include the relationship between the army and the party (China, like other developing socialist countries, has been very successful in avoiding the threat of military coups, compared to the experiences of other kinds of constitutional regimes operating at similar levels of economic development); the relationship between the constitutional state and capitalism; and questions about the fundamental rights of (civil) society in addition to those of individuals.

Constitutional reform proposals from scholars associated with the socialist constitutional school have been submitted to national leaders. But Beijing has neither openly taken up their ideas, nor openly opposed them. In fact, the leadership currently does not permit open public discussions of socialist constitutionalism. But given the modern history of Chinese economic and political reforms, the current censorship on socialist constitutionalism is likely to be temporary. This author is optimistic

[53] Zhou, 'Origin of Constitutional Socialism School', 624.
[54] Hua, *Chaoyue Ziyou Zhuyi* [Beyond Liberalism], ch. 3.

about the future of socialist constitutionalism in China. Despite currently suffering from occasional party criticism and censorship, I believe it will continue to gain traction in the public mind and through that infuse into the CCP political agenda. It may take decades. But enlivening the discourse on socialist constitutionalism now offers a fresh way to not only rethink the current party-state constitutional arrangement, but also to preserve China's rich history and experience (both good and bad) with embedding the values of socialism into the country's constitutional framework.

Perhaps, as suggested by Wang Zhanyang, China will rediscover the true value of Marxism and combine it with liberal constitutionalism to create a new sort of 'mixed constitutionalism'. And indeed, it seems that China has already taken significant steps in this direction. Many socialist constitutionalist arguments contain a core of liberal elements – like democracy and fundamental civil and political rights – on the one hand, while rejecting other liberal elements (like the constitutional elevation of the individual over civil society), on the other. In other words, China is warming up to the idea of constitutional hybridity. It is seeking a constitutional system that incorporates liberal components but is not dominated by them.[55] The general direction of China's political development in recent decades has been along these lines. And while this mixed system approach has its share of problems, I believe it may nevertheless offer the best means of achieving an effective and humane constitutional governance in China.

[55] He Baogang, 'Constitutionalism and Transcending the Competition between the Left and the Right', *Jinyang Journal* [Jingyang xuekan] No. 4 (2010): 21–24.

8

Islamic Constitutionalism Beyond Liberalism

CLARK LOMBARDI

I. Introduction

Constitutions structure governments and create the rules by which they operate. Over the last twenty years, scholars have started to debate with new urgency descriptive and normative questions about constitutions.[1] W*hy* do people write constitutions? Why *should* they write constitutions? What values do good constitutions promote?

During the late twentieth century, many constitutional theorists in the West have suggested that that the primary purpose of a meaningful constitution has always been to limit or restrain government power. More specifically, they assert that constitutions must do this by creating governments with particular structural features – including multiparty electoral democracy, separation of governmental powers, and judicial review of government action to ensure governmental respect for both the principles of legality and of fundamental rights. This is the vision that Dowdle and Wilkinson in Chapter 1 term *structural-liberal constitutions.* Correspondingly, these Western theorists dismiss constitutions that fail to conform to the structural-liberal vision as sham constitutions.

In recent years, however, scholars have challenged those who would appropriate the term *constitution* for structural-liberal constitutions. One such scholar is Nathan Brown. In a monograph titled, provocatively, *Constitutions in a Non-constitutional World*, Brown challenges the idea that constitutions are designed to restrain government.[2] From a very early period, he suggests, people wrote entrenched legal documents called 'constitutions' not for the purpose of limiting government, but rather for strengthening an existing government and making it more efficient. Such

[1] Adapted from Clark Lombardi, 'Can Islamizing a Legal System Ever Help Promote Liberal Democracy? A View from Pakistan', *University of St. Thomas Law Journal* 7 (2010): 647–691. Dedicated to Drs. Ryland Clarke and Massimo Maglione, inspirational teachers of history.

[2] Nathan Brown, *Constitutions in a Non-Constitutional World, Arab Basic Laws and the Prospects for Accountable Government* (Albany: State University of New York Press, 2001).

documents were often accepted by both the rulers and people as superior law, and they often achieved their goal of state empowerment. It would be peculiar, he suggests, to criticize these documents as 'shams' or to dismiss them as 'ineffective'. He thus argues that they should be recognized as what he termed 'non-constitutionalist' constitutions.[3] (Cf. Chapter 9, showing this in Jean-Jacque Rousseau's constitutional understandings.)

Having argued that some constitutions are nonconstraining, Brown also argues that even some constraining constitutions are nevertheless not *liberal* constitutions. That is to say, there are 'constitutionalist' constitutions that were explicitly drafted with an eye to restraining government, but that were designed to ensure that the state respects not liberal values, but rather some other set of values that may or may not overlap in places with liberal values. He describes these constitutions as being constitutionalist, but not *liberal* constitutionalist.

Although Brown does not discuss it, there is a third problem with the simple equation of constitutions with structural-liberal constitutions. Some constitutions are constitutionalist and wish to constrain government in the service of liberal values. However, they do not rely on the traditional *structures* of liberal constitutionalism such as multiparty elections democracy and independent judicial review of fundamental rights, because the drafters felt that such structures are not well suited to protect liberal values in that particular country.

In short, if we look at the things called 'constitutions' around the world that actually shape the behavior of governments and the lives of their subjects, the world turns out to be far more diverse than many liberal constitutional theorists would allow. Alongside structural-liberal, constitutionalist constitutions, we find a wide variety of other Weberian ideal types: nonconstitutionalist constitutions, nonliberal constitutionalist constitutions, and nonstructural but liberal constitutions. Even more perplexing, in practice one finds many constitutions that fall outside even these ideal types – constitutions that combine elements associated with different types of constitution and promoting ends that compromise between governmental strength and restraint, liberal values and some other types of value.

As I will discuss in this chapter, some who embrace such hybrids can be committed liberals. Among them was A. R. (Alvin Robert) Cornelius. Cornelius was an extraordinary person. An Indian convert to Catholicism, he was recruited by the British to join the elite Indian Civil Service's

[3] Id. at 5.

Judicial Branch. Trained at Cambridge, he embraced liberal values, and as he rose to be an important judge in British India, he maintained his fidelity to these principles. After the Partition of the British Indian Empire into the separate sovereign states of India and Pakistan in 1947, Cornelius served in the Pakistani judiciary. There, he began, slowly and painfully, to abandon his reflexive commitment to structural-liberal constitutionalism and came to embrace instead a more diverse and nuanced understanding of what constitutions can be and what, in the context of Pakistan, they should be.

Cornelius never wavered in his commitments to the ideal of a state that was constitutionally constrained; to the idea that those constraints should include a duty to respect a core of liberal values; and to the belief that judges should play a central role in interpreting, elaborating, and policing all constitutional constraints. At the same time, he became convinced that constitutionalism in Pakistan could not survive unless it reimagined itself in a form that was attractive to both Pakistan's elites and masses alike, and he concluded that to do this it must be prepared to jettison its commitment to at least some values that British liberals traditionally held dear. In an extraordinary development, the British-trained Catholic liberal argued that Pakistani judges, lawyers, and intellectuals should explore a form of *Islamic* constitutionalism whose values overlapped in many places with Western liberal values, but that did not accept those liberal values as ends in themselves. Perhaps more unlikely still, his once idiosyncratic argument appears over time subtly to have shaped judicial behavior and public attitudes in Pakistan, with effects that are still being felt today.

Before going on, it is important to note that the term *Islamist* is currently a fraught one. Some use it to refer only to people who believe that the government must govern in a manner that is consistent with a highly illiberal interpretation of Islamic law, and who favor authoritarian governance and the application of laws that are inconsistent with Western liberal values.[4] For reasons that I have discussed in other publications, I find that problematic.[5] This chapter uses the term *Islamist* to refer to *anyone* who believes that state action (including state law) must respect supralegislative principles of Islamic law – what is called the *shari'a* – and thus that courts

[4] See, e.g., Daniel Pipes, 'Distinguishing between Islam and Islamism,' paper presented at the Center for Strategic and International Studies, 1998. http://www.danielpipes.org/954/distinguishing-between-islam-and-islamism. Compare Stephen Cohen, *The Idea of Pakistan*. 2nd ed. (Washington, DC: Brookings Institution Press, 2006), 162.

[5] See Lombardi, 'Can Islamizing a Legal System Ever Help Promote Liberal Democracy?'

or some other forms of independent institution should be empowered to review and void legislation when and if it conflicts with these principles.[6] They are 'Islamists' irrespective of whether their interpretation of Islam is liberal or illiberal.

II. The Education of A. R. Cornelius

Alvin Robert Cornelius was born in 1903 in Allahabad to a family of Indian Protestant academics.[7] As a young adult, Cornelius married a Catholic and converted to Catholicism. From that point forward he remained a practicing, and apparently devout, Catholic.[8] Cornelius was marked early for success in British India. After a superb undergraduate career in India, he was sent on a scholarship to Cambridge University for further education. He entered Selwyn College, which had been created in the nineteenth century to honor one of Victorian England's most notable churchmen and missionaries, Bishop Selwyn. Bishop Selwyn was famous for explaining Britain's success as a nation and as a colonial power by reference to its integration of Christian ideals into its legal and political culture. Not surprisingly, although it was a college devoted to general education rather than theology, Selwyn College had a far more 'Christian' tone than most other Cambridge colleges, and it trained a disproportionate number of clergymen.[9] Judging from his later writings, Cornelius was probably impressed at Selwyn by the idea that a society's stability, strength, and liberty depended upon its maintaining a connection between the nation's law and the religion of the people.

After finishing at Cambridge, Cornelius took a commission in the powerful and prestigious Indian Civil Service (ICS). The ICS was a crucial institution within the British imperial structure, sometimes characterized as the 'steel frame of the British empire'.[10] It was composed of a small cadre of carefully selected and highly trained officials – some British expatriates and some native Indians. British and Indian members of the ICS served

[6] See *id.* Compare with Leonard Binder, *Religion and Politics in Pakistan* (Berkeley: University of California Press, 1961), 102–108, 138–141.

[7] See, generally, Ralph Braibanti, *Chief Justice Cornelius of Pakistan: An Analysis with Letters and Speeches* (Oxford University Press, 1999), 21–24; S. M. Haider, 'Preface', in A. R. Cornelius, *Law and Judiciary in Pakistan* (ed., S. M. Haider) (Lahore: Lahore Law Times Publications, 1981), 1–6

[8] Braibanti, *Chief Justice Cornelius*, 71–72.

[9] See, generally, Owen Chadwick, *Selwyn College, 1882–1973: A Short History* (Cambridge, 1973).

[10] See David Potter, *India's Political Administrators* (Oxford University Press, 1986), 88.

on equal terms, promoted (or not) on the basis of a strictly meritocratic system. The ICS provided the Raj with its administrative and judicial elite.[11]

Like most of the native Indian members of the service, Cornelius was appointed to serve within the judicial rather than the administrative branch of the ICS.[12] Those in the judicial branch served in both legal advisory roles and as judges at every level of the judicial system. As part of his early service, Cornelius rotated through trial courts in the State of Punjab, then one of British India's wealthiest regions.[13] In the 1940s, he was appointed to the prestigious Lahore High Court, which had final appellate jurisdiction over cases from both the State of Punjab and the State of Haryana. Cornelius enjoyed his work on the Court and was happy living in Lahore.[14] His satisfaction with his job and his location would affect his life in important ways.

In 1947, the British decided to leave India and agreed to carve their Indian possessions into two states. The new state of India was to be a multiethnic democracy, but with a population that was overwhelming Hindu majority. The new state of Pakistan was also intended to be a democratic state, but with an overwhelmingly Muslim population. Although it was supposed to provide a place where Muslims could go if they did not want to be governed by a Hindu majority in India,[15] it was not necessarily supposed to be an 'Islamic state'. In fact, those most active in the formation of Pakistan were 'secular' Anglophone members of British India's Muslim elite[16] who supported the creation of Pakistan not out of an ideological commitment to Islam, but because they worried that a Hindu-majority state would discriminate against them and deny them the access to power and prestige that they had previously enjoyed.[17] They imagined Pakistan as a country where a Muslim majority would use representative political mechanisms to determine the types of law that would be applied, while at

[11] See, generally, Bankey Bihari Misra, *The Bureaucracy in India: An Historical Analysis of Development up to 1947* (Oxford University Press, 1977); Roland Hunt and John Harrison, *The District Officer in India 1937–47* (London: Scolar Press, 1980); Potter, *India's Political Administrators*. See also Cohen, *The Idea of Pakistan*, 41.

[12] Cf. Arudra Burra, 'The Indian Civil Service and the Raj: 1919–1950' (unpublished, 2007), 94–100. http://ssrn.com/abstract=2052658.

[13] See Haider, 'Preface', 2, 4–5.

[14] Braibanti, *Chief Justice Cornelius*, 23.

[15] See Chaudhri Muhammad Ali, *The Emergence of Pakistan* (Columbia University Press, 1967), 39; Ian Talbot, *Pakistan: A Modern History*. 2nd ed. (New York: Palgrave Macmillan, 1998), 4–5.

[16] See Tayyab Mahmud, "Freedom of Religion and Religious Minorities in Pakistan: A Study of Judicial Practice," *Fordham International Law Journal* 19 (1995–1996): 51–62; Cohen, *The Idea of Pakistan*, 161. Cf. Binder, *Religion and Politics in Pakistan*, 61–64, 67–69.

[17] See Ali, *The Emergence of Pakistan*, 239.

the same time one with a judiciary ensuring that majoritarian laws did not violate the liberal rights of citizens in the minority – rights were understood particularly in common law terms of natural justice.[18]

Opposed to those championing a 'secular' democratic Pakistan were a group that this chapter has termed 'Islamists' – people including liberals who wanted Pakistan to be constrained by a constitutional principle requiring the state never to act in a way inconsistent with Islamic law, that is, the *shari`a*. Although many of these Pakistani Islamists supported a democratic Pakistan, up to a point, they did not believe that democratically elected legislatures could be trusted always to respect the *shari`a*. They insisted where state laws and administrative actions conflicted with the *shari`a*, Pakistani courts, or some other form of expert institution, should be empowered to strike down the legislation.[19] Even laws designed to realize and preserve fundamental rights might have to give way.

Like all native Indian members of the ICS, Cornelius was given a choice at Partition: He could move to the territories that would become part of India and remain a member of the ICS; or he could stay in Lahore become a member of the Civil Service of Pakistan.[20] Happy in Lahore and comfortable with the philosophy of Pakistan's secular elites, Cornelius chose to serve the new Pakistani government, continuing to serve on the Lahore High Court, and immediately becoming an important member of the legal elite in the new country.[21] In 1954, he was appointed to the Pakistani Supreme Court, becoming its Chief Justice in 1960, where he would remain until 1968.

When Cornelius opted to become a citizen of Pakistan, there was nothing to suggest that he had any personal sympathy for Islamists, Political Islam, or 'Islamism'. Indeed, Cornelius remembered later in life the distaste with which he viewed the calls for the new Pakistani state to be an 'Islamic' state.[22] Yet within fifteen years, he would join those who called for Pakistan to systematically Islamize its legal system. To understand the evolution in Cornelius's thinking, it is important to understand some trends that were taking place in Pakistan and around the contemporary Islamic world.

[18] Id.

[19] See also Binder, *Religion and Politics in Pakistan*, 102–108, 138–141.

[20] See Braibanti, *Chief Justice Cornelius*, 4, 24.

[21] See id.; see also Haider, 'Preface', 3.

[22] Letter from A. R. Cornelius to Ralph Braibanti (Nov. 14, 1977), reprinted in Braibanti, *Chief Justice Cornelius*, 193.

III. Contextualizing Cornelius's Growing Interest in Islamic Constitutionalism: Pakistan in the 1950s

Three developments during the 1950s seem to have pushed Cornelius along the unlikely path toward an idiosyncratic modernist conception of Islamic constitutionalism. Two were unique to Pakistan and one was global. The first was the growth of Islamist political power in Pakistan. The second was the collapse of Pakistan's secular, liberal democratic constitutional order and its apparent replacement by a still secular but now illiberal autocracy. The third was the apparent success of Arab Middle East programs of legal reforms that had reconceptualized the European civil law system in Islamic terms.

A. *The Growing Power of Islamist Discourse in Pakistan*

As already noted, the drive to create a secular Pakistani state was led by secular Muslim members of the economic and administrative elite in British India.[23] These were the people who assumed control of Pakistan after independence in 1947. Almost immediately, their vision of Pakistan as a secular state was severely challenged.

After independence, Islamists quickly demonstrated their broad popularity among the many segments of the Pakistani population. To the distress of many secular elites, no other ideological group appeared so able both to motivate and unify the Pakistani people. Worse, although a significant faction these Islamists in fact embraced political liberalism,[24] there were also numerous *illiberal* factions of Islamists – and it was these illiberal factions that quickly enjoyed the greatest popular support in Pakistan.[25]

As time went on, Pakistan's secular elite increasingly distrusted Islamism. In 1952, a number of illiberal Islamist factions began opposing the Ahmadi sect of Islam[26] – a small and highly controversial Islamic sect whose members included many powerful members of Pakistan's Anglophone elite. These Islamists demanded that the Pakistani government ban the

[23] See Binder, *Religion and Politics in Pakistan*, 117.

[24] See Wilfred Cantwell Smith, *Modern Islam in India: A Social Analysis* (London: V. Gollancz, 1946), 7–135. See also M. K. Masud, 'Rethinking Shari`a: Javed Ahmad Ghamidi on Hudud,' *Die Welt des Islams* 47 (2007): 356–375.

[25] Binder, *Religion and Politics in Pakistan*, 26–33, 70–107.

[26] See, generally, Yohanan Friedmann, *Prophecy Continuous: Aspects of Ahmadi Religious Thought and Its Medieval Background* (Oxford University Press, 2003).

propagation of its doctrines. When the government refused, some of these factions responded with violence, both against the Ahmadi and against the government.[27] After reestablishing order in 1954, the government created a special Court of Inquiry tasked to look into the disturbances. That Court of Inquiry's report – sometimes called the 'Munir Report' after its President, Muhammad Munir – warned that, in Pakistan at least, Islamism was ultimately incompatible with the needs of a modern, liberal state.[28]

The report noted not only that Islamic rhetoric seemed to have significant power to motivate the masses in Pakistan, but that Pakistanis also seemed overwhelmingly to find illiberal versions of Islamism much more compelling than liberal ones.[29] It warned that liberals were naïve if they thought that any form of Islamism would someday evolve to become consistent with the needs of a modern modes or with liberal values.[30] Arguably going beyond their mandate, the authors of the report concluded that Pakistani liberals should resist any attempt to formally modify their existing secular, democratic mode of governance:

> [I]rreconcilables remain irreconcilables even if you believe or wish to the contrary. As long as we rely on the hammer when a file is needed and press Islam into service to solve solutions it was never intended to solve [i.e., the question of what laws to apply in a modern state] frustration and disappointment must dog our steps.[31]

To their dismay, by the early 1960s the famously liberal colleague Cornelius would come to advocate the exact opposite approach from that advocated by the Munir Report, calling for the abandonment of any ideal of traditional secular liberal democracy in favor of an Islamist system that nevertheless embraced liberal democratic ideals.

Cornelius suggested that those committed to upholding liberal democratic ideals should, counterintuitively, embrace the ideal of Islamizing the

27 See Mahmud, 'Freedom of Religion', 65–66; Binder, *Religion and Politics in Pakistan*, 259–296.

28 Muhammad Munir and M. R. Kayani, *Report of the Court of Inquiry Constituted under Punjab Act II of 1954 to Enquire into the Punjab Disturbances of 1953* (Punjab: Superintendent, Government Printing, 1954).

29 Munir and Kayani, *Report*, 231–232. Cf. Seyyed Vali Reza Nasr, *The Vanguard of the Islamic Revolution: The Jama'at-i Islami of Pakistan* (University of California Press, 1994), 138; Barbara Daly Metcalf, *Islam in South Asia in Practice* (Princeton University Press, 2009), 424; John L. Esposito, *Islam and Politics*. 4th ed. (Syracuse, NY: Syracuse University Press, 1998), 119.

30 Munir and Kayani, *Report*, 232.

31 Id. See also Binder, *Religion and Politics*, 343–344.

legal system, so long as the judiciary retained the authority to define the government's official interpretation of Islamic law. At the same time, he urged members of the historically liberal legal profession, both the judiciary and the bar, to study the Arabic language and Islamic law so that they could learn to reconceptualize liberal democratic values in Islamic terms and to articulate arguments in favor of them. This, he believed, would allow them to win over Pakistani's Islamist polity to liberal rather than illiberal interpretations of Islamic law.

To understand Cornelius's thinking, we need to consider two factors. The first is Cornelius's growing distress about the rise of secular authoritarianism in Pakistan and his skepticism that a secular liberal government could ever govern Pakistan effectively. The second is Cornelius's new awareness of liberal Islamic legal reforms occurring in the contemporary Arab Middle East beginning in the late 1940s. The first trend convinced him that liberal secularism could never be as successful as the Munir Report's authors had hoped. The second made him think that Islamism in Pakistan could in fact be implemented in a fashion that was much more liberal than those authors had recognized.

B. The Collapse of Secular Liberal Democracy and Rise of Secular Autocracy in Pakistan

In the years after the publication of the Munir Report, Pakistan went through a period of constitutional turmoil. At independence, Pakistan did not have a constitution and found itself compelled to retain much of the governmental structure of the colonial period.[32] Pakistan's inherited legislature, the Constituent Assembly, then struggled for years to draft a new constitution.[33] But as we saw, by the mid-1950s, the secular, quasi-liberal, quasi-democratic regime that Pakistan had inherited from the British had come under increasing pressure. In response, Pakistan's executive branch – the branch most firmly under the control of Pakistan's secular elites – began to aggrandize itself at the expense of the Constituent

[32] See Donald N. Wilbur, *Pakistan: Yesterday and Today* (New York: Holt Rinehart Winston, 1964), 120; Paula Newberg, *Judging the State: Courts and Constitutional Politics in Pakistan* (Cambridge University Press, 1995), 36–42; Tayyab Mahmud, 'Praetorianism and Common Law in Post-colonial Settings: Judicial Responses to Constitutional Breakdowns in Pakistan', *Utah Law Review* (1993): 1231–1234.

[33] See Newburg, *Judging the State*, 36–42.

Assembly, which was seen as being increasingly sympathetic to regionalists and Islamists.[34]

In 1956, Pakistan finally enacted a constitution, which tried to balance popular Islamist concerns and the liberal concerns of secular elite.[35] It retained Pakistan's representative form of government and provided protections for fundamental liberal rights, while at the same time establishing Pakistan as an 'Islamic Republic' whose laws had to be consistent with the *shari'a*.[36] In 1958, Pakistan scheduled its first set of elections under the new constitution. They did not usher in a period of stability – quite the contrary. As Pakistan descended into increasing ungovernability, its president, Iskander Mirza, declared martial law in October 1958: suspending the constitution, outlawing political parties, and appointing General Ayub Khan, the commander-in-chief of the Pakistani army, as the chief martial law administrator.[37] Some twenty days later, Ayub Khan, supported by a cadre of secularist military officers, staged a military coup, removing Mirza and assuming the office of the presidency himself.[38] The planned elections were canceled. Such was the end of Pakistan's brief constitutional experiment with representative parliamentary democracy.

Having seized power, the new military government sought to establish a secular form of autocratic government sometimes termed 'guided democracy'.[39] In one of its first acts, it abrogated the 1956 Constitution and all laws enacted pursuant to it, while at the same time – to prevent a complete legal vacuum – instructing the courts to enforce all laws that were in force before the coup that were not inconsistent with military orders.

Thereafter, the courts were quickly asked to rule on the scope of the military's new authority. In *State v. Dosso and Another*,[40] several convicted criminals challenged convictions on the ground that their trial violated fundamental rights traditionally protected at common law. The case went to the Pakistani Supreme Court, to which Cornelius had been appointed in 1954. The military ordered the Court not to hear the claim, asserting

[34] See Clark B. Lombardi, 'Islamism as a Response to Emergency Rule in Pakistan: The Surprising Proposal of Justice A. R. Cornelius', in Victor V. Ramraj and Arun K. Thiruvengadam (eds.), *Emergency Powers in Asia: Exploring the Limits of Legality* (Cambridge University Press, 2009), 442–444.

[35] *Constitution of 1956*.

[36] See *Constitution of 1956*, arts. 3–22, 25, 197–98.

[37] See, generally, Cohen, *The Idea of Pakistan*, 56–68.

[38] Id.

[39] See Newberg, *Judging the State*, 24. Cf. Jose Arsenio Torres, 'The Political Ideology of Guided Democracy', *The Review of Politics* 25 (1963) 50–53.

[40] 1958 PLD (Sup. Ct) 533.

that with the abrogation of the 1956 Constitution, the government was no longer bound to respect fundamental rights and that, accordingly, the plaintiffs had no justiciable claim.[41] The Supreme Court agreed, holding that a usurping government could rule indefinitely without recognizing any legal obligation to protect fundamental rights.[42] Cornelius was the lone dissenter.

In 1958, a year after the *Dosso* case, another case came before the Supreme Court, *Province of East Pakistan v. Mehdi Ali Khan*,[43] in which the appellee asked the Court to overrule its earlier *Dosso* ruling and assert that henceforth the government would have to permit courts to issue binding orders protecting citizens from violations of their fundamental rights. Again, the Court refused. Again, the lone objection came from Cornelius.[44] He argued that no government, elected or usurping, can contravene the 'settled expectations' that the people hold for any government that asserts power over them.[45] The military could legitimately dissolve an old constitutional regime and had considerable discretion in shaping a new regime, but at the very least the new regime was still obliged to respect the 'settled expectations' of the people. These included the expectation that the executive would respect the fundamental rights of the common law as they had been elaborated by the judiciary – that is, the fundamental principles of natural justice.[46]

The dissents in *Dosso* and *Mehdi Ali Khan* were sharply worded, and they made clear that Cornelius was disturbed by the Court's failure to assert itself as a guarantor of fundamental rights and as a check on arbitrary power. In 1960, Cornelius, in keeping with Court tradition, became the Chief Justice of the Supreme Court. Upon assuming his new post, Cornelius wrote to General Ayub Khan, still holding the office of the President of Pakistan, appealing that the military government should see itself as bound to respect fundamental common-law rights as traditionally articulated by common-law courts, even notwithstanding the Court's earlier holdings in *Desso* and *Mehdi Ali Khan*.[47] He suggested

[41] See Newburg, *Judging the State*, 73; Mahmud, 'Praetorianism', 1248–1249.

[42] See *Dosso*, 1958 PLD (Sup. Ct) at 541.

[43] 1959 PLD (S.Ct.) 387.

[44] See *Dosso*, 1958 PLD (Sup. Ct) at 553–562 (Cornelius, J. concurring); *Khan*, 959 PLD (S.Ct.) at 435–40 (Cornelius, J., dissenting).

[45] See, e.g., *Khan*, 1959 PLD (S.C.) at 439 (Cornelius, J., dissenting).

[46] See *Khan*, 1959 PLD (S.C.) at 436–442 (Cornelius, J., dissenting).

[47] See 'Some Constitutional Proposals for Pakistan' (1961), reprinted in A. R. Cornelius, *Law and Judiciary in Pakistan* (ed., S. M. Haider) (Lahore Law Times Publications, 1981), 184–201.

that if the military was indeed worried about an open-ended guarantee of 'fundamental rights', it might delineate these rights in a 'bill of rights' modeled after that of the United States.[48] His suggestions fell on deaf ears. In 1962, the General Khan, by executive order, promulgated what I and others have elsewhere termed a 'praetorian constitution'[49] – and it did *not* contain any provision permitting courts to enforce fundamental rights, even those deriving from citizens' settled expectations regarding previous judicial decisions.[50]

Cornelius was probably not surprised. He had already begun to reflect more deeply on his natural rights theory and had started to think about why it had failed to resonate in Pakistan. In a remarkable speech delivered at the Political Science Society of Edwardes College at Peshawar on November 3, 1960, which he entitled 'Law and Liberty', Cornelius commented sourly that he and many other Pakistani liberals had been too quick to assume that fundamental, British common law rights principles would continue to be respected by the non-British rulers who replaced them, because these liberals like himself had forgotten to ask *why* Britons had accepted judicially articulated natural rights principles as legally binding principles independent from (and superior to) positive law in the first place. This had happened, he argued, only because British judges had learned how to articulate their notions of 'justice' in *religious* terms that appealed to the Christian convictions that prevailed in England among both rulers and the ruled.[51] Similarly, in a June 4, 1964 speech to the Pakistan Institute of International Affairs entitled 'The Function of Law as a Link Between Nations', he told his audience:

> In the year 1653 a judge in England did not hesitate to pronounce that: 'There is no law in England, but is as really and truly the law of God as any Scripture phrase, that is by consequence from the very texts of Scripture: for there are very many consequences reasoned out of the texts of Scripture; so is the law of England the very consequence of the very Decalogue itself: and whatsoever is not Consonant to Scripture in the law of England is not the law of England ... be it Acts of Parliament, customs or any judicial acts of the Court, it is not the law of England'. That was said at a stage when the Courts of England being dissatisfied with the legislation of the time were

48 Id. at 187–188.

49 Constitution of 1962 (Pakistan).

50 See, e.g., Lombardi, 'Islamism as a Response to Emergency Rule', 441–451. See, generally, Mahmud, *Praetorianism*, 1223–1251; Newberg, *Judging the State*, 42–93.

51 'Law and Liberty, Speech at the Inauguration of the Political Science Society of Edwardes College at Peshawar (Nov. 3, 1960)', reprinted in Cornelius, *Law and Judiciary in Pakistan*, 47–52. *v.*

searching for grounds on which they could declare the legislative dictates as invalid.[52]

In other words, according to Cornelius, people's belief in the religious grounding of judicially articulated fundamental principles became habitual, and as a result, judges stopped having to justify their laws in religious terms. Fundamental rights principles had come to be recognized in early modern Britain as 'higher law', binding on both ruled and rulers alike, only because England was a Christian society and English judges had been successfully able to 'sanctify' these rights in Christian terms.[53] These fundamental rights principles would only achieve the same status in Pakistan, he argued, if they could be 'resanctified' in Islamic terms, the terms that governed the lives of both the ruled and rulers of Pakistan.[54]

C. *Liberal Middle Eastern Legal Reform and the Rise of the Sanhūrī Codes*

Cornelius drew support for this position from contemporary programs of Arab legal reform in the Middle East, Egypt, and North Africa. To Cornelius, the experience of those countries demonstrated that, contrary to the fears expressed in the Munir Report, lawyers with 'secular' legal training could be taken seriously by the masses as Islamic thinkers and could thereby push the law in liberal directions. In making these claims, Cornelius seems to have been influenced by the work of the Egyptian lawyer, judge, and academic, 'Abd al-Razzaq Ahmad al-Sanhūrī – and in particular from the spread throughout the Arab world of his so-called Sanhūrī codes.[55]

In the 1930s, Egypt had faced a political situation similar, in many ways, to the situation facing Pakistan in the 1950s. The British invasion of Egypt in 1882 led to the abolition of Ottoman Egypt's explicitly Islamic legal system, but kept in place a parallel legal system derived from both French and English law that the Ottomans had set up to hear disputes

52 Id. at 146.

53 See also Braibanti, *Chief Justice Cornelius*, 139.

54 Id.

55 See, generally, Enid Hill, 'Al-Sanhuri and Islamic Law: The Place and Significance of Islamic Law in the Life and Work of 'Abd al-Razzaq Ahmad al-Sanhuri, Egyptian Jurist and Scholar, 1895–1971' [Part I], *Arab Law Quarterly* 3 (1988): 33–64; Enid Hill, 'Al-Sanhuri and Islamic Law: The Place and Significance of Islamic Law in the Life and Work of 'Abd al-Razzaq Ahmad al-Sanhuri, Egyptian Jurist and Scholar, 1895–1971' [Part II], *Arab Law Quarterly* 3 (1988): 182–218; Guy Bechor, *The Sanhuri Code and the Emergence of Modern Arab Civil Law (1932 to 1949)* (Leiden, The Netherlands: Brill, 2007).

involving foreigners.[56] After Britain granted independence to Egypt in 1922, Egyptians began to debate the possible reform of the Egyptian legal system. One of the burning questions was whether Egypt should retain the European-style codes it had developed under English rule or whether it should return to some form of 'Islamic' legal system.[57] At the same time, Egyptian Islamists also debated among themselves what a new 'Islamic' state should look like.[58]

In this fractured political environment, an idiosyncratic member of the Europeanized elite, 'Abd al-Razzāq Ahmad al-Sanhūrī, proposed a grand bargain. A brilliant comparative lawyer, Sanhūrī had completed a PhD in France. During his studies, he had become familiar with (and sympathetic to) some leaders of the 'social law' movement then becoming influential among progressives in both the common law and civil law world.[59] Sanhūrī was also an Islamic modernist. In his French PhD dissertation,[60] he had proposed a novel method of Islamic legal interpretation that he claimed would allow Muslims to accept governments that were simultaneously Islamic, modern, and progressive.[61]

Upon his return from France, Sanhūrī taught at Cairo University Law School and eventually became its dean. Like many legal professionals he also became active in politics.[62] His progressive political and economic views alienated many of Egypt's elites. Sanhūrī knew however, that they were more afraid of populist Islamists than they were of him. In a series of speeches and articles, Sanhūrī played on fears of Islamist unrest in order to get the elites to accept progressive legal reform.[63]

Sanhūrī convinced the Egyptian parliament that it should commission him to revise the Egyptian civil code, promising that his code would

[56] See, generally, Mark S. W. Hoyle, *Mixed Courts of Egypt* (London: Graham and Trotman, 1991).

[57] See Bechor, *The Sanhuri Code*, 21–26.

[58] See Clark B. Lombardi, *State Law as Islamic Law in Modern Egypt* (Leiden, The Netherlands: Brill, 2006), 59–119.

[59] See Amr Shalakany, 'Between Identity and Redistribution: Sanhuri, Genealogy and the Will to Islamise', *Islamic Law and Society* 8 (2001): 201–244.

[60] Subsequently published as A. Sanhoury, *Le califat: son évolution vers une société des nations orientales* (Paris: P. Geuthner, 1926).

[61] Id. at 570–581. See also Abd-el-Razzak Ah. El SANHOURY Bey [Abd al-Razzāq al-Sanhūrī], 'Le droit musulman comme élément de refonte du code civil égyptien', in *Introduction à l'étude du droit comparé: Recuil d'études en l'honneur d'Édouard Lambert.* Vol. 3 (Paris: Librairie générale de droit et de jurisprudence, 1938), 621–642. See, generally, Shalakany, 'Identity and Redistribution', 211–215.

[62] See Hill, 'Al-Sanhuri and Islamic Law' [Part I], 42–43, 53–64.

[63] See, Bechor, *The Sanhuri Code*, 25, 32–35. Cf. Lombardi, *State Law as Islamic Law*, 101–110.

retain much of the current legal system and yet would be accepted by the public as Islamic.[64] In drafting the new code, he reviewed the existing code and kept all rules that could be justified as both progressive and 'Islamic' (according to the modernist method he had developed in his dissertation). Sanhūrī also borrowed from the legal codes of various European states rules that (according to his interpretation of Islamic law) were consistent with principles of justice common to both the European and Islamic traditions.[65] In order to ensure that the code remained flexible enough to adapt to evolving circumstances, he deliberately left some areas of life to be regulated by judge-made law. Judges were instructed to fill in 'gaps' in the code by creating new rules consistent with both 'Islamic' principles and with justice (which Sanhūrī understood to mean).[66]

In short, the code contained many rules that were found in European codes of law and many rules that progressive European jurists would have been happy to include in European codes of law. After completing his draft code in in1942, Sanhūrī spent years trying to convince the public his proposed code was truly 'Islamic'.[67] Eventually, his arguments persuaded clerics, the people, and ultimately the Egyptian parliament.[68] In 1949, his proposed code was adopted into law.[69]

As the new code proved effective and popular, Islamist groups that had initially criticized Sanhūrī's code seemed to grow more comfortable with it, and, more generally, with the idea that a code that shared rules with European codes could be accepted as legitimately Islamic. Sanhūrī and other liberal Islamic legal writers in Egypt and abroad celebrated the success of the code and proselytized throughout the Muslim world for Sanhūrī's project of reconceptualizing in Islamic terms those modern legal institutions and legal rules that had proved effective in Europe. The commentary of such thinkers helped to shape many Arabs' understanding of Islamic law, and Islamists began to incorporate aspects of Sanhūrī's method into

[64] See, e.g., Abd al- Razzāq al-Sanhūri, 'Wujūb Tanqīh al-Qānūn al-Madanī al-Misrī, wa-alaai ay Asā Yakūn Hadha al-Tanqīh', *Majallat al-qānūn wa-l-iqtiṣād* 6 (1936): 114–115, translated in Bechor, *The Sanhuri Code*, 50. See also id. at 87–89.

[65] See Bechor, *The Sanhuri Code*, 88.

[66] See Shalakany, 'Identity and Redistribution', 233–235; Hill, 'Al-Sanhūri and Islamic Law' [Part I], 44.

[67] See Hill, 'Al-Sanhūri and Islamic Law' [Part II], 182–184, Shalakany, 'Identity and Redistribution', 218–219.

[68] See Hill, 'Al-Sanhūri and Islamic Law' [Part I], 50–83; Farhat J. Ziadeh, *Lawyers, the Rule of Law and Liberalism in Modern Egypt* (Palo Alto, CA: Hoover Institution on War, Revolution, and Peace, 1968), 135–147.

[69] See, generally, The Civil Code (Arab Republic of Egypt) (No. 131, 1948).

their own ongoing interpretation of Islamic state law.[70] In short order, numerous postcolonial Arab states struggling to legitimize an inherited legal order also decided to adopt versions of the Sanhūrī code.[71] Bechor comments, '[I]t is impossible to relate to civil law in the Arab world without an acquaintance with the New Egyptian Civil Code'.[72]

In the early 1960s many in the Arab world believed that spread of Sanhūrī codes demonstrated the following core point: that rules developed in European countries and imported into Muslim countries by colonial powers could be reconceptualized as rules consistent with core Islamic principles. Among the influential champions of Sanhūrī's project was the Lebanese lawyer Sobhi Mahmassani – the only leading Arab champion of 'liberal Islam' whose work had been translated into English.[73] Cornelius was reading Mahmassani as early as 1964 and began referring to Mahmassani in his speeches,[74] using both Mahmassani's ideas and the recent successful spread of Sanhūrī-inspired Islamic codes throughout the Middle East as support for Cornelius's own claim that in countries where Islamist pressure was strong, like Pakistan, liberal legal professionals with proper training and drive could build popular support for progressive legal rules. To do so, however, they would first have to reconceptualize those rules in Islamic terms as rules consistent with core Islamic principles and then 'sell' their interpretation of Islamic law to the public.

IV. Cornelius's Argument for Lawyer-Led Islamization in Pakistan

In 1962, Cornelius began explicitly to argue that the only hope for a re-empowerment of the Pakistani judiciary and the legal profession, and for the re-establishment of a liberal constitutionalism would come through liberal Islamization. This, he maintained, meant that Pakistani liberals, and particularly those in the legal profession, needed to engage in a two-part

[70] See Baber Johansen, *Contingency in a Sacred Law: Legal and Ethical Norms in the Muslim Fiqh* (Leiden, The Netherlands: Brill, 1999), 59; see, e.g., Clark B. Lombardi and Nathan J. Brown, 'Do Constitutions Requiring Adherence to Shari'a Threaten Human Rights? How Egypt's Constitutional Court Reconciles Islamic Law with the Liberal Rule of Law', *American University International Law Review* 21 (2006): 433–434.

[71] See Nabil Saleh, 'Civil Codes of Arab Countries: The Sanhūri Codes', *Arab Law Quarterly* 8: (1993): 161–167; see also Bechor, *The Sanhuri Code*, 57.

[72] Bechor, *The Sanhuri Code*, 57.

[73] See Ṣubḥī Rajab Mahmassani, *Falsafat al-Tashrī' fī al-Islām: The Philosophy of Jurisprudence in Islam* (trans., Farhat Ziadeh) (Leiden, The Netherlands: E. J. Brill, 1961).

[74] See, e.g., Cornelius, *Law and Judiciary in Pakistan*, 384.

program. First, they needed to use their institutional prestige to support Islamization – because only through Islamization could a stable legal order emerge. At the same time, they needed to establish themselves as legitimate interpreters of Islamic law, and in the process thereby establish fundamental rights principles as principles essential to Islamic law as well.

Cornelius unveiled his new line of thinking in a daring fashion. In July 1962, just one month after the military had promulgated a new constitution replacing the 1956 Constitution that they had abrogated in 1958, he, as Chief Justice of the Supreme Court, gave a speech before a hostile military command at its headquarters in Rawalpindi.[75] In his speech, Cornelius urged the military to commit itself to respecting the fundamental wishes of the people – which included, he thought, a desire for government that respected traditional fundamental rights and a desire to live under laws that were consistent with Islamic law. He argued that unless the new Pakistani Constitution (which had just gone into effect two months earlier), its laws, and the administration of these laws reflected the fundamental moral beliefs of the people, they would likely be viewed as illegitimate by the people, who – he implied – would disobey them whenever they could.[76] Social stability and public order would be thereby threatened, and the nation might ultimately become ungovernable.[77]

So what was to be done? Drawing upon the writings of Simone Weil, Cornelius argued that after conquering a country, a military could only establish the legitimacy of its rule by demonstrating respect for the 'essential aspirations of the people eternally inscribed in the depths of popular feeling'.[78] In Pakistan, Cornelius said, this principle would require the new military government to establish a regime that respected the people's commitment to Islamic law. It was thus a matter of what he called 'political therapeutics'[79] that the military government both must instruct the judiciary to issue orders and decisions consistent with Islamic law and, at the same time, must respect the authority of an independent judiciary when it does just that:

> [T]here must be restoration of local liberties and power, as nearly as possible on traditional lines, so that the national character may be rebuilt in an atmosphere of freedom, under the age-old incentives and controls. The

[75] 'Address to Officers of the Pakistan Army at General Headquarters in Rawalpindi' (July 11, 1962), reprinted in Braibanti, *Chief Justice Cornelius*, 201–221.

[76] See id. at 204–205.

[77] Id.

[78] Id. at 220 (citing Simone Weil, *The Need for Roots: Prelude to a Declaration of Duties Towards Mankind* [London: Routledge, 2003]).

[79] Id. at 219.

> most important of these [restored] powers, in my opinion, is the judicial power.... It is only necessary to revise them [in Islamic terms]. This is a matter of fundamental importance.[80]

The assembled military officers may have wondered why this Cambridge-educated, Catholic liberal was developing a strategy by which a military government could legitimize its rule through a process of Islamization. In his speech at Rawalpindi, Cornelius did not discuss the content of this new, Islamized law he was proposing. But in speeches to other, less dangerous, audiences, he made clear that this law should enshrine liberal values.

For example, six months after his speech at Rawalpindi, Cornelius gave a speech to Pakistan's national bar association, which was made up primarily of Anglophone, secular members of Pakistan's middle class.[81] There, continuing on the themes he advanced in Rawalpindi, he argued that it was counterproductive for lawyers to ignore the popular calls for Islamization, even if they found most Islamists' understanding of Islamic law to be repugnant. Like it or not, Cornelius contended, Pakistanis would only respect a body of law that was understood to be Islamic:

> There is great weight in the popular demand to bring all laws into the conformity with the dictates of religion. Whatever immediate form the demand may take and from whatever angle it may be represented, it represents the feeling of a people who are seeking to shape their lives according to the Quran and Sunnah.... It is to those cultures that the people of Pakistan owe allegiance. Until the essence of laws to which those cultures have given rise is assimilated into the legal structure of our country, there will be no cessation of this demand.[82]

Along these lines, Cornelius recalled the futility with which the British government tried to end, by force alone, the long-standing and deeply embedded practice of 'honor killing' in rural Pakistan. Whatever Cornelius's views on the morality of honor killing – that is, 'acts of violence, usually murder, committed by male family members against female family members who are perceived to have brought dishonor upon the family'[83] – he came to feel that it was foolish to believe one could simply

[80] Id. at 220.

[81] 'Presidential Address to the All-Pakistan Layers Convention in Decca' (Dec. 23, 1962), reprinted in Cornelius, *Law and Judiciary in Pakistan*, 57–62.

[82] Id. at 58.

[83] Human Rights Watch, 'Integration of the Human Rights of Women and the Gender Perspective: Violence Against Women and "Honor" Crimes, Intervention before the 57th Session of the U.N. Commission on Human Rights' (Apr. 6, 2001).

legislate it out of existence. When a government criminalized acts that 'are esteemed among the highest in their community,'[84] it inspired disrespect for both the law and for judicial orders that applied the law. Ultimately, 'This type of capital punishment is being administered for over a century. It has not resulted in the diminution of the sentiments with which the code of honor is maintained. On the contrary, it is the deterrent effect of the death sentence which has been dulled.'[85]

All-in-all, he argued, if the state did not Islamize its law, then the law was likely to lose its authority. So too would the lawyers and judges who were specialists in that law. By contrast, if the state *did* Islamize the law, then one might see the reestablishment of what in modern parlance is sometimes referred to as a 'thin' rule of law,[86] where the citizenry and the government all respected 'the law' as articulated in written laws and elaborated by judges:

> The people will regard their laws with respect, and will implement them in their lives with honesty and reverence only when they come to recognize the laws as deriving from a true source of sovereignty.... If that ideal is achieved the laws would have a natural force to project and sustain them in the same way as principles are maintained and universally accepted. It will become the delight of the community to live according to their laws.[87]

But what would the content of this new, 'Islamized' law be? Cornelius suggested that it was still evolving and could develop in a liberal fashion. Pakistanis were vigorously debating basic question of Islamic legal authority, Islamic interpretive theory, and thus questions of Islamic law. If lawyers took the initiative to the engage in Islamic debate, they would be able to influence the public's understanding of Islamic law, making the changes less wrenching. To support this claim, Cornelius directed his audience's attention to the success that Sanhūrī codes seemed to be having in many Arab countries:

> I would particularly recommend the study of the historical development and the present condition of the principal laws in force in Middle Eastern countries, in Egypt and in North Africa. It is not generally known that the Codes there prevalent, while based on true Muslim legal concepts, and being fully adapted to the Muslim way of life, are also steadily

[84] Cornelius, *Law and Judiciary in Pakistan*, 59.

[85] 'Presidential Address to the All-Pakistan Layers Convention in Decca' (Dec. 23, 1962), reprinted in Cornelius, *Law and Judiciary in Pakistan*, 57–62.

[86] Cf. Randall P. Peerenboom, *China's Long March towards Rule of Law* (Cambridge University Press, 2002), 55–125.

[87] Cornelius, *Law and Judiciary in Pakistan*, 62.

> assuming a modern form suitable for communities which are emerging into the world of today. Studies of this kind would serve to provide the basis upon which concepts of Middle Eastern fundamental law, being well-adapted to the culture and sentiments of our people could be built into the structure of our laws in replacement of English Common Law principles.[88]

By contrast, Cornelius recognized that a good faith program of Islamization might require some reforms that the liberal and secular jurists of the Pakistani Bar would find personally distasteful. Nevertheless, he urged that they would have to accept such compromises – so long as they were consistent with more fundamental rights – if the law was to be respected by the people. For example, Cornelius suggested that if the assembled members of the bar really wished to reestablish the primacy of law, they should argue for a reform of the criminal codes.[89] Specifically, they should push for abolition of the death penalty in cases of 'honor killings' that the masses (rightly or wrongly) considered to be grounded in Islam.[90] Along similar lines, in a speech given before the Third Commonwealth and Empire Law Conference on August 27, 1965, he created an international uproar when he stated that he could imagine circumstances under which the traditional Islamic punishment of amputating the hand of one who commits theft might be seen as no more cruel than traditional British punishments for the same crime.[91]

Some liberal lawyers and jurists found the supposedly liberal Cornelius's support for such seemingly barbaric punishments to be incoherent. They argued that Cornelius was trying to impose a 'rule of law' without considering whether that rule of law was actually worth imposing.[92] But Cornelius's position was actually more nuanced than many of his critics acknowledged. In particular, he argued that concessions to popular understandings of Islam were generally no more offensive to basic morality than many of the concessions that English law similarly made to realities of human behavior. With respect to abolishing the death penalty for honor killings, for example, he noted that British criminal law already recognized mitigation of punishment for temporary insanity. Given the extreme social

[88] Id.
[89] Id. at 59.
[90] Id. at 62.
[91] 'Crime and Punishment of Crime, A Paper Read at the Third Commonwealth and Empire Law Conference' (Aug. 27, 1965), reprinted in Braibanti, *Chief Justice Cornelius*, 268–271. See also id. at 35–36, 76n53.
[92] Id. at 46–47.

demands that underlie honor killing in some parts of Pakistan, he argued, this behavior might reasonably be seen to be driven by such overwhelming social shame as to effectuate a psychological disposition that is effectively the same as temporary insanity.[93]

Along similar lines, Cornelius's tolerance for punitive amputation was conditioned on a bizarre and Panglossian assumption that doctors, if they put their mind to it, would be able to preserve and reattach the amputated body parts.[94] In other words, he accepted punitive amputation only insofar as the amputation would be temporary. As Cornelius saw it, instead of (temporarily) losing his liberty, as would be the case in England, a person convicted of theft under a 'modern' Islamic state would simply lose temporary use of his hand, which would later be reattached after the period of punishment had run.[95]

For Cornelius, then, the imposition of Islamic law would require changes that might be uncomfortable, but such was necessary to preserve the core values promoted by the common law legal system. Secularist government in Pakistan is simply doomed to be undemocratic and to devalue natural rights. The Pakistani people demanded Islamization, something a secularist government by its very nature could not supply. Thus, the only option such a government had would be to deny the popular will and suppress dissent. Islamic law thus allowed for the reestablishment of core principles of common-law justice that would always lie beyond the reach of secularist government.

Furthermore, Cornelius believed that if they devoted themselves to the task, liberal lawyers and judges would be able to argue convincingly that Islamic law demanded respect for fundamental liberal principles. This point, already implicit in Cornelius's 1962 speeches, was made explicit in numerous later ones. For example, in one speech given at the University of Punjab in April 1964,[96] he cited the Islamic scholar Muhammad Iqbal, one of the modern Islamic thinkers who was most revered among Pakistanis, for the proposition that a 'republican form of government' was 'not only thoroughly consistent with the Spirit of Islam, but also with the new forces that are set free in the word of Islam'.[97] Similarly, in a speech delivered in

[93] See id. at 254–257.

[94] Id. at 269–270.

[95] See id. See also id. at 35–36.

[96] Speech at the University of Punjab: 'Iqbal's Political Message' (April 21, 1964), reprinted in Cornelius, *Law and Judiciary in Pakistan*, 371–378.

[97] Id. at 374.

June 1964 discussing the classical Islamic legal and political thinkers Ibn Khaldun, Ibn Sina, and Ibn Rushd,[98] he concluded:

> It is remarkable that of these great thinkers, the two latter had absorbed to the full all that was of meaning and excellence in the Platonic philosophy on which our modern concepts of democracy are based, but nevertheless they adhered to the view that the integrity of the Muslim State is bound up with adherence to the Shariah.[99]

In short, Cornelius argued that Islamization, and only Islamization, left open the possibility that Pakistan could reestablish a judicially supervised, acceptably liberal democracy. Islamization carried risks and would certainly require nontrivial concessions to illiberal popular beliefs about God's command; nevertheless, it would leave lawyers considerable power to shape people's understanding of what Islamic law required. If they pushed for Islamization while at the same time shaping popular understandings of Islamic values, judges and lawyers might create the conditions under which a liberal rule of law could emerge in Pakistan. Lawyers, he believed, should seize this opportunity:[100]

> The new [1962] Constitution in its Preamble declares that sovereignty over the entire Universe vests in almighty Allah alone, and that Pakistan is to be a democratic State based on Islamic principles of social justice. The lawyers of Pakistan are capable of giving a practical shape to these high principles with the aid of their knowledge and study. The people will regard their laws with respect, and will implement them in their lives with honesty and reverence only when they come to recognize the laws as deriving from a true source of Sovereignty [i.e., Islam].... If that ideal is achieved the laws would have a natural force to project and sustain them in the same way as principles are maintained and universally accepted. It will become the delight of the community to live according to their laws.[101]

From 1964 on, Cornelius continued relentlessly to stress the themes described in the preceding text. Some suggested, however, that Cornelius's radical argument for Islamization had become superfluous. In 1964, the government amended the constitution to make fundamental rights justiciable – thus apparently recognizing the binding quality of these rights. While Cornelius welcomed that move, he was clearly skeptical about the government's *bona*

98 Speech before the Pakistan Institute of International Affairs: 'Function of Law as a Link between Nations' (June 4, 1964), reprinted in Cornelius, *Law and Judiciary in Pakistan*, 141–151.

99 Id. at 149.

100 Id. at 60.

101 Id. at 62.

fides. Having lived through the imposition of both emergency rule and martial law, he was clearly concerned that respect for fundamental rights would cease whenever the military found it to be inconvenient.

Cornelius's enthusiasm for liberal Islamization did not wane after he left the bench – but it did evolve. Over time, he came to frame the need for Islamization in Pakistan in terms of a broader global need. With regard to human right, for example, in a 1977 speech before the Pakistan Academy for Rural Development,[102] he argued that while international human rights documents drafted by Western democracies reflected universally applicable principles, they were drafted in a language that made them unrecognizable and arguably unattractive to the masses in many postcolonial countries. People around the world should strive to translate human rights concepts into a form that resonated with the religious principles that were revered by the majority of the people in a particular country. If they did, the rulers would be more inclined to obey and, if they failed to, the people would be more likely to hold them accountable:

> Organized and established religion, such as we are familiar with, still remains the most powerful safeguard against man's inhumanity to man. It is an open question to me whether, if South Africa were to become a religious state, there would not be that shift of opinion among the ruling class, who all profess Christianity, in favor of free and equal treatment to the underprivileged persons in their midst, which the recently reported resolution of the General Assembly seems scarcely capable of accomplishing.[103]

Cornelius would continue to study Arabic and Islamic law, and to write works trying to demonstrate points of continuity, right up until his death on December 21, 1991.[104]

V. Might Cornelius Have Been on to Something? The Ambiguities of Islamization in Pakistan in the 1970s, 1980s and 1990s

Cornelius's proposal was nothing if not ambitious. He thought that legal professionals would need to take part in a systematic program to study Islamic law, and particularly to study liberal interpretations of Islamic law. They should learn to articulate and proselytize for the values they

[102] Speech delivered before the Pakistan Academy for Rural Development: 'Islam and Human Rights' (Nov. 8, 1977), reprinted in Braibanti, *Chief Justice Cornelius*, 278–296.

[103] Id. at 294 (internal references omitted).

[104] See Braibanti, *Chief Justice Cornelius*, 297–331.

cherished (efficient governance, protection of fundamental rights) using the language of Islamic law. In selling his agenda, Cornelius freely admitted that he was optimistic about two issues. First, he was optimistic that liberal Pakistani legal professionals would be willing to engage in a time-consuming process of reconceptualization. Second, he was optimistic that these legal professionals would be able to convincingly connect liberal constitutional principles to Islamic principles and to develop 'Islamic' justifications for the enforcement of many liberal rights – indeed for all of those that made up the central core.

Less optimistic than Cornelius, secular liberals overwhelmingly resisted his appeal on behalf of Islamization. Even those who were distressed about the illiberal direction that secularism had taken were skeptical about the idea that lawyers in Pakistan could win the public over to a liberal interpretation of Islamic law that would allow for modern government and would serve as a bulwark of fundamental common-law rights.[105] They continued to presume that Islamization would never empower liberal Pakistani voices; that instead it would always empower intolerably illiberal voices. Islamization, the skeptics believed, would always tend to lead to a net loss of individual liberties. Islamic constitutionalism, by this account, was not a meaningful form of constitutionalism at all.

At first glance skeptics might seem to have been proved right. During a period of Islamization in the 1970s, first a populist president (Zulfikar Ali Bhutto) and then a military dictator (Muhammad Zia-ul-Haq) both cooperated with reactionary elements in Pakistani society to impose some self-styled 'Islamic statutes' that were profoundly illiberal.[106] Under Zia in particular, the constitution was amended to empower a special branch of courts to strike down laws on grounds of repugnancy to Islam;[107] and other notorious statutes were passed declaring the Ahmadi sect of Islam to be un-Islamic,[108] criminalizing blasphemy,[109] and imposing traditional

105 See Braibanti, *Chief Justice Cornelius*, 46–47.

106 See, e.g., Talbot, *Pakistan: A Modern History*, 240, 270–283.

107 See The Constitution (Amendment) Order, 1979 (Public Order 3 of 1979); cf. Constitution of the Islamic Republic of Pakistan (1973), art. 203D. See, generally, Talbot, *Pakistan: A Modern History*, at 273–274.

108 See Anti-Islamic Activities of Quadiani Group, Lahori Group and Ahmadis (Prohibition and Punishment) Ordinance 1984 (Ordinance XX of 1984) (now codified in Pakistan Penal Code, chapter XV, sec. 298-B). See, generally, Mahmud, 'Freedom of Religion'.

109 See President's Order 1 of 1982 (Ordinance 1 of 1982); Criminal Law (Amendment) Act (Act 111 of 1986); Pakistan Penal Code (Second Amendment) Ordinance (Ordinance XLIV of 1980); (Prohibition and Punishment) Ordinance (Ordinance XX of 1984) (codified in Pakistan Penal Code, chapter XV, Sections, 295-B, 295-C, and 298-A). See, generally, Osama Siddique and Zahra Hayat, 'Unholy Speech and Holy Laws: Blasphemy

Islamic punishments for fornication.[110] Much of the commentary on these statutes declared them to be disastrous from a human rights perspective.[111]

However, the fact that this particular period of illiberal Islamization had a detrimental effect on individual liberties (and particularly those of women) does not disprove Cornelius's hypothesis. Cornelius always understood that Islamization *could* take place in an illiberal form, and in fact he well recognized that illiberal Islamization is precisely what many in Pakistan hoped to see. He made only the narrow claims: (1) that a liberal Islamization was a realistic possibility in Pakistan; (2) that judges and lawyers could be able to effectively proselytize for liberal interpretations of Islam; and (3) that in Pakistan, a liberal *Islamic* regime was the only type of liberal regime that could withstand pressures from both illiberal secularists and illiberal Islamists.

Recent studies suggest that, if we understand his claim in these narrow terms, Cornelius may have been onto something. Islamization in Pakistan from the 1970s through the present day has been a much more multifaceted process than is often portrayed. General Zia's promulgation of 'Islamic' constitutional amendments and statutes constituted only one facet of it. These amendments and statutes had to be interpreted and applied. Drawing from court records, Charles Kennedy has shown that at least some of Bhutto and Zia's 'Islamic' statutes had less of an impact on people's lives than critics claimed precisely because, as per Cornelius, judges employed progressive interpretations of Islamic law to give creative interpretations of the statutes and to limit the impact of the Islamic amendments and statutes.[112]

This observation is further confirmed in a recent study by Martin Lau that argues that whatever negative impact the conservative Islamic statutes had on the liberal rule of law, they may have been offset by the positive

Laws in Pakistan – Controversial Origins, Design Defects, and Free Speech Implications', *Minnesota Journal of International Law* 17 (2008): 310–322.

110 The Offence of Zina (Enforcement of Hudood) Ordinance, 1979 (Ordinance No. VII of 1979). See also, Jahangir Asma and Hina Jilani, *The Hudood Ordinances: A Divine Sanction? A Research Study of the Hudood Ordinances and Their Effect on the Disadvantaged Sections of Pakistan Society* (Lahore: Sang-e-Meel Publications, 2003). But see Charles Kennedy, 'Islamization in Pakistan: Implementation of the Hudood Ordinances', *Asian Survey* 28 (1988): 307–316.

111 See, e.g., Rashida Patel, *Islamisation of Laws in Pakistan* (Karachi: Faiza Publishers, 1986); Khawar Mumtaz and Farida Shaheed (eds.), *Women of Pakistan: Two Steps Forward and One Step Back?* (London: Zed Books, 1987). But see Kennedy, 'Islamization in Pakistan'.

112 See Charles Kennedy, 'Islamization and Legal Reform in Pakistan, 1979–1989', *Pacific Affairs* 63 (1990): 72–77; Kennedy, 'Islamization in Pakistan', 307, 317–318.

impact of court decisions in which judges used the power of Islamic review to increase judicial power and to employ that power in the service of democracy and fundamental liberal rights.[113] Lau's work is based on an exhaustive survey of all published Pakistani court cases from the 1960s to the present in which judges cite 'Islamic law' as a ground for decision. It identifies a trend that seems to have begun shortly after Cornelius left the bench but before the rise of Zia Islamization program, in which judges increasingly used Islamic arguments to justify opinions that boldly asserted the power of judges to protect natural and fundamental rights, notwithstanding military attempts to restrict their powers. As judges struck down illiberal statutes as un-Islamic, or reinterpreted them to conform to a more liberal Islamic vision, they expanded the power of judges and the scope of fundamental rights even in areas not governed by Islamic statute. Lau's conclusion is unequivocal:

> The Islamisation of laws in Pakistan has been primarily a judge-led process, which was initiated to enhance the power of the judiciary and to expand the scope of constitutionally protected rights.... [T]he role of judges in the Islamization of the [Pakistani] legal system has been largely obscured by the more visible manifestations of Islamisation, namely the promulgation of the infamous hudood ordinances and other isolated pieces of Islamic legislation.... [T]he judicial appropriation of Islam and its integration into the vocabulary of courts was a conscious process aimed not only at the fulfillment of a general desire to indigenise and Islamise the legal system after the end of colonial rule, but it was also a way of enhancing judicial power and independence. The Islamisation of law did, perhaps ironically, not only predate Zia al-Haq's regime, but was used to challenge him.... [It] has become an integral part of the legal discourse being relied on in the context of a wide range of issues, from the permissibility to erect high rise buildings in Karachi to the dismissal of a Prime Minister.[114]

Although Lau's work only covers cases through the early 2000s, judicial use liberal interpretations of Islamic law as a tool to protect constitutional liberties seems to have continued unabated. An examination of Pakistani newspapers reveals that courts today continue to cite Islamic law to justify important rights-protecting decisions. Notably, as illiberal Islamists have become powerful in recent years, judges have nevertheless been striking down self-styled 'Islamic' laws that are based on illiberal interpretations of

[113] Martin Lau, *The Role of Islam in the Legal System of Pakistan* (Leiden, The Netherlands: Martinus Nijhoff, 2006).

[114] Id. at 1.

Islam by arguing that such laws are inconsistent with Islamic justice properly understood.

For example, Pakistan's Federal Shariat Court (FSC) – which handles crimes under Islamic criminal laws governing, *inter alia*, rape or sexual harassment and has jurisdiction to hear challenges to laws on the grounds of their repugnancy – recently overturned article 154(4) of the Qanun-e-Shahadat Law, which is an Islamized version of the law of evidence. The overturned article permitted men accused under the Islamic criminal laws governing rape or sexual harassment to bring in evidence of the woman's 'character'. Although the law was consistent with some widely held interpretations of Islam, the FSC overturned the law on the ground that this interpretation relied on misinterpretations of the Islamic tradition.[115]

Pakistan is not the only country in which judicial application of Islamic legal principles has occasionally been used to protect natural and fundamental rights from both secular and religious enemies. My own research on Egyptian constitutional court cases involving Islamic law shows that in Egypt too, liberal judges have successfully used Islamic legal arguments to justify a policy of expanding the scope of constitutional rights.[116]

None of this proves conclusively that Cornelius was correct to hypothesize that, in a Muslim world, liberalization *requires* Islamization in order to be effective. It is possible that judicial empowerment and judicial liberalization would have taken place in Pakistan and Egypt even if judges had not chosen to harness Islamic arguments in their favor. But at the very least, the recent histories of Pakistan and Egypt do suggest that as argued by Cornelius, in some Islamic countries there can be particular approaches to Islamization that can generate meaningful 'constitutional' constraints on government that overlap – in function if not in form – with those of liberal constitutionalism.

VI. Conclusion

A. R. Cornelius was a Catholic liberal jurist who had once found public discussions of Islam's role in the state 'repellent'. In the 1950s, however, Cornelius observed how Islamists were able successfully to take advantage of popular appetite for Islamic political discourse, and by monopolizing the field of Islamist political discourse had been able to shape

[115] See 'Shahadat Law against Quran, Sunnah: FSC', *The News International*, Feb. 12, 2009.

[116] See, generally, Lombardi, *State Law as Islamic Law*; Lombardi and Brown, 'Do Constitutions Requiring Adherence to Shari`a Threaten Human Rights?'

public understandings of Islamism and to convince many Pakistanis that authentic Islamism was necessarily antiliberal. Cornelius drew from this experience, however, a very different lesson than did his judicial colleagues. He concluded that if lawyers and judges wanted to maintain something approaching the liberal rule of law in an Islamizing world, they should not reject their obligation to respect the people's core demand for Islamization, but rather they should try to influence the people's understanding of Islamic government and Islamic law.

Subsequent developments in Pakistan and the Middle East give some degree of support to Cornelius's vision. But they also leave us with many more questions. Was Cornelius correct that liberal Islamists could win a war of ideas with their illiberal rivals, and that a state could establish itself on a liberal version of Islamic constitutional law? Are there other types of society in which structural constitutionalism can only be effective if it is conceptualized as a system that constrains a state to act in accordance with religious or cultural values? If so, can those religious values also be conceptualized in ways that overlap significant with liberal values? Can we argue that at some broader level, some non-European societies (and perhaps some European ones as well) may need to go 'Beyond Liberalism' if they wish to enjoy on an ongoing basis a critical mass of liberal rights that are effectively protected by both political and judicial institutions?

These questions are not solely of academic interest. We live in an age in which democracy and rule of law promotion are not only objects of academic study, but are also explicit foreign policy goals of the United States, the European Union, and powerful multilateral institutions such as the World Bank.[117] Billions of dollars are spent every year with the explicit goal of promoting the rule of law, often defined in thick terms as the practice of government constrained by what Dowdle and Wilkinson in Chapter 1 call a structural-liberal constitution.[118] Much of this money is spent in regions where religious revival is taking place: Muslim, Christian, Buddhist, or Hindu, and in many of these areas, self-styled 'secular' actors have historically been antiliberal. It is important to ask how actors should promote

[117] See Patrícia Galvão Teles, 'EU Presidency Statement – United Nations 6th Committee: Rule of Law at National and International Levels' (New York: European Union Delegation to the United Nations, PRES07-320EN, Oct. 25, 2007); David Trubek, 'The "Rule of Law" in Development Assistance: Past, Present, and Future', in David M. Trubek and Alvaro Santos (eds.), *The New Law and Economic Development: A Critical Appraisal* (Cambridge University Press, 2006), 74.

[118] Trubek, 'Rule of Law', 74.

the 'rule of law' in such areas.[119] Cornelius would suggest that in such areas, the best alternative might be some self-consciously religious form of governance.[120] Consider Cornelius's question to his colleagues: Is it possible that under some conditions, liberal constitutionalists are better off under a government effectively constrained by a structural religious constitution than they are under a government ineffectively constrained by a structural-liberal one?

If Cornelius *was* correct, then those involved in the process of building constitutionalism in the Muslim world should treat Islamization as a double-edged sword. Under some circumstances, Islamization can result in laws and applications of law that are repugnant to liberal understandings of law. Under other circumstances, however, it can result in laws and applications of law that may not embrace liberalism for its own sake, but nevertheless produce results that are more liberal in practice than any stable secular constitutional order is likely to be. It remains a provocative possibility that, as Cornelius suggested, in some countries some kinds of Islamization – and beyond that, *some kinds of religious constitutionalism* – might be something not simply to tolerate, but also to encourage and facilitate.

[119] See, e.g., Robin Bush, Philip Fountain, and Michael Feener (eds.), *Religion and the Politics of Development: Critical Perspectives on Asia* (New York: Palgrave Macmillan, 2015).

[120] See e.g., Jan Michiel Otto, *Sharia and National Law in Muslim Countries: Tensions and Opportunities for Dutch and EU Foreign Policy* (Amsterdam University Press, 2008), 11–14.

PART IV

Solidarity

9

Rousseau's Radical Constitutionalism and Its Legacy

MARCO GOLDONI

I. Introduction: Rousseau and Liberal Political Philosophy

The modern constitutional tradition has been dominated by liberal political theory. Alternative interpretations have, however, emerged from time to time, like a Carsic river, offering views of modern constitutionalism that are not based on liberal assumptions.[1] This chapter will offer a reconstruction of Jean-Jacques Rousseau's constitutional thought – drawing not only on his political theory but also on his critique of modern political economy, private property, and social inequality – as a source of inspiration for an alternative to the dominant liberal paradigm.

In light of allegations that Rousseau's philosophy is illiberal[2] and even totalitarian,[3] this might appear a redundant operation. But such critiques, even if defensible, are of little analytic utility from a constitutional perspective: Because in presenting Rousseau in terms of what he is not, that is, liberal, these critiques tell us nothing about what he is. To show that Rousseau did not contribute to the liberal constitutional tradition is not to show that he has not contributed to constitutionalism at all.[4] As this chapter will demonstrate, such critiques, in and of themselves, serve principally to impoverish both our appreciation for Rousseau and, more importantly insofar as this volume is concerned, our appreciation for the possibilities of constitutionalism.

[1] Cf. Antonio Negri, *Insurgencies: Constituent Power and the Modern State* (trans., M. Boscagli) (Minneapolis: University of Minnesota Press, 1999).

[2] See, generally, Jean Roussel, *Jean-Jacques Rousseau en France après la Révolution* (Paris: Colin, 1972), 497–499.

[3] See, generally, Jacob Talmon, *The Origins of Totalitarian Democracy* (London: Secker and Warburg, 1950).

[4] But see Ruzha Smilova, 'The General Will Constitution: Rousseau as a Constitutionalist', in Denis Galligan (ed.), *Constitutions and the Classics* (Oxford University Press, 2014), 265–289; Martin Loughlin, *Foundations of Public Law* (Oxford University Press, 2010), ch. 4.

This chapter will show that, in fact, Rousseau's constitutionalism belongs to an alternative constitutional tradition of what we might call 'radical' constitutionalism – a tradition that is best interpreted as a form of republicanism, but which is highly sensitive to social conditions and substantive equality. To see this, we will first need to examine his germinal work, *The Social Contract* (1762) (hereinafter *SC*),[5] as it relates to his earlier and more overtly political works – primarily the *Discourse on the Origin and Basis of Inequality among Men* (*DOI*)[6] and the *Discourse on Political Economy* (*DPE*),[7] both published in 1755. We will then track Rousseau's contribution to other versions of non-liberal constitutionalism – to that of the French Revolution (and specifically on the Jacobin constitutional model); then, more obliquely, to that of the Marxist political tradition; and, finally, to contemporary republican constitutionalism. And moreover, and unlike critiques that simply present Rousseau as illiberal, it will show how recognising Rousseau as representative of an alternative constitutional tradition shows us something very important about the possibilities of constitutionalism that liberal visions of constitutionalism cannot see.

II. Rousseau's Constitutional Question: Liberty *and* Equality

The key to the anti-liberal interpretation of Rousseau's constitutionalism lies in Rousseau's ambitious attempt to reconcile (political) freedom and substantive equality. But this is also one of Rousseau's most original contributions to modern constitutionalism. This chapter will show how substantive equality is the key concept in tracing a radical critique of the classical political economy. And from this critique stems a radical overcoming of liberal constitutionalism.

The quest of uniting freedom and substantive equality lies at the heart of Rousseau's most constitutionalist work, *The Social Contract*. In the second book of *SC* we are famously told that:

> if we seek to define precisely the greatest good of all, the necessary goal of every system of legislation, we shall find that the main objectives are limited to two only: *liberty* and *equality*; liberty, because any form of

[5] See, generally, Jean-Jacques Rousseau, 'The Social Contract', in *The Social Contract* (trans., Christopher Betts) (Oxford University Press, 1994), 43–168.

[6] See, generally, Jean-Jacques Rousseau, *A Discourse on Inequality* (trans., Maurice Cranston) (London: Penguin, 1984).

[7] See, generally, Jean-Jacques Rousseau, 'Discourse on Political Economy', in *The Social Contract* (trans., Christopher Betts) (Oxford University Press, 1994), 1–42.

> particular subordination means that the body of the state loses some degree of strength; and equality because liberty cannot subsist without it.[8]

To grasp why the composition of freedom and substantive equality is Rousseau's key constitutional question requires understanding his criticism of political economy. This is not to say that the relation between freedom and equality is ever fully settled by Rousseau. Recently, Frederick Neuhouser has put forward a solid argument that equality (and in particular economic equality) has only instrumental value in Rousseau's constitutionalism, with freedom alone having intrinsic value.[9] While this reading cannot be ruled out, it nevertheless downplays the role that substantive equality has in the structuring of Rousseau's constitutionalism.

To avoid any misunderstanding, two points must be highlighted. Rousseau himself refers to the impossibility of a perfect substantive equality just after the *SC* passage quoted in the preceding paragraph: 'as for equality, the word must not be taken to mean that the degrees of power and wealth should be exactly the same'.[10] In fact this point was already fully recognised in the last section of *DOI*: 'moral inequality, authorised by positive law alone, is contrary to natural right, whenever it is not matched in exact proportion with physical inequality'.[11] Equality has a significant substantive dimension, but it cannot be measured using some rigorous mathematical weighing. Along these lines, Rousseau also recognises the existence of diverse forms of substantive equality – such as where, in a language later taken up by Pierre Bourdieu, symbolic or social capital, rather than material welfare, is at stake.[12] As evident from Rousseau's discussion of the role of private property, for example, equality is directly addressed to the conditions of subsistence, but not just that. Equality in power and education are all immanent to the shaping of a specific type of citizen without whom a truly political constitution would be impossible.

The second remark, which follows, is that equality plays a guiding role in Rousseau's work. At a critical level, it is the basis upon

[8] Rousseau, *Social Contract*, 86–87 (bk. 2, ch.11).

[9] Frederick Neuhouser, 'Rousseau's Critique of Economic Inequality', *Philosophy and Public Affairs* 41 (2013): 193–215. But see Stephen Ellenburg, 'Rousseau and Kant: Principles of Political Right', in Ralph Leigh (ed.), *Rousseau after Two Hundred Years* (Cambridge University Press, 1982), 3–22.

[10] Rousseau, *Social Contract*, 87.

[11] Rousseau, *Discourse on Inequality*, 137.

[12] See also Eoin Daly, 'Austerity and Stability in Rousseau's Constitutionalism', *Jurisprudence* 5 (2013): 191–192.

which the Geneva philosopher erects his criticism of modern forms of socialisation. At a normative level, it is the bedrock of his constitutional ideal: 'instead of destroying natural equality, the fundamental contract substitutes moral and legal equality for whatever degree of physical inequality nature has put among men; they may be unequal in strength or intelligence, but all become equal through agreed convention and by right'.[13] In other words, equality serves a double function in his work: It illuminates the shortcomings of the political economy of modern society, and it provides the ground for a more radical type of constitutionalism.

Such emphasis on substantive equality remains largely missing in the tradition of classical liberal constitutionalism, except in its formalist legalist guise.[14] The radical consequence of the focus on substantive equality takes the form of an alternative view of the relation between society and constitutionalism. The lesson to learn from this reading of Rousseau's work is that the modern development of society brings about the dominance of particular and selfish interests, blocking any possible reconciliation with more authentic forms of individual and collective participation (i.e., the value of self-government) with claims of equality (i.e., the value of justice). In this light, Rousseau's constitutionalism is decidedly anti-liberal because he grasps (whether fully realising it or not) the dilemma of modern liberal society, exposing the inadequacy of its formalistic solution to the problem of equality.

This reading brings Rousseau's work closer to an anticipation of the Marxist critique of ideology. Both thinkers share the idea that the realisation of a truly political constitution (i.e., one that restores political power directly to the citizens while respecting substantial equality) entails the transformation of society and its foundational economic structure. Procedural or formal democracy, although necessary, is insufficient to resolve the dilemma of self-government and substantive equality. This way of framing the constitutional question does, of course, raise an obvious problem: How can freedom and substantive equality be concretely reconciled with one another? Even after Rousseau, the tension between these two poles remains. But as we shall see immediately below, Rousseau's attempt is nonetheless valuable because he incorporates a critique of classical political economy into his constitutional theory.

[13] Rousseau, *Social Contract*, 62.

[14] See, e.g., Jeremy Waldron, *Liberal Rights* (Cambridge University Press, 1993), ch. 16.

III. The Political Economy of Constitutionalism: The Function of Private Property

Along these lines, the best starting point to grasp Rousseau's alternative constitutionalism is to look at how property is defined. For it is in this that we can see how Rousseau's constitutionalism derives from his critique of classical political economy (although is arguable how much Rousseau himself *knew* modern political economy[15]) and how alternative it is to Locke's constitutionalism. In brief, the key contrast is that Locke's liberal constitutionalism is organised as a device for protecting the right to private property.[16] Of course, as Peter Laslett reminds us, Locke's use of property has to be retrieved carefully because the word is often employed in its wide sense to include the idea of self-ownership. In this sense, property extends to life and liberty as well as estates or goods.[17] But as noted by Macpherson, most of the references to property in the Second Treatise are to material or real goods.[18] Thus, it is still material property that is the focal point of the constitution and is protected more fiercely than life or liberty. Estates and goods are defined as untouchable because they constitute the main glue of the family, even more than the components of the family itself. Last but not least, we might also note that according to Locke, the creation of government is the effect of a *second* social contract, after the one instituting society, and the rationale for this need for a second contract derives from the special capacity of the government to protect property rights from socially driven encroachments.

As is well known, title to property, according to Locke, is acquired in the first place through labour. Yet, after the initial appropriation, and despite the notion of limits imposed upon it, a silent consensus accrues on the possibility and desirability of unlimited accumulation of wealth. In this way, legal entitlement to property becomes subject to exchange through contract. Circulation of property, and hence the development of an exchange economy, is enabled by the creation of money.[19] This is a key passage in Locke's reasoning because the introduction of money is seen as a neutral act supported by a consensus to pursue unlimited accumulation: 'and thus

[15] See Birtel Friden, *Rousseau's Economic Philosophy* (Dordrecht, The Netherlands: Kluwer 1998); see also Céline Spector, 'Rousseau et la critique de l'économie politique', in Bruno Bernardi (ed.), *Rousseau et les sciences* (Paris: L'Harmattan, 2003), 237–256.

[16] Jeremy Waldron, *The Right to Private Property* (Oxford University Press, 1988), ch. 6.

[17] Peter Laslett, 'Introduction', in John Locke, *Second Treatise on Civil Government* (ed. Peter Laslett) (Cambridge University Press, 1980), 102–104.

[18] Crawford Macpherson, *The Political Theory of Possessive Individualism* (Oxford University Press, 1962), 232–233.

[19] See also Ellen Meiksins Wood, *Liberty and Property* (London: Verso, 2012), 266–283.

came in the use of Money, some lasting thing that Men might keep without spoiling, and that by mutual consent Men would take in exchange for the truly useful'.[20] The emergence of money is presented as a harmless outcome of the creation of exchange value.

Locke disentangles labour from money only by omitting to note that labour itself is generative of exchange value and not only an activity capable of use value.[21] Inequality in property and wealth is justified through the fiction of a silent consensus with regard to the introduction of exchange value and its unit of measurement, that is, money. The natural limits imposed on the personal labour of an owner can be overcome by allowing the appropriation of the fruits of somebody else's work. Such a move is justified by the industriousness of the owner, which can improve the value of the object of property.

In contrast to Locke, Rousseau's constitutionalism is not conceived as a device for protecting a natural right to property. It is oriented toward the general interest, with private property assuming a derivate form.[22] This contrast is highlighted in their treatment of land. There are two aspects to this, both announced in *SC* where Rousseau discusses the touchstone of property, and most particularly land:

> In general, the following conditions are required in order to justify the right of first occupancy for a given piece of land. First, the land must as yet be uninhabited; secondly, no more must be occupied than is needed for subsistence; and in the third place, possession must be taken not by empty ceremonies but by work and cultivation, the only mark of ownership which ought, in default of juridical title, to be respected by others.[23]

The first theme is the limitation of private property in accordance with the needs of each, a theme linked, through the *DOI*, to the subsistence of each citizen and its family. The criterion of subsistence operates in two directions: It establishes a threshold that cannot be overcome, but it also introduces a minimum standard necessary to achieve independence. A passage from the Geneva Manuscript of the *SC* addressing the situation of a cession of land that would leave the seller in a situation of dependence demonstrates that without leaving a minimum amount of property, there

[20] John Locke, *Two Treatises of Government* (ed. Peter Laslett) (Cambridge University Press, 1980), 300–301.

[21] Cf. Karl Marx, *Capital* (Oxford University Press, 1988), part I, chs. 1–3.

[22] See also Robert Derathé, *Jean-Jacques Rousseau et la science politique de son temps* (Paris: Presses Universitaires de France, 1950), 113–120.

[23] Rousseau, *Social Contract*, 60–61.

can be no meaningful citizenship: 'As for what concerns the conditions of this agreement, it is clear that they are illegitimate and void [Quant aux conditions de cet accord, il est très évident qu'elles sont illégitimes et nulles].'[24] Just as in the case of the alienation of freedom, the cession of a minimum quantity of land necessary for subsistence is not valid. This is the basis of a concrete conception of freedom: without a minimum amount of property there is no space for self-government because relations of domination easily spread across society.

The second main difference is found in the idea of labour as a source of legitimacy for the original acquisition of property. While Locke introduces, after the original appropriation, the conditions of use and improvement that allow him to shift attention to the preservation of land's fertility and then the possibility of appropriating other people's work through contract and money, Rousseau maintains that personal labour remains the legitimating factor for property. The right to property, therefore, comes from one's continuous personal labour in utilising and maintaining it, it is the 'only mark of ownership'. This ensures that the cycle of production is directly tied to consumption and subsistence and not to accumulation. As emphasised in *DOI*,[25] the great transformation occurs when men decide to start accumulating resources not for immediate but for future consumption, and instrumental rationality opens up a space for an autonomous form of economic activity.

Contrary to Locke's irenic account of the legitimacy of social inequality, Rousseau locates the seeds of the further corruption of men in the process of social differentiation. Division of labour, uneven distribution of wealth, and the rise of a distorted form of pride (*amour propre*) become co-extensive with society. Far from Locke's pacified presentation of the emergence of private property, the prose of the *DOI*, with its dramatic overtones, identifies property as corrosive and an obstacle to the end of equality:

> [F]rom the instant one man needed the help of another, and it was found to be useful for one man to have provisions enough for two, equality disappeared, property was introduced, work became necessary, and vast forests were transformed into pleasant fields which had to be watered with the sweat of men, and where slavery and misery were soon to germinate and flourish with crops.[26]

[24] Alberto Burgio, *Eguaglianza, interesse, unanimità. La politica di Rousseau* (Napoli: Bibliopolis, 1989), 191 (translation by author).

[25] Rousseau, *Discourse on Inequality*, 116–120.

[26] Id. at 116.

Rousseau offers a historical approach to labour in contrast to Locke's naturalistic approach. According to Locke, labour is any process of altering a thing from its original indistinct condition. This can be equivalent to mere acquisition: collecting walnuts, boiling them, or even eating and digesting them – all are activities that amount to labour. In other words, labour is a natural activity. In Rousseau's philosophy, by contrast, labour is conceived as socially constructed from the very beginning.[27] The moment of appropriation, according to Rousseau, takes its meaning vis-à-vis the social context. It is the functional link of appropriation to the common good of society that justifies the connection between the owner and the things that are regarded as being her 'property'.

Locke cannot account for the role of labour in the formation of exchange value because he does not examine the consequences of the commodification of labour. In Marxist terms, one could say that Locke postulates the move from labour as source of use value to labour as source of exchange value without further enquiring on the constitutive role of abstract labour as the enabling condition for the creation of economic value. In fact, he does not thematise the creation of wage labour (i.e., abstract labour subject to market transaction in the form of a commodity) and he justifies the employment relation simply on the basis of the consent given by the worker through contract. Had Locke taken the *social meaning* of property into account, he would have had to explain inequality as something created by the social contract itself.

Obviously, this choice would have made it much more difficult for him to justify the social status quo and would have pushed him toward a critical analysis of the commercial society. Locke cannot treat the roots of social inequality because his basic assumptions make them invisible or irrelevant, as is evident from one of the few passages (§ 54) where the issue of difference (of age, talent, and virtue) is addressed, but immediately rationalised as consistent with men's equality before the law:

> Though I have said above.... *That all men by nature are equal*, I cannot be supposed to understand all sorts of *equality*: *age* or *virtue* may give men a just precedency: *excellency* of *parts* and *merit* may place others above the common level: *birth* may subject some, and *alliance* or *benefits* others, to pay an observance to those to whom nature, gratitude, or other respects, may have made it due: and yet all this consists with the *equality*, which all men are in, in respect of jurisdiction or dominion one over another; which was the equality I there spoke of, as proper to the business in hand, being

[27] See also Victor Goldschmidt, *Anthropologie et politique. Les principes du système de Rousseau* (Paris: Vrin, 1974), 527.

> that *equal right*, that every man hath, to his *natural freedom*, without being subjected to the will or authority of any other man.[28]

All this reinforces Locke's assumption that there is continuity between the natural and the civil condition of human beings. Such continuity is achieved using a common denominator of freedom expressed through consent. If there is poverty and unemployment, it is only because of some men's moral ineptitude and laziness.[29]

Rousseau's treatment of social inequality, by contrast, gives him a firm grounding from which to criticise the rise of the commercial society in a way that Locke cannot see. Rousseau's republic does not leave any legitimate space for the financial appropriation of labour. Such appropriation is not grounded on consent, as per Locke, but on the financial codification of uneven and unfair social relations. In a discussion devoted to the perverse effects of representation, Rousseau notes:

> [when] service done in person is changed into money because people are busy with their trade or craft, greedily self-interested for profit, lovers of comfort and material possessions ... pay out money and soon you will be in chains. The word *finance* is for slaves, it is unknown in a real state. In a truly free state, the citizens do everything with their own hands, and nothing with money.[30]

Rousseau's vehement denunciation of finance shows not only the stark rejection of an economy of signs and symbols, but also an acute awareness of money as a vector of concrete power relations. In that respect, Rousseau's constitutional thought is driven by a conscious and material criticism of classical political economy. Famously, he describes his contemporary societies as associations 'which powerfully protect(s) the rich man's immense possessions, while scarcely permitting the poor man the enjoyment of the cottage which he has built with his own hands'.[31] Here, the structural difference between the rich and the poor is still at the forefront of the argument: 'Are not all the advantages of society for the rich and powerful? Are not all the lucrative posts filled by them alone?'[32] Once this difference is introduced, there is no possibility of avoiding the corruptive

28 Locke, *Two Treatises of Government*, 309.

29 Cf. Maurice Cranston, *John Locke: A Biography* (London: Longmans, 1957), 88–89. See also Peter Laslett, 'John Locke, the Great Recoinage and the Origins of the Board of Trade: 1695–1698', *William and Mary Quarterly* 14 (1957): 370–402.

30 Rousseau, *Social Contract*, 126.

31 Rousseau, 'Discourse on Political Economy', 34.

32 Id. See also id. at 36.

consequences, and even an equal distribution of wealth is 'chimerique', as Rousseau notes in this enticing unpublished short piece on luxury:

> [E]ven if this wealth is distributed equally, it is still sure that it will spread unequally eventually. This is because either wealth will not naturally remain in a state of equality or its value will become irrelevant for its owners. In fact, for the wealth beyond necessity, it is only because of the differences that the advantages of fortune become effective.[33]

Rousseau's conceptualisation of property needs to be interpreted through the lens of his key notion of the general will, introduced for the first time in *DEP*.[34] Overall, he does recognise property as a 'right', but only to a limited level – that level necessary for an independent life. In other words, one's right to property only extends to that amount of property necessary for subsistence.[35] This led him, in contrast to Locke,[36] to see both the right to property and consent to taxation as properly deriving from the general will and not the individual will. This is because of the psychological dynamics that he sees attending to wealth accumulation. In one of Rousseau's unpublished works provisionally entitled *Discours sur les richesses*[37] (possibly written around the same time of the *DOI*), Rousseau sets up an imaginary interlocutor, Crisophile, attributing to him the desire to become wealthy for philanthropic reasons. Only in this way, so the argument goes, will he be able to help the poor. Rousseau's confutation of this argument is merciless: It is impossible to be rich and virtuous, or rich and happy. The logic behind the accumulation of wealth is the denial of the humanity of the poor; the human condition of affluence denies the possibility of individual autonomy because the rich end up in the grip of its logic. Similarly, in a fragment on luxury and the arts, possibly written around the same time of the *DPE*, Rousseau makes explicit the sources of gratification attached to the condition of personal affluence. The main benefit given by wealth is privilege, that is, the valorisation of the superfluous through the exclusion of the poor. One can enjoy the status of being wealthy only as long as there are others excluded from it.

It is important to note that Rousseau's political economy is remarkably distinct not only from liberal constitutionalism, but also from his

33 Jean-Jacques Rousseau, 'Le luxe, le commerce et les arts', in *Ouevres completes*. Vol. 2 (Paris: Gallimard, 1959), 522 (translation by author).

34 See, generally, Patrick Riley, 'Rousseau's General Will', in *Cambridge Companion to Rousseau* (ed., Patrick Riley) (Cambridge University Press, 2001) 124–155.

35 Rousseau, 'Discourse on Political Economy', 34; see also id. at 36.

36 Compare Locke, *Two Treatises of Government*, 138.

37 See also John O'Neal, 'Rousseau's Theory of Wealth', *History of European Ideas* 7 (1986): 453.

contemporaries in the republican tradition. Whereas in eighteenth-century republicanism, trade and commerce are accepted as the building blocks of political economy and incorporated into republican constitutional projects,[38] Rousseau's political economy advocates agriculture and craftsmanship as the central economic activities, and shows an acute awareness that commercial exchange beyond the threshold of the means of subsistence leads to corruption and the reification of power differentials. Rousseau cannot accept the argument – advanced by Montesquieu, Hume, and Smith, among many others – of the '*doux commerce*' because he rejects the postulate of a harmonic composition of different interests.[39]

The centrality attributed to agriculture should not, however, confuse Rousseau for an ally of the Physiocrats, whose constitutional doctrine might still be compatible with liberal constitutionalism.[40] Although certain key themes are treated in similar ways, two differences set him apart. First, Rousseau assumes an incompatibility between agriculture and commerce. Second, Rousseau cannot accept the idea of a *natural* economic order. Therefore, although this opens Rousseau to the critique of primitivism (usually associated with his alleged incompetence in the economic sciences), his political economy is not grounded on exchange and accumulation. On the contrary, Rousseau's political economy is first of all a theory of government where what we would define today as 'the economic system' is given a subsidiary role. In this way, Rousseau avoids disentangling the economic from the political and, whether intentionally or not, provides a material basis for his constitutionalism. Following this path, the value of political equality is linked to social equality in a way that foreshadows Marx's critique of a formalist interpretation of the 'rights of man' in *On the Jewish Question*.[41]

IV. The Pathologies of the Liberal Social Contract

At first sight, one might perceive a common thread between Rousseau and classic contractualist authors such as Hobbes, Pufendorf, and Locke.

[38] See J. G. A. Pocock, *Virtue, Commerce and History* (Cambridge University Press, 1985); see also Adam Tomkins, 'On Republican Constitutionalism in the Age of Commerce', in Samantha Besson and José Marttí (eds.), *Legal Republicanism* (Oxford University Press, 2009), 316–336.

[39] Spector, 'Rousseau et la critique de l'economie politique', 242.

[40] See, generally, Catherine Larrére, *L'invention de l'économie aux XVIIIeme Siécle* (Paris: Presses Universitaires de France, 1992).

[41] See also David Leopold, *The Young Marx* (Cambridge University Press, 2007), 198.

Rousseau's social contract narrative looks similar to theirs: sharing an individualistic premise based on the strategic rationality of human beings facing the undesirability of the state of nature:

> I make the assumption that there is a point in the development of mankind at which the obstacles to men's self-preservation in the state of nature are too great to be overcome by the strength that any one individual can exert in order to maintain himself in this state. The original state can then subsist no longer, and the human race would perish if it did not change its mode of existence.[42]

Rousseau resorts here to the language of costs and benefits in order to explain why human beings opt for the social contract. The rational actors see it as a beneficial exchange:

> [N]othing is truly renounced by private individuals under the social contract ... instead of abandoning anything they have simply made a beneficial transfer, exchanging an uncertain and precarious mode of existence for a better and more secure one, natural independence for liberty, the power of hurting others for their own safety.[43]

But it does not take long for the reader to discern that this individualistic language is misleading, employed tactically to enable Rousseau to position himself within the social contract tradition. In fact, another logic is at play: It is actually through the negation of individual autonomy – that is, through renouncing completely to the natural right to freedom – that the social contract is realised:

> If individuals retained some rights, there being no common superior to give judgment between them and the public, each would make his own judgement on certain points, and would soon aspire to do so on all of them: the state of nature would remain in force, and the association would become, necessarily, either tyrannical or meaningless.[44]

In fact, there is much more going on in Rousseau's social contract than the mere deployment of strategic rationality. The move from the state of nature to society is driven not by individual autonomy and private interest, but rather by the general constraint of the common interest. The primacy of the common over the private interest is demonstrated by the transformative aspect of the social contract. This is not an external dynamic – that is, the simple act of agreeing with some other (or, at least, it is

[42] Rousseau, *Social Contract*, 54.

[43] Id. at 70.

[44] Id. at 55.

not only that) – but an internal process: a transforming of one's identity.[45] The complete alienation of one's rights brings about nothing less than a profound change in the subject, realising what Balibar calls 'political individuality'.[46] Rousseau's social contract thus foreshadows a critique of instrumental reasoning and its reductive depiction of social relations.

In other words, in contrast to Hobbes and Locke, Rousseau's social contract requires an anthropological mutation. The individual emerges from it radically transformed into a citizen, 'replacing instinct by justice in his behaviour, and conferring on his actions the moral quality that they had lacked before'.[47] The transformation entails no less than the acquisition of moral status. In light of this consideration, Rousseau's effort aims at transcending, if not utterly dismissing, the liberal version of the social contract: The only way to overcome the corruptive and dysfunctional logic of liberal (economic) autonomy is to build a different social being upon the bases of the primacy of the public interest and a strong and substantial conception of equality.

Three further aspects of Rousseau's notion of the social contract, articulated in the *SC* and in later works, confirm the insufficiency of the liberal, contractarian logic for the construction of a society. First, the figure of the 'Legislator', who is supposed to frame the fundamental laws and submit them for the community's approval,[48] exists outside the reach of social contract. To establish a proper constitution, a legislator external to society is necessary. Although the precise nature of the Legislator is something of a mystery,[49] the combination of its foundational necessity for the social contract together with its essential existence outside that contract represents a fundamental denial of the social contract's grounding in individual autonomy. Second, political association in Rousseau does not simply reify in the social context what is already available in the state of nature. His social contract is much more demanding: As we saw, it requires the transformation of the individual herself into a fully conscious citizen. Third, from his description of the role played by the

[45] Luc Vincenti, *Jean-Jacques Rousseau. L'individu et la république* (Paris: Kimé, 2001), 159.

[46] Etienne Balibar, *La crainte des masses: Politique et philosophie avant et après Marx* (Paris: Galilée, 1997), 102.

[47] Rousseau, *Social Contract*, 59.

[48] See also Melissa Schwartzberg, 'Rousseau on Fundamental Law', *Political Studies* 51 (2003): 387–403.

[49] See Raymond Polin, *Jean-Jacques Rousseau et son oeuvre* (Paris: Klincksieck, 1964) 231–247; Harvey Fireside, 'The Concept of the Legislator in Rousseau's Social Contract', *The Review of Politics* 82 (1970): 191–216; Maurizio Viroli, *Jean-Jacques Rousseau and the 'Well-Ordered Society'* (Cambridge University Press, 2003), 185–186.

customs and the morals of the people, it is clear that Rousseau understands the state's laws as reflecting a concrete community ethos.[50] Laws are clearly 'general' in a double sense: (1) because of their general subjects and objects; but also (2) because they have to rest upon the general customs and virtues of citizens, otherwise they will have no traction.

V. The Constitution of the General Will

How is Rousseau's critique of political economy translated into constitutional thought? The starting point is given by the non-liberal assumption that the sovereign power is immanent to society, in the form of the general will. There is no *pactum subjectionis*. Neither the government nor the general will is constituted by a pact. Instead, Rousseau invents a particular figure he calls 'the Legislator', a figure that exists outside of the general will and calls it into being, and in doing so separates, or draws a distinction, between sovereignty and government.[51] And the purpose of the constitution is to allow and guarantee the realisation of that law. Under this vision, the ultimate purpose of the constitution is to enable, rather than constrain.[52]

Two principal goals animate Rousseau's constitutional model. The first, to be achieved by the essential building block, the concept of the general will, which squares the constitutional circle of (positive) freedom and substantive equality. The second is to frame the relation between government and sovereign power.

First, the lawmaking process, which is the supreme constitutional function, is to be governed by the general will. Sovereignty is manifested through the exercise of the general will and has a 'general' character, it cannot be represented or transferred.[53] Of course, one available interpretation, one with some textual grounding, pits the contrast between particular interests and the common interest in a moral fashion. Accordingly, the general will would function as the moral interpretation of what ought to be the case *in abstracto*. The radical potential of Rousseau's understanding of the social contract is lost in this reading, and reduced to a moral denunciation of the corruption of modern times. What is missing from

[50] Rousseau, *Social Contract*, 89–90.

[51] Id. at 16.

[52] Cf. Emile Durkheim, *Montesquieu and Rousseau: Forerunners of Sociology* (Ann Arbor: University of Michigan Press, 1960).

[53] Rousseau, *Social Contract*, 63.

this interpretation is the material dimension of the conflict between the two wills.

The crux of the concept of the general will lies in the relationship between common and individual interest. Read in continuity with the *DOI* and *DEP*, the general will should not be understood as an abstract or transcendental normative standard. The common interest springs out of a conflict, one of the central conflicts in modernity, because the general will is opposed to the 'will of all' (*volonté de tous*). The general will legislates from the perspective of a critique of modernity, which means *against* a model of political economy based on exchange, division of labour, and the anti-social understanding of private property.

The vantage point for grasping the concept of the general will is the historical experience of domination. In other words, the conflict between the will of all and the general will is a material conflict in which the general will is that universalisable will that includes the experiences of the poor and the dispossessed. The concrete experiences that give rise to this conflict do not necessarily generate full awareness of the structural condition of domination from the side of the dominated, or at least not at that stage. But at the very least, they do give rise to a claim to equality. And this in turn allows the articulation of a *common* interest of the community that transcends mere aggregation of preferences or political compromises.

The second concern of Rousseau's theory lies clearly within the wider tradition of modern constitutionalism: to avoid the illegitimate cession of the people's sovereignty and prevent arbitrary and absolutist uses of its power. In that respect, Rousseau remains a thinker in the constitutionalist tradition, concerned with the limitation of governmental power. But unlike classical, Anglo liberalism, Rousseau does not locate the need to limited government in the need to protect the rights of individual autonomy, but in the need to protect the authority of the sovereign.[54] For Rousseau, 'limited government' is functional to sovereign power because it does not restrain it.

We see this distinction most clearly in contrasting Rousseau's vision of 'separation of power' with that of his contemporary, the Baron de Montesquieu. Montesquieu's constitutional thought pivots on an ideal of moderate government through which capacity for social change is limited in order to avoid disorder and to make efficient use of a scarce good such as civic virtue. Hence, the separation of powers is really a particular form

[54] See also Bruno Bernardi, *La fabrique des concepts. Recherches sur l'invention conceptuelle chez Rousseau* (Paris: Champion, 2006).

of 'mixed government' where only the most powerful estates (*puissances*) really enjoy a share in the governing function. Albeit a precious deposit of a series of brilliant insights,[55] the *Spirit of the Laws* remains an in-between work, torn between medieval and modern constitutionalism,[56] where the principle of the separation of powers actually operates as a constitutional tool for preserving social inequality.[57]

Rousseau's constitutional model, by contrast, is much more radical. It aims at transforming society, not constraining the sovereign. Rousseau does believe that government ought to be constrained, not because it might otherwise bring about unwise social change, but because it might obstruct the demands of the general will. The principle of separation of powers does not constitute a negative device, but precisely a way of empowering the people by keeping sovereignty and government apart. The following sections will show the reasons why authors or political actors in search of an alternative to liberal constitutionalism looked at its work as a source for inspiration.

While Rousseau is not always consistent in the way he treats the relationship between sovereignty and government, his definition of government stands out: 'it is an intermediate body set up between subjects and sovereign to ensure their mutual correspondence, and is entrusted simply with the *execution* of laws and with the maintenance of liberty, both social and political'.[58] The government is not involved in the construction or approval of the laws; it is not involved in the expression of the general will.[59] To separate and subordinate government from and to the law-making function (which is expressive of the general will) is the only way to preserve popular sovereignty from corruption or decadence:

> It is not good that the person who makes laws should execute them, nor that the body of the people should turn its attention from general considerations towards particular matters. Nothing is more dangerous than the influence of private interests in public affairs, and the abuse of law by the

[55] See Louis Althusser, *Politics and History: Montesquieu, Rousseau, Marx* (London: Verso, 2007), ch. 1.

[56] But see Judith Shklar, *Montesquieu* (Oxford University Press, 1987).

[57] See also Charles Eisenmann, '*L'Esprit des lois* et la separation des pouvoirs', in *Mélanges R. Carré de Malberg* (Paris: Duchemin, 1933), 165–192.

[58] Rousseau, *Social Contract*, 92.

[59] Cf. John Scott, 'Rousseau's Anti-Agenda Setting and Contemporary Democratic Theory', *American Political Science Review* 99 (2005): 137–144; Ethan Putterman, 'Rousseau on the People as Legislative Gatekeepers, Not Framers', *American Political Science Review* 99 (2005): 145–151.

government is a lesser evil than the corruption of the legislative body, to which particular considerations inevitably lead.[60]

To further constrain the government, Rousseau also suggests fixed periodic assemblies of the people where they can express the general will.[61] In the fourth book of the *SC*, he introduces another institutional 'body', the Tribunate, whose function is to preserve the laws and the legislative power, in particular in their relations with government: 'sometimes its role is to protect the sovereign body from the government'.[62] The Tribunate prevents abuses of power and its constitutional function is fully preventive, that is, it can stop other bodies from acting, but it cannot take any initiative.

VI. Rousseau in the Jacobin Experience: The Radical Model of Constitutionalism

Rousseau is often characterised as setting the stage for the political philosophy of the French Revolution.[63] The French Revolution was (and is) an enormous repository of constitutional projects and ideas,[64] which are often expressed with key Rousseauvian concepts. For example, the essential idea of the general will seemed to have been accepted by all major actors of the revolution. A classic instantiation is Article 6 of the 1789 Declaration of the Rights of Man, which states that 'Law is the expression of the general will'.

On a shallow reading, one might find Rousseau's influence pervasive and effective in all French revolutionary traditions, but apart for a superficial reception of some of his main ideas, not all revolutionaries adopted Rousseau's constitutional model. It is tempting to see the general will as being synonymous with 'sovereign will'.[65] But the concept of the general will cannot be easily transposed into a constitutional system founded on majority rule, division of labour, and the politics of liberal freedoms. Among the main revolutionary traditions, the Jacobins were the most receptive to Rousseau's constitutional lessons. His influence operated at

60 Rousseau, *Social Contract*, 101. See also Derathé, *Rousseau et la science politique*, 307.

61 Rousseau, *Social Contract*, 123. See also Judith Shklar, *Men and Citizens* (Cambridge University Press, 1969), 20.

62 Rousseau, *Social Contract*, 151.

63 See, generally, Joan MacDonald, *Rousseau and the French Revolution: 1762–1791* (London: Athlon Press, 1965).

64 Egon Zweig, *Die Lehre vom Pouvoir Constituant* (Tübingen, Germany: Mohr, 1909), 28.

65 Cf. McDonald, *Rousseau and the French Revolution 1762–1791*, 11–13. See also Iring Fetscher, *Rousseaus Politische Philosophie* (Berlin: Neuwied, 1960).

a double level: on the formation of the political thought of the Jacobin leaders, and on the formulation of the Constitution of Year I (June 24, 1793). In that respect, it is easy to agree with François Furet when he writes that Rousseau's 'political thought set up well in advance the conceptual framework of what was to become Jacobinism and the language of Revolution'.[66]

The Jacobins' constitution represents the most accomplished instantiation of the radical model of modern constitutionalism.[67] And herein lies the source of Rousseau's appeal. Among the Jacobins, Jean-Paul Marat, Louis Antoine de Saint-Just, and obviously Maximilien Robespierre were the leading figures for whom Rousseau's political philosophy was a fix point of reference. Marat acknowledged explicitly Rousseau's influence on his work. This influence is obvious in his main work, *The Chains of Slavery*, published originally in English in 1774, but it can also be found in earlier in other writings published in the decade before the inception of the Revolution. Marat shares Rousseau's views on nature and history,[68] and the stark criticism of luxury and commerce; he endorses the basic tenets of Rousseau's constitutional thought, like the admiration for the Spartan and Roman models and the primacy of direct self-government. In the wake of the Revolution, when popular sovereignty is conceived in the context of the modern state, Marat proposes a conception of political representation highly indebted to the *Considerations on the Government of Poland* (1772): The legislature has to be separated from the executive; legislative representatives have to be elected with an imperative mandate;[69] but they also must function as commissaries, because – as per Rousseau – there can be no real delegation of sovereign power.[70]

Saint-Just's relation to Rousseau was more complex, and it changed during his revolutionary experience (possibly around the second half of 1793).[71] His first writings deal with numerous Rousseauvian themes and adopt the general will as their key normative reference. But he sees the general will as almost anti-volontaristic, as an objective and rational phenomenon. References to other Rousseauvian ideas are also frequent and

66 Francois Furet, *Interpreting the French Revolution* (Cambridge University Press, 1981), 31.

67 Maurizio Fioravanti, *Costituzionalismo* (Bari: Laterza, 2009), 108.

68 See, generally, Jean Ehrard, *L'idée de nature en France dans la 1e moitié du XVIIIe siècle* (Paris: Flammarion, 1963).

69 See Jean-Paul Maret, *La constitution, ou projet de declaration des droits de l'homme et du citoyen* (Paris: Chez Buisson, 1789).

70 See Ehrard, *L'idée de nature en France*, 22–23.

71 See, generally, Norman Hampson, *Saint-Just* (Oxford: Blackwell, 1991).

relevant. Among many other signs of Rousseau's influence, the definition of the republic is rather revealing in its Rousseauvian overtones:

> I define republic a sacred confederation of men who recognize themselves as similar and brothers, of equal, independent and wise men, who do not recognise any master but the law emanating from the *general will*, as freely expressed by the representatives of the whole republic.[72]

In the discourse for the Constitution of Year I, Saint-Just still affirms that 'the principle of legislation in a free State is the *general will*'.[73] However, as the situation deteriorates, his position gets closer to a naturalistic critique of politics and history.[74] Conventions and artifice become culprits for the failure of the revolutionary government. Political institutions corrupt the original freedom of human beings and they threaten their natural rights. Rousseau becomes, at this point, one of his targets. The social contract, being a convention, amounts to a form of oppression. Rousseau's mistake is that 'he turns his eyes constantly toward nature, looking for an independent society, but this cannot be reconciled in any way with the strong government he envisages'.[75] The general will cannot be the building block of legislation any longer because, being a political artifice, it exercises a corruptive force upon society.

Robespierre's appropriation of Rousseau represents the most paradigmatic case among the revolutionaries of the radical model of constitutionalism. His main points of reference are the *SC* and the *Considerations on the Government of Poland*, but it is clear that he is well acquainted with the whole corpus of Rousseau's writings. His evaluation of political representation seems to distance him from Rousseau, but it is precisely on this point of departure from his main intellectual source that the debt to the Geneva philosopher is confirmed. While it is the case that the question of representative government is at the core of Robespierre's enterprise, such government remains nonetheless conceived in terms of giving expression to the general will. The idea of the general will provides guidance for the conception of a legitimate representative government.

The draft of a declaration of the rights of man contains important insights into Robespierre's reading of the general will. Article XIV of the draft states that 'the people are sovereign: The government is its product

[72] Louis Antoine de Saint-Just, *Oeuvres* (Paris: Folio, 2004), 369–370.

[73] Saint-Just, *Oeuvres*, 422.

[74] Miguel Abensour, 'La philosophie politique de Saint-Just', *Annales historiques de la Révolution Française* 38 (1964): 24.

[75] Saint-Just, *Oeuvres*, 929.

and its property, public officials are its assistants. The people may, if it wishes, change its government and revoke its representatives'. The following article (XV) adds that '[t]he law is the free and solemn expression of the people's will'.[76] Pushing further Rousseau's interpretation of the people (*le peuple*) as the honest and frugal part of the population, Robespierre assumes that the 'people are good and its delegates corruptible'.[77] A comment on the *Social Contract* reveals the extent of Robespierre's identification of the general will with an objective common good: 'the people always want their good but not always see it'. It follows that the people must never cease to oversee the activities of its mandataries.

The idea of the general will is further elaborated when Robespierre takes up the question of the foundation of the republic in the context of an emergency situation. Rousseau's general will is raised to a more abstract and objective level, permitting a contemptuous criticism of political representation. But by 1792, protecting the unity and stability of the state becomes the higher law: 'The State has to be saved, whatever it takes'.[78] It is telling that in one of his last speeches to the *Convention nationale*, Robespierre delivers a pompous tribute to Rousseau, pitting his work against those of the Encyclopaedists. It is in that famous intervention that Robespierre introduces the cult of the Supreme Being, trying to square the constitutional circle by resorting, *à la Rousseau*, to a civil religion.

The Jacobin draft *Constitution of Year I* (which never went into force[79]), sometimes labelled '*la constitution selon Rousseau*'[80], is possibly the closest instantiation of a radical model of constitutionalism. Its effort to combine elements of strong political participation with measures in support of substantive equality echoes Rousseau's constitutional alternative to liberalism.[81] Although representative politics is recognised, the constitution corrects it by introducing channels of direct popular participation. The purpose is to affirm the primacy of the lawmaking power and to reduce to a minimum its delegation. First of all, the representative's mandate was very short, only one year (art. 40), providing

[76] Maximillien Robespierre, *Virtue and Terror* (ed., Jean Ducange; trans., John Howe) (London: Verso, 2007), 70.

[77] Robespierre, *Virtue and Terror*, 72.

[78] Maximilien de Robespierre, 'Des maux et des ressources de l'état', in *Oeuvres de Maximilien Robespierre*. Vol. 1 (ed., Albert Laponneraye) (Paris: Albert Laponneraye, 1840), 45–68.

[79] Cf. Olivier Juanjan, 'La suspension de la constitution de 1793', *Droits* 10 (1993): 125–138.

[80] Francis Hamon and Michel Troper, *Droit constitutionnel* (Paris: LGDJ, 2003), 328. Cf. Pierre Bodineau and Michel Verpeaux, *Histoire constitutionnelle de la France* (Paris: PUF, 2013), 23.

[81] Cf Juanjan, 'La suspension de la constitution', 125–138.

the possibility of removing representatives that would not follow their mandates. Second, the lawmaking process would always be connected to popular sovereignty: Article 26 establishes the role of the primary assemblies as forums for direct popular participation. Third, the constitution of 1793 introduces an essential difference between *lois* (statutes) and *décrets* (decrees), according to their subjects (arts. 54 and 55), with the legislative process changing according to the nature of its output: In the case of the *décrets*, the representatives could pass them without resorting to popular approval; while for the *lois* their competence was limited to drafting. But in any event, legislative proposals required popular ratification to come into force.[82] Draft statutes were first deliberated by the representatives after the submission of a report (arts. 56 and 57). But then, they were sent in printed form to the primary assemblies of the departments. If, after forty days, less than one-tenth of the primary assemblies had advanced any objection, the law would be considered approved (art. 59). Otherwise, the statute would be submitted to a popular referendum (art. 60). A similar procedure would be followed for constitutional revision (art. 115), but in this case the question would revolve around the opportunity of forming a national convention, separate from the legislative assembly, with a strict mandate for changing the constitution (arts. 116 and 117).

The executive power, again in a very Rousseauvian fashion, was constituted by an Executive Council comprised of twenty-four members, half of them renewed each year at the end of the legislative term on the basis of proposals coming from the primary meetings (arts. 61, 62, and 63). The council would exercise the executive function and would still have foreign policy competences, such as the appointment of the ambassadors, but could not be involved in the legislative function. Article 65 states this separation of functions in the clearest way: 'The executive council has the management and supervision of the general administration. Its activity is limited to the execution of laws and decrees of the legislative'. The rigid separation between the two functions, coupled with a clear hierarchy of norms, is a constitutional translation of Rousseau's legal theory: The sovereign legislative function is superior to the executive function; and this entails that laws are superior to decrees.

The Jacobin *Declaration of the Rights of Man of 1793* also evinces a pronounced Rousseauvian influence in comparison with the earlier

[82] See also Marco Fioravanti, 'Aspetti del costituzionalismo giacobino. La funzione legislativa nell'*acte constitutionnel* del 24 giugno 1793', *Historia del costitucionalismo* 8 (2007): 123–142.

Declaration of the Rights of Man of 1789, bearing a much more radical view of the relation between society and constitution.[83] This view entails that society is not fully realised in advance of the constitutional order. To the contrary, the specific aim of the constitution is the transformation of society, substantiated by the principle of popular participation. Along these lines, citizens are not the passive recipient of individual rights. Rather, the rights of the citizenry are to, and realised only through, the *active* engagement of citizens and through the ongoing legislative function: 'the action of all to secure to each the enjoyment and the maintenance of his rights' (art. 23).

Overall, the basic principles of the Jacobins' constitution were directly inspired by Rousseau's work. Instead of focusing on the balance of powers, they saw in the sovereignty of the people the only guarantee against the arbitrariness even of the supreme legislative function. For this reason, the Jacobins tried to reduce the distance between representatives and represented by encouraging popular participation while at the same time trying to change society through the constitution.

The Jacobins were not the only constitutionalists inspired by Rousseau during the late eighteenth century. Some of the constitutions written in the North of Italy after the French Thermidor bear the marks of Rousseau's key idea of popular sovereignty. The most notable is the Bolognese Constitution of 1796, in particular its emphasis on the entitlement of all citizens to participate in making laws.[84]

VII. Rousseau and Marx: Affinities

In light of the previous reconstruction of Rousseau's critique of political economy it should not be surprising that some of its elements were immediately appealing to parts of the Marxist constellation, as the many commentaries written on the topic demonstrate.[85] On the specific relation between Rousseau and Marx, three issues can be addressed:[86] familiarity (Marx's

[83] See, generally, Stephan Rials, *La déclaration des droits de l'homme et du citoyen* (Paris: Presses Universitaires de France, 1988).

[84] See also, Augusto Barbera, 'La prima costituzione italiana: La costituzione di Bologna del 1796', *Clio: rivista trimestrale di studi storici* 21 (1998): 218–41. Cf. Chris Thornhill, *A Sociology of Constitutions: Constitutions and State Legitimacy in Historical- Sociological Perspective* (Cambridge University Press, 2011), 220.

[85] See, e.g., Lucio Colletti, *From Rousseau to Lenin* (London: Penguin, 1975), 179.

[86] Cf. Leopold, *The Young Marx*, 262.

knowledge of Rousseau's work), acknowledgment (Marx's recognition of Rousseau's work), and affinity (Marx's intellectual proximity to Rousseau).

We know that Marx had read Rousseau extensively between 1843 and 1844. In fact, the second of his notebooks – where Marx, starting from July 1843, used to collect extracts and notes from his readings – contains numerous annotations and extracts from *SC* and the *DPE*.[87] There are around 103 excerpts from the *SC*, including passages on the nature of sovereignty, the distinction between sovereignty and government, and the impossibility of representing the sovereign.[88] It is also certain that he was familiar with the *Considerations on the Government of Poland*, but, despite certain similarities in the arguments on property and accumulation, there is no certainty that he had studied the *DOI*.

With regard to acknowledgment, Marx's explicit engagement with Rousseau is limited. It has been estimated that the author of *Das Kapital* only referred to Rousseau around twenty-two times in his writings.[89] And when Marx quotes or refers to Rousseau, it is not always in positive terms. Marx's explicit comments on the *SC* in particular, while sometimes ambiguous,[90] leave the overall impression that he did not think highly of that work.

Nonetheless, the attention given to the Rousseau-Marx nexus is indicative of the potential affinities between these two authors. Even though it may not have informed much of Marx's own constitutional thinking, it has certainly informed many of Marx's followers.[91] Apart from Engels's praise of Rousseau as a precursor to Marx in his *Anti-Dühring*,[92] even a cursory look at a list of themes tackled with the same type of sensitivity by both authors suggests a visible intellectual proximity: Rousseau's criticism of the political economy undergirding liberal constitutionalism is echoed

[87] See Francesco Trincia, 'Marx lettore di Rousseau', *Critica marxista* 31 (1985): 97–127.

[88] Leopold, *The Young Marx*, 262.

[89] Robert Wokler, 'Rousseau and Marx', in David Miller and Larry Siedentop (eds.), *The Nature of Political Theory* (Oxford University Press, 1983), 221. But see Leopold, *The Young Marx*, 270.

[90] See Jean-Louis Lecercle, 'Rousseau et Marx', in R. A. Leigh (ed.), *Rousseau after 200 Years: Proceedings of the Cambridge Bicentennial Colloquium* (Cambridge University Press, 2010), 67–86.

[91] See, e.g., Galvano della Volpe, *Rousseau and Marx, and Other Writings* (trans. John Fraser) (London: Lawrence and Wishart, 1978); see also John Fraser, *An Introduction to the Thought of Galvano della Volpe* (London: Lawrence and Wilshart, 1977).

[92] See Yves Vargas, 'Marx et Engels, lecteurs de Rousseau', in Guglielmo Forni Rosa and Frédréric Lefevbre (eds.), *Rousseau dans le XIXe siècle* (Montmorency: Musée Jean-Jacques Rousseau, 2007), 98.

in Marx' rejection of the liberal conception of the rights of man. The phenomenology of an economy based on private property and contractual social relations is addressed by both philosophers and takes the form of a critique of ideology.[93] Moreover, Marx's preoccupations with direct democracy and popular empowerment – evident, for example, in the *Critique of Hegel's Doctrine of the State* and in the *Eighteenth Brumaire* – bear traces of Rousseau's influence.[94] The same is true for the historical anthropology undergirding his conception of labour.[95]

At the constitutional level, Marx's reflections present several affinities with Rousseau's radical constitutionalism. Both authors share a sceptical attitude toward the virtues of political representation, and they both conceive government as a commission. The young Marx, in particular, is adamant in stressing the point that legislative power (but, note, not parliamentary politics!) constitutes the major force for social change while government is depicted as a conservative or at least ineffective institution:

> The legislature made the French Revolution; in fact, wherever it has emerged as the dominant factor it has brought forth great, organic, universal revolutions. It has not attacked the constitution as such but only a particular antiquated constitution; this is because the legislature acted as the representative of the people, of the *species-will* [*gattungswillen*]. In contrast to this, the executive has made all the petty revolutions, the retrograde revolutions, the reactions.[96]

As Max Adler aptly pointed out, one might find further echoes of Rousseau's writings on radical constitutionalism in Marx's considerations on the Parisian Commune,[97] even though, it should be added, without any explicit mention of the Genevan philosopher.

In conclusion, while the direct influence of Rousseau's radical constitutionalism upon Marx's reflections on democracy and constitutions is questionable, their affinities are undeniable and they have represented a constant source of inspiration for authors in the variegated Marxist tradition. Both thinkers consider substantive equality as the lodestar of their constitutional reflections.

[93] Nicholas Dent, *A Rousseau Dictionary* (Oxford: Blackwell, 1992), 22.

[94] Lucio Colletti, 'Introduction', in *Karl Marx, Early Writings* (London: Penguin, 1975), 45.

[95] Asher Horowitz, *Rousseau, Nature and History* (University of Toronto Press, 1987), 75.

[96] Karl Marx, *Early Writings* (trans., Rodney Livingstone and Gregor Benton) (London: Penguin, 1975), 119–120.

[97] Max Adler, *Démocratie et conseils ouvriers* (Paris: Maspero [French translation], 1967), 55.

VIII. The Republican Revival, without Rousseau

The link between constitutionalism and the general will outlived the Jacobin experience, at least in its formal version. In the history of French constitutionalism, the seeds planted by the radical model germinated during the third republic, as, for example, in the work of its main constitutional theorist, Raymond Carré de Malberg.[98] Tied to the reception of the idea of the law as general will was a rejection of judicial review of state action, clearly in tune with the French adversion against the '*gouvernement des juges*'. Relatedly, distrust of judicial power, although not given proper treatment in the *SC*,[99] begins with the Jacobins and runs through the French republican tradition.[100]

As identified at the outset of this chapter, Rousseau's radical version of republican constitutionalism can be read as a point of reference for alternatives to the liberal model. In fact, as the engagement with Marx demonstrates, Rousseau's radical constitutionalism can serve as a bedrock for imagining constitutional models in both the republican and socialist traditions. One might have thought that the same could be said of the republican revival of the last three decades. However, Rousseau's republicanism seems, on the contrary, to be incompatible with the neo-republican revival.

The so-called neo-roman version of republicanism (sometimes dubbed 'civic republicanism')[101] has presented itself as an original political theory, based on a different modern tradition, and independent from mainstream contemporary liberal constitutionalism.[102] But the neo-republicans have not adopted or revived Rousseau's theory. On the contrary, their conception of freedom as absence of non-domination has been pitted against the participatory kind of freedom advocated by the author of the *SC*.[103]

Philip Pettit, for example, believes that Rousseau's republicanism is very close to a form of communitarianism and that for this reason Rousseau does not belong to the 'Italian-Atlantic' republican tradition. At the

[98] See Raymond Carré de Malberg, *La loi expression de la volonté générale* (Paris: Sirey, 1931). See also Eric Maulin, *La théorie de l'état de Carré de Malberg* (Paris: PUF, 2003), 251–255.

[99] See also Ethan Putterman, *Rousseau, Law and the Sovereignty of the People* (Cambridge University Press, 2010), 146–151.

[100] Marcel Gauchet, *La Révolution des droits de l'homme* (Paris: Gallimard, 1995), 55.

[101] See also Iseult Honohan, *Civic Republicanism* (London: Routledge, 2002).

[102] See, e.g., Philip Pettit, *Republicanism* (Oxford University Press, 1997); Quentin Skinner, *Liberty before Liberalism* (Cambridge University Press, 1998).

[103] Philip Pettit, 'Two Republican Traditions', in Andreas Niederberger and Philipp Schink (eds.), *Republican Democracy: Liberty, Law and Politics* (Edinburgh University Press, 2012), 169–204.

constitutional level, according to Pettit, Rousseau's main problem lies in his rejection of mixed government and his endorsement of popular sovereignty, which Pettit equates to a betrayal of the republican tradition. Rousseau starts from freedom as non-domination – each citizen ought to be independent of all the others – but ends up with the absolutism of modern sovereignty and the cult of the community. He thus sacrifices non-dominated freedom to the god of the public persona. Pettit sees in the link between the general will and legislation a reversal of republican ideas, because under this linkage, laws, once enacted, appear sacred and untouchable. No space is left, in this reconstruction, for contestatory citizenship. Citizens are 'lawmakers but not law-checkers'.[104]

Pettit's dismissive remarks ignore the key role played by equality in Rousseau's constitutionalism. In Pettit's reconstruction, Rousseau is a romantic thinker obsessed with political participation.[105] Such a reading is clearly partial and does not do justice to the richness of Rousseau's constitutionalism. Pettit is perhaps too quick to infer a rejection of republicanism from Rousseau's disapproval of the mixed constitution. From the point of view of the Genevan philosopher, the mixed constitution is equivalent to the preservation of the status quo. It hampers the possibility of social change and, crucially, the promotion of substantive equality. The problem is that the neo-republicans adopt a very formal conception of equality (see also Chapter 5).[106] From such a perspective, it is impossible to register the key position occupied by substantive equality in Rousseau's work. The latter is basically reduced to either an anti-modern or a utopian proposal. In light of the argument presented here, it should be evident that, unlike Rousseau's own project, neo-republican constitutionalism remains within the constellation of modern liberalism, as many of its authors are actually keen to stress.[107]

IX. Conclusion: The Continuing Relevance of Rousseau

Rousseau's constitutionalism represents a compelling source of inspiration in the search for contemporary alternatives to liberal approaches. His ideas offer valuable insights at the methodological, normative, and doctrinal levels. His philosophy offers an encompassing critical perspective on

104 Philip Pettit, *On the People's Terms* (Cambridge University Press, 2012), 15.

105 See id. at 227.

106 See, e.g., Frank Michelman, 'Law's Republic', *Yale Law Journal* 97 (1988): 1493–1535.

107 See, e.g., Bruce Ackerman, *We, the People, Volume 1: Foundations* (Cambridge [MA]: Belknap Press, 1991), ch. 1.

the discontents of modernity and more specifically on the vices of modern political economy and its apparatuses of domination (see also Chapter 2). In that respect, his work entails a critical approach to the dominant liberal political economy and, at the level of methodology, incorporates this into constitutional thinking. From this perspective, Rousseau's political philosophy provides a double lesson to the contemporary constitutionalist: (1) constitutional analysis ought always to start from a criticism of the underlying political economy and its rationalistic assumptions; (2) constitutions are strictly tied to society, hence, constitutional analysis ought not be limited to the formal and legalistic dimension, but it should enquiry into the undergirding socio-economic and psychological dynamics (see also Part II).

These methodological insights pave the way for Rousseau's more radical contribution to contemporary constitutionalism. To the critical approach to methodology corresponds a demanding ideal at the normative level: The critique of modern political economy invites us to conceive constitutionalism as being founded on the general will. The general will is a vector for individual and societal *transformation*, not just realisation. The departure from the main tenets of liberal constitutionalism is obvious. What makes Rousseau's constitutionalism much more radical than other proposals is the primary role attributed to substantial equality and its relation to self-government (cf. Chapter 5).

Of course, one cannot find in Rousseau's work a full-fledged constitutional doctrine. As already noted, one cannot find, for example, a developed conception of judicial power. But this would be an anachronistic critique and, also, a misdirected quest for a doctrine that was not Rousseau's main aim to formulate. Taken at its own terms, Rousseau's most constitutionally relevant works have a great deal to offer to the contemporary debate. In particular, his ideas on the role of lawmaking as a synthesis between the requests of self-government and substantive equality is commendable for those who have a political conception of constitutionalism (again, see Chapter 5).[108] The same applies to his strongly political definition of citizenship and his views on constitutional guardianship that still prove to be a repository of ingenious constitutional ideas.

[108] Cf. Jeremy Waldron, 'Can There Be a Democratic Jurisprudence?', *Emory Law Journal* 58 (2009): 675–712.

10

Constitutional Trajectory in Malaysia: Constitutionalism without Consensus?

ANDREW HARDING

I. Introduction

This chapter takes a long view of the evolution of constitutional ordering in Malaysia, with particular reference to the evolving concept of the state. The interest of this case in the context of the present volume is that competing interpretations of, and demands for, constitutional ordering occur here within a multi-cultural context that has stretched debate as far as it conceivably could be stretched within the broad acceptance of a single constitutional order. Something of this kind is true everywhere, even within classically liberal-democratic orders such as those of the United States or Canada; but in Malaysia we can see an especially heady and contested mix of ethnicities, religions, and competing socio-economic interests in one of the world's most pluralist nation-states. This pluralism is reflected in sharply contradictory constitutional ideologies and discourses. In this context the law and the constitution become the rope on which a tug of war takes place. In this chapter, this constitutional conflict is explored by attempting to examine the evolution of the Malaysian State over a period of almost sixty years. (By the 'the State', I mean the executive power of the Malayan/Malaysian federation since 1957. Because Malaysia is a federation, I use the uncapitalised word 'state' to indicate the sub-jurisdictions of that federation.)

What I will suggest is that the perpetual pluralist conflict that characterises Malaysia's surprisingly long history of constitutionalism may itself be a particular form of constitution order – a kind of conflictual equilibrium, as it were.[1] In other words, in such a highly polarised society as Malaysia, pluralist 'conflict' may actually contain stabilising elements. If so, it represents a kind of constitutionalism that is not wholly captured by traditional, liberal models, which invariably locate constitutional stability and order

[1] Cf. Michael W. Dowdle, 'On the Public Law Character of Competition Law': A Lesson from Asian Capitalism', *Fordham International Law Journal* 38 (2015): 355–359.

in consensus rather than in conflict.[2] On this view, even conflict embraces elements of consensus around implied limits within which conflict can take place. There may, for example, be no meeting of minds on constitutional questions, but still an understanding that physical violence is not acceptable at any level.

Malaysia has one of the most diverse societies in the world. Out of a population of approximately 28.4 million people, 60 percent are Muslim and 40 percent are non-Muslim. These non-Muslims include Buddhists (19 percent), Christians (9 percent), Hindus (6.3 percent), and Sikhs (0.4 percent). The members of the native tribes of East Malaysia (Sabah and Sarawak) and of the *orang asli* (original inhabitants) of West Malaysia profess animistic religions, although large numbers of Dayaks, Ibans, and Kadazans in East Malaysia have converted to Islam and Christianity. The largest ethnic group in Malaysia are the Malays (50 percent), followed by the Chinese (24 percent), the indigenous people (11 percent), and 'Indians' (i.e., those of South Asian heritage, 8 percent). Bahasa Malaysia is the official language, but English, Chinese (mainly in Cantonese and Hokkien dialect), Tamil, Telugu, Malayalam, Panjabi, Thai, and several indigenous languages in Eastern Malaysia are also widely spoken in places.[3] This was the challenge presented to constitution-makers in the 1950s and 1960s, and that still makes the discovery of common conceptions of constitutional order elusive and controversial.

Along these lines, the Malaysian constitution is infused with traditional elements, modified according to the perceived needs of a new polity deeply divided by religion and ethnicity, and confronted by terrorism (the so-called Malayan Emergency of 1948–1960,[4] a persistent communist insurgency that finally ended only with the surrender of the communist party in 1989[5]). Although amended frequently, and being the site of continual and intense struggle, the constitution survived to celebrate its fiftieth anniversary on August 31, 2007.[6] Despite its colonial origins and its continually disputed interpretation and relevance, the constitution has achieved, due to its longevity and in spite of its colonial origins, a status quite rare in the

[2] See, e.g., John Rawls, *A Theory of Justice* (Cambridge [MA]: Harvard University Press, 1971).

[3] See, generally, Andrew Harding, *The Constitution of Malaysia: A Contextual Analysis* (Oxford: Hart Publishing), 1.

[4] See Karl Hacka, 'The Malayan Emergency as Counter-Insurgency Paradigm', *Journal of Strategic Studies* 32 (2009): 383–414.

[5] See K. S. Nathan, 'Malaysia in 1989: Communists End Armed Struggle', *Asian Survey* 30 (1990): 210–220.

[6] See, generally, Andrew J. Harding and H. P. Lee (eds.), *Constitutional Landmarks in Malaysia: The First 50 Years, 1957–2007* (Kuala Lumpur: LexisNexis, 2007).

contemporary world: that of an embedded, and in a sense autochthonous – no longer colonial – constitution. In other words, after half a century it is meaningful to refer to 'Malaysian constitutional traditions'.[7]

It is with this story of constitutional continuity along with continued constitutional struggle that Malaysia offers a fascinating glimpse into the possibility of stability within perpetual conflict. In contemporary Malaysia we find a lively democracy in perpetual motion; authoritarian nationalism; rapid economic development; social change and urbanisation; and ethnic tension heightened by an intense dialogic clash and competition for religious converts. All of these elements have deeply affected the contours of the constitution as it has been contested and interpreted. More than this, the constitution has not just provided a battlefield for, but has also shaped continuing political struggle. Malaysian public life often resembles a fierce struggle between different groups over the essence and meaning of the constitution: a struggle in which almost every controversial issue, it seems, is or is capable of being framed as a constitutional issue.

Constitutional change in Malaysia demonstrates what James Tully has called a 'strange multiplicity'.[8] It is a constitutionalism in constant, pluralist motion. It does not settle or seem likely to settle on any universal set of foundational principles. And yet, it is the oldest constitution in East Asia, and has already survived three times as long as the average life constitutional life span of nineteen years.[9]

In this discussion I focus on competing constitutional claims around religion and ethnicity; developmentalism; and democratic aspiration, as expressed through three processes – protest, election, and constitutional litigation. I conclude that, rather than being disruptive or destabilising of constitutional order, these forms of contestation may be responsible for preserving that order. Contrary to liberal presumptions, there is in this case no ultimate resolution point of consensus, and therefore a form of constitutional unity arises from the constant jostling and re-jostling of forces – always changing, but at the same time continuing to define a stable boundary of constitutional practices and sustainability.

[7] See Andrew Harding, *Law, Government and the Constitution in Malaysia* (Kuala Lumpur: Malayan Law Journal Sdn. Bhd., 1996), 271.

[8] James Tully, *Strange Multiplicity: Constitutionalism in an Age of Diversity* (Cambridge University Press, 1995).

[9] See Tom Ginsburg, Zach Elkinsy, and James Meltonz, 'The Lifespan of Written Constitutions', paper no. 33 presented at the 17th American Law and Economics Association Annual Meeting 2007 (New York: Columbia Law School, May 16–17, 2008), at 1.

II. The Post-Colonial Liberal-Democratic State of 1957–1971

Understanding the complexity of Malaysia constitutionally and politically requires a brief historical introduction. The State (the Federation of Malaya 1957–1963) was conceived in liberal-democratic terms at the point at which it formally attained independence under the influence of that arch-constitution-maker Sir Ivor Jennings.[10] This version of the State, defined in the decolonisation process, was ascendant between 1957 and 1969 under the premiership of the first Prime Minister, Tunku Abdul Rahman (universally known as 'the Tunku'). The federation became the Federation of *Malaysia*, with the addition of three new states – Singapore, Sabah, and Sarawak – in 1963, but Singapore left the federation in 1965.[11]

This evolution from Malaya to Malaysia under the liberal-democratic State, gave way after the May 13, 1969 ethnic riots to increased authoritarianism during the '*rukunegara*' (national ideology) period that followed that incident.[12] This second iteration of the State, which I will call 'the Developmental State', was ascendant between 1971 and 2008. These different iterations of the State will be explained and discussed further in the next two parts. The fourth part will examine the evolution of the State since 2008 in order to reach some conclusions about its now highly contested constitutional evolution. The critical juncture here is the general election of 2008, which appeared to create almost instantaneously a two-party – and highly polarised – political system in which two coalitions contest for power at federal and state levels.[13]

The main tenets of the independence constitution were worked out in an imperial constitutional conference in London in 1956 and were based on a memorandum from the Alliance parties under the Tunku's leadership.[14] As a result of the terms of reference drawn up by the conference, an independent commission was established, known as the Reid Commission, to

[10] Joseph M. Fernando, 'Sir Ivor Jennings and the Malayan Constitution', *The Journal of Imperial and Commonwealth History* 34 (2006): 577–597.

[11] Harding, *The Constitution of Malaysia*, 42–45.

[12] See, generally, Andrew Harding, 'The Rukunegara Amendments of 1971', in Andrew Harding and H. P. Lee (eds.), *Constitutional Landmarks in Malaysia: The First 50 Years, 1957-2007* (Singapore: LexisNexis, 2007), 115–134.

[13] Andreas Ufena, 'The Transformation of Political Party Opposition in Malaysia and Its Implications for the Electoral Authoritarian Regime', *Democratization* 16 (2009): 604–627.

[14] See Colonial Office [Great Britain], *Report of the Federation of Malaya Constitutional Conference Held in London in January and February, 1956* (London: Her Majesty's Stationary Office, 1956).

draft the constitution. The resulting constitution evinces a Westminster-style structure familiar across the British Empire and Commonwealth during the 1950s and 1960s.[15] It reflected Anglo-Indian constitutional ideas of the 1950s, adapted in some respects to local traditions such as Islam and Malay monarchy. It embodied Westminster-type constitutional ideas and traditions, but also embraced constitutional supremacy, constitutional monarchy, federalism, and a bill of rights, as well as other ideas squarely based on the Indian Constitution of 1950.[16]

Nonetheless there were issues relating to the key problems of ethnicity and religion that had specifically local resonance. Prior to the London Conference, the three Alliance parties – the United Malays National Organisation (UMNO), the Malaysian Chinese Association (MCA), and the Malaysian Indian Congress (MIC) – had over some months negotiated behind the scenes a common position on the future Constitution, resulting in a memorandum being submitted to the commission.[17] The memorandum's most important proposals involved a compromise: The rights of non-Malays to citizenship, and their constitutional guarantees, would be strengthened in return for the acceptance of special privileges for the Malays.[18] It also dealt with such issues as the national language and the monarchy. This position was destined to become in effect the cornerstone of the nation and the *Merdeka* Constitution, and is now often referred to in popular discourse as 'the social contract'[19]: a social contract not in Rousseau's sense of a notional contract explaining philosophically the relationship between individuals and the state, but rather a politically negotiated contract between ethnic communities, indigenous and

[15] See Colonial Office [Great Britain], *Report of the Federation of Malaya Constitutional Commission 1957* (London: Her Majesty's Stationary Office, 1957). See, generally, Rais Yatim, 'The Road to Mardeka', in Andrew J. Harding and H. P. Lee (eds.), *Constitutional Landmarks in Malaysia: The First 50 Years, 1957–2007* (Kuala Lumpur: LexisNexis, 2007), 16–20.

[16] See R. H. Hickling, 'An Overview of Constitutional Change in Malaysia: 1957–1977', in Tun Mahamed Suffian, H. P. Lee, and F. A. Trindade (eds.), *The Constitution of Malaysia: Its Development, 1957–1977* (Kuala Lumpur: Oxford University Press, 1978), 3.

[17] See 'Alliance Memorandum to the Reid Commission' (Sept. 27, 1956), reprinted in *British Documents on the End of Empire, Series B Vol. 3: Malaya. Part III – The Alliance Route to Independence 1955–1957* (ed., A. J. Stockwell) (London: Her Majesty's Stationary Office, 1995), 307–317.

[18] See also Harding, *The Constitution of Malaysia*, 30–31.

[19] See Mavis C. Puthucheary, 'Malaysia's "Social Contract": The Invention and Historical Evolution of an Idea', in Norani Othman, Maris C. Puthucheary, and Clive Kessler (eds.), *Sharing the Nation: Faith, Difference and Power in the State 50 Years after Merdeka* (Petaling Jaya: Strategic Information and Research Development Centre, 2008), 1–28.

migrant, planning to live under a newly independent state that had not previously existed as a single entity.[20]

An inevitable consequence of the Constitutional Commission's terms of reference was the espousal of a Westminster-style executive based on the British model of constitutional monarchy. The new office of 'Supreme Head of the Federation' (*Yang di-Pertuan Agong* in Malay) was given powers resembling those of the British Crown.[21] Given nine existing monarchies within the federation, the rulers (sultans of the states that had protected status during the colonial period) favoured a rotation of office among them on the basis of five years' tenure. The rulers each were to remain 'Heads of Islam' in their respective states, and a Conference of Rulers (in existence already since 1948) was given some special functions, including the right to withhold its consent to the passing of certain laws, for example legislation affecting the special position of the Malays and the legitimate interests of the other communities (i.e., the social contract).[22]

The commission failed to address some rather obvious arguments in favour of entrenchment of fundamental rights. Malaya was a diverse society with many races, religions, and languages – a condition that required a more positive reassurance, especially to minority groups, that their rights would not be removed, whoever was in power. As a result of the spineless approach adopted by the commission, the government was emboldened after 1957 to impose important and far-reaching restrictions on fundamental rights, both by amending the draft constitution, and subsequent to its passage by frequent, almost routine, legislative amendments – especially after 1971 as the developmental state replaced the liberal-democratic.[23]

The commission also had to deal with even more thorny questions of ethnicity and religion, and in particular the issue of special privileges. It was obvious to all that the diversity of Malaya presented several constitutional problems. The underlying problem was that the Malays, as the majority population, were far behind other communities, especially the Chinese, economically. Colonial rule had given the Malays some special privileges to avoid their being eclipsed economically in their own country by large or even larger numbers of migrant people who controlled most of the economy. For example, most positions in the police and the public service went to Malays, while in 1957 the economy was controlled

[20] See also Harding, *The Constitution of Malaysia*, 69–82.

[21] See Federal Constitution of Malaysia, arts. 39–40.

[22] See also Harding, *The Constitution of Malaysia*, 116–123.

[23] See id. at 41, 47–48.

almost entirely by Chinese and British interests.[24] The issue was whether the special privileges should continue, and if so in what form and for how long. At issue was in fact the entire principle of the rule of law and a citizen's equality before it.

The commission recognised the inheritance of an ethnic-managment framework that gave special privileges to Malays with regard to land acquisition, admission into the public service, access to business licences, and state-funded scholarships. Because there was no opposition to these privileges for the time being, the commission recommended their continuance, subject to review by parliament after fifteen years. They clearly viewed the special privileges as 'sunset legislation', whose necessity would decline rapidly when the consequent laws and policies took effect, and as aspects of government that were essentially incompatible with the overriding principle of equality. But after the commission issued its report, the Colonial Office created a 'Working Party', comprising representatives of the British government, the Malay rulers, and the Alliance Coalition, to review its constitutional draft. Disagreeing with the Reid Commission, the Working Party thought that the government should be required to review this issue 'from time to time', with no time limitation. It was the Working Party view that prevailed.[25]

The debates concerning religion in and around the commission's report are also important to understand. Constitutional interpretation has become the weapon of choice in the struggle over the constitutional position of religion. Given the penumbra of ambiguity, or at least alleged ambiguity, of several provisions, the thinking of those involved in the drafting process becomes preeminently important. The Tunku's Alliance parties wanted Islam to be the official religion of the federation. The rulers disagreed, reasoning that as Heads of Islam, being the religion of all the Malay States, they could not countenance religion being made in any sense a federal matter, which would be radical and also undermine their position, because being head of Islam was one of the few powers left in their hands. Moreover at the time Muslims were actually in a minority, so there was no real case for making Islam the official religion based on it being the majority's religion. It is no doubt that under Jennings's guidance, the commission discerned a contradiction between the notion of a secular state and having an official religion. This distinction indicates Jennings's extreme foresight:

[24] See Jomo K. S. and Chang Yii Tan, 'The Political Economy of Post-Colonial Transformation', in Jomo K. S. and Wong Sau Ngan (eds.), *Law, Institutions and Malaysian Economic Development* (Singapore: NUS Press), 27.

[25] See Harding, *The Constitution of Malaysia*, 38–39.

As he feared, this issue has come to divide Malaysia as no other. Thus the majority of the commission recommended that the federation should have a secular state, and that there should be no official religion, as was the case in India. The commission considered that a secular state did not sit well with an official religion.[26]

Predictably the Alliance leaders were displeased with the outcome and demanded a provision on official religion. As a result, the stipulation in the current Article 3 of the Constitution that 'Islam is the religion of the Federation'[27] was inserted during the constitutional review process following the commission's report. The Tunku's party, UMNO, stuck to its demand for an official-religion provision, and the other component parties of the Alliance were disposed not to unravel the carefully negotiated Alliance compromise – no doubt also recognising, in their own interests, the political inexpediency of exposing UMNO to electoral problems. The Tunku was in favour of Article 3 on the grounds that the provision was innocuous; would not prevent the state from being secular in nature; was similar to provisions in constitutions of Muslim countries; was found in the constitutions of some of the Malay States; and was agreed to unanimously by the Alliance, which also included non-Muslim parties.[28]

The non-Muslims' acceptance of Islam as the official religion was in essence a part of the social contract, from which they obviously derived other benefits. It was also clear in statements of the Alliance position that the enshrinement of Islam as simply 'the religion of the Federation' – as opposed to as a 'state religion' – would not create a theocracy.[29] Nor would it affect the secular nature of the state, alter the rights of the rulers as heads of Islam, or abridge the religious rights of non-Muslims. It was therefore in essence symbolic. The official Working Party in reviewing the draft constitution also went along with the Alliance view. Even Malay opposition parties agreed with the Alliance view on religion and non-Malay opposition parties did not raise the issue, preferring to attempt to safeguard economic, language, and education rights.

All in all, the Chinese and Indian populations gained some access to the political system through the extension of their citizenship rights and

[26] See, generally, id. at 226–229.

[27] Federal Constitution of Malaysia, art. 3.

[28] See, generally, Joseph M. Fernando, 'The Position of Islam in the Constitution of Malaysia', *Journal of Southeast Asian Studies* 37 (2006): 257–260.

[29] See, e.g., Colonial Office [Great Britain], *Constitutional Proposals for the Federation of Malaya* (London: Her Majesty's Stationary Office, 1957), 20. See generally Fernando, 'The Position of Islam', 260–265.

their participation in the Alliance victory in the constitutional debates, but at a cost. Their property and businesses were protected, and their cultures and languages recognised and tolerated (it was to prove otherwise in Indonesia). But they would not necessarily be equal citizens in all respects: The Malays' had their language serve as the official language; their status and religion, in contrast to those of the Indians and Chinese, were *constitutionally* recognised and associated with the state; and they were guaranteed an increasing share of the economy.

Moreover, by allowing the constitution to be amended simply by approval of two-thirds majority of parliament,[30] the Malaysian constitutional-amendment provision effectively gave the Malay-dominated Alliance Party control over the constitution, given the electoral dominance of that political coalition.[31] This gave it extremely wide powers with little accountability for their exercise. Malaysia's liberal democracy therefore contained the seeds of authoritarianism. Like Banquo in Macbeth, let us now proceed to 'look into the seeds of time and see which will grow and which will not'.[32]

III. The Developmental State, 1971–2008

Within twelve years of the coming into being of the *Merdeka* Constitution, internal problems led to a crisis, the 'May 13' incident, that narrowly failed to propel Malaysia into either permanent dictatorship or military rule.[33] While the continued relevance of that incident has probably been exaggerated, it remains the most traumatic episode in Malaysia's history, one that threatened to eclipse completely the constitution and democratic, parliamentary government. The incident was sparked by the outcome of particularly tense and racially charged election in Kuala Lumpur.[34] The resulting ethnic violence spread rapidly throughout Kuala Lumpur to other urban centres. In response, the State was dramatically redefined with changes to the social contract; the emergence of new, discriminatory, policies;

[30] Federal Constitution of Malaysia, art. 159.

[31] See Lim Hong Hai, 'Electoral Politics in Malaysia: "Managing" Elections in a Plural Society', in Aurel Croissant, Gabriele Bruns, and Marei John (eds.), *Electoral Politics in Southeast and East Asia* (Singapore: Friedrich Ebert Stiftung, 2002), 105–113.

[32] William Shakespeare, *Macbeth*, act. 1, scene 3.

[33] See National Operations Council, *The May 13 Tragedy: A Report of the National Operations Council* (Kuala Lumpur: Government Printer, 1969). See, generally, Cyrus Das, 'The May 13th Riots and Emergency Rule', in Andrew Harding and H .P. Lee (eds.), *Constitutional Landmarks in Malaysia: The First 50 Years, 1957–2007* (Singapore: LexisNexis, 2007), 103–114.

[34] See Das, 'The May 13th Riots', 104–105.

the instigation of emergency rule; and new restrictions on the scope of free expression. On May 15, 1969, a state of emergency was proclaimed under Article 150 of the constitution, extending to the entire federation, on grounds of a threat to national security.[35] Emergency rule continued for twenty-two months before parliament was eventually summoned. During this period, the entire executive and legislative power of the federation was vested in a Director of Operations (Tun Abdul Razak, also Deputy Prime Minister and then Prime Minister, 1971–1976).[36]

Elections resumed in 1971, which gave the Alliance Party a two-thirds majority in parliament. The administrative structure of emergency rule was dismantled, but the emergency powers it had bestowed on the government still remained. The return to some kind of normality was not a return to the pre-1969 constitution, but to a radically altered version of constitutionality: This was the price, in effect and in the judgment of UMNO leaders, of a return to any kind of constitutional government. With its two-thirds majority, the Alliance Party was able to push through a number of constitutional amendments – often termed the '*Rukunegara* amendments' (after the Malay name for the national ideology[37]) – that fundamentally altered the nature of the State.[38]

The *Rukunegara* amendments took Malaysia a significant step away from several of the key tenets of the *Merdeka* Constitution. Principally, the amendments redefined the social contract so as to give more special privileges to the Malays; extended the scope of these privileges to include natives (indigenous peoples) of Sabah and Sarawak; and entrenched those privileges even further than was already the case.[39] They also allowed for legislation that would make the social contract a 'sensitive issue' that could not be discussed, except as to policy implementation, in any forum, including even on the floors of the federal parliament of Malaysia or of the state legislatures.[40]

These changes were the foundation of what was termed the 'New Economic Policy' (NEP), designed to secure thirty percent ownership of the economy for what were called the '*bumiputera*' – that is, the Malays

[35] See id. at 106.

[36] See id. at 109–112.

[37] See, generally, Muhammad Ghazali bin Shafie, *Rukunegara: A Testament of Hope* (Kuala Lumpur: Creative Entreprise Sdn. Bhd., 1985).

[38] See, generally, Harding, 'Rukunegara Amendments'.

[39] See id. at 120–127.

[40] See Federal Constitution of Malaysia, art. 10(4); Sedition Act 1948 (Act 15) s. 3(1)(f) (as amended).

and other scheduled populations who enjoyed to special status under the constitution – within twenty years.[41] At a stroke, the *Rukunegara* amendments redefined ethnic relations and the political economy of Malaysia, in the process greatly increasing the powers of government and the restrictions on freedom of expression. They had in effect converted a liberal democracy observing basic rights into an authoritarian State that subjected those rights to a large range of exceptions.

The Malaysian State that resulted from the *Rukunegara* period and the NEP exhibited the principal features of what have been called the 'developmental states' of East Asia.[42] Accordingly, the term 'Malaysian Developmental State' will be used here to indicate that the State under the post-1971 model has peculiarly Malaysian but also strongly developmental characteristics.[43] This Malaysian Developmental State proved both stable and successful in orchestrating Malaysia's economic development.[44] Four decades on, it cries out for renovation and in some respects it has been reformed. But there is no real agreement as to the type or extent of renovation that is needed.[45] This issue has been the source of an acute form of political polarisation since 2008 between the Barisan Nasional (BN), Malaysia's ruling coalition and the successor to the Alliance Party, and the opposition Pakatan Rakyat (PR) coalition.[46]

Malaysia's second prime minister, Tun Abdul Razak (who also had managed the emergency situation as Director of Operations) died in office in 1976, by which time he had redesigned the State, and laid the foundations for the new social contract under the NEP and the modern developmental state. However, the Malaysian Developmental State evolved to its fullest extent under the twenty-two years of the premiership of its fourth prime minister, Tun Dr Mahathir Mohamad (1981–2003), who imposed his personal and controversial stamp on the polity as no other prime minister did, not even the Tunku.[47] He launched Malaysia on a path towards striking economic growth. He survived many political crises, taking Malaysia much further towards authoritarian government than any of his predecessors or successors. As with 'Thatcherism' in the United Kingdom and

[41] See, generally, Jomo and Tan, 'Political Economy', 27–30.

[42] Cf. Mark Beeson, 'Mahathir and the Markets: Globalisation and the Pursuit of Economic Autonomy in Malaysia', *Pacific Affairs* 73 (2000): 326–348.

[43] See also Jomo and Tan, 'Political Economy', 30–34.

[44] See id. at 39.

[45] See id. at 39–41.

[46] See Abdul Rashid Moten, '2008 General Elections in Malaysia: Democracy at Work', *Japanese Journal of Political Science* 10 (2009): 35.

[47] Cf. Jomo and Tan, 'Political Economy', 30–52.

'Reaganomics' in the United States, 'Mahathirism' defined the Malaysia of the 1980s and 1990s. Its main features were nationalism, developmentalism, and authoritarian government.[48]

Mahathir's premiership expanded even the already extensive power of the prime minister. Unlike his predecessors he was not a lawyer, and perhaps for this reason proved more impatient than his predecessors with regard to constitutional checks and balances. In particular he challenged the power of the judiciary in 1988, the rulers in 1983 and 1993, and dissent within UMNO in 1987 and 1998 – and got his way in all of these instances. He also held important ministerial portfolios during his premiership, taking over Finance, Home Affairs, and Defence during the period from 1998 to 2003. He not only had virtually unlimited power, but exercised it extensively and personally, playing a significant role even in planning and executing major projects such as the Multimedia Super Corridor, Kuala Lumpur International Airport, the Petronas Twin Towers, and the new administrative capital of Putrajaya. He also orchestrated Malaysia's response to the financial crisis of 1997–1998, successfully resisting international criticism and demands.[49] Mahathir stepped down as prime minister in 2003 but remains a caustic critic of anything that deviates from his legacy. In 2016, he established a new party opposed to Prime Minister Najib Razak.

Pursuing the theme of the Malaysian Developmental State, we can note how even today large numbers of federal agencies, and even state agencies, are described as having an explicitly development-related function. To take the example of information and communications technology, which is regarded as a critical aspect of Malaysia's development,[50] no less than fifteen agencies have significant regulatory jurisdiction over this sector. They range from the Ministry of Information and Communications to the Malaysian Communications and Multimedia Commission, the Malaysian Technology Development Corporation, the Multimedia Development Corporation, and the Multimedia Super Corridor. They involve a federal ministry and statutory agencies as well as a government-linked company. One obvious feature of all of these agencies is their lack of independence.

[48] See, generally, Khoo Boo Teik, *Paradoxes of Mahathirism: An Intellectual Biography of Mahathir Mohamad* (Kuala Lumpur: Oxford University Press, 1995).

[49] See R. S. Milne and Diane K. Mauzy, *Malaysian Politics under Mahathir* (London: Routledge, 1999), 67–8, 75–76, 175–178.

[50] See Abu Bakar Munir, 'Privatisation in Malaysia: A Case Study of the Telecommunications Department', in Euston Quah and William Neilson (eds.), *Law and Economic Development: Cases and Materials from South East Asia* (Singapore: Longman, 1993), 169–176.

All are under the control of the federal government either directly through lines of responsibility leading to a minister and the Cabinet, or else through the government's power to appoint their members or executives. This is true even of government-linked companies.[51] In practice the operation of ministerial responsibility insulates administrative agencies from parliamentary criticism. Even agencies that are formally independent of the government are often nonetheless treated as if the minister has to answer for them in parliament.[52] The Malaysian Developmental State resists power slipping away to statutory and privatised agencies.[53]

Ironically, however, Mahathir's fierce political contest with his popular Deputy Prime Minister Datuk Seri Anwar Ibrahim during the Asian Economic Crisis of the late 1990s, and his unsuccessful attempts to destroy Anwar's political career (at least until 2015 when Anwar was finally convicted and jailed on a charge of sodomy) by having questionable criminal charges be brought against him, ultimately led to a sea change in Malaysian politics.[54] After being removed from UMNO and the BN, Anwar set up a new political party – the National Justice Party (*Parti Keadilan Nasional*) – which was able for the first time to form a viable opposition coalition capable of winning elections. The narrowness of the BN's victory in the 2008 and 2013 general elections, with the loss of several state governments by the BN and its drastically reduced parliamentary majority, has made the government significantly more responsive to public opinion than previously; and the loss of the two-thirds parliamentary majority has taken constitutional amendments out of the equation: It is now impossible to increase the constitutional powers of the State, but it is also impossible to decrease them.

Hence the legal foundations of the State, although deeply contested, have not altered much since 2008, except in that some reforms have reduced the State's armoury of legal weaponry to a certain degree. Nonetheless the political system has been shaken to its foundations in a manner that opens up the possibility of the emergence of a new kind of State. Before we rush to the conclusion that the original liberal-democratic State is being dusted

[51] See Michael B. Likosky, *The Silicon Empire: Law, Culture and Commerce* (Aldershot, UK: Ashgate, 2005), 169.

[52] See also Mavis Puthucheary, 'Ministerial Responsibility in Malaysia', in Tun Mahamed Suffian, H. P. Lee, and F. A. Trindade (eds.), *The Constitution of Malaysia: Its Development, 1957–1977* (Kuala Lumpur: Oxford University Press, 1978), 123–135.

[53] See also Harding, *The Constitution of Malaysia*, 64.

[54] See, generally, James Chin and Wang Chin Huat, "Malaysia's Electoral Upheaval', *Journal of Democracy* 20.3 (2009): 73–76.

off and revived, it would be well to see how the issues of religion and the role of Islam in the constitutional identity of the State have divided society equally deeply but along somewhat different lines from the ethnic cleavages described in the preceding text.

IV. The Evolving Social Contract

Since 1971 the making and implementation of Malaysia's social contract through the NEP was the State's all-consuming task, involving the creation of prosperity, the reduction of poverty, and the providing of opportunity to the Malay/Muslim majority.[55] We have seen earlier the general rationale for its creation. But what exactly are its terms? Who are its parties? How is it implemented? Can it be changed? Confusion surrounds these issues. The lack of any real freedom to address these issues (being deemed 'sensitive issues', discussing them gives rise to possibly seditious speech[56]) has proved not so much a necessity of pluralism as a dysfunctional form of political process. The social contract is not contained in any particular document, and has to be construed mainly from the provisions of the constitution and the circumstances surrounding their adoption.[57]

The original terms of the social contract, crystallised in the *Merdeka* Constitution in 1957, were reasonably clear. The contract was concluded between leaders representing the three communities in their capacity as leaders of the three main political parties in the Alliance (UMNO, MCA, and MIC). They could fairly claim to negotiate on behalf of their respective ethnic communities because they had demonstrated that, collectively, they had the overwhelming support of the electorate. This was an electorate to which the idea of being represented communally but in a manner that embraced accommodation and compromise was perennially appealing.[58]

The social contract has to be understood as a response to the deep fears of all communities that existed in the early decades of Malaysia and that still persist today. In 1957 the Malays owned about 1 percent of Malaysia's corporate equity. By 1969, that figure had risen to just 2.5 percent.[59] In 1957, and even, one might argue, in 1969, the Malays were in danger

[55] See Jomo and Tan, 'Political Economy', 47.

[56] See Federal Constitution of Malaysia, art. 10(4); Sedition Act 1948 (Act 15) s. 3(1)(f) (as amended).

[57] See, generally, Puthucheary, 'Malaysia's "Social Contract"'; see, especially, id. at 19, 22–23.

[58] See Karl von Vorys, *Democracy without Consensus: Communalism and Political Stability in Malaysia* (Princeton University Press, 1975), 105–142.

[59] Jomo and Tan, 'Political Economy' 27.

of losing not just political status, their *ketuanan Melayu*, but even their aspirations for development. The non-Malays stood to lose their own economic position, their cultural and language rights, and even possibly their membership in the country. The memory of post-war ethnic reprisals was also still fresh. The social contract was not seen as a dangerously discriminatory new order, but rather as a mercy – the best compromise that could be expected in fraught circumstances in a deeply fractured society. Whatever the objections, it was thought better for those disadvantaged to live within its constraints than risk losing all.

The social contract is a compromise that *balances* the rights and interests of different communities, and the constitution, while preserving some traditional elements and special privileges, does not in essence embody Malay dominance but a pluralist democracy.[60] The concessions given by all sides are significant. Malays accepted the possibility of becoming a political minority in their own country in exchange for constitutional acknowledgment that their position was special. Non-Malays conceded the special constitutional status of Malays in exchange for being able to enjoy citizenship themselves. Beyond that, it was clear from the retention of the States and their Malay monarchies in a federal structure, the designation of *Bahasa Melayu* (the Malay language) as the national language, and the establishment of Islam as the official religion, that the State as a pluralist artefact was nevertheless underpinned by a substratum of Malay culture.[61]

The social contract was reflected principally in Article 153 of the constitution. Article 153 established and protected the 'special position' of the Malays. But the practices that constituted the social contract pre-date that amendment – such as reserving for Malays positions in the public service, certain scholarships and licences, and ownership of certain kinds of land – actually commenced during the immediate post-war period under the English colonial government.[62] The principal effect of Article 153 was to clarify and extend these practices, and most importantly give them constitutional legitimacy and through that constitutional-political embeddedness.

[60] See Jaclyn Ling-Chien Neo, 'Malay Nationalism, Islamic Supremacy and the Constitutional Bargain in the Multi-ethnic Composition of Malaysia', *International Journal on Minority and Group Rights* 13 (2006): 95–118; but see Puthucheary, 'Malaysia's "Social Contract"', 13–14.

[61] Abdul Aziz Bari, *Malaysian Constitution: A Critical Introduction* (Kuala Lumpur: The Other Press, 2003), 43–50.

[62] See Gordon P. Means, 'Malaysia: Islam in a Pluralist Society', in Carlo Caldarola (ed.), *Religions and Societies: Asia and the Middle East* (Berlin: Walter de Gruyter, 1983), 474.

A. The Social Contract Amended

The political settlement of 1971, which brought some degree of political stability following ethnic violence stemming from the May 13 incident, made changes to the terms of the social contract, which had the effect a remaking it along somewhat different terms. Principally, it expanded the scope of its protections to include the indigenous populations of Sabah and Sarawak (which together with the Malays are now referred to as the *bumiputera*); it added admission to tertiary education to its list of quotas reserved for protected classes.[63] As we saw previously, it also entrenched the social contract by essentially immunising it from political debate using the threat of bringing sedition charges.[64] These changes configured a Developmental State that was largely typical of Asian developmental states in subordinating all elements of the State to the demands of development, while at the same time being one that, by restricting criticism of its use of ethnic quotas, was particular to Malaysia's multi-cultural society.

It is important to understand, however, that Article 153 is not a licence to ignore the constitution or the rights of citizens, or to indulge generally in official or institutionalised discrimination. Article 153 represents a significant but nevertheless balanced exception to equality before the law. It authorises the use of quotas in specified areas of public decision making affecting individual opportunities. But at the same time, it forbids unequal treatment of federal employees based on race. For example, it forbids the government and parliament from 'depriv[ing] or authoris[ing] the deprivation of any person of any right, privilege, permit or licence accrued to or enjoyed or held by him'[65]; it forbids parliament from restricting 'business or trade solely for the purpose of [quota] reservations'.[66]

As noted in the preceding text, with the application of Article 153 to 'natives of Sabah and Sarawak', these communities too were made parties to the social contract, and the communities protected by Article 153 are now routinely referred to in Malaysia as '*bumiputera*' (although not in Article 153 itself). Although the meaning of this term fluctuates somewhat in common usage, from an official perspective it includes Malays – who are in turn defined by the constitution as Muslims habitually using the Malay language and Malay customs and domiciled in Malaysia, and anyone

[63] See Harding, 'Rukunegara Amendments', 121–122.

[64] See also id. at 122–127.

[65] Federal Constitution of Malaysia, art. 153 (7).

[66] Federal Constitution of Malaysia, art. 153 (9).

with one Malay parent;[67] and natives of Sarawak and Sabah belonging to a scheduled list of indigenous groups, or whose parent belonged thereto. Essentially it is for the particular department overseeing some particular quota to decide if a given applicant is a *bumiputera* or not, and they have little incentive to find against inclusion. Given the indelibly mixed nature of Malaysia's diverse society, this issue is clearly an official headache embodying little in the way of social or economic logic. But the essential point is that through this broadening of the *bumiputera* class, that class is now able to constitute a clear majority of the Malaysian population, especially give Singapore's departure from the federation in 1965.

As we have seen, there was no agreement among the Alliance parties in 1956–1957 as to the duration of the special privileges under the provision that became Article 153. The drafting commission had proposed that parliament reconsider these special privileges after fifteen years, but that proposal was rejected, and so no duration was fixed. Given that this proposal would have demanded parliamentary reconsideration in 1972, its rejection was probably fortunate, as parliament during that time was expanding and entrenching these privileges, through the NEP, rather than shepherding them towards their sunset. No particular duration was set for the NEP (although its targets were set to be achieved by 1990). Moreover, parliament made all potential amendments to the *Rukunegara* amendments subject not simply to the usual two-thirds parliamentary majority required for ordinary constitutional amendments, but requiring also the consent of the Conference of Rulers.[68] This makes the revision of the post-1971 social contract extremely difficult.

There is another dark side to the remodelled social contract. Its initial remodelling took place under the cloud of emergency rule, with parliamentary democracy suspended, elections uncompleted, and citizens preventively detained without trial under the Internal Security Act. Agreements reached behind the closed doors of inter-party meetings were placed beyond public debate. The foundations were laid for an authoritarian style of government that contradicted many of the basic tenets or assumptions of the liberal-democratic order under the *Merdeka* Constitution. All this establish precedent for the construction of a Developmental State that denied basic civil liberties and entrenched the Alliance Party, later to become the BN, in power.[69]

67 Federal Constitution of Malaysia, art. 160 (2).

68 Art. 159 (5).

69 See also Das, 'The May 13th Riots', 112–113.

B. *The Social Contract Questioned*

The Malaysian Developmental State has indeed achieved development. Since 1970, and especially after Mahathir became prime minister in 1981, economic growth rates have been high, albeit not consistently so. Recessions in 1985/6 and 2008/9, in addition to the Asian currency crisis of 1997/8, have held back economic development, but the overall trajectory represents notable achievement.[70] Malaysia no longer appears on most lists of 'developing countries', and poverty has been very substantially reduced.[71]

At the same time the consequences of the NEP have by no means received universal applause. It is criticised for contributing to growing wealth inequality among the Malay population.[72] Corruption and cronyism in government are other phenomena that have spurred criticism.[73]

Indeed, since the 2000s signs have appeared that the NEP's star is waning. The government is cautiously and by degrees addressing dysfunctional aspects of the *bumiputera* preference policy, no doubt aware of its need to satisfy non-*bumiputera* voters given the splintering of the Malay vote since 1999 between UMNO and opposition parties (PAS and PKR). The '30 percent bumiputera' rule in foreign investment approvals was rescinded in 2009, and earlier, for all investments, in the MSC and other special zones. Quotas for university admission were abolished in 2004, and in 2008 the scholarship quota was adjusted from 90 to 10 percent to 55 to 45 percent in favour of *bumiputera*.[74] There is clearly widespread belief that the social contract is outdated and changes are required.[75]

Central to all of these changes, we have noticed, is Malaysia's often problematical attempt to secure its own vision of development as a stabilising factor for its fraught and fractious pluralism. Here the social contract has been the real test of its success. Clearly there have been positive and negative aspects of this attempt. Malaysia's unique development trajectory

70 See Jomo and Tan, 'Political Economy', 39.

71 See Anoma Abhayaratne, 'Economic Growth and Poverty Reduction: Lessons from the Malaysian Experience', FEA working paper no. 2004–13 (Kuala Lumpur: University of Malaya Faculty of Economics and Administration, 2004).

72 A. H. Roslan, 'Income Inequality, Poverty and Development Policy in Malaysia', paper presented at the conference on *Poverty and Sustainable Development* (Pessac, Fr.: Université Montesquieu-Bordeaux, Nov. 22–23, 2002), 18–20.

73 But see Jomo and Tan, 'Political Economy', 47.

74 Center for Public Policy Studies, 'CPPS Policy Factsheet: National Unity', www.cpps.org.my/downloads/factsheets/National%20unity%20factsheet.pdf (undated).

75 See id.

remains an excruciatingly important matter but one for implicit not explicit debate. This brings us to the final but most important piece of the Malaysia jigsaw puzzle – religion.

V. Religion and the State

In recent years Malaysia's reputation for religious tolerance and cultural diversity has become tarnished by images of an intolerant form of Islamisation and of inter-religious strife. In particular, the tragic case of Muslim apostate Lina Joy in 2007 (discussed in the following text) drew attention to the great hostility towards a woman whose campaign simply to choose her own religion led to rejection by the courts and her flight overseas to escape death threats that extended to her Christian fiancé and even to the Muslim human rights lawyer involved in the case. Debates and controversies around religion and the constitution appear to have intensified significantly since the millennium. Of particular relevance here are the debates concerning Malaysia as an 'Islamic state'; jurisdictional contradictions between the civil and Syariah courts ('Syariah' being the Malay spelling of what in English is normally spelled 'sharia'); and the related issue of religious freedom. All of these are exemplified by the case of Lina Joy. Some background needs to be sketched.

With the aim of undercutting the Islamist appeal of the opposition Islamic party, the Pan-Malaysian Islamic Party (*Parti Islam Se-Malaysia*) (PAS), the BN-controlled government from the early 1980s mounted its own programme of Islamisation.[76] With regard to the legal system, this involved the harmonisation of Islamic law across the thirteen states, and institutional reform within the Syariah courts and legal profession, and the religious bureaucracy.[77] In 1988, the BN succeeded in amending Article 121 of the constitution, which sets out the jurisdictional competencies of the Syariah courts and the civil courts, by providing that civil courts could not exercise jurisdiction in any case falling under the Syariah courts' jurisdiction. Article 121 has proved highly problematical in terms of religious freedom, giving rise to endless litigation seeking to test the limits of civil and Syariah court jurisdiction.[78]

[76] Jason P. Abbott and Sophie Gregorios-Pippas, 'Islamization in Malaysia: Processes and Dynamics', *Contemporary Politics* 16 (2010): 135–151.

[77] See, generally, Farid S. Shuaib, 'The Islamic Legal System in Malaysia', *Pacific Rim Law and Policy Journal* 21 (2012): 85–113.

[78] See Li-ann Thio, 'Jurisdictional Imbroglio: Civil and Religious Courts, Turf Wars and Article 121 (1A) of the Federal Constitution', in Andrew Harding and H. P. Lee (eds.), *Constitutional*

The PAS's electoral and legislative successes, particularly in the state legislatures, created a new and controversial environment for the discussion of the role of Islamic law in in Malaysia's constitutional system. In recent years, for example, there has been public debate about the concept of Malaysia as an Islamic state.[79] This started in 1999 and intensified following an announcement by Prime Minister Mahathir in June 2002 that Malaysia indeed was an 'Islamic state'.[80] Succeeding prime ministers have followed the same line, but have stressed moderation as the characteristic of the Malaysian Islamic state. These statements have sparked great controversy. Catholic bishops and non-Muslim parties, for example, denounced them as creating a climate of fear and discrimination in a society that has always embraced religious and ethnic pluralism, and as being factually and legally incorrect.[81]

This description of Malaysia as an Islamic state, as well as attempts to mould the common law to Islamic principles (or substitute the common law with Islamic law) have been strenuously resisted by the legal profession, which relies on constitutional history and the foundational nature of the social contract to resist a theocratic state or any deviation from the constitution or the common law.[82]

The PAS, by contrast, while adhering to the concept if not to an actual concrete policy of creating an Islamic state, has been forced to reach political accommodation with other opposition parties in the interest of gaining power. This has caused it to split into an *ulama* faction, which is fundamentalist, and an 'Erdogan' faction, which is pragmatic. For this reason, the PAS has refrained from making clear what an Islamic state would look

Landmarks in Malaysia: The First 50 Years, 1957–2007 (Singapore: LexisNexis, 2007), 197–226.

79 Andrew J. Harding, 'The Keris, the Crescent and the Blind Goddess: The State, Islam and the Constitution in Malaysia', *Singapore Journal of International and Comparative Law* 6 (2002): 154–180; see, generally, Abdul Razak Baginda and Peter Schier (ed.), *Is Malaysia an Islamic State? Secularism and Theocracy – A Study of the Malaysian Constitution* (Kuala Lumpur: Malaysian Strategic Research Centre and Konrad Adenauer Foundation, 2002).

80 'Mahathir: Malaysia Is "Fundamentalist State"', *CNN.com*, June 18, 2002, http://edition.cnn.com/2002/WORLD/asiapcf/southeast/06/18/malaysia.mahathir/. See, generally, Liew Chin Tong, 'PAS Politics: Defining an Islamic State', in Edmund Terence Gomez (ed.), *Politics in Malaysia: The Malay Dimension* (London: Routledge, 2007), 112–113.

81 See Tommy Thomas, 'Is Malaysia an Islamic State', *Malayan Law Journal* 14 (2006): 15–46.

82 See Andrew Harding and Amanda Whiting, '"Custodians of Civil Liberties and Justice in Malaysia": The Malaysian Bar and the Moderate State', in Terence C. Halliday, Lucien Karpik, and Malcolm M. Feeley (eds.), *Fates of Political Liberalism in the British Post-Colony: The Politics of the Legal Complex* (Cambridge University Press, 2012), 288–296.

like,[83] and accepts that its proposals need to be negotiated in terms of the existing constitution and political process.[84]

A. *The Constitutional Structure of Constitutional Islam in Malaysia*

This is made difficult by the fact that from a religious perspective, the constitution's structuring of the State is somewhat ambiguous. The state governments (or federal government insofar as the Federal Territories are concerned) are responsible for the regulation of Islam within their respective jurisdictions. Their powers and responsibilities in this regard are defined exhaustively in Schedule 9 of the constitution. Paraphrased here, they include administering the personal and family laws of Muslims; overseeing charitable and religious endowments and places of Islamic worship; creating and punishing of offences by Muslims against Islamic law; organising the constitution and procedure of Islamic (*syariah*) courts; overseeing the propagation of Islamic doctrines and beliefs among Malays; and deciding on matters of Islamic law and doctrine and Malay custom. The issue of propagation is the item on this list that affects non-Muslims most deeply. Each state maintains an extensive religious bureaucracy, which even includes religious police.[85]

Beyond the structure of religious jurisdiction, Article 3 of the constitution, while enshrining Islam as 'the religion of the Federation' adds that 'other religions may be practised in peace and harmony'.[86] To understand Article 3 further we need to refer also to Article 11, which guarantees freedom of religion and is discussed further. According to Article 11, 'Every person has the right to profess and practice his religion and, subject to Clause (4), to propagate it'. Clause (4) provides that '[s]tate law [and in respect of the Federal Territories, federal law] may control or restrict the

[83] See Liew, 'PAS Politics', 113–130.

[84] See id.

[85] Shuaib, 'The Islamic Legal System', 94–97.

[86] Compare Jamila Hussain, 'Freedom of Religion in Malaysia: The Muslim Perspective', in Wu Min Aun (ed.), *Public Law in Contemporary Malaysia* (Petaling Jaya: Longman Malaysia, 1999), 107–133, with Poh-ling Tan, 'Prime Suspect or Potential Witness? Paying the Price for Religious Freedom: A Non-Muslim Perspective', in Wu Min Aun (ed.), *Public Law in Contemporary Malaysia* (Petaling Jaya: Longman Malaysia, 1999), 137–177. See also Andrew Harding, 'Malaysia: Religious Pluralism and the Constitution in a Contested Polity', *Middle East Law and Governance* 4 (2012): 356–385; Andrew Harding, 'Constitutionalism, Islam and National Identity in Malaysia', in Rainer Grote and Tilmann Röder (eds.), *Constitutionalism in Islamic Countries: Between Upheaval and Continuity* (Oxford University Press, 2012), 201–219.

propagation of any religious doctrine or belief among persons professing the religion of Islam'. Article 11 also attaches religious freedom to religious communities by guaranteeing the rights of religious communities to manage their own affairs. Under Article 12 discrimination against any citizen on the grounds of religion is prohibited in relation to the administration of public education, and every religious group has the right to establish and maintain institutions for educating children in its own religion. It is, however, lawful under Article 12 for the federal and state governments to maintain Islamic institutions. But no person shall be required to receive instruction in or to take part in any ceremony or act of worship of a religion other than his or her own.

These provisions have in practice raised a large number of practical dilemmas with which we cannot here be concerned in any detail, but that go the heart of the State's very identity. They encompass jurisdictional issues in a bifurcated legal system; the status of Islam under the constitution; the religious rights of both Muslims and non-Muslims; and the nature of Malaysian citizenship.[87]

Beyond this there is a sharp division of opinion between those who consider that Article 3 has no effect other than symbolic or ceremonial, that is, that the State is essentially secular, and those who consider that Article 3 effectively and substantively establishes Malaysia as an Islamic state.[88] There is also a variety of views that sit in between these positions. Resort is often had to the drafting process of the 1950s, discussed at the outset of this chapter.[89] While it might seem odd to examine the minutiae of what are now rather ancient discussions, interpretation of the constitution is critical. Ironically, this constitutional-history debate has the incidental benefit of entrenching the constitution as an immovable feature of public discourse.

Litigation around Article 3 and Article 121 has been extensive and tightly fought, but without clarifying many general propositions. It can be seen that the courts have moved away from seeing Islamic law as operating in a personal-law-for-Muslims niche towards seeing it as a defining element in the polity and the constitution. In one High Court decision, *Meor Atiqulrahman v. Fatimah binte Sihi*, the judge even stated that 'Islam in the Constitution [is] a complete way of life and not just a mere set of rituals ... [it] is the primary religion which takes precedence over other religions

[87] See, generally, Harding, 'The Keris, the Crescent and the Blind Goddess'.

[88] See, e.g., Jaclyn L. Neo, 'Competing Imperatives: Conflicts and Convergences in State and Islam in Pluralist Malaysia,' *Oxford Journal of Law and Religion* 4 (2015): 1–25.

[89] See, e.g., Fernando, 'The Position of Islam'.

in Malaysia, and this is the implication of the stipulation of Islam as the religion of the Federation'.[90]

B. A Case Study: *The Allah Case*

In the place of an explication of the complex case law that surrounds the jurisdictional divide between Syariah courts and the civil courts, which is the subject of a large amount of legal literature, we will instead examine the place of Islam and fundamental rights through study of a recent case.

In 2009 objections were made about a Catholic publication, the *Herald*, which in its Malay edition used the word 'Allah' to indicate the Christian God. It is accepted that for a long time Malay-speaking Christians have used 'Allah' in this way. The Minister for Home Affairs, using his powers under the Publications and Printing Presses Act 1984, banned the publication.[91] The publishers of the *Herald* applied for judicial review, and the High Court issued a powerful judgment striking down the minister's ban on the ground that it violated the right to practice religion 'in peace and harmony' under Article 3(1), and the right of freedom of expression under Article 10.[92] This decision was then overturned by the Federal Court of Malaysia, which emphasised the need for public order in these decisions, and which also adopted a restrictive interpretation of the 'peace and harmony' provision, which places both the protection of Islam against proselytisation by other religions, and religious confusion among Muslims, above respect for other religions. The Federal Court then by a 4–3 decision refused leave to appeal against this decision, despite the High Court's decision and a split decision in the Federal Court itself, which went far beyond the legitimate parameters of a leave application to consider the merits of the case.[93]

The issue was extremely divisive, and resulted in the government issuing an unusual '10-point solution' to guide decisions of executive bodies

[90] *Meor Atiqulrahman bin Ishak* v *Fatimah binte Sihi* [2000] 5 *MLJ*: 375, 381 (High Court of Malaysia); see also Abdul Aziz Bari, 'Islam in the Federal Constitution: A Commentary on the Decision of Meor Atiqulrahman' [2000] 2 *MLJ* cxxx.

[91] See Baradan Kuppusamy, 'Can Christians Say "Allah"? In Malaysia, Muslims Say No', *Time*, Jan. 8, 2010.

[92] *Titular Roman Catholic Archbishop of Kuala Lumpur* v *Menteri Dalam Negeri* [2010] 2 MLJ 78 (High Court of Malaysia).

[93] See *Titular Roman Catholic Archbishop of Kuala Lumpur v Menteri Dalam Negeri & Ors* [2014] 4 MLJ 765 (Federal Court of Malaysia).

on religious matters.[94] (What seems conspicuously lacking from Malaysia's constitutional/political system is any constitutionally mandated process whereby the various religious communities can negotiate a mutually acceptable solution to issues such as proselytisation, conversion, doctrinal schisms, religious critiques, and the use of religious texts. Litigation seems to encourage paranoia rather than tolerance.[95]) Underlying this divisiveness is that there seems to be a real fear among some Muslims that unless there are severe limits on conversion from Islam, very large numbers of people will desert the faith, which accordingly needs protection and doctrinal clarity.[96] In response to some troubling incidents and in an attempt to provide a mechanism for non-confrontational resolution of inter-religious differences, in 2010 the government set up under the Prime Minister's Department a 'Special Committee to Promote Understanding and Harmony Among Religious Adherents', comprising thirty-five representatives of various religious organisations.[97]

The case law on Article 121(1A) reached a critical juncture with the decision of the Federal Court (the highest court) in the case of *Lina Joy v. Federal Territory Islamic Council* in May 2007, relating to an attempt by a Muslim woman to change the religious affiliation listed on her identity card.[98] Lina Joy was brought up as a Muslim (her original name was Azlina Binti Jailani), but as an adult she converted to Christianity, and changed her name to Lina Joy. When she requested that here National Identity Card be changed to show her new religion, the National Registration Department (NRD) refused to accept her statutory declaration that she was now a Christian, saying that she needed to obtain further documentary evidence of conversion, such as a statement of apostasy from the Syariah court saying that she was no longer a Muslim. However, the National Registration Regulations 1990, which governed the issue, made no such requirement,

94 See Letter from Prime Minister Najib Razak to Bishop Ng. Moon Hing, April 11, 2011, reprinted in 'Bahasa Malaysia Bibles: The Cabinet's 10-point solution', *Aliran*, Jan. 25, 2014, http://aliran.com/web-specials/bahasa-malaysia-bibles-10-point-solution/.

95 Cf. Robert A. Kagan, *Adversarial Legalism: The American Way of Law* (Cambridge, MA: Harvard University Press, 2003).

96 'See '"Illogical" That 250,000 Muslims Have Left Faith, Says Perlis Mufti', *The Malaysian Insider*, Oct. 18, 2011, http://www.themalaysianinsider.com/malaysia/article/illogical-that-250000-muslims-have-left-faith-says-perlis-mufti.

97 See Debra Chong, 'Interfaith Panel Back in Saddle Next Month, Says New Chief', *The Malaysian Insider*, Oct. 17, 2011, www.themalaysianinsider.com/mobile/malaysia/article/interfaith-panel-back-in-saddle-next-month-says-new-chief/.

98 See, generally, Steven Thiru and Ben Dawson, 'The Lina Joy Case and the Future of Religious Freedom in Malaysia', *Lawasia Journal* (2007): 151–162.

and she was understandably unwilling to do so because applying to the Syariah court would not only imply that she herself accepted her Muslim identity, but would also raise the possibility of her being prosecuted for apostasy.

Her application for judicial review of the NRD's decision continuously preoccupied and inflamed public opinion as it proceeded through the courts from 2004 through 2007. A majority of the Federal Court (two to one) ultimately rejected her appeal, deciding that the NRD had acted lawfully.[99] The majority judgment proceeded on the basis that if a Muslim wanted to leave Islam this was a question of Islamic law, and Article 121(1A) of the constitution gave Syariah courts, not civil courts, jurisdiction over questions of apostasy. The Federal Court also held that the freedom of Malay/Muslims to leave their religion was qualified by Articles 3 and 160(2) of the Malaysian Constitution. Article 3, as we have seen, makes Islam the 'religion of the federation', and this protected status justifies subjecting decisions by Malays, who are defined to be Muslims by Article 160(2), to leave Islam to review by the Syariah Courts, given the negative and contra-constitutional effect such decisions might have for Islam.

By so deciding, the Court had in effect, by reference to Article 121(1A), elevated Article 3's recognition of Islam above Article 11's right to choose one's religion, something not envisaged when the constitution was drafted. However, Justice Richard Malanjum (the only non-Muslim judge hearing the appeal) registered a passionate dissent, arguing that the superior civil courts should not decline jurisdiction over apostasy cases, because Article 121(1A) only provided for the jurisdiction of Syariah courts over issues of Islamic law, it did not give those courts authority to interpret constitutional provisions, and where restrictions on fundamental rights are involved, constitutional interpretative authority has to be express, not implied. The majority, he argued, failed to grasp that the jurisdiction of Islamic law is conditioned on the constitutional right of an individual, under Article 10, to choose her or his religion.

This case created an unprecedented degree of passion among the public. The plaintiff, her fiancé, and a human rights lawyer were the objects of death threats.[100] For many Muslims, the suit threated an attack on Islam that could lead to unrestricted apostasy. For many non-Muslims, the

[99] See *Lina Joy v. Majlis Agama Islam Wilayah Persekutuan* [2007] 4 MLJ 585 (Federal Court of Malaysia).

[100] 'Once Muslim, Now Christian and Caught in the Courts', *New York Times*, Aug. 24, 2006.

decision undermined the secular state and their constitutional right to freedom of religion.[101] The outcome of this and other recent cases is that the jurisdiction of the syariah courts has been increased by resolving any doubts in their favour. The result is a worrying, deepening polarisation of a society that has generally prided itself on its multi-culturalism and its mutual tolerance.

VI. The State after 2008: Beyond What, Leading to What?

Malaysia remains deeply divided; but it is divided along more than one axis. The divisions are political, ethnic, and religious; but they intertwine other divisions over, for example, governance and the electoral system, the federal structure, the political economy of development, national identity, and the constitutional roles of the monarchy. The religious divide between Muslims and non-Muslims appears to be deepening, moving from one social arena to another with no effective mediatory mechanism apparent other than litigation. To some extent this divide functions as a surrogate for ethnic divisions. But even beyond this, ethnicity is still a very divisive issue, as we have seen. We therefore have to confront the questions whether this situation represents a contest within an accepted range of norms; or a volatile situation that lurches outside this range of norms into new modes of governance – and what such modes of governance might look like in future.

Along these lines, there are some positive signs not often recognised by those partaking in this tug-of-war. These conflicts take place for the most part on the assumption that the constitution (despite whatever list of faults it is seen as being guilty of) is the basis for discussion and the conflict is over its meaning or its reform, not over its legitimacy as such. Indeed, it is revealing that the discourse is so often around constitutional history and interpretation, as opposed to the possibility of constitutional revision (or suspension). The frequent resort to litigation is, of course, highly divisive, and ultimately threatening to public confidence in judicial independence. But constitutional litigation does offer the possibility of closure, allowing for constitutional growth as grounds of contestation move from one issue to another overlapping issue. The other positive indication is that these conflicts have never (at least since 1969) involved significant

[101] See, generally, Yang Lai Fong and Md. Sidin Ahmad Ishak, 'Framing Religious Disputes: A Comparative Analysis of the Lina Joy Controversy Reported by Malaysian Newspapers', *The Journal of the South East Asia Research Centre for Communication and Humanities* 3.2 (2011): 21–37.

physical violence – although incidents have sometimes involved damage to property, in particular church arson.

Indeed, the cognitive and political chaos these conflicts present can itself be seen as a process of generating a new species of constitutional order.[102] It is a process similar to that described by James Tully, one that takes 'religious law out from under the conceptual framework of modern secular law, [making] it possible to understand it in its own terms and compare it with others'.[103] This is clearly a positive move. In the short run, it may heighten political conflict between the two legal systems. But there may be no clearer way forward on this issue.

What can be seen in this story is thus a tension between three different conceptions of constitutional order: liberal democracy based on and defending the Westminster constitution; Malay nationalist/monarchist domination of the institutions of power under a restricted form of developmental constitutionalism; and an ambitious Islamic-state constitutional ideology that attempts to reinterpret the constitution in line with its agenda of desecularising the State. Only in the first case does the conception of 'constitution' or 'constitutionalism' involve restricting the power of the State.

This does not in my view quite represent a pluralist ideology: rather it represents a *pluralism of ideologies* in a relatively stable state of tension. Malaysia is often seen as an example of ethnic and religious accommodation – a 'moderate' (according to President Obama and some Malaysian government rhetoric that emphasises 'moderate' Islam) State making the best of a difficult situation. This is not correct. It is not accommodation but rather a perpetual conflict in which there are, so far at least, no final winners and no final losers, but only marginal gains, sustainable losses, and the possibility of something better.

The question then arises whether this position is sustainable. Few in 1957 or in 1969 would have given much chance of success in dealing with the acute social divisions effectively in what has been and still is a deeply fractured society. Fewer still would have envisaged that this could be done within the confines (albeit confines stretched almost to breaking point on more than one occasion) of a colonially devised constitution. However, the historical basis and practical consequences of inter-ethnic accommodation seem not to be accepted by newer generations of Malaysians.

[102] Cf. Harding, 'Malaysia: Religious Pluralism and the Constitution in a Contested Polity'.

[103] James Tully, 'Middle East Legal and Governmental Pluralism: A View of the Field from the Demos', *Middle East Law and Governance* 4 (2012): 260.

Development, education, and urbanisation have also brought about closer proximity, more religious competition and conversions, and larger numbers of mixed marriages. These factors have also, ironically perhaps, heightened inter-communal tensions. The previously docile Indian community, for example, has in recent years started to assert its religious (Hindu) and socio-economic rights.[104]

In the long run, this constant acrimonious, arms-length, intellectual skirmishing may turn out to be simply the way in which Malaysians 'do' constitutional evolution. This may not be completely apparent, but in examining this process one has to be aware of what opposed forces agree about as well as what they disagree about. The agreements can be stated as a belief, even if a purely pragmatic one, that the issues can only be determined constitutionally; that violent direct action other than protest (including illegal protest) is largely impossible; and that democracy is the only avenue by which the state can make change changes in the law and the constitution. Ironically, the post-2008 period is the only period of Malaysian history in which the constitution could not effectively be amended; yet it is also the period in which the most positive and potentially far-reaching changes have taken place. Time alone will tell, but it is probably simply unavoidable that a single notion of constitutionalism is unlikely to be able to prevail.

[104] See, e.g., Farish A. Noor, 'The Hindu Rights Action Force (HINDRAF) of Malaysia: Communitarianism across Borders?', RSIS Working Paper Series No. 163 (Singapore: Nanyang Technological University, S. Rajaratnam School of International Studies [RSIS], July 2008).

11

A Sense of Grievance and the Quest for Freedom: South Africa's Constitution – the Struggle Continues

HUGH CORDER

I. Introduction

In an endeavour to situate South Africa's constitutional history[1] into the general themes of this volume, I argue that what characterises the history of public governance in South Africa, and thus its 'constitution', is a complex series of interactions between two key elements: a sense of grievance and the quest for freedom. Both these notions manifested themselves in many forms at different times, and it is sometimes difficult in any particular circumstance to identify whether some sense of grievance gave rise to a corresponding quest for freedom, or the other way around.

To take just two examples: The arrival in the southwestern Cape of the French Huguenots in the 1670s was a result of their seeking freedom from persecution in Europe, but after their settlement and their becoming part of the 'establishment' at the Cape, they developed grievances with the governing Dutch East India Company (the *Vereenigde Oostindische Compagnie*, hereinafter VOC).[2] On the other hand, an increasing sense of grievance felt by the mainly Dutch-speaking and slave-owning farmers after the British took power in 1806 led directly to these farmers' own quest for freedom as expressed by their trekking away from the

[1] See, generally, Carolyn Hamilton, Bernard K. Mbenga, and Robert Ross (eds.), *The Cambridge History of South Africa*. Vol. 1, *From Early Times to 1885* (Cambridge University Press, 2014); and Robert Ross, Anne Kelk Mager, and Bill Nasson (eds.), *The Cambridge History of South Africa*. Vol. 2, *1885–1994* (Cambridge University Press, African ed., 2014).

[2] See, generally, Robert Ross, 'Khoesan and Immigrants: The Emergence of Colonial Society in the Cape 1500–1800', in Carolyn Hamilton, Bernard K. Mbenga, and Robert Ross (eds.), *The Cambridge History of South Africa*. Vol. 1, *From Early Times to 1885* (Capetown: Cambridge University Press, 2014), 168–210.

English imperial stranglehold and forming independent republics in the hinterland.[3]

I use the indefinite article to precede 'sense of grievance' to draw attention to the multiplicity of complaints and dissatisfaction that existed, and the definite article before 'quest for freedom' because, although the exact form of the ultimate state of freedom would certainly have differed among the various groups seeking it, the quality expressed by that notion seems more universally applicable.

I start by exploring these two central notions in a little more detail in the section that follows. I then attempt to periodise the history of human settlement and interactions in a way that demonstrates most vividly both senses of grievance and the corresponding quest for freedom, identifying key moments that, I would argue, mark particular shifts in discourse about the relations of power between important groups. I shrink from using the word *development*, lest it be implied that in some way I am making a normative assessment, that there has been a gradual process of improvement of the standards of public governance, in alignment with some sort of unifying and progressive political ideology: If this has happened at all in the dominant political culture of the country, it has only been in the last two decades. Of course, at the same time, the particular methodology I use to develop this periodisation itself expresses a choice of values.

I engage in this analysis not only to sketch the outline of the main reasons for constitutional change, but also because I maintain that a knowledge of this history is an essential element, as I will explain in the concluding section, in understanding the structure and content of the current constitutional democracy. The 1993 and 1996 Constitutions respond to, confront, and seek to transcend much that is 'wicked' in that history, while building on whatever 'good' elements there may have been. Yet many senses of grievance remain, some old, some revived, some new, and the quest for freedom remains the central element in much political rhetoric in the public domain.

The exercise in periodisation also assists, furthermore, to identify the complex nature of any ideas that may have informed such constitutional history over the period of about 180 years that is reviewed here. Much more attention needs to be given to these ideas. Nevertheless, I end by drawing some extremely provisional conclusions.

[3] See Martin Legassick and Robert Ross, 'From Slave Economy to Settler Capitalism: The Cape Colony and Its Extensions, 1800–1854', in Carolyn Hamilton, Bernard K. Mbenga, and Robert Ross (eds.), *The Cambridge History of South Africa*. Vol. 1, *From Early Times to 1885* (Cambridge University Press, 2014), 253–318.

II. The Ideas Central to the Constitutional Enterprise in South Africa

As introduced, South Africa's long-term constitutional-evolutionary development and trajectory can be seen as having been driven by the interplay between two epistemic dynamics: 'a sense of grievance' and 'the quest for freedom'. In this section, I will introduce each in turn.

A. *'A Sense of Grievance'*

Life in South Africa reflects a rich diversity of unhappiness. Underlying much of the unhappiness are the fundamental organising realities of *exclusion* and *inequality*. These, in turn, lead to conditions conducive to exploitation, suspicion and violent confrontation, and easy resort to physical and psychological force. Yet at the same time, perhaps not paradoxically, they also give rise to astonishing displays of heroic courage; tight communal relationships; a remarkably tenacious belief in formal religious faiths (of all varieties); and, as we shall see, a similarly tenacious belief in the capacity of the law to deliver justice.[4]

Evidence of this set of ideas is to be found, I would argue, in the myriad criteria according to which the population of South Africa has classified itself over the decades. These include classifications according to race, ethnicity, sex, gender, class, religious and political belief, sexual orientation, national origin, subjection to customary or religious personal law, and so on. Such classifications frequently became the basis for both informal and formal differentiations and even exclusions from resource allocation or access to social benefits. So one is always conscious of the 'other' all around one, and this may have the effect of wanting a constitutional order that cabins and confines the population, so to protect and advance one's own interests by protecting and advancing those of one's own particular group (not that South Africa is necessarily unique in this regard).

At this point, a note on South Africa's racial nomenclature is essential. No discussion about South Africa and its people can proceed without a common understanding of how notions of 'race' have been conceptualised, nominalised, and applied throughout its history.[5]

[4] Jens Meierhenrich, *The Legacies of Law: Long-Run Consequences of Legal Development in South Africa, 1652–2000* (Cambridge University Press, 2008).

[5] See John Dugard, *Human Rights and the South African Legal Order* (Princeton University Press, 1978), 59–63.

There have always been essentially four identifiable racial groups, although the precise labels have changed over the decades. None of this usage implies that such divisions are in any manner either scientific, nor easily demarcated, nor remotely acceptable, in any frame of reference. They are, however, an inalienable reality in any account such as the current one, and so will be resorted to when necessary.

In present-day South Africa, the most frequently used social classifications and divisions are as follows (with earlier usage bracketed in parentheses): 'black African', i.e., those people who in the main are descended from the 'tribes' that migrated south-westwards into the current South African state, particularly from 1600 to 1850 (earlier referred to as 'natives' and 'Bantu'); 'white', i.e., descendants of migrants from Europe (known formerly as 'Europeans'); 'Asian', i.e., descendants of persons drawn largely from the Indian sub-continent through indentured labour contracts, and who then remained in the country, as well as some professionals and traders (previously referred to as 'Indians'); and 'coloured', which includes persons descended from the ancient indigenous people of South Africa (usually called the 'Khoesan'), the slave populations brought in from 1652 till the early 1800s, and the product of racially mixed partnerships.

More broadly, South Africans also use the term *black* to signifying anyone who is not of 'white' European descendant.

Particularly when paired with segregation and apartheid, such classifications worked to enhance the capitalist exploitation of both resources and labour, so as to produce long-standing and frankly obscene levels (and displays) of wealth juxtaposed with dire and degrading poverty. And what is perhaps more surprising is that the gap between the wealthy and the poor has widened since 1994, despite a partial blurring of the racial composition of the 'black' and 'white' classifications. According to a report compiled by Statistics South Africa, in 2011 South Africa had a Gini coefficient of 0.69, making it one of the most unequal countries in the world.[6] Against such a background, it is inevitable that strong expressions of grievance would become and will continue to be the stock-in-trade of South African political and constitutional discourse. These various senses of grievance would in turn impact on the type of freedom sought by those expressing them.

[6] Statistics South Africa, *Poverty Trends in South Africa: An Examination of Absolute Poverty between 2006 and 2011* (Report No. 03-10-06 2014) (Pretoria: Statistics South Africa, 2014), 14.

B. 'The Quest for Freedom'

This ultimate objective of constitutional development has been expressed in many ways throughout South Africa's history, some of them antithetical to more common understandings of liberal constitutionalism. Among the many incidents in South African history that exemplify such a longing for freedom – albeit sometimes on a limited, 'sectoral' level – are:

- The ultimately futile struggles of the indigenous inhabitants of what became the Cape Colony to maintain their pastoral and nomadic lifestyles when confronted by evermore violent encroachments on their territory by settlers from Europe during the seventeenth and eighteenth centuries;[7]
- The constant tensions between the rule of the settlement at the Cape by the Dutch VOC and attempts by those who were granted 'free burger' status to farm and trade with the VOC to gain political autonomy;
- The longing for freedom of those brought to South Africa as slaves;
- The desire among the trek-boers to escape British colonial rule (in part so that they could continue to own slaves) and to establish their own republics during the nineteenth century;
- The staunch defence of freedom of expression and the press in the first half of the 1800s both by members of the British 1820 settler community and by farmers of Dutch extraction who remained within the territories under the control of the British;
- The agitation by the growing permanent settler population for representative and responsible government for the Cape in the mid-nineteenth century;
- The Xhosa Wars from 1779 to 1879, in which the amaXhosa resisted imperial expansion first by Boer frontiersmen and later by English imperialism into the Eastern Cape;
- Boer efforts to escape British colonial and economic imperialism by establishing independent Boer Republics in the centre and north of the South African interior in the early 1850s (albeit bringing with them the subjugation of the local black population),[8] culminating in the Anglo-Boer War of 1899 to 1902 (which witnessed the ruthless extinction of

[7] See Ross, 'Khoesan and Immigrants'.

[8] See L. M. Thompson, 'Constitutionalism in the South African Republics', *Butterworths South African Law Review* (1954): 49–73. See generally H. R. Hahlo and Ellison Kahn, *The Union of South Africa: The Development of Its Laws and Constitution* (London: Stevens, 1960). See especially chs. 2,3, and 4.

much of what the Boers had held sacred, in a material, cultural and spiritual sense);

- The passage of the *South Africa Act 1909*[9] by the Imperial (British) Parliament, leading to the formation of a new nation-state – the Union of South Africa – albeit one whose legislative autonomy was still subordinated to that of the imperial British Parliament through the Colonial Laws Validity Act 1865;[10]
- The imperial British Parliament's passage of the Statute of Westminster 1931,[11] which after ratification by the South African Parliament through the Status of the Union Act, 1934,[12] repealed the Colonial Laws Validity Act and gave the Union of South Africa complete legislative autonomy, albeit still a commonwealth nation under the nominal sovereignty of the British monarch;
- The establishment in 1912 of the South African Native National Congress – renamed the African National Congress in 1923 – to fight for the freedom of blacks within the Union after they were denied the right to vote in the South Africa Act 1909;
- The drafting and promulgation of the *Africans' Claims in South Africa* by the African National Congress in 1943,[13] a report by the Congress's Atlantic Charter Committee proposing a South African bill of rights in the spirit of the 'Atlantic Charter' advanced in 1941 by Franklin Roosevelt and Winston Churchill;
- The adoption in 1955 by the Congress of the People (a meeting of more than three thousand democrats from all four main 'racial' groups in South Africa) of the *Freedom Charter*,[14] a programme for the construction of a non-racial South Africa that would later serve as an inspiration for South Africa's first post-apartheid constitution of 1994;
- The cathartic effect for many Afrikaner nationalists of leaving the British Commonwealth in 1961 and establishing a now fully sovereign nation, the Republic of South Africa. accompanied by the adoption of South Africa's second constitution, the Republic of South Africa Constitution Act;[15] and

[9] 7 Edw VII, c 9.
[10] 28 & 29 Vict. c. 63.
[11] 22 Geo V, c 4.
[12] Act No. 69 of 1934.
[13] See Hassen Ebrahim, *The Soul of a Nation: Constitution-Making in South Africa* (Cape Town: Oxford University Press, 1998), 396–414.
[14] Id. at 415–419.
[15] Act No. 32 of 1961.

The countless other entreaties, letters, petitions, campaigns, marches, strikes, and boycotts throughout this period, often led in the main by black-African South Africans but increasingly supported by members of all races, that continually pushed the advancement of freedom.[16]

Most of the events mentioned above represent important milestones in South Africa's constitutional history. They show in many different guises how diverse senses of grievance underlay the expression both in words and deeds of the quest for freedom. Out of this can be constructed a compelling narrative of the complex process of South Africa's constitutional unfolding, one that by identifying moments at which the balance of these forces – sense of grievance and quest for freedom – seemed to shift to cause clear changes in the form and/or substance of constitutional governance in the political territory now known as the Republic of South Africa.

III. A Periodisation of South Africa's Constitutional History

I identify six periods in the constitutional history of South Africa. These are characterised by particular constellations of social and political interaction, in which different internal constituencies and forces form alliances with, test, confront, exploit, and fight each other as the grievances of one group collide with the quests for freedom of others.

A. *Laying the Foundations of European Domination (1808–1902)*

This first period of South Africa's constitutional history is defined by struggles between the British imperial invaders and local populations of European origin – initially primarily of Dutch origin but later of British origin as well – that had grown to think of themselves as 'South African'. Equally important were tensions between both of these European groups and indigenous African populations that gradually moved south-westwards and that increasingly came into contact with the north-easterly expansion of the Europeans.[17] A third set of conflicts, arising particularly

[16] See, generally, Thomas Karis and Gwendolyn M. Carter (eds.), *From Protest to Challenge: A Documentary History of African Politics in South Africa 1882–1990* (Stanford, CA: Hoover Institution Press [Vol. 1–5]) (Capetown: University of South Africa Pres [Vols. 5–7], 1971–1997).

[17] See John Wright, 'Turbulent Times: Political Transformations in the North and East 1760s–1830s', in Carolyn Hamilton, Bernard K. Mbenga, and Robert Ross (eds.), *The Cambridge History of South Africa*. Vol. 1, *From Early Times to 1885* (Cambridge University Press, 2014), 211–252.

during the 1800s, is to be seen in the anomalous and uneasy position of those who did not 'fit' into either of these dominant groups, persons regarded as 'coloured' and those of Asian origin from 1864 onwards. For these latter groups, the quest for freedom was from slavery and indenture, and the sense of grievance was chiefly the ambivalence with which they were regarded by the colonial masters, being used as a 'buffer' against black Africans, sometimes even in armed conflict, but simultaneously being denied full membership of the ruling establishment through both social sanction and operation of the law.

Within this period, one can identify five catalytic moments that I argue represent key points or phases that significantly reframed the nature of constitutional governance in some form or another.

1. The Abolition of Slavery and the 'Great Trek'

Slaves had been imported from Asia by the VOC since settlement in 1652. Slaves were part of the workforce both in the towns and on almost all the farms owned and run by European settlers. Few slaves were freed, and there was much agitation (including several revolts) regarding their conditions and their desire for freedom. The British, having taken over the Cape in 1795, outlawed the importation of slaves in 1808,[18] although not ownership per se. Slavery at the Cape ceased by law in 1834,[19] which led directly to the large-scale departure of many of the rural, slave-holding Dutch settlers from the Cape – a movement that became known as the 'Great Trek'. The Great Trek can be seen, somewhat paradoxically, as a quest for freedom resulting from a sense of grievance that had been triggered in significant part by another group's quest for freedom. And it would have significant consequences for the shape of constitutional development over the next sixty years at least.

2. The Establishment of the Boer Republics

The Trekkers (or 'trekboers') moved both northwards and eastwards. By the mid-1830s, one group settled in what would become became Natal, inflicting significant defeats on a large force of black African (Zulu) warriors en route. The British were not prepared to tolerate this, however. Invading from the coast, they pushed the trekboers through the Drakensberg Mountains into the interior of the subcontinent. In 1852, these trekkers established the South African Republic (ZAR) in what

[18] Slave Trade Act 1807 (47 Geo 3 Sess 1 c 36).
[19] Slavery Abolition Act 1833 (3 & 4 Will. IV c. 73).

later became Transvaal Province. Other trekboers settled in the area of the Orange and Vaal rivers, where they established the Orange Free State (OFS) in 1854.[20]

These two, independent 'Boer republics' both adopted roughly American-style constitutions – which included a listing of protected fundamental rights, and which gave the judiciary authority to review both legislative and executive action. But their experience under these constitutions varied greatly. The OFS Constitution was much more effective in providing 'citizens' with an effective rule-of-law – although such citizenship was almost exclusively granted only to male European trekkers.[21] Government in the ZAR, on the other hand, was much more oppressive. Its executive branch refused to accept the judiciary's power to pronounce decisions of the *Volksraad* (People's Assembly, or parliament) to be unconstitutional.[22] But all in all, both these republics satisfied the quest for freedom insofar as the ruling groups were concerned.

Of course, such 'freedom' came at significant cost both to the indigenous Africans living in or migrating into the territories of those republics, and to the 'coloured' people, many of whom had been brought into the territories as slaves, and who in any event continued, along with the blacks, to be denied the most basic protections of citizenship. The ZAR Constitution was particularly oppressive along these lines, stating that there was to be no 'equality in church or state' between white and black.[23] As we shall see, in this way, one group's quest for freedom ended up bringing new senses of grievance to other groups.

3. Resistance against Imperial Authority

Back in the Cape, beginning around 1820, new waves of European immigrants, particularly those who settled the eastern districts of the colony, began pursuing their own quest for freedom from the British imperial government in London, in the form of increasing self-government by the local European population. One of the most celebrated incidents of this involved clashes between the imperial authorities and the settlers centred on freedom of expression and the press in Grahamstown in the

[20] See also Norman Etherington, Patrick Harries, and Bernard K Mbenga, 'From Colonial Hegemonies to Imperial Conquest, 1840–1880,' in Carolyn Hamilton, Bernard K. Mbenga, and Robert Ross (eds.), *The Cambridge History of South Africa*. Vol. 1, *From Early Times to 1885* (Cambridge University Press, 2014), 319–391.

[21] See Thompson, 'Constitutionalism in the South African Republics'.

[22] See, e.g., *Brown v. Leyds NO* (1897) 4 Off Rep 17.

[23] See the Grondwet (Constitution) of 1858, article 6.

eastern part of the Cape, in which the settlers triumphed.[24] This and other pressures duly led to the granting by the British first of representative government status to the Cape Colony in 1853[25] and to Natal in 1856, and then of responsible government in the Cape in 1872 and Natal in 1893.[26]

While the imperial power in London retained ultimate legislative authority (as exercised through the Parliament at Westminster) and executive authority (through the appointment and control of the colonial governor), both the Cape and Natal enjoyed a fair degree of autonomy in day-to-day governmental business. There were no specially protected substantive (fundamental) rights, and the superior courts exercised judicial review of administrative but not legislative action. Nevertheless, the quality of justice dispensed by the courts came to secure at least a significant measure of the rule of law and an observance of formal equality before the law. There were several landmark cases that emphasised the limits of governmental authority.[27] Lines of race discrimination began to blur, at least on the edges, and educated 'coloured' and African inhabitants found some degree of social and legal acceptance.

4. Continued Influx of African Populations

In both the English colonies and the Boer republics, hunger for land led to the fourth major set of flashpoints. Africans continued to move steadily south and westwards in the southern-African sub-continent, motivated both by the need for pasture and grazing lands for their livestock, and by the need to escape the acquisitive aggression of powerful autocrats such as Shaka (the legendary Zulu leader of the 1820s).[28] In both Boer republics, and in the British colony of Natal, such groups enjoyed few if any rights of citizenship, engendering massive resentment and a sense of grievance at the European invaders, both Dutch- and English-speaking.[29]

5. Unification, Resentment, and the Creation of a 'White' South Africa

The last and perhaps most critical episode in this period that impacted conclusively on the constitutional history of South Africa had its origins

[24] See Legassick and Ross, 'Slave Economy', 269–274.
[25] Order in Council of 11 March 1853, section 2 of the Schedule (July 1853).
[26] See Hahlo and Kahn, *The Union of South Africa*, ch 3.
[27] E.g., *In re Willem Kok and Nathaniel Balie*, 1879 Buch 45.
[28] See Wright, 'Turbulent Times', 228–231.
[29] See Dugard, *Human Rights and the South African Legal Order*, 17–21.

in the quest for freedom, detailed in the preceding text, which led the trekboers to leave their farms in the Cape and establish their own independent republics in the hinterland. Initially, the British authorities were prepared to let this be (although they occupied the ZAR for a while in the early 1880s, before returning it to independent rule). Everything changed, however, with the discovery of massive reserves of diamonds in Kimberley in the northernmost part of the Cape Colony in 1867, bordering the ZAR. This was followed almost some twenty years later by the even more significant discovery of huge deposits of gold and other precious metals deep within the territory of the ZAR itself.

The economic impact of these discoveries was more than significant – it changed the game entirely. British imperial capital moved in with a vengeance, and countless investors, adventurers, and work-seekers flocked to the diamond and gold fields. Political power in the Cape was ruthlessly pursued by those with economic power, as was the case with C. J. (Cecil John) Rhodes. Rhodes was able to monopolise the global diamond market in the 1880s (he was one of the founders of DeBeers). He became prime minister of the Cape in 1890, and used his position to promote mining interests.

His infamous raid on the ZAR, led by his close accomplice, Jameson, in 1895–1896, and intended to overthrow the then republican government and replace it with a regime more accommodating of his own mining interests, ultimately occasioned the Anglo-Boer War. The Jameson Raid was an ignominious failure, and Rhodes resigned the office of prime minister in disgrace. But the continuing domination of Cape politics by mining interests caused the British and their surrogates at the Cape to exert intolerable pressure on the ZAR government to allow wholesale British exploitation of ZAR mineral resources. The ZAR government resisted this pressure, and in late 1899 resorted to war to try to keep the imperial enemy at arm's length.[30] This marked the start of the Anglo-Boer War. The OFS joined the ZAR in this campaign, with great success on the battlefield initially, but by the second half of 1900, the British had taken the capital cities and most urban areas in both republics, and their Boer governments had

[30] See Stanley Trapido, 'Imperialism, Settler Identities, and Colonial Capitalism: The Hundred-Year Origins of the 1899 South African War', in Robert Ross, Anne Kelk Mager, and Bill Nasson (eds.), *The Cambridge History of South Africa*. Vol. 2, *1885–1994* (Cambridge University Press, 2014), 66–101; Shula Marks, 'War and Union 1899–1910', in Robert Ross, Anne Kelk Mager, and Bill Nasson (eds.), *The Cambridge History of South Africa*. Vol. 2, *1885–1994* (Cambridge University Press, 2014), 157–210. See also Bill Nasson, *The War for South Africa* (Cape Town: Tafelberg, 2010).

fled. The Boers resorted very effectively to guerrilla warfare, to which the British responded with a scorched earth policy (burning most farmhouses and crops, while driving off the livestock) and confining the (European) civilian population and their servants to concentration camps in which at least twenty-seven thousand people perished.[31] On May 31, 1902, the leadership of the Boer commando forces agreed to an uneasy peace treaty with the British, who thus took formal control of the ZAR and OFS, which together with the Cape and Natal form the territory that now constitutes the South African state.

The brutality of the British campaign, especially their treatment of the civilian population, magnified the distrust and bitterness that the trekboers had always felt towards the British, and cemented a deep-seated sense of grievance towards them that became fundamental to nationalist Afrikaner politics in the twentieth century. While there were probably an equal number of Afrikaners, particularly in the Cape, who had a less extreme sense of anger towards the imperial power, the yearning for self-determination and the freedom of the Afrikaner 'volk' became the dominant narrative of 'white' politics in South Africa for the next seventy-five years.

Black Africans and 'coloureds' were not centrally drawn into the Anglo-Boer War as combatants, although many became casualties as servants of the women and children imprisoned in the concentration camps or as servants of the regular and commando forces on both sides of the conflict. The war brought no alleviation to their plight, however. Indeed, in seeking to unite 'white' power in South Africa, the British-Boer pact of 1902 even further marginalised the position of those not of the 'white race'.[32]

B. Consolidating White Power and Further Dispossessing Blacks (1902–1936)

The end of the Anglo-Boer War resulted in British rule throughout the territory that is now South Africa: the former Afrikaner republics (now styled the Orange River Colony [ORC] and the Transvaal) were initially ruled directly by British officials, but in 1907 were granted responsible government status (the same as existed in the Cape and Natal). At the same time, a National Convention, consisting only of English- and Dutch-speaking

[31] See Elizabeth van Heyningen, *The Concentration Camps of the Anglo-Boer War: A Social History* (Johannesburg: Jacana, 2013).

[32] See, generally, Marks, 'War and Union 1899–1910'.

whites, was formed to work towards the constitutional consolidation of Britain's imperial power in the form of a South African nation-state.[33]

This convention resulted in agreement on the constitutional union (not federation) of the four British colonies, with effective parliamentary sovereignty and a racially exclusionary franchise entitlement in three of the four provinces of the Union (the exception being the Cape). This agreement was formalised in an Act of the British Parliament at Westminster, the South Africa Act of 1909.[34]

Legalised racism was a key element of this constitutional compact. Prior to Union, the Cape granted the franchise to all adult males who qualified on either educational or wealth grounds. 'Non-white' males who met these requirements not only could exercise the vote, but could even serve as members of representative institutions in government, and during the convention Cape representatives argued strongly in favour of extending this non-racial approach to the whole of the new nation. However, the deep-seated racism pervading the Transvaal, ORC, and Natal resisted such an approach, and a compromise was reached that allowed the Cape to retain its non-racial franchise, but did not mandate it elsewhere. This Cape franchise was even protected by providing that this arrangement could not be removed except by a law approved by a two-thirds majority in a special, unicameral sitting of both houses of the South African Parliament.

Convention proponents of the less racist policy of the Cape hoped that over time the Cape's less-restrictive franchise would spread to the other three provinces. So too, they hoped that the institution of provincial governments would develop towards a federalism rather than a more centralised union. At the time, however, their thinking was also that the greater 'good' of uniting the 'white races' (Dutch- and English- speaking republicans and colonials) and seeking to overcome the horror of the recent war should take immediate precedence over their more liberal agenda.

The exclusion of all those not regarded as 'white' from discussions about the future nation was naturally a source of great discontent among these groups. Indeed, the last episode of armed resistance to imperial power, the Bambata rebellion led by King Dinizulu in northern Natal, coincided with the convention. Paradoxically, this caused perhaps the most articulate proponent of the non-racial franchise in the Cape, W. P. (William Philip) Schreiner, to miss key sessions of the convention in order to

[33] See, generally, Martin Chanock, *The Making of South African Legal Culture 1902–1936: Fear, Favour and Prejudice* (Cambridge University Press, 2001).

[34] 7 Edw VII, c 9.

serve as counsel for the defence in Dinizulu's subsequent trial for treason (Dinizulu was found guilty and sentenced to four years' imprisonment in March 1908).[35]

After it became clear that the convention would enshrine racial subjugation in its constitutional draft, black South Africans sent a delegation to Westminster in 1909, accompanied by some whites and by Mahatma Gandhi, to attempt to persuade the British government not to approve the proposed constitution – but to no avail. This led to the founding of the South African Native National Congress in 1912, which consisted primarily of professional and formally educated black South Africans, and that tried in a respectful and non-violent manner to persuade the leaders of the nascent state to give blacks and 'coloureds' formal access to the political process and institutions.[36]

The new South African state, the Union of South Africa, came into being on May 31, 1910. It was unstable at the outset, for a number of reasons, but perhaps the most powerful being the lingering and strongly held resentment stemming from the terrible ill-treatment by the British of many who were on the losing side of the Anglo-Boer War only eight years previously.[37] Most of the working farms in the former Boer republics were devastated and unviable, and the highly disaffected former owners drifted to the towns and cities to seek wage labour. The British imperial authorities took a high-handed and arrogant attitude towards their former adversaries, including the large-scale imposition of English as the medium of government, public life, and education. Among the local colonists, both English-speaking and Dutch-speaking, the defeated Boer/Afrikaner side probably enjoyed more political sympathy than the prevailing British.[38]

Even in the Cape, there had been many Dutch-speaking residents who had rebelled and joined the Boer forces during that war, as well as much agitation against the war by influential English-speakers. Much tension surrounded the position of those of Asian origin, with Gandhi leading a number of passive resistance campaigns against their exclusion from effective citizenship. On the Witwatersrand, a short-lived experiment

35 For further details, see Dugard, *Human Rights and the South African Legal Order*, 27, 251–252.

36 See Marks, 'War and Union, 1899–1910'.

37 See Chanock, *The Making of South African Legal Culture*, ch. 1.

38 See also Philip Bonner, 'South African Society and Culture, 1910–1948', in Robert Ross, Anne Kelk Mager, and Bill Nasson (eds.), *The Cambridge History of South Africa*. Vol. 2, *1885–1994* (Cambridge University Press, 2014), 254–318.

with the large-scale importation of Chinese labour to work in the mines in the immediate aftermath of the Anglo-Boer War led to massive tensions between the largely white artisanal work force – who, deeply influenced by early forms of socialism, rallied to the plight of the imported Asians – and the rampantly capitalist mine owners.

These tensions translated into severe challenges to central governmental authority, and produced major social upheavals – including an armed rebellion by disaffected Boer fighters at the outbreak of World War I in 1914 that threatened to tear apart the newly formed South African Defence Force; and substantial labour unrest by white workers and a militant trade union movement, with intermittent outbreaks of violent worker action culminating in the Rand Revolt in 1922 (to which the government responded with aerial bombardments).

Paradoxically, there were no notable incidents of serious resistance from non-European South Africans during this period, other than the mobilisation of the Asian population by Gandhi referred to previously. This is not to argue that these people were somehow satisfied with their lot. But before the major shifts to urbanisation that began during World War II, black life, confined as it was primarily to rural areas, continued largely as it had been prior to Union. The most common sentiment during this period seemed to have been a willingness to embrace education and religion as a means of escaping the strictures of 'tribal' customs and practices, and thus to seek acceptance from the ruling white establishment, in whose ranks some allies were to be found.

In 1924, the accession to power of the Afrikaner National Party in coalition with the largely English-speaking Labour Party – also known as the 'Pact Government' – further excluded the 'native' (black African) population from any meaningful possibility of participating in public governance and sharing in the economic development of the country. It did this in order to promote the political and economic conditions of poorer whites, mainly but not exclusively Afrikaans-speaking – many of whom had been badly affected by economic depression during that decade. This further exclusion of blacks was chiefly to be seen in the Native Trust and Land Act of 1936,[39] which reserved 87 percent of the land in the country for whites and Asians. It could also be seen in the exclusion of black workers from the definition of 'employee' in the Industrial Conciliation Act[40] and myriad segregationist interventions across the Cape and Natal that emulated the

[39] Act 18 of 1936.
[40] Act 11 of 1924.

tools for racial segregation and oppression adopted by the former Boer republics.[41]

Outside of the northern provinces of the Transvaal and OFS – which prohibited Asian from owning land or even, in the case of the OFS, simply staying overnight in the province (a law that survived until 1985) – the treatment of Asian and 'coloured' people was somewhat more ambivalent. Neither Asians nor 'coloured' people (always regarded as separate from a governmental point of view) exercised a major influence on the body politic. But most coloured people saw themselves as more closely allied with the whites, while most Asians showed little direct interest in politics and focussed primarily on educational and economic advancement, as professionals and traders.

The 'Pact' government of 1924 was followed by the accession to power in 1934 of the United Party (formally called the United National South African Party), a new party that was created when the National Party merged with the remnants of the former South African Party. The United Party stressed a common 'white' South African-ness, to the partial exclusion of 'coloureds' and the more complete exclusion of Asians and blacks. Racially preferential labour policies, especially within the public enterprises that the state used to control the economy (such as the railways, harbours, and the iron and steel industry), and a far-reaching set of national cooperative schemes in the agricultural sector, worked to 'uplift' poor white South Africans at the further expense of other, non-white groups.

At a formal level, the most significant constitutional events of this period were the relaxation of British imperial supervision over colonial legislative authority through the Statute of Westminster of 1932, which to all intents and purposes granted full legislative authority to all Dominion Parliaments. Lest there be any attempt to re-assert such imperial supervision in the future, the South African Parliament passed the Status of the Union Act of 1934,[42] which essentially repeated the language of the Statute of Westminster but in the form of an act of the national parliament. Supporters of Afrikaner nationalism, who dominated the United Party at this time, regarded this as a much longed-for assertion of national independence. For those on the more extreme end of Afrikaner nationalism, however, only full republican status would suffice, due both to resentment at imperial meddling in the politics of South Africa, and to lasting bitter memories of the Anglo-Boer War.

[41] See Dugard, *Human Rights and the South African Legal Order*.

[42] Act 69 of 1934.

On the other hand, while a few black political leaders continued to harbour illusions that the British government would somehow intervene on their behalf and upset the racist constitutional compromise of 1909, the vast majority of the black population interpreted the relinquishing of a residual imperial authority to intervene in South African policies and practices as meaning that they would have to deal with a new reality. Within two years of the adoption of the Status of the Union Act, the South Africa Parliament had removed all black African voters from the common voters' roll (with the Supreme Court upholding this initiative).[43] After 1936, it was clear that a relatively un-tempered racial discrimination would become the dominant policy tool of successive governments, together with further forms of legislative and executive dispossession of whatever rights and freedoms black South Africans still possessed.

All in all, by 1936, white domination of all spheres of constitutional governance was even more secure than it had been in 1910. The courts played no small part in promoting this consolidation – appearing on the one hand to be seeking reconciliation between opposing groups of whites, while, on the other, endorsing at key moments the racist basis on which the constitution and society were founded.[44] It is not suggested that this was some kind of express and deliberate judicial policy. Rather, it was due simply to the fact that the judges shared the racist presumptions of general society; the growing emergence of a more positivist approach to judging; and an unwillingness to second-guess parliament or the executive.

C. *Breaking the Colonial Bonds and Entrenching Apartheid (1936–1982)*

South Africa's decision to enter World War II in support of Britain and the Allies in September 1939 split the ruling party, causing remnants of the old National Party – which opposed entry into the war – to disassociate themselves from the ruling United Party and reform the National Party. Random and relatively unstructured acts of resistance by those sympathetic with Nazi ideology were dealt with through emergency measures endorsed by parliament. However, many South African men and women, drawn from a broad spectrum of society and including many black South African males, volunteered to serve in the armed forces and their support

[43] See Hugh Corder, *Judges at Work: The Role and Attitudes of the South African Appellate Judiciary, 1910–1950* (Claremont, SA: Juta and Co., 1984), 152–155.

[44] See id. 231–244.

units. These forces saw service in east and north Africa, the Middle East, and Western Europe.

Paradoxically, in 1948, as the developed world responded to the horrors of the war by setting up the United Nations and adopting the Universal Declaration of Human Rights, South Africa – now led by the newly reformed 'National Party' dominated by extreme Afrikaner nationalists – began 'refining' and extending to all aspects of social life the policy of legislated segregation and race-determinism known as apartheid.

Apartheid, which literally means 'separateness' in Afrikaans, is the umbrella term for a system of laws and policies whose purpose is to separate as much as possible people of different race-groups, forcing them to live, be educated, be entertained, be hospitalised, and be buried in separate areas and facilities. The ideology behind apartheid was based on a belief in the inherent and evolutionary inferiority of black people, but as a political-economic tool it was intended primarily to oppress blacks in order to promote the socio-economic interests of working class and unemployed whites, the vast majority of whom were Afrikaners.[45] To this end, it advocated massive separation of the various 'race-groups' as categorised by the Population Registration Act.[46] The two main race-groups were called 'Europeans' (i.e., whites) and 'natives' (i.e., black Africans). Those of Asian descent constituted a third group, while everyone else was placed into one of the seven sub-groups that constituted a fourth race-group called 'coloured'. This and related legislation – such as the Group Areas Act enforcing residential separation,[47] the Prohibition of Mixed Marriages Act prohibiting marriage across race-groups,[48] and the Immorality Act making sexual relations across race lines unlawful[49] – formally entrenched at the national level the kind of informal and localised segregation found in white South African society before then.

The ideology of apartheid found its most definitive expression in what was known as 'grand apartheid'. This involved subdividing the black-African race-group into what were called 'tribes', loosely based on 'ethnic' differences, and assigning each tribe a particular 'homeland' located in unproductive, underdeveloped, and often fractured rural areas. All this

[45] See Deborah Posel, 'The Apartheid Project, 1948–1970', in Robert Ross, Anne Kelk Mager, and Bill Nasson (eds.), *The Cambridge History of South Africa*. Vol. 2, *1885–1994* (Cambridge University Press, 2014), 319–368.

[46] Act 30 of 1950.

[47] Act 36 of 1966.

[48] Act 55 of 1949.

[49] Act 23 of 1957.

was done under the pretence of granting them 'self-determination', but its actual purpose was to bring about the complete and total exclusion of all black South-Africans from the public-political arena.[50] Movement by black-Africans outside of their designated tribal homeland was strictly controlled by what were termed 'pass laws'.[51]

Predictably, the institution of apartheid strengthened the sense of political grievance that had been catalysed by the racist constitutional compromise of 1910 among all 'non-white' South Africans. Those grievances first expressed themselves through large-scale passive resistance, and then later erupted into furious resistance. This was met with the brutal deployment of discretionary executive power in the name of 'national security' and 'suppression of communism and terrorism'. As a result, detention without trial; social bannings (effective civil imprisonment); banishment (deportation to an isolated rural area far from home); and intimidation by the police of government opponents of all races, but particularly those who were not white, became common practice. On extreme occasions, such as the Sharpeville Massacre of 1960 (which ultimately forced South Africa out of the British Commonwealth – see following text), such responses involved governmental deployment of lethal violence.[52]

South Africa became a republic through the Republic of South Africa Constitution Act of 1961.[53] For many South Africans, this meant that South Africa was now finally a completely independent nation with its own 'homegrown' constitution – albeit a constitution that in almost all respects replicated in its structure the South Africa Act of 1909. Tellingly, in abolishing the old colonial post of governor general, the new republic replaced it with a 'State President' – a title that harked back to the Boer republics of the late nineteenth century.

Those opposed to apartheid naturally resorted to legal process whenever they could to attempt to stay if not to defeat the many measures used to implement apartheid and crush dissent. In the early 1950s, such strategies were often successful. But gradually, judicial space to oppose the executive and parliament in this area was reduced, both by parliamentary and executive action, and by changes in the ideologies and mind-sets of

[50] See Laurence Boulle, Bede Harris, and Cora Hoexter, *Constitutional and Administrative Law: Basic Principles* (Cape Town: Juta, 1989).

[51] See Hugh Corder, 'The Right of Africans to Remain in Urban Areas', *Responsa Meridiana* (1977): 213–227.

[52] Dugard, *Human Rights and the South African Legal Order*, 325–365; A. S. Mathews, *Freedom, State Security and the Rule of Law* (Cape Town: Juta, 1986)

[53] Act 32 of 1961.

judges appointed since 1948.[54] In the process, the capacity of the law and the judiciary to achieve justice was severely undermined. The courts lost legitimacy, and appeared to acquiesce to the executive and parliament in upholding of the policies of apartheid.

Opponents of apartheid also responded organisationally. Opposition forces reinvigorated organisations founded long before, most notably the African National Congress (discussed in preceding text). They also formed new organisations to oppose particular initiatives. A particularly important event along these lines was the 'Congress of the People', which convened near Johannesburg in mid-1955, and that brought together four different 'congress' organisations representing the four main race groups. The Congress of the People was convened to adopt the 'Freedom Charter' – a demand for basic rights under a democratic government, starting with the ringing phrase: 'South Africa belongs to all the people who live in it, black and white'.[55]

These organisations held marches and protests, labour unrest rose in frequency and intensity, and passive resistance campaigns were mounted against the pass laws. In all, 156 leaders of anti-apartheid organisations were put on trial for treason during the late 1950s. All were acquitted.[56] But many others who challenged apartheid were convicted of crimes against 'public safety', or were detained without trial.[57]

On March 21, 1960, this escalating tension erupted in what became known as the Sharpeville Massacre, in which South African police opened fire on a crowd of about six thousand black Africans protesting the pass laws, killing sixty-nine people. The event isolated South Africa on the world stage and made opposition to apartheid a global movement. It led directly to South Africa being expelled from the British Commonwealth in 1961. The South African government's response to the massacre, however, was to outlaw several popular anti-apartheid organisations, including the ANC and the Pan Africanist Congress (the Communist Party of South Africa had been declared unlawful as early as 1950). There then ensued the high-profile (and largely successful) criminal prosecutions of many leaders of those organisations, the most famous of which was the Rivonia trial in which Nelson Mandela and the top leadership of the ANC were found guilty of treason for their part in launching the armed wing of the ANC to carry out acts of sabotage and

[54] See Christopher Forsyth, *In Danger for Their Talents: A Study of the Record of the Appellate Division of the Supreme Court of South Africa 1950–1980* (Cape Town: Juta, 1985).

[55] See Ebrahim, *The Soul of a Nation.*

[56] See Phyllis Naidoo, *156 Hands That Built South Africa* (Cape Town: Stephan Phillips, 2006).

[57] See Dugard, *Human Rights and the South African Legal Order.*

related activities.[58] Riding on ever-growing parliamentary majorities from the white voting public, and on South Africa's rapidly growing economy and prosperity, the National Party systematically adopted ever more stringent limits on black political activity, including laws that allowed increasingly long periods of detention without trial, culminating in the Terrorism Act of 1967,[59] which authorised police to detain indefinitely, without trial, those suspected of 'endanger[ing] the maintenance of law and order'.[60]

From 1965 to 1972, there was a lull in political contestation as the state's draconian crackdown on black resistance took its toll; strong economic growth placated the population's sense of grievance; and the leading nations of Western Europe and North America provided strong support to the South African regime as an ally against communism in the context of the Cold War (by contrast, exiled resistance movements, like the ANC, received support from the Soviet Union).

Socio-political agitation began to increase, however, from late 1972, due primarily to changes in the geo-politics of southern Africa. This included the appearance of new labour activism in Namibia (then effectively a South African colony) and the Natal city of Durban; the granting of sovereign independence to the former Portuguese colonies of Mozambique in 1974 and Angola in 1975; and an escalating guerrilla war in Zimbabwe (then known as Rhodesia) fuelled by the same kind of white oppression of the black African population found in South Africa. During that time, a new spirit and philosophy gripped the imagination of many black South African student leaders in the form of the black consciousness movement, with popular organisations mushrooming in support of its basic tenets.[61] These currents culminated in the Soweto uprising of June 1976, and the national revolt, which ensued over the next three years.

This revitalisation in the expression of grievances and the quest for freedom was led from within the country, with very little overt identification with the exiled political movements. Its campaigns and acts of resistance were spearheaded mainly by the black youth and black trade union leaders. While black African (but not coloured and Indian) workers had been excluded by law from the state-sanctioned industrial unions since the 1920s,[62] there was no formal prohibition against black

[58] See Nelson Mandela, *Long Walk to Freedom* (Johannesburg: Macdonald, 1994), 297–364; see also Bob Hepple, *Young Man with a Red Tie* (Johannesburg: Jacana, 2013).

[59] Act 83 of 1967.

[60] Sec. 6.

[61] See, e.g., Steven Bantu Biko, *I Write What I Like* (London: Heinemann, 1978).

[62] See Industrial Conciliation Act, No. 11 of 1924.

African workers forming their own trade unions. And they did so. These unions became a focal point of progressive white student activism from the early 1970s, with great courage and commitment being shown by black workers.

This shift towards more oppositional politics shared little in common with the strategies and tactics for expressing black-African grievances (and the grievances of Asian and 'coloureds') used by such groups prior to the 1970s. The sense of grievance had become more radical, with the corresponding quest for freedom more confident, despite seemingly insurmountable obstacles. Opposition to apartheid began to focus, not simply on strategies of resistance borne of grievance, but also on what the future face of freedom would look like, that is, on what form of governance South Africa should construct once racial oppression had ended.

The effect of this renewed and intensified resistance was twofold. First, this new and increasingly confident focus on the future prospects of freedom served to unite black activists in South Africa. Second, the radicalisation of black-African grievances made black urban areas increasingly difficult for government to manage. In the rural areas, the implementation of 'grand apartheid' in the guise of the granting of notional constitutional self-government to identified ethnic 'homelands' found some marginal support among traditional black-African leadership.[63] But this attempt to divide and rule by granting a sham freedom generated increasing anger among largely urban black Africans who lived outside their designated homelands, but were forced by law nevertheless to be 'citizens' of one of these homelands, and thus be subject to the often-corrupt demands of their government.

In sum, no amount of political and security-force clamp down could suppress the growing resistance, especially as the tide of independence in Africa moved ever closer. In 1980, anti-apartheid guerrillas finally succeeded in overthrowing the white government of (internationally unrecognised) Rhodesia, and establishing in its stead the newly independent nation of Zimbabwe. But in South Africa, by contrast, it would ultimately be through constitutional intervention, rather than military force, that the next phase in South Africa's quest for freedom would be expressed.

[63] See, e.g., M. P. Vorster, M. Wiechers, and D. J. van Vuuren, *The Constitutions of Transkei, Bophuthatswana, Venda and Ciskei* (Durban: Butterworth, 1985).

D. *Unravelling the Web: Compromise in Search of Progress (1983–1993)*

This constitutional intervention took the form of the Republic of South Africa Constitution Act of 1983,[64] which established a unique 'tricameral' parliamentary structure – a real departure from the Westminster model that had been used to govern British South Africa since union in 1910. This structure involved the establishment of a three-house parliament, with separate houses for whites, coloured, and Indian citizens. The ratio of representation between the three race-groups was 4:2:1 (white/coloured/Indian), so that whites always held a majority of the votes when the houses voted collectively. Collective voting was used to decide issues involving 'general affairs', such as defence and foreign affairs. Issues involving what were called the 'own affairs' of the represented racial groups, such as health and education, were notionally the preserve of each house independently.

As is evident from the preceding, this tricameral arrangement continued to exclude black Africans from any form of political participation in central government, the fiction being that black Africans were represented by their homeland governments, as well as virtually by the state president in his capacity as head of state, head of government, and leader of the ruling party. While occasionally portrayed as an articulation of consociational democracy,[65] the actual intent of this structure was to co-opt the coloured and Indian sections of the population as minority allies of the whites, by giving them better access to better-quality social services and some limited sectoral authority.

But this arrangement was ultimately stillborn. Only a derisory percentage of the coloured and Indian race-groups was willing to participate in this new form of government, despite the perks. This was primarily because the vast majority of those 'race-groups' was by that stage so embittered by the racist abuse they had suffered over the decades that there was no way they could be assuaged by this transparent confidence trick. Also, by that point a substantial degree of trans-racial solidarity had emerged between these groups and black Africans – especially in the urban areas, and also on the shop floor, as the organising mantra of the independent (black) trade union movement was overtly non-racialism. This sham was also abhorred by many democratically

[64] Act 110 of 1983.

[65] See L. J. Boulle, *South Africa and the Consociational Option: A Constitutional Analysis* (Johannesburg: Juta, 1984).

minded white South Africans (as well as by an appreciable number of far right-wing whites who rejected even a *de minimis* deviation from the apartheid ideology).

Indeed, the all-encompassing intensity of political opposition to this arrangement forced the apartheid regime to resort once again to emergency powers.[66] First proclaimed in Natal in July 1985, the 'state of emergency' became a constant national presence from mid-1986 through 1990. The practical effect of this was to suspend the rule of law, because the powers given to the executive by this emergency rule were so invasive of citizens' rights and were so supportive of completely unlimited discretion as to amount to capitulation to administrative fiat. The courts from time to time attempted to constrain the exercise of those powers, but eventually capitulated and were of only limited utility. This period has been characterised as one of 'state lawlessness',[67] and it fed further resentment across a vast swath of the population, of all race-groups.

The debilitating political estrangements brought about by these four years of emergency rule, coupled with increasing political pressures to end apartheid – in the form of financial and trade sanctions and cultural and other forms of boycott – from 'friendly' Western nations (whose earlier willingness to turn a blind eye to South African apartheid had faded together with the collapse of the Soviet empire), led the South African regime to come to realise that apartheid was unsustainable. Beginning in 1990, it would begin to pursue ending apartheid seriously, a process that would culminate in the constitutional compact of 1993.

The constitutional compact negotiated in 1993 was the culmination of the process of reform initiated by the National Party regime. It began in the mid-1980s with a series of secret talks between the National Party leadership and the imprisoned leadership of the ANC. It was then given manifest and dramatic shape when State President F. W. (Frederik Willem) de Klerk announced on February 2, 1990 his decision to free Nelson Mandela, to unban the ANC and all other prohibited political organisations, and to negotiate a common future on the future of South Africa. There followed almost four years of talks and bargaining, leading to the formation of the Multi Party Negotiating Forum in April 1993, which drafted and then on November 18, 1993 approved a transitional or interim Constitution for the Republic of South Africa.

[66] See the Public Safety Act, 3 of 1953.

[67] See Geoff Budlender, 'Law and Lawlessness in South Africa', *South African Journal on Human Rights* 4 (1988): 139–152.

The Interim Constitution of 1993 was formally passed into law by the tricameral parliament in January of 1994.[68] This constitution necessitated deep levels of compromise on all sides, but particularly from those who had suffered the most under the racist exploitation of the past centuries. Many in the liberation movements in exile, and many active inside the country in opposition to apartheid, expected some form of capitulation by the regime, an abrupt break with the past, and a no-holds-barred takeover of every aspect of public governance. For reasons that are too numerous and complex to detail here, the brutal reality was that, despite its substantial weakening through sanctions and internal dissent over the previous fifteen years or so, the minority regime still had immense military and other forms of power at its disposal, which it used surreptitiously to destabilise its opponents throughout the negotiation process, and which it could have released to devastating effect for all concerned had it wished to. This would admittedly have left the country, its infrastructure, and its economy barely functioning, and countless numbers of ordinary people, mostly black, would have suffered hugely. But it was an ever-present threat during the negotiations.[69]

On the other hand, of course, once the ban on anti-apartheid political action was lifted, the course of these negotiations could not be controlled and directed as the apartheid government wished it to, which was a calculated risk on it part. If it could not through negotiations retain some form of majority stake in post-apartheid government, the second-best prize was a constitution that subjected the future government's exercise of power to constitutional constraints, enforced by an independent judicial system. Pragmatism dictated the outcome, as well as the reluctant acceptance by the ANC in mid-1993 that there would be a two-stage transition to the final form of a democratic constitution: with the first stage being characterised by a transitional government of national unity; by a fairly rigid constitution (although one that would establish the framework for the negotiated drafting of the 'final' constitution by the popularly elected first parliament within two years); and by the necessity for that 'final' constitution to be 'certified' by the Constitutional Court as being compliant with thirty-four 'constitutional principles' that the Interim Constitution of 1993 listed as being a necessary basis for any final constitution.[70] These principles ranged

[68] The Republic of South Africa Constitution Act, 200 of 1993.

[69] For further details of these negotiations, see Richard Spitz with Matthew Chaskalson, *The Politics of Transition: A Hidden History of South Africa's Negotiated Settlement* (Johannesburg: Wits University Press, 2000); Ebrahim, *The Soul of a Nation*; Hugh Corder 'Towards a South African Constitution', *Modern Law Review* 57 (1994): 491–533.

[70] See Constitutional Principles Schedule 4 of the Interim Constitution. Act 200 of 1993.

from the broad and general (e.g., 'There shall be a separation of powers between the legislature, executive and judiciary, with appropriate checks and balances to ensure accountability, responsiveness and openness'[71]) to the very particular (e.g., 'Every member of the public service shall be entitled to a fair pension'[72]).

It seemed, therefore, that despite the many contradictions and compromises enshrined in the Interim Constitution, the price was worth paying, particularly given the relatively low levels of violence that accompanied the hand-over of formal governmental authority to the majority of the population.

E. *The Dream Realised? (1993–1999)*

The Interim Constitution of 1993 was a remarkably progressive instrument, and departed entirely from the patterns of abuse of public power that had characterised most of the preceding eighty-four years of so-called constitutional government in South Africa. The vast majority of the South African population clearly saw things this way: There was a massive turnout of eligible voters in the first free and universal election in South African history in April 1994, and the newly elected government enjoyed a degree of legitimacy rarely seen in modern democracies.

In form, the 1993 transitional constitution was a substantial departure from anything that had gone before, and embraced both liberal democratic and social democratic objectives. Perhaps the single most emphatic change was the inclusion of a bill of rights,[73] and granting the judiciary the authority to test all exercises of public power against the standards of the constitution. The South African judiciary had always been formally independent and impartial, but in substance, as many studies showed, it had become associated with the racist excesses of the apartheid era, and the fact that it was staffed almost exclusively by white males made it unlikely that it would be trusted as impartial by black South Africans. Its track record in cases in which citizens seeking to realise common-law rights in the face of executive and legislative injustice was patchy at best, and constituted rank capitulation at worst.[74]

[71] Schedule 4 of the Interim Constitution, Principle VI.

[72] Schedule 4 of the Interim Constitution, Principle XXX.

[73] See, generally, Lourens du Plessis and Hugh Corder, *Understanding South Africa's Transitional Bill of Rights* (Cape Town: Juta, 1994).

[74] See Stephen Ellmann, *In a Time of Trouble: Law and Liberty in South Africa's State of Emergency* (Oxford: Clarendon Press, 1992).

However, as the past twenty years have shown, it had nevertheless been able to retain during that dark period sufficient professional independence and sufficient popular belief in the law as an instrument to achieve justice to allow the courts to quickly develop after 1994 a remarkable reputation for courage and independence in standing against abuses of all forms in the exercise of public power. The fact that this was achieved despite the continuation in office of every judge appointed before 1994 makes this an even more astonishing fact. In this, the leadership role of the newly established Constitutional Court of South Africa in ensuring this outcome cannot be underestimated.

Nelson Mandela became South Africa's first post-apartheid president after the 1994 general election, as leader of the dominant party, the ANC. He and his cabinet, which contained several ministers who had served in government during apartheid, appeared to deliver much of what most South Africans, including many whites, had only dared dream about over the prior decades. Part of this achievement must be attributed to the astonishing style of leadership of President Mandela, as well as to the calibre of his ministers. Together, they constantly confounded and exceeded expectations and skilfully managed both deep-seated historic grievances as well as newfound fears. The sense of catharsis that set in after the awfulness of the preceding decades, and particularly after the immediately previous fifteen years, was strengthened immeasurably by the activities of the Truth and Reconciliation Commission,[75] under the leadership of Archbishop Desmond Tutu, from 1995 to 1998.

Another signal achievement of this period was the drafting and adoption of the 'final' constitution by parliament in 1996,[76] which incorporated both liberal and social democratic goals, as well as many elements that point to its 'transformative' nature. So, for example, the constitution is founded on the supremacy of the constitution and the rule of law, non-racialism and non-sexism, and universal adult suffrage. It aims to achieve a system of democratic government that must ensure 'accountability, responsiveness, and openness'.[77] The Bill of Rights provides for several socio-economic rights, such as the rights to housing, health care, food, water, and social security[78] – albeit in a less-demanding manner than it does the more traditional, civil and political rights that are included in that bill. In the light of

[75] Promotion of National Unity and Reconciliation Act, Act 34 of 1995.

[76] Constitution of the Republic of South Africa, Act 108 of 1996. See also *Re Certification of the Amended Text of the Constitution of the Republic of South Africa*, 1997 (2) SA 97 (CC).

[77] See Constitution of the Republic of South Africa, sec. 1.

[78] Constitution of the Republic of South Africa, sec. 26 and sec. 27.

the subsequent record of public governance in South Africa, this period will go down as South Africa's 'golden period': Although by no means perfect, all three branches of the first post-apartheid government far exceeded expectations, and the spirit of freedom was almost intoxicating. It was as though the centuries of multiple grievances and the bitter struggles for freedom, resisted in the most violent manner, were now something of the past, now entirely submerged beneath a generous sea of reconciliation and unity (even though very little had changed in a socio-economic sense over these first five years). The years succeeding this golden age show the extent of the challenges that remain to be addressed – how, in fact, the grievances of the past continue to reverberate, despite the attainment of formal freedom for all.

F. Challenging the Compromises: The Struggles Continue (1999-present)

Elements of this 'rainbow nation' atmosphere carried over into the beginning of the tenure of President Thabo Mbeki, who succeeded President Mandela in 1999. This was because during much of the time of the Mandela administration, Mbeki – then deputy president – ran the day-to-day business of government. Mbeki retained some ministers from other political parties in his cabinet, and his years as president witnessed strong economic development and an increasingly prominent role for the country in international forums, particularly on the African continent.

However, the magnanimous atmosphere of the Mandela years soon began to break down as Mbeki's secretive, relatively authoritarian and unaccountable style of leadership eroded good governance within the ANC and within parliament, and as his highly suspect stance that HIV does not because AIDS took its toll both on popular support and international goodwill. Public procurement practices began to attract allegations of corruption and favouritism, most significantly the massive 'arms deal' of 1998–1999, which indirectly led to the dismissal of Deputy President Jacob Zuma in 2002. This action came back to haunt Mbeki, however, as the popular and wily Zuma managed to harness the grievances of the many people and groups within the party who had been alienated by the Mbeki administration, and through that unseat Mbeki as party leader at the ANC Congress in December 2007. This indirectly caused the ANC to 'recall' the president by decision of the party executive in September 2008, without recourse to the formal processes demanded by the constitution. A constitutional crisis was averted by Mbeki's acceptance of the decision and his resignation from the presidency on September 24, 2008. This was followed by a 'holding government' led by President Kgalema Motlanthe, which lasted until the 2009 election and which resulted in the appointment of Zuma as president. Zuma is still in office.

Like the period immediately after Union in 1910, the years since the Mandela administration have been marked by instability and potential danger for the state and for the development of socio-political cohesion – and again it seems as if the courts, and particularly the newly created Constitutional Court, are the principal actors attempting to foster reconciliation and the achievement of the constitutional values.[79] From time to time, their judgments have found both the executive and parliament wanting in their compliance with the demands of the constitution. This has angered those institutions, which have responded – much as was the case sixty years earlier – by complaining of judicial contravention of the separation of powers, and even by issuing veiled threats to re-examine the limits of judicial authority. While such threats have not yet become a reality (although some strange judicial appointments have recently been made), they do give cause for concern.[80]

The highly controversial manner in which President Mbeki was deposed, to be replaced after the next general election by Zuma, whose immediate past was strewn with allegations of improper (e.g., being the corrupt beneficiary of proceeds from one of the foreign companies that won one of the contracts in the arms deal) if not criminal (he was charged with but acquitted of the rape of the daughter of a friend of his) conduct, dealt severe blows to the legitimacy of the constitutional and governmental order in South Africa. There have been few moments since Zuma's accession to power in mid-2009 that have dispelled such concerns, and his political style as well as weak leadership have created the opportunity for populist demagogues to dominate political discourse.[81]

The Zuma administration's attacks on the judiciary and other independent pillars of the constitutional order – such as the National Prosecuting Authority, the Public Protector (the South African ombudsman), and the South Africa Broadcasting Corporation (the national public broadcaster) – have had a deleterious effect on the constitutional order. While

[79] See Hugh Corder, '"Building a Nation": The Judicial Role in South Africa', *Law in Context* 28 (2012): 60–75.

[80] See Hugh Corder and Jason Brickhill, 'The Constitutional Court', in Cora Hoexter and Morne Olivier (eds.), *The Judiciary in South Africa* (Cape Town: Juta, 2014), 355–402; see also Theunis Roux, *The Politics of Principle: The First South African Constitutional Court, 1995–2005* (Cambridge University Press, 2013).

[81] See, generally, Richard Calland, *The Zuma Years* (Cape Town: Zebra, 2013).

these attacks have been resisted – by those attacked, opposition parties, and civil society in general – and while court judgments continue frequently to find government conduct to be unconstitutional or otherwise unlawful, it remains to be seen what long-term damage all this is inflicting on the fabric of the constitution. There can be no doubt, however, that a long road of continuing struggle lies ahead, before it can possibly be claimed that the constitutional democratic order of South Africa is secure.

IV. Evaluation: On the Need to Transform History and Transcend Liberalism

South Africa has had five formal constitutional instruments since the formation of a unified state within its current borders 105 years ago (i.e., those of 1909, 1961, 1983, 1993, and 1996). The first two were informed by the history that immediately preceded their enactment, but they did little to confront that history. The 1983 tricameral constitution, whatever its many grievous shortcomings, was a deliberate attempt to mark the end of one approach to constitutional governance, and the beginning of another. On this view, black African citizens were forced down one constitutional road to desolate poverty and tin-pot tyranny in the rural fringes, while whites with their unwilling coloured and Indian allies pursued the golden treasure of constitutional governance in the wealthy heartland. Again, one cannot but wonder at the galvanising effect of this wildly dishonest scheme in provoking even the mildest opponent of apartheid into intense rage, which collectively shipwrecked the whole edifice and opened the way to another chance for all South Africans.

The transitional (1993) and final (1996) constitutions finally ushered in constitutional democracy, and seized the opportunity to do two other things. First, they – for the first time – challenged and responded to many of South Africa's historical evils. Examples are legion in both texts, but include the right to freedom from slavery and from servitude in the Bill of Rights; the provision for the necessity of the return and redistribution of land; and in the 'Postamble/Afterword' to the transitional Constitution of 1993, which required parliament to establish a 'truth and reconciliation' process. So the new constitutional theme is 'catalogue, confront, accept responsibility, then move on,' in a spirit of memory with reconciliation and a determination never to allow such excesses again.

Second, the constitutional drafters and those negotiating their texts were deeply aware of both the strengths and limits of liberal democratic structures. One of its greatest perceived shortcomings these drafters needed to address was liberalism's inability to provide the tools to transcend the gross inequalities that pervaded almost every aspect of socio-economic life in the country. Their underlying goal was to seek, through constitutional process, to transform the existing patterns of allocation and distribution of resources and services, and in so doing to transcend the limits of liberalism. This would be a tall order in any country's book: Its achievement on such arid soil as that of South Africa is more than a challenge.

V. Conclusion

So perhaps the phrase that best sums up the final steps in the historical record outlined in this chapter is that the constitutional order in South Africa seeks to be both *transformative*[82] and *transcending*. These qualities are necessary in order to begin to allay and address the multiple expressions of grievance that have marked that history, and to seek to achieve the quest for freedom that underlies most of those complaints.

Whether this will be achieved is worth debating, while the struggle continues. For the present, I think that the following four points are worth further discussion:

- First, it seems that the device of putting in place a transitional/interim constitutional regime provided the essential, stable, and democratically responsive space within which a lasting constitutional order could be safely attempted. By demarcating the interim constitution as an avowedly temporary measure, yet at the same time containing within its four corners the guaranteed essence of any lasting constitutional dispensation, it provided a way forward that every negotiating group could at least live with, if not wholeheartedly embrace. For those who foresaw a loss of power and influence, as well as for those who were frustrated at not obtaining all that they had aspired to, it was a device that promised another opportunity to get things right – within certain broad limits to be sure, but nevertheless on firm foundations.
- Second, there is evident in this history, despite the substantial shifts over time and especially given the 'revolutionary' nature of the change of the constitutional grundnorm in 1994, a formal legislative continuity that ought not to be disregarded: even the transitional constitution of 1993 was ultimately the product of the last, tricameral, apartheid parliament. This gave comfort to those who wished to deny that a revolution had

[82] Karl Klare, 'Legal Culture and Transformative Constitutionalism', *South African Journal on Human Rights* 12 (1998): 146–188.

occurred, while at the same time serving as only a minor irritant to the rest of the political forces. It may also have played some kind of reassuring role for those observing the process nervously from abroad, including those with substantial financial resources invested in the country.

- Third, there are clear traces of all three of the great constitutional initiatives of the late eighteenth century outlined in the introductory chapter to this volume – that is, the Whiggish (later Diceyan) constitution of England, the liberal Madisonian constitution of the United States, and the revolutionary *Rousseauian* constitutionalism of republican France – in South Africa's current constitutional order. But it is the liberal American model that is perhaps the least influential. The English influence can be ascribed to South Africa's 180-year British-colonial and commonwealth heritage. The French influence is more evident though the substantial role played by modern European constitutionalism, and the pan-European developments of the post-war era (such as the rise of a European human rights jurisprudence based on the European Convention and associated treaties, and decisions of the European Court of Human Rights). For its part, the relatively minor role played by the American constitutional model can be attributed to the manner in which and the extent to which South African nationalism manifested itself during the negotiations – its overwhelming desire to produce a homegrown constitutional product shaped by and suited to the extraordinary history described, and its correspondingly stubborn unwillingness to be dictated to from outside. The style of presentation of ideas and advice from beyond the United States tended to be more informal and subtle, reflecting sensibilities that are more European and English than American. And in the atmosphere in which the 1993 negotiations took place, this was not insignificant.
- Fourth, the predominant structural principle in the final South African Constitution has moved beyond liberalism to what is commonly accepted now as the 'transformative' agenda, albeit based on a liberal democratic foundation.[83] This is to be seen in many aspects of the constitution, how it has been read, and how the judges have interpreted it in most of the leading cases. While the politicians have, from time to time, used the constitution as a scapegoat to seek to avoid being held accountable for their own shortcomings, few serious observers accept such excuses.

[83] See id.; Dennis M. Davis and Karl Klare, 'Transformative Constitutionalism and the Common and Customary Law', *South African Journal on Human Rights* 26 (2010): 403–509.

The foundations thus exist for finally eliminating over the coming decades the many grievances that have been explored in the preceding text – including the newer ones that have arisen in the post-apartheid era, mainly among those without ready access to political power and patronage – and for the achievement of freedom for most South Africans. Yet a long and hard road still lies ahead, and strong and visionary leadership is required on all fronts to achieve these ideals.

BIBLIOGRAPHY

Abbott, Jason P., and Sophie Gregorios-Pippas. 'Islamization in Malaysia: Processes and Dynamics'. *Contemporary Politics* 16 (2010): 135–151.

Abensour, Miguel. 'La philosophie politique de Saint-Just'. *Annales historiques de la Révolution Française* 38 (1964): 24.

Abhayaratne, Anoma. 'Economic Growth and Poverty Reduction: Lessons from the Malaysian Experience'. FEA working paper no. 2004–13. Kuala Lumpur: University of Malaya Faculty of Economics and Administration, 2004. Available at http://asianscholarship.org/asf/AnnualFellows/download_Fifth/Abhayaratne,%20Anoma-Economic%20Growth%20and%20Poverty%20Reduction.doc.

Abraham, Ann. 'The Ombudsman as Part of the UK Constitution: A Contested Role?' *Parliamentary Affairs* 61 (2008): 206–215.

Ackerman, Bruce. 'The Rise of World Constitutionalism'. *Virginia Law Review* 83 (1997): 771–797.

We, the People, Volume 1: Foundations. Cambridge, MA: Belknap Press, 1993.

Adler, Max. *Démocratie et conseils ouvriers*. French translation. Paris: Maspero, 1967.

Akita, George. *Foundations of Constitutional Government in Modern Japan, 1868–1900*. Cambridge, MA: Harvard University Press, 1967.

Alexander, Larry, (ed.). *Constitutionalism: Philosophical Foundations*. Cambridge University Press, 1998.

Ali, Chaudhri Muhammad. *The Emergence of Pakistan*. New York: Columbia University Press, 1967.

'Alliance Memorandum to the Reid Commission' (Sept. 27, 1956). Reprinted in *British Documents on the End of Empire, Series B Vol. 3: Malaya. Part III – The Alliance Route to Independence 1955–1957*. A. J. Stockwell (ed.). London: Her Majesty's Stationary Office, 1995. 307–317.

al-Sanhūri, 'Abd al-Razzāq. 'Wujūb Tanqīh al-Qānūn al-Madanī al-Misrī, wa-alaai 'Ay Asā Yakūn Hadha al-Tanqīh'. *Majallat al-qānūn wa-l-iqtiṣād* 6 (1936): 114–115.

Althusser, Louis. *Politics and History: Montesquieu, Rousseau, Marx*. Translated by Ben Brewster. London: Verso, 2007.

Amar, Akhil Reed. 'Some New World Lessons for the Old World'. *University of Chicago Law Review* 58 (1991): 483–510.

Anderson, Gavin. 'Societal Constitutionalism, Social Movements, and Constitutionalism from Below'. *Indiana Journal of Global Legal Studies* 20 (2013): 881–906.

'Beyond Constitutionalism beyond the State'. *Journal of Law and Society* 39 (2012): 359–383.

Anderson, Perry. *New Old World*. London: Verso, 2009.

Anechiarico, Frank, and James B. Jacobs. *The Pursuit of Absolute Integrity: How Corruption Control Makes Government Ineffective*. University of Chicago Press, 1996.

Ansari, Iqbal. 'Minorities and the Politics of Constitution Making in India'. In D. Sheth and Gurpreet Mahajan (eds.), *Minority Identities and the Nation-State*. Oxford University Press, 1999. 111–123.

Arendt, Hannah. *On Revolution*. London: Penguin, 2006.

The Origins of Totalitarianism. New York : Harcourt, Brace & World, 1968.

Asma, Jahangir, and Hina Jilani. *The Hudood Ordinances: A Divine Sanction? A Research Study of the Hudood Ordinances and Their Effect on the Disadvantaged Sections of Pakistan Society*. Lahore: Sang-e-Meel Publications, 2003.Austin, John. *The Province of Jurisprudence Determined*. Edited by W. Rumble. Cambridge University Press, 1996.

Austin, John L. *How to Do Things with Words*. Oxford: Clarendon, 1975.

Aviation Safety Reporting System [ASRS]. 'ASRS: The Case for Confidential Incident Reporting Systems'. ASRS Research Papers. No. 60 (2001). Available at http://asrs.arc.nasa.gov/docs/rs/60_Case_for_Confidential_Incident_Reporting.pdf.

Ayres, Ian, and John Braithwaite. *Responsive Regulation: Transcending the Deregulation Debate*. Oxford University Press, 1995.

Backer, Larry Catá. 'The Party as Polity, the Communist Party, and the Chinese Constitutional State: A Theory of State-Party Constitutionalism'. *Journal of Chinese and Comparative Law* 16 (2009): 101–164.

'Theocratic Constitutionalism: An Introduction to a New Global Legal Ordering'. *Indiana Journal of Global Legal Studies* 16 (2008): 85–172.

'The Rule of Law, the Chinese Communist Party, and Ideological Campaigns: Sange Daibiao (The "Three Represents"), Socialist Rule of Law, and Modern Chinese Constitutionalism'. *Journal of Transnational Law and Contemporary Problems* 19 (2006): 29–102.

Baginda, Abdul Razak, and Peter Schier (ed.). *Is Malaysia an Islamic State? Secularism and Theocracy – A Study of the Malaysian Constitution*. Kuala Lumpur: Malaysian Strategic Research Centre and Konrad Adenauer Foundation, 2002.

'Bahasa Malaysia Bibles: The Cabinet's 10-point Solution', *Aliran*, Jan. 25, 2014. Available at http://aliran.com/web-specials/bahasa-malaysia-bibles-10-point-solution/.
Bajpai, Rochana. *Debating Difference: Group Rights and Liberal Democracy in India*. Oxford University Press, 2011.
Baker, Keith Michael. *Inventing the French Revolution: Essays on French Political Culture in the Eighteenth Century*. Cambridge University Press, 1990.
Baker, Ray S. *Woodrow Wilson: Life and Letters, Youth, 1856–1890*. Westport, CT: Greenwood Press, 1968.
Balakrishnan, Gopal. *The Enemy: An Intellectual Portrait of Carl Schmitt*. London: Verso, 2000. 101–115.
Bali, Asli U. 'Justice under Occupation: Rule of Law and the Ethics of Nation-Building in Iraq'. *Yale Journal of International Law* 30 (2005): 431–472.
Balibar, Etienne. *La crainte des masses: Politique et philosophie avant et après Marx*. Paris: Galilée, 1997.
Balme, Stéphanie, and Michael W. Dowdle (eds.). *Building Constitutionalism in China*. New York: Palgrave Macmillan, 2009.
Barbera, Augusto. 'La prima costituzione italiana: La costituzione di Bologna del 1796'. *Clio: rivista trimestrale di studi storici* 21 (1998): 218–241.
Bari, Abdul Aziz. *Malaysian Constitution: A Critical Introduction*. Kuala Lumpur: The Other Press, 2003.
'Islam in the Federal Constitution: A Commentary on the Decision of Meor Atiqulrahman'. [2000] 2 *MLJ:* cxxix–cxlii.
Beatty, David. *The Ultimate Rule of Law*. Oxford University Press, 2005.
Beaud, Olivier. 'Reframing a Debate among Americans: Contextualising a Moral Philosophy of Law'. *International Journal of Constitutional Law* 7 (2009): 53–68.
La puissance de l'état. Paris: Presses Universitaires de France, 1994.
Bechor, Guy. *The Sanhuri Code, and the Emergence of Modern Arab Civil Law (1932 to 1949)*. Leiden, The Netherlands: Brill, 2007.
Beck, Ulrich. *German Europe*. London: Polity Press, 2013.
Beeson, Mark. 'Mahathir and the Markets: Globalisation and the Pursuit of Economic Autonomy in Malaysia'. *Pacific Affairs* 73 (2000): 335–351.
Bellamy, Richard. *Political Constitutionalism: A Republican Defence of the Constitutionality of Democracy*. Cambridge University Press, 2007.
Bendersky, Joseph. 'Introduction: The Three Types of Juristic Thought in German Historical and Intellectual Context'. In Carl Schmitt, *On the Three Types of Juristic Thought*. Westport, CT: Praeger, 2004.
Berger, Peter L., and Thomas Luckmann. *The Social Construction of Reality: A Treatise in the Sociology of Knowledge*. New York: Anchor Books, 1967.
Bernardi, Bruno. *La fabrique des concepts. Recherches sur l'invention conceptuelle chez Rousseau*. Paris: Champion, 2006.

Bhattacharya, Sabyasachi. *Mahatma and the Poet; Letters and Debates between Gandhi and Tagore, 1915–1941*. New Dehli: National Book Trust, 1997.

Bickerton, Chris. *European Integration: From Nation-State to Member State*. Oxford University Press, 2013.

From Nation-States to Member States. Oxford University Press, 2013.

Biko, Steven Bantu. *I Write What I Like*. London: Heinemann, 1978.

Bilgrami, Akeel. 'Gandhi (and Marx)'. In *Secularism, Identity, and Enchantment*. Cambridge, MA: Harvard University Press, 2014. 122–174.

Binder, Leonard. *Religion and Politics in Pakistan*. University of California Press, 1961.

bin Shafie, Muhammad Ghazali. *Rukunegara: A Testament of Hope*. Kuala Lumpur: Creative Entreprise Sdn. Bhd., 1985.

Blyth, Mark. *Austerity: The History of a Dangerous Idea*. Oxford University Press, 2013.

Bobbitt, Philip. *The Shield of Achilles*. New York: Alfred Knopf, 2002.

Böckenförde, Ernst-Wolfgang. 'Die verfassunggebende Gewalt des Volkes. Ein Grenzbegriff des Verfassungsrechts'. In *Staat, Verfassung, Demokratie: Studien zur Verfassungstheorie und zum Verfassungsrecht*. 2nd ed. Frankfurt: Suhrkamp, 1992. 90–112.

State, Society, Liberty: Studies in Political Theory and Constitutional Law. Oxford: Berg, 1981.

Bodin, Jean. *The Six Bookes of a Commonweale*. Translated by R. Knolles. Cambridge, MA: Harvard University Press, 1962.

Bodineau, Pierre, and Michel Verpeaux. *Histoire constitutionnelle de la France*. Paris: Presses Universitaires de France, 2013.

Bomhoff, Jacco. *Balancing Constitutional Rights*. Cambridge University Press 2013.

Bomhoff, Jacco, and Anne Meuwese. 'The Meta-Regulation of Transnational Private Regulation'. *Journal of Law and Society* 38 (2011): 138–162.

Bonefeld, Werner. 'Freedom and the Strong State: On German Ordo-Liberalism', *New Political Economy* 17 (2012): 633–656.

Bonner, Philip. 'South African Society and Culture, 1910–1948'. In Robert Ross, Anne Kelk Mager. and Bill Nasson (eds.), *The Cambridge History of South Africa*. Vol. 2, *1885–1994*. Cambridge University Press, 2014. 254–318.

Bork, Robert H. *The Antitrust Paradox: A Policy at War with Itself*. 2nd ed. New York: Simon and Schuster, 1993.

Boulle, L. J. *South Africa and the Consociational Option: A Constitutional Analysis*. Johannesburg: Juta, 1984.

Boulle, Laurence, Bede Harris, and Cora Hoexter. *Constitutional and Administrative Law: Basic Principles*. Cape Town: Juta, 1989.

Bovens, Mark. 'Public Accountability: A Framework for the Analysis and Assessment of Accountability Arrangements in the Public Domain'. *European Law Journal* 13 (2007): 447–468.

Bovens, Mark, Thomas Schillemans, and Paul 'T Hart. 'Does Public Accountability Work? An Assessment Tool'. *Public Administration* 86 (2008): 225–242.

Braibanti, Ralph. *Chief Justice Cornelius of Pakistan: An Analysis with Letters and Speeches*. Oxford University Press, 1999.

Braithwaite. John. 'Accountability and Responsibility through Restorative Justice'. In Michael W. Dowdle (ed.), *Public Accountability: Designs, Dilemmas and Experiences*. Cambridge University Press, 2006. 33–51.

Braithwaite, John, Valerie Braithwaite, Michael Cookson, and Leah Dunn. *Anomie and Violence: Non-truth and Reconciliation in Indonesian Peacebuilding*. Canberra: ANU E Press, 2010.

Breslin, Shaun. 'The 'China Model' and the Global Crisis: From Friedrich List to a Chinese Mode of Governance?' *International Affairs* 87 (2011): 1323–1343.

Brown, Nathan. *Constitutions in a Non-Constitutional World, Arab Basic Laws and the Prospects for Accountable Government*. Albany: State University of New York Press, 2001.

Bryde, Brun-Otto. 'The ECJ's Fundamental Rights Jurisprudence – A Milestone in Transnational Constitutionalism'. In Miguel Poiares Maduro and Loïc Azoulai (eds.), *The Past and Future of EU Law: The Classics of EU Law Revisited on the 50th Anniversary of the Rome Treaty*. Oxford: Hart Publishing, 2010. 119–130.

Budlender, Geoff. 'Law and Lawlessness in South Africa'. *South African Journal on Human Rights* 4 (1988): 139–152.

Bui Ngoc Son. 'The Introduction of Modern Constitutionalism in East Asian Confucian Context: The Case of Vietnam in the Early Twentieth Century'. *National Taiwan University Law Review* 7 (2012): 423–463.

Burgio, Alberto. *Eguaglianza, interesse, unanimità. La politica di Rousseau*. Napoli: Bibliopolis, 1989.

Burke, Edmund. *Reflections on the Revolution in France* (ed. J.G.A. Pocock). Indianapolis and Cambridge: Hackett Publising Company, 1987 (originally published in 1790).

Burra, Arudra. 'The Indian Civil Service and the Raj: 1919–1950'. Unpublished, dated Feb. 11, 2007. Available at http://ssrn.com/abstract=2052658.

Bush, Robin, Philip Fountain, and Michael Feener (eds.). *Religion and the Politics of Development: Critical Perspectives on Asia*. New York: Palgrave Macmillan, 2015.

Buti, Marco, and Lucio R. Pench. 'Why Do Large Countries Flout the Stability Pact? And What Can Be Done About It?' *JCMS: Journal of Common Market Studies* 42 (2004): 1025–1032.

Byertz, Kurt (ed.), *Solidarity*. Dordrecht, The Netherlands: Kluwer Academic Publishers, 1999.

Calhoun, Craig. 'Constitutional Patriotism and the Public Sphere: Interests, Identity, and Solidarity in the Integration of Europe'. *International Journal of Politics, Culture, and Society* 18 (2005): 257–280.

Calland, Richard. *The Zuma Years*. Cape Town: Zebra, 2013.

Carothers, Thomas. 'The Rule of Law Revival'. *Foreign Affairs* 77 (2) (Mar.–Apr. 1998): 95–106.

Carré de Malberg, Raymond. *La loi expression de la volonté générale*. Paris: Sirey, 1931.

Contribution à la Théorie générale de l'Etat. Paris: Sirey, 1922.

Casper, Steven. 'The Legal Framework for Corporate Governance: The Influence of Contract Law on Company Strategies in Germany and the United Stated'. In Peter A. Hall and David Soskice (eds.), *Varieties of Capitalism: The Institutional Foundations of Comparative Advantage*. Oxford University Press, 2001. 387–416.

'German Industrial Associations and the Diffusion of Innovative Economic Organization: The Case of JIT Contracting'. *WZB Working Paper*, FS I 96–306. Berlin: Wissenschaftszentrum, 1996.

Center for Public Policy Studies [Malaysia]. 'CPPS Policy Factsheet: National Unity'. www.cpps.org.my/downloads/factsheets/National%20unity%20factsheet.pdf (undated).

Chadwick, Owen. *Selwyn College: 1882–1973 A Short History*. [Cambridge], 1973. Also available at http://www.sel.cam.ac.uk/wp-content/uploads/Selwyn-1882-1973.pdf.

Chamberlin, Edward Hastings. *The Theory of Monopolistic Competition: A Re-Orientation of the Theory of Value*. 8th ed. Cambridge, MA: Harvard University Press, 1965.

Chambers, Simone. 'Democracy, Popular Sovereignty, and Constitutional Legitimacy'. *Constellations* 11 (2004): 153–173.

Chandler, Alfred D., Jr. 'The Emergence of Managerial Capitalism'. *The Business History Review* 58 (1984): 473–503.

Chang, Williamson B. C., and Manuel U. Araujo. 'Interpreters for the Defense: Due Process for the Non-English-Speaking Defendant'. *California Law Review* 63 (1975): 801–823.

Chanock Martin. *The Making of South African Legal Culture 1902–1936: Fear, Favour and Prejudice*. Cambridge University Press, 2001.

Chêne, Marie. 'Anti-Corruption Clauses in Constitutions'. Berlin: Transparency International, 2013. Available at http://www.transparency.org/files/content/corruptionqas/Anti-corruption_constitutional_clauses_2014.pdf.

Chin, James, and Wang Chin Huat. "Malaysia's Electoral Upheaval'. *Journal of Democracy* 20. 3 (2009): 71–85.

Chong, Debra. 'Interfaith Panel Back in Saddle Next Month, Says New Chief'. *The Malaysian Insider*, Oct. 17, 2011, www.themalaysianinsider.com/mobile/malaysia/article/interfaith-panel-back-in-saddle-next-month-says-new-chief/.

Choudhury, G. W. *Documents and Speeches on the Constitution of Pakistan*. Dhaka: Green Book House, 1967.

Christodoulidis, Emilios. 'The European Court of Justice and "Total Market" Thinking'. *German Law Journal* 14 (2013): 2005–2020.

Cohen, Antonin. 'Constitutionalism without Constitution: Transnational Elites between Mobilisation and Legal Expertise in the Making of a Constitution for Europe (1940s–1960s)'. *Law and Social Enquiry* 32 (2007): 109–135.

Cohen, Ellie. 'The Euro, Economic Federalism, and National Sovereignty'. In Anthony Pagden (ed.), *The Idea of Europe: From Antiquity to the European Union*. Cambridge University Press, 2002. 260–286.

Cohen, Stephen. *The Idea of Pakistan*. 2nd ed. Washington, DC: Brookings Institution Press, 2006.

Colby, Thomas, and Peter J. Smith. 'The Return of Lochner'. *Cornell Law Review* 100 (2015): 527–602.

Colletti, Lucio. 'Introduction'. In Karl Marx, *Early Writings*. London: Penguin, 1975. 7–56.

From Rousseau to Lenin. London: Penguin, 1975.

Collins, Richard B. 'Economic Union as a Constitutional Value'. *New York University Law Review* 63 (1988): 43–129.

Colonial Office [Great Britain], *Constitutional Proposals for the Federation of Malaya*. London: Her Majesty's Stationary Office, 1957.

Colonial Office [Great Britain]. *Report of the Federation of Malaya Constitutional Commission 1957*. London: Her Majesty's Stationary Office, 1957. Available at http://www.slideshare.net/mbl2020/the-reid-commission-report-1957.

Colonial Office [Great Britain]. *Report of the Federation of Malaya Constitutional Conference Held in London in January and February, 1956*. London: Her Majesty's Stationary Office, 1956. Available at http://filestore.nationalarchives.gov.uk/pdfs/small/cab-129-79-cp-56-47-47.pdf.

Colón-Ríos, Joel I. *Weak Constitutionalism: Democratic Legitimacy and the Question of Constituent Power*. London: Routledge, 2012.

Constituent Assembly Debates: Official Report. New Dehli: Lok Sabha Secretariat, 1999.

Corder, Hugh. '"Building a Nation": The Judicial Role in South Africa'. *Law in Context* 28 (2012): 60–75.

'Towards a South African Constitution'. *Modern Law Review* 57 (1994): 491–533.

Judges At Work: The Role and Attitudes of the South African Appellate Judiciary, 1910–1950. Claremont, SA: Juta and Co., 1984.

'The Right of Africans to Remain in Urban Areas'. *Responsa Meridiana* (1977): 213–227.

Corder, Hugh, and Jason Brickhill. 'The Constitutional Court'. In Cora Hoexter and Morne Olivier (eds.), *The Judiciary in South Africa*. Cape Town: Juta, 2014. 355–402.

Cornelius, A. R. *Law and Judiciary in Pakistan*. Edited by S. M. Haider. Lahore: Lahore Law Times Publications, 1981.

Coupland, Reginald. *Report on the Constitutional Problem in India: The Indian Problem, 1833–1935*. Oxford University Press, 1943.

Courville, Sasha. 'Understanding NGO-Based Social and Environmental Regulatory Systems: Why We Need New Models of Accountability'. In Michael W. Dowdle (ed.), *Public Accountability: Designs, Dilemmas and Experiences*. Cambridge University Press, 2006. 271–300.

Cranston, Maurice. *John Locke: A Biography*. London: Longmans, 1957.

Cristi, Renato. *Carl Schmitt and Authoritarian Liberalism*. Cardiff: University of Wales Press, 1998.

Crotty, James. 'Core Industries, Coercive Competition and the Structural Contradiction of Global Neoliberalism'. In Nicholas Phelps and Philip Raines (eds.), *The New Competition for Inward Investment: Companies, Institutions and Territorial Development*. Cheltenham, UK: Edward Elgar, 2003. 9–38.

Curtin, Deirdre. 'The Constitutional Structure of the Union: A Europe of Bits and Pieces'. *Common Market Law Review* 30 (1993): 17–69.

Czapracka, Katarzyna. *Intellectual Property and the Limits of Antitrust: A Comparative Study of US and EU Approaches*. Cheltenham, UK: Edward Elgar, 2009.

Dai Jietao. 'The Constitutional Meaning of Wukan Event'. *Xianzheng Shehui Zhuyi Luncong* [Constitutional Socialism Series] 3–4 (2012): 505–509.

Daintith, Terence. 'Regulation'. In Richard Buxbaum and Ferenc Mádl (eds.), *International Encyclopedia of Comparative Law*. Vol. 17. Tubingen, Germany: Mohr Siebeck, 1997, ch. 10.

'The Techniques of Government'. In Jeffrey Jowell and Dawn Oliver (eds.), *The Changing Constitution*. Oxford University Press, 1994. 212–213.

Daly, Eoin. 'Austerity and Stability in Rousseau's Constitutionalism'. *Jurisprudence* 5 (2013): 191–192.

Das, Cyrus. 'The May 13th Riots and Emergency Rule'. In Andrew Harding and H. P. Lee (eds.), *Constitutional Landmarks in Malaysia: The First 50 Years, 1957–2007*. Singapore: LexisNexis, 2007. 103–114

Davidson, Donald. *Inquiries into Truth and Interpretation*. 2nd ed. Oxford: Clarendon, 2001.

Davidson, Kenneth M. 'Creating Effective Competition Institutions: Ideas for Transitional Economies'. *Asian-Pacific Law and Policy Journal* 6 (2005): 71–129.

Davis, Dennis M., and Karl Klare. 'Transformative Constitutionalism and the Common and Customary Law'. *South African Journal on Human Rights* 26 (2010): 403–509.

Dawson, Mark, and Floris De Witte. 'Constitutional Balance after the Euro-Crisis'. *Modern Law Review* 76 (2013): 817–844.

della Volpe, Galvano. *Rousseau and Marx, and Other Writings*. Translated by John Fraser. London: Lawrence and Wishart, 1978.

DeLong, J. Bradford, and Lawrence H. Summers. 'The "New Economy": Background, Historical Perspective, Questions, and Speculations'. *Economic Review* (Federal Reserve Bank of Kansas City) 29.4 (2001): 33–34

Dent, Nicholas. *A Rousseau Dictionary*. Oxford: Blackwell, 1992.

Derathé, Robert. *Jean-Jacques Rousseau et la science politique de son temps*. Paris: Presses Universitaires de France, 1950.

Derrida, Jacques. 'Declarations of Independence'. *New Political Science* 15 (1986): 7–15.

Desika Char, S. V. (ed.). *Readings in the Constitutional History of India 1757–1947*. Oxford University Press, 1983.

Devereux, Robert. *The First Ottoman Constitutional Period: A Study of the Midhat Constitution and Parliament*. Baltimore: The Johns Hopkins University Press, 1963.

Dewey, John. *The Public and Its Problems*. New York: Holt Publishing, 1927.

Dezalay, Yves, and Bryant G. Garth (eds.). *Global Prescriptions: The Production, Exportation, and Importation of a New Legal Orthodoxy*. Ann Arbor: University of Michigan Press, 2002.

Dhareshwar, Vivek. 'Politics, Experience and Cognitive Enslavement: Gandhi's Hind Swaraj'. *Economic and Political Weekly* 45 (2010): 51–58.

Dicey, A. V. *Lectures on the Relation between Law and Public Opinion in England during the Nineteenth Century*. Edited by Richard VandeWetering. Indianapolis: Liberty Fund, 2008.

Introduction to the Study of the Law of the Constitution. 10th ed. (ed., E. C. S. Wade). London: Macmillan, 1982.

Dorf, Michael C., and Charles F. Sabel. 'A Constitution of Democratic Experimentalism'. *Columbia Law Review* 98 (1998): 267–473.

Dowdle, Bentham Li. *High School Star*. Edited by Jing Li and M. Dowdle. In press.

Dowdle, Michael W. 'China's Present as the World's Future: China and "Rule of Law" in a Post-Fordist World'. In Leigh K. Jenco (ed.), *Chinese Thought as Global Theory: Diversifying Knowledge Production in the Social Sciences and Humanities*. New York: SUNY Press, 2016. 207–230.

'On the Public-Law Character of Competition Law: A Lesson from Asian Capitalism'. *Fordham International Law Journal* 38 (2015): 301–386.

'The Peripheral Regulatory State'. In Navroz K. Dubash and Bronwen Morgan (eds.), *The Rise of the Regulatory State of the South: Infrastructure and Development in Emerging Economies*. Oxford University Press, 2013. 209–224.

'Constitutional Listening'. *Chicago-Kent Law Review* 88 (2012): 115–155.

'Popular Constitutionalism and the Constitutional Meaning of Charter 08'. In Jean-Philippe Béja, Fu Hualing, and Eva Pils (eds.), *Liu Xiaobo, Charter 08, and the Challenges of Political Reform in China*. Hong Kong: Hong Kong University Press, 2012. 205–228.

Dowdle, Michael W. 'Of Comparative Constitutional Monocropping: A Reply to Qianfan Zhang'. *International Journal of Constitutional Law* 8 (2010): 977–984.

'Public Accountability in Alien Terrain: Exploring for Constitutional Accountability in the People's Republic of China'. In Michael W. Dowdle (ed.), *Public Accountability: Designs, Dilemmas and Experiences*. Cambridge University Press, 2006. 332–333.

'Public Accountability: Conceptual, Historical, and Epistemic Mappings'. In Michael W. Dowdle (ed.), *Public Accountability: Designs, Dilemmas and Experiences*. Cambridge University Press, 2006. 1–32.

(ed.). *Public Accountability: Designs, Dilemmas and Experiences*. Cambridge University Press, 2006.

'Of "Socialism" and "Socialist" Legal Transformations in China and Vietnam'. In John Gillespie and Pip Nicholson (eds.), *Asian Socialism and Legal Change: The Dynamics of Vietnamese and Chinese Reform*. Canberra: ANU E Press, 2005. 21–44.

Dowdle, Michael W. 'Of Parliaments, Pragmatism and the Dyanamics of Constitutional Development: The Curious Case of China'. *New York University Journal of International Law and Politics* 35 (2002): 1–200.

Drewry, Gavin. 'Public-Private Partnerships: Rethinking the Boundary between Public and Private Law'. In Stephen Osborne (ed.), *Public-Private Partnerships: Theory and Practice in International Perspective*. London: Routledge, 2000. 57–69.

Dugard, John. *Human Rights and the South African Legal Order*. Princeton University Press, 1978.

Dullien, Steph, and Ulrike Guérot. 'The Long Shadow of Ordoliberalism: Germany's Approach to the Euro-crisis'. *European Council of Foreign Relations Policy Brief*. London: European Council on Foreign Relations, 2012. Available at http://www.ecfr.eu/page/-/ECFR49_GERMANY_BRIEF.pdf.

Dunn, John. 'Situating Democratic Political Accountability'. In Adam Przeworski, Susan Stokes, and Bernard Manin (eds.), *Democracy, Accountability, and Representation*. Cambridge University Press, 1999. 329–344.

Durkheim, Emile. *Montesquieu and Rousseau: Forerunners of Sociology*. Ann Arbor: University of Michigan Press, 1960.

Dworkin, Ronald. *A Matter of Principle*. Cambridge, MA: Harvard University Press, 1986.

Law's Empire. Cambridge, MA: Harvard University Press, 1986.

'What Is Equality? Part 1: Equality of Welfare'. *Philosophy and Public Affairs* 10 (1981): 185–246.

'What Is Equality? Part 2: Equality of Resources'. *Philosophy and Public Affairs* 10 (1981): 283–345.

Taking Rights Seriously. Cambridge, MA: Harvard University Press, 1978.

Dyzenhaus, David. 'Constitutionalism in an Old Key: Legality and Constituent Power'. *Global Constitutionalism* 1 (2012): 233.

'The Question of Constituent Power'. In Martin Loughlin and Neil Walker (eds.), *The Paradox of Constitutionalism: Constituent Power and Constitutional Form*. Oxford University Press, 2007. 129–145.

East India (advisory and legislative councils, &c.), vol. 1: *Proposals of the Government of India and despatch of the Secretary of State : in continuation of Cd. 3710 of 1907*. London: House of Commons, 2008.

Ebrahim, Hassen. *The Soul of a Nation: Constitution-Making in South Africa*. Cape Town: Oxford University Press, 1998.

Ehrard, Jean. *L'idée de nature en France dans la 1e moitié du XVIIIe siècle*. Paris: Flammarion, 1963.

Eichengreen, Barry. *The European Economy since 1945: Co-ordinated Capitalism and Beyond*. Princeton University Press, 2007.

Eilstrup-Sangiovanni, Mette, and Daniel Verdier. 'European Integration as a Solution to War', *European Journal of International Relations* 11 (2005): 99–135.

Eisenmann, Charles. '*L'Esprit des lois* et la separation des pouvoirs'. In *Mélanges R. Carré de Malberg*. Paris: Duchemin, 1933. 165–192.

Elhauge, Einer, and Damien Geradin. *Global Competition Law and Economics*. Oxford: Hart Publishing, 2007.

Ellenburg, Stephen. 'Rousseau and Kant: Principles of Political Right'. In Ralph Leigh (ed.), *Rousseau after Two Hundred Years*. Cambridge University Press, 1982. 3–22.

Ellmann, Stephen. *In a Time of Trouble: Law and Liberty in South Africa's State of Emergency*. Oxford: Clarendon Press, 1992.

Elster, Jon. *Ulysses Unbound: Studies in Rationality, Precommitment, and Constraint*. Cambridge University Press, 2000.

'Strategic Uses of Argument'. In Kenneth J. Arrow, Robert H. Mnookin, Lee Ross, Amos Tversky, and Robert B. Wilson (eds.), *Barriers to Conflict Resolution*. New York: W. W. Norton, 1995. 236–258.

Elster, Jon, and Rune Slagstaad (eds.). *Constitutionalism and Democracy*: Cambridge University Press, 1993.

Epp, Charles. *The Rights Revolution: Lawyers, Activists, and Supreme Courts in Comparative Perspective*. University of Chicago Press, 1998.

Epstein, Richard A. 'Foreword: Unconstitutional Conditions, State Power, and the Limits of Consent'. *Harvard Law Review* 102 (1988): 4–104.

Esposito, John L. *Islam and Politics*. 4th ed. Syracuse, NY: Syracuse University Press, 1998.

Etherington, Norman, Patrick Harries, and Bernard K. Mbenga. 'From Colonial Hegemonies to Imperial Conquest, 1840–1880'. *The Cambridge History of South Africa, Vol. 1, From Early Times to 1885*. Cambridge University Press, 2014. 319–391.

Eule, Julian N. 'Laying the Dormant Commerce Clause to Rest'. *Yale Law Journal* 91 (1982): 425–485.

Evans, Peter. 'Collective Capabilities, Culture, and Amartya Sen's *Development as Freedom*'. *Studies in Comparative International Development* 37 (2002): 54–60.

Fabio, Udo di. 'Karlsruhe Makes a Referral'. *German Law Journal* 15 (2014): 107–110.

Farber, Daniel A. 'Another View of the Quagmire: Unconstitutional Conditions and Contract Theory'. *Florida State University Law Review* 33 (2005): 913–952.

Farrand, Max. *The Fathers of the Constitution: A Chronicle of the Establishment of the Union*. New Haven, CT: Yale University Press, 1921.

Facey, Brian A., and Dany H. Assaf. 'Monopolization and Abuse of Dominance in Canada, the United States, and the European Union: A Survey'. *Antitrust Law Journal* 70 (2002): 513–591.

Fauvarque-Cosson, Bénédicte, and Anne-Julie Kerhuel. 'Is Law an Economic Contest? French Reactions to the *Doing Business* World Bank Reports and Economic Analysis of the Law'. *American Journal of Comparative Law* 57 (2009): 811–830.

Feldman, Noah. 'Imposed Constitutionalism'. *Connecticut Law Review* 37 (2005): 857–889.

Fernando, Joseph M. 'Sir Ivor Jennings and the Malayan Constitution'. *The Journal of Imperial and Commonwealth History* 34 (2006): 577–597.

'The Position of Islam in the Constitution of Malaysia'. *Journal of Southeast Asian Studies* 37 (2006): 249–266.

Fetscher, Iring. *Rousseaus Politische Philosophie*. Berlin: Neuwied, 1960.

Fioravanti, Marco. 'Aspetti del costituzionalismo giacobino. La funzione legislativa nell'*acte constitutionnel* del 24 giugno 1793'. *Historia del costitucionalismo* 8 (2007): 123–142.

Fioravanti, Maurizio. *Costituzionalismo*. Bari, Italy: Laterza, 2009.

Fireside, Harvey. 'The Concept of the Legislator in Rousseau's Social Contract'. *The Review of Politics* 82 (1970): 191–216.

Fischer, Joscka. 'From Confederacy to Federation: Thoughts on the Finality of European Integration'. In Yves Mény, Christian Joerges, and Joseph Weiler (eds.), *What Kind of Constitution for What Kind of Polity: Responses to Joschka Fischer*. Cambridge, MA: Harvard Law School, 2001. 19–31.

Foerster, Heinz von. *Understanding Understanding: Essays on Cybernetics and Cognition*. New York: Springer, 2003.

Observing Systems. Seaside, CA: Intersystems Publications, 1981.

Forsyth, Christopher. *In Danger for Their Talents: A Study of the Record of the Appellate Division of the Supreme Court of South Africa 1950–1980*. Cape Town: Juta, 1985.

Foucault, Michel. *The Birth of Biopolitics: Lectures at the College de France, 1978–1979*. Translated by Graham Burchell. New York: Palgrave MacMillan, 2008.

Fox, Eleanor M. 'US and EU Competition Law: A Comparison'. In J. David Richardson and Edward M. Graham (eds.), *Global Competition Policy*. Washington, DC: Peterson Institute for International Economics, 1997. 339–354.

Frank, Jason. *Constituent Moments: Enacting the People in Postrevolutionary America*. Durham, NC: Duke University Press, 2010.

Frankenberg, Günter. 'Constitutional Transfer: The IKEA Theory Revisited'. *International Journal of Constitutional Law* 8 (2010): 563–579.

'Comparing Constitutions: Ideas, Ideals and Ideologies – Towards a Layered Narrative'. *International Journal of Constitutional Law* 4 (2006): 439–459.

Fraser, John. *An Introduction to the Thought of Galvano della Volpe*. London: Lawrence and Wilshart, 1977.

Freeman, Jody. 'Extending Public Accountability through Privatization: From Public Law to "Publicization"'. In Michael W. Dowdle (ed.), *Public Accountability: Designs, Dilemmas and Experiences*. Cambridge University Press, 2006. 83–114.

French, Rebecca. *The Golden Yoke: The Legal Cosmology of Buddhist Tibet*. Ithaca, NY: Cornell University Press, 1995.

Friden, Birtel. *Rousseau's Economic Philosophy*. Dordrecht, The Netherlands: Kluwer, 1998.

Friedman, Milton. *Capitalism and Freedom*. University of Chicago Press, 1962.

Friedmann, Yohanan. *Prophecy Continuous: Aspects of Ahmadi Religious Thought and Its Medieval Background*. Oxford University Press, 2003.

Friedrich, Carl J. 'The Political Thought of Neo-liberalism'. *American Political Science Review* 49 (1955): 509–525.

Fukuyama, Francis. *The End of History and the Last Man*. New York: Simon and Schuster, 1992.

Fuller, Lon. 'Positivism and Fidelity to Law – a Reply to Professor Hart'. *Harvard Law Review* 71 (1958): 630–672.

Fuller, Lon L. *The Morality of Law*. 2nd ed. New Haven, CT: Yale University Press, 1969.

Furet, Francois. *Interpreting the French Revolution*. Cambridge University Press, 1981.

Galanter, Marc. 'Hinduism, Secularism, and the Indian Judiciary'. In Rajeev Bhargava (ed.), *Secularism and Its Critics*. Oxford University Press, 1999. 233–267.

Gallie, Walter B. 'Essentially Contested Concepts'. *Proceedings of the Aristotelian Society* 56 (1956): 167–198.

Gandhi, M. K. *Hind Swaraj and Other Writings*. Edited by Anthony Parel. Cambridge University Press, 1997.

Gandhi, Mahatma. *Hindu Dharma*. New Delhi: Orient Paperbacks, 1978.

Gao Fang. 'Party-dominated Constitutionalism Is Not the Essence of Constitutionalism'. *Xianzheng Shehui Zhuyi Luncong* [Constitutional Socialism Forum] 3–4 (2012): 627–633.

Gardner, John. 'The Mark of Responsibility (with a Postscript on Accountability)'. In Michael W. Dowdle (ed.), *Public Accountability: Designs, Dilemmas and Experiences*. Cambridge University Press, 2006. 220–242.

Gauchet, Marcel. *La Révolution des droits de l'homme*. Paris: Gallimard, 1995.

Gazley, Beth. 'Beyond the Contract: The Scope and Nature of Informal Government–Nonprofit Partnerships'. *Public Administration Review* 68 (2008): 141–154.

Geertz, Clifford. *Local Knowledge: Further Essays in Interpretive Anthropology*. 3rd ed. New York: Basic Books, 2000.

Geng Guojie. 'The Transformation of the Party and the Reconstruction of China's Governance Model'. *Xianzheng Shehui Zhuyi Luncong* [Constitutional Socialism Forum] 3–4 (2012): 438–460.

Genovese, Michael A. *The Watergate Crisis*. Westport, CT: Greenwood, 1999.

Gerber, David J. *Global Competition: Law, Markets, and Globalization*. Oxford University Press, 2010.

'Constitutionalizing the Economy: German Neo-liberalism, Competition Law and the 'New' Europe'. *American Journal of Comparative Law* 42 (1998): 25–84.

Gill, David. *Power and Resistance in the New World Order*. New York: Palgrave Macmillan, 2003.

Gilmour, Robert S., and Laura S. Jensen. 'Reinventing Government Accountability: Public Functions, Privatization, and the Meaning of "State Action"'. *Public Administration Review* 58 (1998): 247–257.

Gilson, Ronald J., and Curtis J. Milhaupt. 'Sovereign Wealth Funds and Corporate Governance: A Minimalist Response to the New Mercantilism'. *Stanford Law Review* 60 (2007): 1349–1350.

Ginsburg, Tom, (ed.). *Comparative Constitutional Design*. Cambridge University Press, 2014.

Ginsburg, Tom, and Alberto Simpser (eds.). *Constitutions in Authoritarian Regimes*. Cambridge University Press, 2014.

Ginsburg, Tom, Zach Elkinsy, and James Meltonz. 'The Lifespan of Written Constitutions'. Paper no. 33. Presented at the 17th American Law and Economics Association Annual Meeting 2007 (New York: Columbia Law School, May 16–17, 2008. Available at http://law.bepress.com/alea/17th/art33.

Glasman, Maurice. *Unnecessary Suffering*. London: Verso, 1995.

Glencross, Andrew, and Alexander H. Trechsel (eds.). *EU Federalism and Constitutionalism: The Legacy of Altiero Spinelli*. Lanham, MD: Lexington Books, 2010.

Glendon, Mary Ann. 'Rights in Twentieth-Century Constitutions: The Case of Welfare Rights'. *Journal of Policy History* 6 (1994): 140–156.

'Rights in Twentieth-Century Constitutions'. *University of Chicago Law Review* 59 (1992): 519–538.

Glyn, Andrew. *Capitalism Unleashed: Finance Globalisation and Welfare*. Oxford University Press, 2006.

Godley, Wynn. 'Maastricht and All That'. *London Review of Books* 14 (1992): 3–4.

Goldschmidt, Victor. *Anthropologie et politique. Les principes du système de Rousseau*. Paris: Vrin, 1974.

Goodin, Robert E., Bruce Headey, Ruud Muffels, and Kenk-Jan Dirven. *The Real Worlds of Welfare Capitalism*. Cambridge University Press, 1999.

Graham, Cosmo, and Fiona Smith (eds.). *Competition, Regulation and the New Economy*. Oxford: Hart Publishing, 2004.

Griffith, John A. G. 'The Political Constitution'. *The Modern Law Review* 42 (1979): 1–21.

Grossman, Brian R., Erica Solway, Brooke A. Hollister, Carroll L. Estes, and Leah Rogne. 'One Nation, Interdependent: Exploring the Boundaries of Citizenship in the History of Social Security and Medicare'. In Leah Rogne, Carroll L. Estes, Brian R. Grossman, Brooke A. Hollister, and Erica Solway (eds.), *Social Insurance and Social Justice: Social Security, Medicare, and the Campaign Against Entitlements*. New York: Springer, 2009. 115–148.

Guo Daohui. 'The Constitutionality of Social Management and Socialization'. *Xianzheng Shehui Zhuyi Luncong* [Constitutional Socialism Forum] 3–4 (2012): 462–466.

'An Outline of Constitutional Socialism'. *Xianzheng Shehui Zhuyi Luncong* [Constitutional Socialism Forum] 2 (2011): 453–459.

'Realizing Historical Change from Revolutionary Party to Constitutional Party'. *Xianzheng Shehui Zhuyi Luncong* [Constitutional Socialism Forum] 2 (2011): 169–170.

'Authority, Power, or Rights? A Legal Reflection on the Relationship between the Party and People's Congress'. *Legal Studies* [Fa Xue] No. 1 (1994): 3–11.

Gurung, D. B., Narad Bharadwaj, Khagendra Neupane, and Aparajita Acharya. *Towards a Federalized Democratic Nepal*. Kathmandu: Friends for Peace Publishers, 2009.

Haakonssen, Knud. *Natural Law and Moral Philosophy from Grotius to the Scottish Enlightenment*. Cambridge University Press, 1996.

Haas, Ernst B. *The Uniting of Europe*. Stanford University Press, 1958.

Habermas, Jurgen. *The Crisis of the European Union: A Response*. London: Polity, 2012.

Habermas, Jürgen, and Jacques Derrida. 'February 15th or What Binds European Together?' *Constellations* 10 (2003): 291–297.

Hacka, Karl. 'The Malayan Emergency as Counter-Insurgency Paradigm'. *Journal of Strategic Studies* 32 (2009): 383–414.

Hahlo, H. R., and Ellison Kahn. *The Union of South Africa: The Development of Its Laws and Constitution*. London: Stevens, 1960.

Haider, S. M. 'Preface'. In A. R. Cornelius, *Law and Judiciary in Pakistan*. Edited by S. M. Haider. Lahore: Lahore Law Times Publications, 1981. 1–45.

Hairi, Abdul-Hadi. 'European and Asian Influences on the Persian Revolution of 1906'. *Asian Affairs* 6 (1975): 155–164.

Hall, Peter A., and David Soskice (eds.). *Varieties of Capitalism: The Institutional Foundations of Comparative Advantage*. Oxford University Press, 2001.

Hall, Richard L., and Frank W. Wayman. 'Buying Time: Moneyed Interests and the Mobilization of Bias in Congressional Committees'. *American Political Science Review* 84 (1990): 797–820.

Hamilton, Alexander. 'Federalist No. 1'. In Alexander Hamilton, James Madison, and John Jay, *The Federalist Papers*. Edited by Clinton Rossiter. New York: Signet Classics, 2003. 27–31.

Hamilton, Carolyn, Bernard K. Mbenga, and Robert Ross (eds.). *The Cambridge History of South Africa*. Vol. 1, *From Early Times to 1885*. Cambridge University Press, 2014.

Hamon, Francis, and Michel Troper. *Droit constitutionnel*. Paris: LGDJ, 2003.

Hampson, Norman. *Saint-Just*. Oxford: Blackwell, 1991.

Harding, Andrew J. *The Constitution of Malaysia: A Contextual Analysis*. Oxford: Hart Publishing, 2012.

'Constitutionalism, Islam and National Identity in Malaysia'. In Rainer Grote and Tilmann Röder (eds.), *Constitutionalism in Islamic Countries: Between Upheaval and Continuity*. Oxford University Press, 2012. 201–219.

'Malaysia: Religious Pluralism and the Constitution in a Contested Polity'. *Middle East Law and Governance* 4 (2012): 356–385.

'The Rukunegara Amendments of 1971'. In Andrew Harding and H. P. Lee (eds.), *Constitutional Landmarks in Malaysia: The First 50 Years, 1957–2007*. Singapore: LexisNexis, 2007. 115–134.

'The Keris, the Crescent and the Blind Goddess: The State, Islam and the Constitution in Malaysia'. *Singapore Journal of International and Comparative Law* 6 (2002): 154–180.

Law, Government and the Constitution in Malaysia. Kuala Lumpur: Malayan Law Journal Sdn. Bhd., 1996.

Harding, Andrew J., and H. P. Lee (eds.). *Constitutional Landmarks in Malaysia: The First 50 Years, 1957–2007*. Singapore: LexisNexis, 2007.

Harding, Andrew, and Amanda Whiting. '"Custodians of Civil Liberties and Justice in Malaysia": The Malaysian Bar and the Moderate State'. In Terence C. Halliday, Lucien Karpik, and Malcolm M. Feeley (eds.), *Fates of Political Liberalism in the British Post-Colony: The Politics of the Legal Complex*. Cambridge University Press, 2012. 247–304.

Harding, Andrew. *The Constitution of Malaysia: A Contextual Analysis*. Oxford: Hart Publishing, 2012.

Hardt, Michael, and Antonio Negri. *Empire*. Cambridge, MA: Harvard University Press, 2001.

Harrington, Christine B., and Z. Umut Turem. 'Accounting for Accountability in Neoliberal Regulatory Regimes'. In Michael W. Dowdle, (ed.), *Public*

Accountability, Designs, Dilemmas and Experiences. Cambridge University Press, 2006. 195–219.

Hart, H. L. A. *The Concept of Law*. 2nd *ed*. Oxford: Clarendon, 1994.

Harter, Philip J. 'Negotiating Regulations: A Cure for Malaise'. *Georgetown Law Journal* 71 (1986): 2–113.

Hauriou, Maurice. *Précis de Droit Constitutionnel*. 2nd ed. Paris: Sirey, 1929.

Hausner, Karl Heinz, and Silvia Simon. 'Experiences with Budget Rules in Switzerland and Germany'. *Intereconomics* 50 (2015): 99–107.

He, Baogang. 'Constitutionalism and Transcending the Competition between the Left and the Right'. *Jinyang Journal* [Jingyang Xuekan] 4 (2010): 21–24.

'Intra-Party Democracy: A Revisionist Perspective from Below'. In Kjeld Erik Broedsgaard and Yongnian Zheng (eds.), *The Chinese Communist Party in Reform*. London: Routledge, 2006. 192–209.

Hegel, Georg Wilhelm Friedrich. *Hegel: Political Writings*. Edited by Laurence Kickey and H. B. Nisbet, translated by H. B. Nisbet. Cambridge University Press, 1999.

Hegel's Philosophy of Right. Translated by T. M. Knox. Oxford: Clarendon Press, 1952.

Held, David, Anthony G. McGrew, David Goldblatt, and Jonathan Perraton. *Global Transformations: Politics, Economics and Culture*. Stanford University Press, 1999.

Helleiner, Eric. 'Economic Nationalism as a Challenge to Economic Liberalism? Lessons from the 19th Century'. *International Studies Quarterly* 46 (2002): 307–329.

Heller, Hermann. 'Authoritarian Liberalism?' *European Law Journal* 21 (2015): 295–301 (translated by S. Paulson).

'Political Democracy and Social Homogeneity'. In Arthur Jacobson and Bernhard Schlink (eds.), *Weimar: A Jurisprudence of Crisis*. New ed. Berkeley: University of California Press, 2002. 256–264.

'The Nature and Structure of the State'. *Cardozo Law Review* 18 (1996): 1139–1216. Translated by David Dyzenhaus.

Gesammelte Schriften. Leiden, The Netherlands: A. W. Sijthoff, 1971.

'Autoritärer Liberalismus', *Die Neue Rundschau* 44 (1933): 289–298.

Hemert, Dianne van. *Patterns of Cross-Cultural Differences in Psychology: A Meta-Analytic Approach*. Amsterdam, The Netherlands: Dutch University Press, 2003.

Henkin, Louis. *Foreign Affairs and the United States Constitution*. 2nd ed. Oxford: Clarendon Press, 1997.

'A New Birth of Constitutionalism: Genetic Influences and Genetic Defects'. In Michel Rosenfeld (ed.), *Constitutionalism, Identity, Difference, and Legitimacy*. Durham, NC: Duke University Press, 1994. 39–53.

Hepple, Bob. *Young Man with a Red Tie*. Johannesburg: Jacana, 2013.

Hervey, Tamara. 'Social Solidarity: A Buttress against Internal Market Law?' In Jo Shaw (ed.), *Social Law and Policy in an Evolving European Union*. Oxford: Hart Publishing, 2000. 31–48.

Heyningen, Elizabeth van. *The Concentration Camps of the Anglo-Boer War: A Social History*. Johannesburg: Jacana, 2013.

Hickling, R. H. 'An Overview of Constitutional Change in Malaysia: 1957–1977'. In Tun Mahamed Suffian, H. P. Lee, and F. A. Trindade (eds.), *The Constitution of Malaysia: Its Development, 1957–1977*. Kuala Lumpur: Oxford University Press, 1978. 1–26.

Hill, Clanspeter, and Jors Menzel (eds.). *Constitutionalism in Southeast Asia*. Vol. 2, *Reports on National Constitutions*. Singapore: Konrad-Adenauer-Stiftung and Time Edge Publishing, 2010.

Hill, Enid. 'Al-Sanhuri and Islamic Law: The Place and Significance of Islamic Law in the Life and Work of 'Abd al-Razzaq Ahmad al-Sanhuri, Egyptian Jurist and Scholar, 1895–1971' [Part I]. *Arab Law Quarterly* 3 (1988): 33–64.

'Al-Sanhuri and Islamic Law: The Place and Significance of Islamic Law in the Life and Work of'Abd al-Razzaq Ahmad al-Sanhuri, Egyptian Jurist and Scholar, 1895–1971' [Part II]. *Arab Law Quarterly* 3 (1988): 182–218.

Hodge, Graeme A. 'Tendering and Contracting Out: Rhetoric or Reality?' *Public Productivity and Management Review* 22 (1999): 455–469.

Hodge, Graeme A., and Carsten Greve. 'Public-Private Partnerships: An International Performance Review'. *Public Administration Review* 67 (2007): 545–558.

Hogan, Joyce, and Ann M. Quigley. 'Physical Standards for Employment and the Courts'. *American Psychologist* 41 (1986): 1193–1217.

Holmes, Stephen. *Passions and Constraint: On the Theory of Liberal Democracy*. University of Chicago Press, 1995.

Honig, Bonnie. *Political Theory and the Displacement of Politics*. Ithaca, NY: Cornell University Press, 1993.

Honohan, Iseult. *Civic Republicanism*. London: Routledge, 2002.

Horowitz, Asher. *Rousseau, Nature and History*. University of Toronto Press, 1987.

Horowitz, Morton. *The Transformation of American Law, 1870–1960: The Crisis of Legal Orthodoxy*. Oxford University Press, 1992.

Horwitz, Morton J. 'The History of the Public/Private Distinction'. *University of Pennsylvania Law Review* 130 (1982): 1423–1428.

Hou Ruili. 'Rule of Law Takes Center Stage'. *China Today*, Nov. 11, 2014. At 4. Available at http://epaper.chinadailyasia.com/asia-weekly/article-3509.html.

Hoyle, Mark S. W. *Mixed Courts of Egypt*. London: Graham and Trotman, 1991.

Hu Deping. 'Study the Urgently Needed Big Topic in Our Time'. *Xianzheng Shehui Zhuyi Luncong* [Constitutional Socialism Forum] 3–4 (2012): 1–4.

Hua Bingxiao. 'Local Governance and the Grassroots of Constitutional Socialism', *Xianzheng Shehui Zhuyi Luncong* [Constitutional Socialism Series] 3–4 (2012): 476–485.

'On the Constructive Reform Path of Constitutional Socialism'. Paper presented at the 2011 China's Reform Summit: Present and Future (Beijing, 2011).

Chaoyue Ziyou Zhuyi: *Xianzheng Shehui Zhuyi de Sixiang Yanshuo* [Beyond Liberalism: A Discourse on Constitutionalism]. Xian: Northwest University Press, 2011.

Human Rights Watch. 'Integration of the Human Rights of Women and the Gender Perspective: Violence against Women and "Honor" Crimes, Intervention before the 57th Session of the U.N. Commission on Human Rights', Apr. 6, 2001. Available at http://www.hrw.org/news/2001/04/05/item-12-integration-human-rights-women-and-gender-perspective-violence-against-women.

Hunt, Roland, and John Harrison. *The District Officer in India 1937–47*. London: Scolar Press, 1980.

Hussain, Jamila. 'Freedom of Religion in Malaysia: The Muslim Perspective'. In Wu Min Aun (ed.), *Public Law in Contemporary Malaysia*. Petaling Jaya: Longman Malaysia, 1999. 107–133.

'"Illogical" That 250,000 Muslims Have Left Faith, Says Perlis Mufti'. *The Malaysian Insider*, Oct. 18, 2011. http://www.themalaysianinsider.com/malaysia/article/illogical-that-250000-muslims-have-left-faith-says-perlis-mufti.

Inglehart, Ronald, and Daphna Oyserman. 'Individualism, Autonomy and Self-Expression: The Human Development Syndrome'. In Henk Vinken, Joseph Soeters, and Peter Ester (eds.), *Comparing Cultures, Dimensions of Culture in a Comparative Perspective*. Leiden, The Netherlands: Brill, 2004. 74–96.

Jackson, Sherman A. *Islamic Law and the State: The Constitutional Jurisprudence of Shihāb Al-Dīn Al-Qarāfī*. Leiden, The Netherlands: Brill, 1996.

Jacobs, Francis. *Sovereignty of Law: The European Way*. Cambridge University Press, 2007.

James, Harold. 'Economic Reasons for the Collapse of the Weimar Republic'. In Ian Kershaw (ed.), *Weimar: Why Did German Democracy Fail?* New York: St. Martin's Press, 1990. 30–57.

Jayasuriya, Kanishka. 'Globalisation, Sovereignty and the Rule of Law: From Political to Economic Constitutionalism'. *Constellations* 8 (2001): 442–460.

'Introduction: A Framework for the Analysis of Legal Institutions in East Asia'. In Kanishka Jayasuriya (ed.), *Law, Capitalism and Power in Asia: The Rule of Law and Legal Institutions*. London: Routledge, 1999. 1–23.

Jefferson, Thomas. *Notes on the State of Virginia*. New York: Digireads.com Publishing, 2004.

Jenco, Leigh K. *Making the Political: Founding and Action in the Political Theory of Zhang Shizhao*. Cambridge University Press, 2010.

Jessop, Bob, and Ngai-Ling Sum. *Beyond the Regulation Approach: Putting Capitalist Economies in Their Place*. Cheltanham, UK: Edward Elgar, 2006.

Jiang Haisong, and Su Dan. 'The Unique Features of the Rule of Law in Hunan'. *Xianzheng Shehui Zhuyi Luncong* [Constitutional Socialism Forum] 3–4 (2012): 495–504.

Jiang Qing. *A Confucian Constitutional Order: How China's Ancient Past Can Shape Its Political Future*. Edited by Daniel A. Bell and Ruiping Fan, translated by Edmund Ryden. Princeton University Press, 2012.

Jiang Ping. 'On Constitutional Socialism'. *Xianzheng Shehui Zhuyi Luncong* [Constitutional Socialism Forum] 1 (2011): 3–6.

Joerges, Christian. 'Europe's Economic Constitution in Crisis and the Emergence of a New Constitutional Constellation'. ZenTra Working Paper in Transnational Studies No. 06/2012. Oldenberg and Bremen: ZenTra Centre for Transnational Studies, 2012. Available at http://papers.ssrn.com/sol3/papers.cfm?abstract_id=2179595.

'What Is Left of the European Economic Constitution?' European University Institute Working Papers Law 2004/13. Florence, Italy; European University Institute, 2004. Available at http://cadmus.eui.eu/bitstream/handle/1814/2828/law04-13.pdf.

Johansen, Baber. *Contingency in a Sacred Law: Legal and Ethical Norms in the Muslim Fiqh*. Leiden, The Netherlands: Brill, 1999.

John, Mathew. 'Identity and the Social Revolution: On the Political Sociology of Constitutionalism in Contemporary India'. Jawaharlal Nehru University Centre for the Study of Law and Governance Working Paper No. CSLG/WP/18. New Delhi: Jawaharlal Nehru University 2012. Available at http://www.jnu.ac.in/cslg/workingPaper/18-Identity%20%28John%29.pdf.

Jomo K. S., and Chang Yii Tan. 'The Political Economy of Post-Colonial Transformation'. In Jomo K. S. and Wong Sau Ngan (eds.), *Law, Institutions and Malaysian Economic Development*. Singapore: NUS Press. 22–53.

Juanjan, Olivier. 'La suspension de la constitution de 1793. *Droits* 10 (1993): 125–138.

Judt, Tony. *Ill Fares the Land*. London: Penguin, 2010.

Kagan, Robert A. *Adversarial Legalism: The American Way of Law*. Cambridge, MA: Harvard University Press, 2003.

Kahn, Paul. *Political Theology: Four New Chapters on the Concept of Sovereignty*. New York: Columbia University Press, 2011.

Kamman, Michael. *A Machine That Would Go of Itself: The Constitution in American Culture*. New York: Alfred A. Knopf, 1986.

Kaplan, Edward. *The Bank of the United States and the American Economy*. Westwood, CT: Greenwood Press, 1999.

Kaplow, Louis, and Steven Shavell. *Fairness versus Welfare*. Cambridge, MA: Harvard University Press, 2009.

Karis, Thomas, and Gwendolyn M Carter (eds.). *From Protest to Challenge: A Documentary History of African Politics in South Africa 1882–1990*. Stanford, CA: Hoover Institution Press (Vols. 1–5); Capetown: University of South Africa Press (Vols. 5–7), 1971–1997.

Kelsen, Hans. *Introduction to the Problems of Legal Theory*. Translated by B. L. Paulson and S. L. Paulson. Oxford: Clarendon Press, 1992.

Pure Theory of Law. Translated by Max Knight. Berkeley: University of California Press, 1967.

Kennedy, Charles. 'Islamization and Legal Reform in Pakistan, 1979–1989'. *Pacific Affairs* 63 (1990): 62–77.

'Islamization in Pakistan: Implementation of the Hudood Ordinances'. *Asian Survey* 28 (1988): 307–316.

Ketcham, Ralph, (ed.). *The Anti-Federalist Papers and the Constitutional Debates*. New York: New American Library, 1986.

Keynes, John Maynard. 'A Short View of Russia'. In *The Collected Writings of John Maynard Keynes*. Vol. 9. London: Macmillan, 1971. 253–271.

'National Self-Sufficiency'. *The Yale Review* 22 (1933): 755–769.

Khoo Boo Teik. *Paradoxes of Mahathirism: An Intellectual Biography of Mahathir Mohamad*. Kuala Lumpur: Oxford University Press, 1995.

Kilpatrick, Claire. 'On the Rule of Law and Economic Emergency: The Degradation of Basic Legal Values in Europe's Bailouts'. *Oxford Journal of Legal Studies* 35 (2015): 325–353.

'Are the EU Bail-Outs Immune to Social Challenge Because They Are Not EU Law?' *European Constitutional Law Review* 10 (2014): 393–421.

'Constitutions, Social Rights and Sovereign Debt States in Europe: A Challenging New Area of Constitutional Inquiry'. European University Institute Working Papers Law 2015/34. Florence, Italy: European University Institute, 2004. Available at http://cadmus.eui.eu/bitstream/handle/1814/36097/LAW_2015_34.pdf?sequence=1.

Klare, Karl. 'Legal Culture and Transformative Constitutionalism'. *South African Journal on Human Rights* 12 (1998): 146–188.

Klotz, Audie. 'Norms Reconstituting Interests: Global Racial Equality and U.S. Sanctions against South Africa'. *International Organization* 49 (1995): 451–478.

Koh, Harold Hongju. *The National Security Constitution: Sharing Power after the Iran-Contra Affair*. New Haven, CT: Yale University Press, 1990.

Komarek, Jan, and Matej Avbelj (eds.). *Constitutional Pluralism in the European Union and Beyond*. Oxford: Hart Publishing, 2012.

Kommers, Donald P., and Russell A. Miller. *The Constitutional Jurisprudence of the Federal Republic of Germany*. Durham, NC: Duke University Press, 2012.

Kong, Tao, and Arief Ramayandi. 'Survey of Recent Developments'. *Bulletin of Indonesian Economic Studies* 44 (2008): 25–28.

Koskenniemi, Martti. 'Histories of International law: Dealing with Eurocentrism'. *Rechtsgeschichte* 19 (2011): 152–176.

Kostal, R. W. 'The Alchemy of Occupation: Karl Loewenstein and the Legal Reconstruction of Nazi Germany, 1945–1946'. *Law and History Review* 29 (2011): 1–52.

Kovacic, William E. 'A Regulator's Perspective on Getting the Balance Right'. In R. Ian McEwin (ed.), *Intellectual Property, Competition Law and Economics in Asia*. Oxford: Hart Publishing, 2011. 23–34.

Krajewski, Markus, Ulla Neergaard, and Johan van de Gronden (eds.). *The Changing Legal Framework for Services of General Interest in Europe: Between Competition and Solidarity*. The Hague: T. M. C. Asser Press, 2009.

Kramer, Larry D. *The People Themselves: Popular Constitutionalism and Judicial Review*. Oxford University, 2004.

Krugman, Paul, 'Secular Stagnation in the Euro Area'. *New York Times*, May 17, 2014. Reprinted at http://krugman.blogs.nytimes.com/2014/05/17/secular-stagnation-in-the-euro-area/?_php=true&_type=blogs&_r=o.

Kumm, Matthias. 'Rebel without a Good Cause: Karlsruhe's Misguided Attempt to Draw the CJEU into a Game of "Chicken" and What the CJEU Might Do About It'. *German Law Journal* 15 (2014): 203–216.

'The Best of Times and the Worst of Times: Between Constitutional Triumphalism and Nostalgia'. In Martin Loughlin and Petra Dobner (eds.), *The Twilight of Constitutionalism*. Oxford University Press, 2012. 201–220.

'How Does European Union Law Fit into the World of Public Law'. In Jürgen Neyer and Antje Wiener (eds.), *Political Theory of the European Union*. Oxford University Press, 2010. 111–139.

Kuppusamy, Baradan. 'Can Christians Say "Allah"? In Malaysia, Muslims Say No'. *Time*, Jan. 8, 2010. Available at http://content.time.com/time/world/article/0,8599,1952497,00.html.

Lakoff, George, and Mark Johnson. *Metaphors We Live By*. University of Chicago Press, 1980.

Lang, Andrew. *World Trade Law after Neo-Liberalism: Re-Imagining the Global Economic Order*. Oxford University Press, 2011.

Larrére, Catherine. *L'invention de l'économie aux XVIIIeme Siécle*. Paris: Presses Universitaires de France, 1992.

Laslett, Peter. 'Introduction'. In John Locke, *Second Treatise on Civil Government*. Edited by Peter Laslett. Cambridge University Press, 1980. 102–104.

'John Locke, the Great Recoinage and the Origins of the Board of Trade: 1695–1698'. *William and Mary Quarterly* 14 (1957): 370–402.

Lasser, Mitchell. *Judicial Transformations: The Rights Revolution in the Courts of Europe*. Oxford University Press, 2009.

Lau, Martin. *The Role of Islam in the Legal System of Pakistan*. Leiden, The Netherlands: Martinus Nijhoff, 2006.

Lavenex, Sandra. 'Mutual Recognition and the Monopoly of Force: Limits of the Single Market Analogy'. *Journal of European Public Policy* 14 (2007): 762–779.

Lecercle, Jean-Louis. 'Rousseau et Marx'. In R. A. Leigh (ed.), *Rousseau after 200 Years: Proceedings of the Cambridge Bicentennial Colloquium*. Cambridge University Press, 2010. 67–86.

Lefort, Claude. 'The Permanence of the Theological-Political?' In *Democracy and Political Theory*. Translated by D. Macey. Cambridge: Polity Press, 1988.

Legassick, Martin, and Robert Ross. 'From Slave Economy to Settler Capitalism: The Cape Colony and Its Extensions, 1800–1854'. In Carolyn Hamilton, Bernard K. Mbenga, and Robert Ross (eds.), *The Cambridge History of South Africa, Vol. 1, From Early Times to 1885*. Cambridge University Press, 2014. 253–318.

Legrand, Pierre. 'What "Legal Transplants?"' In David Nelken and Johannes Feest (eds.), *Adapting Legal Cultures*. Oxford: Hart Publishing, 2001. 55–68.

Leopold, David. *The Young Marx*. Cambridge University Press, 2007.

Lerner, Abba P. 'The Economics and Politics of Consumer Sovereignty'. *American Economic Review* 62 (1972): 258–266.

Levin, Robert A., and Laurie Moses Hines. 'Educational Television, Fred Rogers, and the History of Education'. *History of Education Quarterly* 43 (2003): 262–275.

Lewis, Norman. 'Regulating Non-Government Bodies: Privatization, Accountability and the Public-Private Divide'. In Jeffrey Jowell and Dawn Oliver (eds.), *The Changing Constitution*. 2nd ed. Oxford: Clarendon Press, 1989. 219–247.

Li Yang, 'The Heated Debate Arising from the Constitutionalist Socialism Study', *Xianzheng Shehui Zhuyi Luncong* [*Constitutional Socialism Forum*] 2 (2011): 164–169.

Liddle, William D. '"A Patriot King, or None": Lord Bolingbroke and the American Renunciation of George III'. *The Journal of American History* 65 (1979): 951–970.

Lienesche, Michael. 'Reinterpreting Rebellion: The Influence of Shays's Rebellion on American Political Thought'. In Robert A Gross (ed.), *In Debt to Shays: The Bicentennial of an Agrarian Rebellion*. Charlottesville: University Press of Virginia, 1993. 161–182.

Liew Chin Tong. 'PAS Politics: Defining an Islamic State'. In Edmund Terence Gomez (ed.), *Politics in Malaysia: The Malay Dimension*. London: Routledge, 2007. 107–137.

Likosky, Michael B. *The Silicon Empire: Law, Culture and Commerce*. Aldershot, UK: Ashgate, 2005.

Lim Hong Hai. 'Electoral Politics in Malaysia: "Managing" Elections in a Plural Society'. In Aurel Croissant, Gabriele Bruns, and Marei John (eds.), *Electoral Politics in Southeast and East Asia*. Singapore: Friedrich Ebert Stiftung, 2002.

Lin, Li-Wen, and Curtis J. Milhaupt. 'We Are the (National) Champions: Understanding: The Mechanisms of State Capitalism in China'. *Stanford Law Review* 65 (2013): 697–759.

Lindahl, Hans. 'A-Legality: Postnationalism and the Question of Legal Boundaries'. *Modern Law Review* 73 (2010): 30–56.

'Constituent Power and Reflexive Identity: Towards an Ontology of Collective Selfhood'. In Martin Loughlin and Neil Walker (eds.), *The Paradox of*

Constitutionalism: Constituent Power and Constitutional Form. Oxford University Press, 2007. 9–27.

'Sovereignty and Representation in the EU'. In Neil Walker (ed.), *Sovereignty in Transition*. Oxford: Hart Publishing, 2003. 87–115.

Lindseth, Peter. *Power and Legitimacy: Reconciling Europe and the Nation-State*. Oxford University Press, 2010.

Lippmann, Walter. *Drift and Mastery: An Attempt to Diagnose the Current Unrest*. New York: Prentice Hall, 1961.

List, Friedrich. 'The National System of Political Economy'. Reprinted in Lars Magnusson (ed.), *Free Trade: 1793–1886*. Vol. 2. London: Routledge, 1997. 72–214.

Liu, Lawrence S. 'In Fairness We Trust? – Why Fostering Competition Law and Policy Ain't Easy in Asia' (Oct. 19, 2004). Available at http://ssrn.com/abstract=610822.

Li Yang, 'The Heated Debate Arising from the Constitutionalist Socialism Study', *Xianzheng Shehui Zhuyi Luncong* [Constitutional Socialism Forum] 2 (2011): 164–169.

Locke, John. *Two Treatises of Government*. Edited by P. Laslett. Cambridge University Press, 1998.

Loewenstein, Karl. 'Militant Democracy and Fundamental Rights, Part 1'. *The American Political Science Review* 3 (1937): 417–432.

'Autocracy versus Democracy in Contemporary Europe, Part 2'. *The American Political Science Review* 29 (1935): 571–593.

Lombardi, Clark B. 'Can Islamizing a Legal System Ever Help Promote Liberal Democracy? A View from Pakistan'. *University of St. Thomas Law Journal* 7 (2010): 647–691.

Lombardi, Clark B. 'Islamism as a Response to Emergency Rule in Pakistan: The Surprising Proposal of Justice A. R. Cornelius'. In Victor V. Ramraj and Arun K. Thiruvengadam (eds.), *Emergency Powers in Asia: Exploring the Limits of Legality*. Cambridge University Press, 2009. 436–65.

State Law as Islamic Law in Modern Egypt. Leiden, The Netherlands: Brill, 2006.

Lombardi, Clark B., and Nathan J Brown. 'Do Constitutions Requiring Adherence to Shari`a Threaten Human Rights? How Egypt's Constitutional Court Reconciles Islamic Law with the Liberal Rule of Law'. *American University International Law Review* 21 (2006): 379–435.

Loughlin, Martin. 'The Constitutional Imagination'. *Modern Law Review* 78 (2015): 1–25.

'Nomos.' In Thomas Poole and David Dyzenhaus (eds.), *Theorists of Constitutional Crisis: Oakeshott, Hayek and Schmitt on Law, Liberty and State*. Cambridge University Press, 2015. 65–95.

'The Concept of Constituent Power'. *European Journal of Political Theory* 13 (2014): 218–237.

The British Constitution: A Very Short Introduction. Oxford University Press, 2013.

'What Is Constitutionalisation?' In Martin Loughlin and Petra Dobner (eds.), *The Twilight of Constitutionalism*. Oxford University Press, 2012. 47–69.

Foundations of Public Law. Oxford University Press, 2010.

'In Defence of Staatslehre'. *Der Staat* 48 (2009): 1–28.

'Constituent Power Subverted: From English Constitutional Argument to British Constitutional Practice'. In Martin Loughlin and Neil Walker (eds.), *The Paradox of Constitutionalism*. Oxford University Press, 2007. 27–49.

The Idea of Public Law. Oxford University Press, 2004.

'Ten Tenets of Sovereignty'. In Neil Walker (ed.), *Sovereignty in Transition*. Oxford: Hart Publishing, 2003. 55–86.

Loughlin, Martin, and Neil Walker (eds.). *The Paradox of Constitutionalism: Constituent Power and Constitutional Form*. Oxford University Press, 2007.

Ludwig-Erhard-Stiftunge e. V. Bonn. *Standard Texts on the Social Market Economy: Two Centuries of Discussion*. Edited by Horst Friedrich Wünsche, translated by Derek Rutter. Stuttgart: Gustav Fisher Verlag, 1982.

Luhmann, Niklas. *Law as a Social System*. Oxford University Press, 2004.

Die Politik der Gesellschaft. Frankfurt: Suhrkamp, 2000.

Die Wissenschaft der Gesellschaft. Frankfurt: Suhrkamp, 1990a.

'Two Sides of the State Founded on Law'. In *Political Theory in the Welfare State*. Berlin: de Gruyter, 1990b. 187–202.

'Der Staat als Historischer Begriff'. In Marcel Storme (ed.), *Mijmeringen van een Jurist bij 1984*. Antwerp: Kluwer Publishers, 1984. 139–154.

MacCormick, John P. 'The Dilemmas of Dictatorship: Carl Schmitt and Constitutional Emergency Powers'. *Canadian Journal of Law and Jurisprudence* 10 (1997): 163–189.

MacDonald, Joan. *Rousseau and the French Revolution: 1762–1791*. London: Athlon Press, 1965.

Macpherson, Crawford. *The Political Theory of Possessive Individualism*. Oxford University Press, 1962.

Madan, T. N. *Modern Myths, Locked Minds: Secularism and Fundamentalism in India*. 2nd ed. Oxford University Press, 2009.

Maddox, Graham. 'Constitution'. In Terence Ball, James Farr, and Russell L. Handon (eds.), *Political Innovation and Conceptual Change*. Cambridge University Press, 1989. 50–67.

Madison, James. 'Federalist No. 10'. In Alexander Hamilton, James Madison, and John Jay, *The Federalist Papers*. Edited by Clinton Rossiter. New York: Signet Classics, 2003. 71–79.

'Federalist No. 52'. In Alexander Hamilton, James Madison, and John Jay, *The Federalist Papers*. Edited by Clinton Rossiter. New York: Signet Classics, 2003. 322–327.

'Federalist No. 57'. In Alexander Hamilton, James Madison, and John Jay, *The Federalist Papers*. Edited by Clinton Rossiter. New York: Signet Classics, 2003. 348–353.

'Mahathir: Malaysia Is "Fundamentalist State"'. *CNN.com*, June 18, 2002. Available at http://edition.cnn.com/2002/WORLD/asiapcf/southeast/06/18/malaysia.mahathir/.

Maher, Imelda. 'The Institutional Structure of Competition Law'. In Michael W. Dowdle, John Gillespie, and Imelda Maher (eds.), *Asian Capitalism and the Regulation of Competition: Towards a Regulatory Geography of Global Competition Law*. Cambridge University Press, 2013. 61–75.

Mahmassani, Ṣubḥī Rajab. *Falsafat al-tashrī fī al-Islām: The Philosophy of Jurisprudence in Islam*. Translated by Farhat Ziadeh. Leiden, The Netherlands: Brill, 1961.

Mahmud, Tayyab. 'Freedom of Religion and Religious Minorities in Pakistan: A Study of Judicial Practice'. *Fordham International Law Journal* 19 (1995–1996): 40–100.

'Praetorianism and Common Law in Post-colonial Settings: Judicial Responses to Constitutional Breakdowns in Pakistan'. *Utah Law Review* (1993): 1225–1305.

Maistre, Joseph de. 'Study on Sovereignty'. In *The Works of Joseph de Maistre*. Edited and translated by Jack Lively. London: Unwin Brothers Ltd, 1965. 93–129.

Majone, Giandomenico. *Rethinking the Union of Europe Post-Crisis*. Oxford University Press, 2014.

Mancini, Federico. 'The Case for Statehood'. *European Law Journal* 4 (1998): 29–42.

Mandela, Nelson. *Long Walk to Freedom*. Johannesburg: Macdonald, 1994.

Mann, Michael. *The Dark Side of Democracy: Explaining Ethnic Cleansing*. Cambridge University Press, 2005.

'The Autonomous Power of the State: Its Origins, Mechanisms and Results'. *European Journal of Sociology* 25 (1984): 185–213.

Marks, Gary, and Lisbet Hooghe. 'A Postfunctionalist Theory of European Integration: From Permissive Consensus to Constraining Dissensus'. *British Journal of Political Science* 39 (2009): 1–23.

Marks, Shula. 'War and Union 1899–1910'. In Robert Ross, Anne Kelk Mager, and Bill Nasson (eds.), *The Cambridge History of South Africa*. Vol. 2, *1885–1994*. Cambridge University Press, 2014. 157–210.

Marshall, T. H. *Citizenship and Social Class, and Other Essays*. Bloomington: University of Illinois Press, 1950.

Marx, Karl. *Capital*. Oxford University Press, 1988.

Early Writings. Translated by Rodney Livingstone and Gregor Benton. London: Penguin, 1975.

Mashaw, Jerry L. 'Accountability and Institutional Design: Some Thoughts on the Grammar of Governance'. In Michael W. Dowdle (ed.), *Public Accountability: Designs, Dilemmas and Experiences*. Cambridge University Press, 2006. 115–156.

Masud, M. K. 'Rethinking Shari`a: Javed Ahmad Ghamidi on Hudud'. *Die Welt des Islams* 47 (2007): 356–375.

Mathews, A. S. *Freedom, State Security and the Rule of Law*. Cape Town: Juta, 1986.

Maulin, Eric. *La théorie de l'état de Carré de Malberg*. Paris: Presses Universitaires de France, 2003.

Mayer, Jurgen. 'Rebels without a Cause? A Critical Analysis of the German Constitutional Court's OMT Reference'. *German Law Journal* 15 (2014): 111–146.

Mazower, Mark. *Dark Continent: Europe's Twentieth Century*. London: Penguin, 1999.

McCormick, John. *Machiavellian Democracy*. Cambridge University Press, 2011.

McIlwain, Charles Howard. *Constitutionalism: Ancient and Modern*. Ithaca, NY: Cornell University Press, 1958.

Means, Gordon P. 'Malaysia: Islam in a Pluralist Society'. In Carlo Caldarola (ed.), *Religions and Societies: Asia and the Middle East*. Berlin: Walter de Gruyter, 1983. 445–496.

Mehta, Uday Singh. 'Constitutionalism'. In Niraja Gopal Jayal and Pratap Bhanu Mehta (eds.), *The Oxford Companion to Politics in India*. Oxford University Press, 2010. 15–27.

'Gandhi on Democracy, Politics and the Ethics of Everyday Life'. *Modern Intellectual History* 7 (2010): 355–371.

Meierhenrich, Jens. *The Legacies of Law: Long-Run Consequences of Legal Development in South Africa, 1652–2000*. Cambridge University Press, 2008.

Menendez, Agustín José. 'The Existential Crisis of the European Union'. *German Law Journal* 14 (2013): 453–526.

Metcalf, Barbara Daly. *Islam in South Asia in Practice*. Princeton University Press, 2009.

Michelman, Frank. 'Law's Republic'. *Yale Law Journal* 97 (1988): 1493–1537.

Milne, R. S., and Diane K. Mauzy. *Malaysian Politics under Mahathir*. London: Routledge, 1999.

Milward, Alan. *The European Rescue of the Nation-State*. London: Verso, 1992.

Misra, Bankey Bihari. *The Bureaucracy in India: An Historical Analysis of Development up to 1947*. Oxford University Press, 1977.

Möllers, Christoph. ' "We Are (Afraid of) the People": Constituent Power in German Constitutionalism'. In Martin Loughlin and Neil Walker (eds.), *The Paradox of Constitutionalism: Constituent Power and Constitutional Form*. Oxford University Press, 2007. 87–107.

"The Scope and Legitimacy of Judicial Review in German Constitutional Law - The Court versus the Political Process'. In Hermann Punder and Christian Waldhoff (eds.), *Debates in German Public Law* (Oxford: Hart Publishing, 2014).

Mollers, Kai. *The Global Model of Constitutional Rights*. Oxford University Press, 2012.

Montagu Chelmsford Report on Indian Constitutional Reform. Superintendent, Government of India Press, 1918.

Morgan, Bronwen. 'Technocratic v. Convivial Accountability'. In Michael W. Dowdle (ed.), *Public Accountability, Designs, Dilemmas and Experiences*. Cambridge University Press, 2006. 243–268.

Morison, John, Kieran McEvoy, and Gordon Anthony (eds.). *Judges, Transition, and Human Rights*. Oxford University Press, 2007.

Moten, Abdul Rashid. '2008 General Elections in Malaysia: Democracy at Work'. *Japanese Journal of Political Science* 10 (2009): 21–42.

'Mr. Fred Rogers: Senate Statement on PBS Funding, Delivered 1 May 1969'. American Rhetoric Online Speech Bank. Available at http://www.americanrhetoric.com/speeches/fredrogerssenatetestimonypbs.htm.

Mulgan, Richard. 'Contracting Out and Accountability'. *Australian Journal of Public Administration* 56 (1997): 106–116.

Müller, Jan-Werner. *Contesting Democracy: Political Ideas in Twentieth Century Europe*. Revised edition. New Haven: Yale University Press, 2013.

Contesting Democracy: Political Ideas in Twentieth Century Thought. Princeton University Press, 2012.

Mumtaz, Khawar, and Farida Shaheed (eds). *Women of Pakistan: Two Steps Forward and One Step Back?* London: Zed Books, 1987.

Munir, Abu Bakar. 'Privatisation in Malaysia: A Case Study of the Telecommunications Department'. In Euston Quah and William Neilson (eds.), *Law and Economic Development: Cases and Materials from South East Asia*. Singapore: Longman, 1993. 169–176.

Munir, Muhammad, and M. R. Kayani. *Report of the Court of Inquiry Constituted under Punjab Act II of 1954 to Enquire into the Punjab Disturbances of 1953*. Punjab: Superintendent, Government Printing, 1954. Reprinted at http://aaiil.org/text/books/others/misc/munirreport/munirreport.shtml.

Naidoo, Phyllis. *156 Hands That Built South Africa*. Cape Town: Stephan Phillips, 2006.

Nakano, Takeshi. 'Theorising Economic Nationalism'. *Nations and Nationalism* 10 (2004): 211–229.

Nandy, Ashish. 'The Politics of Secularism and the Recovery of Toleration'. In Rajeev Bhargava (ed.), *Secularism and Its Critics*. Oxford University Press, 1999. 321–344.

Napoleon I. *The Corsican: A Diary of Napoleon's Life in His Own Words*. Edited by R. M. Johnston. Boston: Houghton Mifflin Co., 1910.

Nasr, Seyyed Vali Reza. *The Vanguard of the Islamic Revolution: The Jama'at-i Islami of Pakistan*. University of California Press, 1994.

Nasson, Bill. *The War for South Africa*. Cape Town: Tafelberg, 2010.

Nathan, K. S. 'Malaysia in 1989: Communists End Armed Struggle'. *Asian Survey* 30 (1990): 210–220.

National Operations Council [Malaysia]. *The May 13 Tragedy: A Report of the National Operations Council*. Kuala Lumpur: Government Printer, 1969.

Negri, Antonio. *Insurgencies: Constituent Power and the Modern State*. Translated by M. Boscagli. Minneapolis: University of Minnesota Press, 1999.

Neo, Jaclyn L. 'Competing Imperatives: Conflicts and Convergences in State and Islam in Pluralist Malaysia'. *Oxford Journal of Law and Religion* 4 (2015): 1–25.

Neo, Jaclyn Ling-Chien. 'Malay Nationalism, Islamic Supremacy and the Constitutional Bargain in the Multi-ethnic Composition of Malaysia'. *International Journal on Minority and Group Rights* 13 (2006): 95–118.

Neuhouser, Frederick. 'Rousseau's Critique of Economic Inequality'. *Philosophy and Public Affairs* 41 (2013): 193–215.

Neumann, Franz. 'On the Preconditions and Legal Concept of an Economic Constitution'. In Otto Kirchheimer and Franz Neumann (eds.), *Social Democracy and the Rule of Law*. Edited by Keith Tribe. London: Allen and Unwin, 1987. 44–65.

Newberg, Paula R. *Judging the State: Courts and Constitutional Politics in Pakistan*. Cambridge University Press, 1995.

Noor, Farish A. 'The Hindu Rights Action Force (HINDRAF) of Malaysia: Communitarianism across Borders?' RSIS Working Paper Series No. 163. Singapore: Nanyang Technological University, S. Rajaratnam School of International Studies (RSIS), July 2008. Available at https://www.rsis.edu.sg/rsis-publication/idss/163-wp163-the-hindu-rights-actio/#.VZ3g9fmm3o4.

Norton, Michael I. 'Unequality: Who Gets What and Why It Matters'. *Policy Insights from the Behavioral and Brain Sciences* 1 (2014): 151–155.

Oakeshott, Michael. *On Human Conduct*. Oxford University Press, 1975.

Oakley, Francis. 'The Absolute and Ordained Power of God and King in the Sixteenth and Seventeenth Centuries: Philosophy, Science, Politics, and Law'. *Journal of the History of Ideas* 59 (1998): 669–690.

Offe, Claus. 'Europe Entrapped: Does the EU Have the Political Capacity to Overcome Its Political Crisis'. *European Law Journal* 19 (2013): 595–611.

Oklopcic, Zoran. 'Constitutional (Re)vision: Sovereign Peoples, New Constituent Powers, and the Formation of Constitutional Orders in the Balkans'. *Constellations* 19 (2013): 81–101.

Okun, Arthur. *Equality and Efficiency: The Big Tradeoff*. Washington, DC: Brookings Institution Press, 1975.

'Once Muslim, Now Christian and Caught in the Courts', *New York Times*, Aug. 24, 2006. Available at http://www.nytimes.com/2006/08/24/world/asia/24malaysia.html?_r=0.

O'Neal, John. 'Rousseau's Theory of Wealth'. *History of European Ideas* 7 (1986): 453.

Orbach, Barak. 'How Antitrust Lost Its Goal'. *Fordham Law Review* 81 (2013): 2253–2278.

Otto, Jan Michiel. *Sharia and National Law in Muslim Countries: Tensions and Opportunities for Dutch and EU Foreign Policy*. Amsterdam University Press, 2008.

Panitch, Leo, and Sam Gindin. *The Making of Global Capitalism: The Political Economy of American Empire*. London: Verso, 2012.

Park, Donghyun, and Gemma Bolotaulo Estrada. 'Developing Asia's Sovereign Wealth Funds and Outward Foreign Direct Investment'. Asian Development Bank Economics Working Paper Series No. 169. Manila: Asian Development Bank, 2009. Available at http://www.adb.org/publications/developing-asias-sovereign-wealth-funds-and-outward-foreign-direct-investment.

Patel, Rashida. *Islamisation of Laws in Pakistan*. Karachi: Faiza Publishers, 1986.

Pathan, Sufiya. 'A Historical and Theoretical Investigation into Communalism'. Manipal, India: Manipal University PhD thesis, 2009. Available at http://cscs.res.in/dataarchive/textfiles/a-historical-and-theoretical-investigation-into-2018communalism2019/view.

Peacock, Alan T., and Hans Willgerodt. *Germany's Social Market Economy*. London: MacMillan for the Trade Policy Research Centre, 1989.

Peerenboom, Randall P. *China's Long March towards Rule of Law*. Cambridge University Press, 2002.

Pennock, J. Roland, and John W. Chapman (eds.). *Nomos XX: Constitutionalism*. New York University Press, 1979.

Perry, Michael. *The Constitution, The Courts, and Human Rights*. New Haven, CT: Yale University Press, 1982.

Pettit, Philip. On the People's Terms. Cambridge University Press, 2012.

'Two Republican Traditions'. In Andreas Niederberger and Philipp Schink (eds.), *Republican Democracy: Liberty, Law and Politics*. Edinburgh University Press, 2012. 169–204.

On the People's Terms. Cambridge University Press, 2012.

Republicanism. Oxford University Press, 1997.

Phongpaicht, Pasuk, and Chris Baker. *Thailand's Crisis*. Singapore: Institute of Southeast Asian Studies, 2000.

Piketty, Thomas. *Capital in the 21st Century*. Cambridge, MA: Harvard University Press, 2014.

Pinker, Steven. *The Blank Slate: The Modern Denial of Human Nature*. London: Penguin, 2002.

Piore, Michael J., and Charles F. Sabel. *The Second Industrial Divide: Possibilities for Prosperity*. New York: Basic Books, 1984.

Pipe, Daniel. *Distinguishing between Islam and Islamism*. Paper Presented at Center for Strategic and International Studies, Washington, DC, June 30, 1998. Available at http://www.danielpipes.org/954/distinguishing-between-islam-and-islamism.

Plehwe, Dieter. 'Introduction'. In Philip Mirowski and Dieter Plehwe (eds.) *The Road from Mont Pélerin: The Making of the Neoliberal Thought Collective*. Cambridge, MA: Harvard University Press, 2009. 1–44.

Plessis, Lourens du, and Hugh Corder. *Understanding South Africa's Transitional Bill of Rights*. Cape Town: Juta, 1994.

Pocock, J. G. A. *Virtue, Commerce and History*. Cambridge University Press, 1985.

Polanyi, Karl. *The Great Transformation: The Political and Economic Origins of Our Time*. 2nd ed. Boston: Beacon Press, 2001.

Polin, Raymond. *Jean-Jacques Rousseau et son oeuvre*. Paris: Klincksieck, 1964.

Poole, Thomas. 'Back to the Future: Unearthing the Theory of Common Law Constitutionalism'. *Oxford Journal of Legal Studies* 23 (2003): 435–454.

Posel, Deborah. 'The Apartheid Project, 1948–1970'. In Robert Ross, Anne Kelk Mager, and Bill Nasson (eds.), *The Cambridge History of South Africa*. Vol. 2, *1885–1994*. Cambridge University Press, 2014. 319–368.

Potter, David. *India's Political Administrators*. Oxford University Press, 1986.

Power, Michael. *The Audit Society: Rituals of Verification*. Oxford University Press, 1997.

Prandini, Riccardo. 'The Morphogenesis of Constitutionalism'. In Petra Dobner and Martin Loughlin (eds.), *The Twilight of Constitutionalism?* Oxford University Press, 2010. 309–326.

Preuss, Ulrich. 'Constitution-Making and Nation-Building: Reflections on Political Transformations in East and Western Europe'. *European Journal of Philosophy* 1 (1993): 81–92.

Preuss, Ulrich K. 'Constitutional Power-Making for the New Polity: Some Deliberations on the Relations between the Constituent Power and the Constitution'. *Cardozo Law Review* 14 (1992–1993): 639–660.

Prosser, Tony. *The Economic Constitution*. Oxford University Press, 2014.

'Models of Economic and Social Regulation'. In Dawn Oliver, Tony Prosser, and Richard Rawlings (eds.), *The Regulatory State: Constitutional Implications*. Oxford University Press, 2010. 34–49.

The Limits of Competition Law: Markets and Public Services. Oxford University Press, 2005.

Przeworski, Adam, Susan Stokes, and Bernard Manin (eds.). *Democracy, Accountability, and Representation*. Cambridge University Press, 1999.

Pufendorf, Samuel. *On the Law of Nature and Nations*. Translated by C. H. and W. A. Oldfather. Oxford: Clarendon Press, 1934.

Pusey, Michael. 'Economic Rationalism, Human Rights and Civil Society'. *Australian Journal of Human Rights* 4 (1998): 131–153.

Puthucheary, Mavis. 'Ministerial Responsibility in Malaysia'. In Tun Mahamed Suffian, H. P. Lee, and F. A. Trindade (eds.), *The Constitution of Malaysia: Its Development, 1957–1977*. Kuala Lumpur: Oxford University Press, 1978. 123–135.

Puthucheary, Mavis C. 'Malaysia's "Social Contract": The invention and Historical Evolution of an Idea'. In Norani Othman, Maris C. Puthucheary, and Clive Kessler (eds.), *Sharing the Nation: Faith, Difference and Power in the State*

50 Years after Merdeka. Petaling Jaya: Strategic Information and Research Development Centre, 2008. 1–28.

Putterman, Ethan. *Rousseau, Law and the Sovereignty of the People*. Cambridge University Press, 2010.

'Rousseau on the People as Legislative Gatekeepers, not Framers'. *American Political Science Review* 99 (2005): 145–151.

Qianfan Zhang. 'A Constitution without Constitutionalism? The Paths of Constitutional Development in China'. *International Journal of Constitutional Law* 8 (2010): 950–976.

Qing, Jiang. *A Confucian Constitutional Order: How China's Ancient Past Can Shape Its Political Future*. Edited by Daniel A. Bell and Ruiping Fan; translated by Edmund Ryden. Princeton University Press, 2012.

Radhakrishnan, Survepalli. *Indian Philosophy*. London: George Allen and Unwin Ltd., 1948.

Rakove, Jack N. *Original Meanings: Politics and Ideas in the Making of the Constitution*. New York: Vintage Books, 1996.

Ramraj, Victor V. 'No Doctrine More Pernicious? Emergencies and the Limits of Legality'. In Victor V. Ramraj (ed.) *Emergencies and the Limits of Legality*. Cambridge University Press, 2008. 3–29.

Rao, B. Shiva, and others. *The Framing of India's Constitution*. New Dehli: Indian Institute of Public Administration, 1966.

Rapaczynski, Andrzej. 'Constitutional Politics in Poland: A Report on the Constitutional Committee of the Polish Parliament'. *University of Chicago Law Review* 58 (1991): 595–631.

Rawls, John. *A Theory of Justice*. Cambridge, MA: Harvard University Press, 1971.

Raz, Joseph. *The Authority of Law: Essays on Law and Morality*. 2nd ed. Oxford University Press, 2009.

'The Identify of Legal Systems'. *California Law Review* 59 (1971): 795–815.

Rials, Stephan. *La déclaration des droits de l'homme et du citoyen*. Paris: Presses Universitaires de France, 1988.

Richards, David A. J. *Foundations of American Constitutionalism*. Oxford University Press, 1989.

Ricoeur, Paul. *Critique and Conviction*. Translated by K. Blaney. New York: Columbia University Press, 1998.

'Narrative Identity'. *Philosophy Today* 35 (1991): 73–81.

History and Truth. Translated by C. A. Kelbley. Evanston, IL: Northwestern University Press, 1965.

'The Symbol ... Food for Thought'. *Philosophy Today* 3 (1960): 196–207.

Riley, Patrick. 'Rousseau's General Will'. In Patrick Riley (ed.), *Cambridge Companion to Rousseau*. Cambridge University Press, 2001. 124–155.

Risse, Thomas, and Daniela Engelmann-Martin. 'Identity Politics and European Integration: The Case of Germany'. In Anthony Pagden (ed.), *The Idea of Europe: From Antiquity to the European Union*. Cambridge University Press, 2002. 287–317.

Ritchie, David. 'Organic Constitutionalism: Rousseau, Hegel and the Constitution of Society'. *Journal of Law and Society* 6 (2005): 36–81.

Robespierre, Maximillien. *Virtue and Terror*. Edited by Jean Ducange; translated by John Howe. London: Verso, 2007.

Oeuvres de Maximilien Robespierre. Edited by Albert Laponneraye. Paris: Albert Laponneraye, 1840.

Rodrik, Dani. 'The Social Cost of Foreign Exchange Reserves'. *International Economic Journal* 20 (2006): 253–266.

Ropke, Wilhelm. 'Economic Order and International Law'. *Recuil des Cours, Academie de Droit Internationale* 86, no. 2 (1954): 207–271.

Roslan, A. H. 'Income Inequality, Poverty and Development Policy in Malaysia'. Paper presented at the conference on *Poverty and Sustainable Development* (Pessac, Fr.: Université Montesquieu-Bordeaux, Nov. 22–23, 2002). Available at http://ged.u-bordeaux4.fr/SBROSLAN.pdf.

Ross, Robert. 'Khoesan and Immigrants: The Emergence of Colonial Society in the Cape 1500–1800'. In Carolyn Hamilton, Bernard K. Mbenga, and Robert Ross (eds.), *The Cambridge History of South Africa*. Vol. 1, *From Early Times to 1885*. Cambridge University Press, 2014. 168–210.

Ross, Robert, Anne Kelk Mager, and Bill Nasson (eds.), *The Cambridge History of South Africa*. Vol. 2, *1885–1994*. Cambridge University Press, 2014.

Rousseau, Jean-Jacques. *The Social Contract*. In *The Social Contract and Other Later Political Writings*. Translated by V. Gourevitch. Cambridge: Cambridge University Press, 1997.

'Discourse on Political Economy'. In *The Social Contract*. Translated by Christopher Betts. Oxford University Press, 1994. 1–42.

'The Social Contract'. In *The Social Contract*. Translated by Christopher Betts. Oxford University Press, 1994. 43–168.

A Discourse on Inequality. Translated by Maurice Cranston. London: Penguin, 1984.

Ouevres completes. Paris: Gallimard, 1959.

Roussel, Jean. *Jean-Jacques Rousseau en France après la Révolution*. Paris: Colin, 1972.

Roux, Theunis. *The Politics of Principle: The First South African Constitutional Court, 1995–2005*. Cambridge University Press, 2013.

Sahlins, Marshall. *Stone Age Economics*. London: Tavistock, 1974.

Saint-Just, Louis Antoine de. *Oeuvres*. Paris: Folio, 2004.

Saleh, Nabil. 'Civil Codes of Arab Countries: The Sanhuri Codes'. *Arab Law Quarterly* 8 (1993): 161–167.

Sampford, Charles. 'Law, Institutions and the Public/Private Divide'. *Federal Law Review* 20 (1991): 185–222.

Sangiovanni, Andrea. 'Solidarity in the European Union: Problems and Prospects'. In Julie Dickson and Pavlos Eleftheriadis (eds.), *Philosophical Foundations of European Union Law*. Oxford University Press, 2012. 384–411.

Sanhoury, A. ['Abd al-Razzāq al-Sanhūrī]. *Le califat: son évolution vers une société des nations orientales*. Paris: P. Geuthner, 1926.

Sanhoury Bey, Abd-el-Razzak Ah. El['Abd al-Razzāq al-Sanhūrī]. 'Le droit musulman comme élément de refonte du code civil égyptien'. In *Introduction à l'étude du droit comparé: Recuil d'études en l'honneur d'Édouard Lambert*. Vol. 3. Paris: Librairie générale de droit et de jurisprudence, 1938. 621–642.

Schama, Simon. *Citizens: A Chronicle of the French Revolution*. New ed. London: Penguin, 2004.

Scharpf, Fritz. 'After the Crash: A Perspective on Multi-Level European Democracy'. *European Law Journal* 21 (2015): 393.

'The Asymmetry of European Integration: Or Why Europe Can't Have a Social Market Economy'. *Socio-Economic Review* 8 (2010): 211–250.

'Legitimacy in the Multi-Level European Polity'. In Petra Dober and Martin Loughlin (eds.) *Twilight of Constitutionalism* (Oxford University Press, 2010), 89–120.

'The Asymmetry of European Integration: Or Why Europe Can't Have a Social Market Economy'. *Socio-Economic Review* 8 (2010): 211–250.

Scheuerman, William. 'The Unholy Alliance of Carl Schmitt and Friedrich Hayek', *Constellations* 4 (1997): 172–188.

Schmitt, Carl. *Dictatorship: From the Origin of the Modern Concept of Sovereignty to Proletarian Class Struggle*. Translated by M. Hoelzl and G. Ward. Cambridge: Polity Press, 2014.

Constitutional Theory. Translated by J. Seitzer. Durham, NC: Duke University Press, 2008.

Verfassungslehre. Translated by J. Seitzer. Durham, NC: Duke University Press, 2008.

Political Theology: Four Chapters on the Concept of Sovereignty. Translated by G. Schwab. University of Chicago Press, 2005.

Legality and Legitimacy. Translated by J. Seitzer. Durham, NC: Duke University Press, 2004.

On the Three Types of Juristic Thought. Translated by J. Benderskey. Westport, CT: Praeger, 2004.

The Nomos of the Earth in the International Law of the Jus Publicum Europeaum (trans., G. L. Ulmen). New York: Telos Press, 2003.

State, Movement, People: The Triadic Structure of the Political Unity. Translated by S. Draghici. Corvallis, OR: Plutarch Press, 2001.

The Concept of the Political. Translated by G. Schwab. University of Chicago Press, 1996.

The Crisis of Parliamentary Democracy. Translated by E. Kennedy. Cambridge, MA: MIT Press, 1985.

Schmitter, Philippe C. 'Still the Century of Corporatism?' *The Review of Politics* 36 (1974): 85–131.

Schmitter, Philippe C., and Gerhard Lehmbruch (eds.). *Trends toward Corporatist Intermediation*. New York: Sage, 1979.

Schneiderman, David. 'A. V. Dicey, Lord Watson, and the Law of the Canadian Constitution in the Late Nineteenth Century'. *Law and History Review* 16 (1998): 495–526.

Schönberger, Christoph. '"L'Etat de la 'Theorie Generale de l'Etat": Remarkes Comparatives sur un Discipline Specifiquement Allemand'. In Alain Chatriot und Dieter Gosewinkel (eds.), *Figurationen des Staates in Deutchsland und Frankreich 1870–1945*. Munich: R. Oldenbourg Verlag, 2006. 257–275.

Schumpeter, Joseph A. *Capitalism, Socialism, and Democracy*. 3rd ed. New York: Harper and Row, 1975.

Schwartzberg, Melissa. 'Rousseau on Fundamental Law'. *Political Studies* 51 (2003): 387–403.

Sciulli, David. *Theory of Societal Constitutionalism: Foundations of a Non-Marxist Critical Theory*. Cambridge University Press, 1992.

Scott, Colin. 'Spontaneous Accountability'. In Michael W. Dowdle (ed.), *Public Accountability: Designs, Dilemmas and Experiences*. Cambridge University Press, 2006. 174–191.

Scott, Joanne, and David M. Trubek. 'Mind the Gap: Law and New Approaches to Governance in the European Union'. *European Law Journal* 8 (2002): 1–18.

Scott, John. 'Rousseau's Anti-Agenda Setting and Contemporary Democratic Theory'. *American Political Science Review* 99 (2005): 137–144.

'Shahadat Law against Quran, Sunnah: FSC'. *The News International*, Feb. 12, 2009. Available at http://www.thenews.com.pk/TodaysPrintDetail.aspx?ID=162186&Cat=5&dt=2/13/2009.

Shalakany, Amr. 'Between Identity and Redistribution: Sanhuri, Genealogy and the Will to Islamise'. *Islamic Law and Society* 8 (2001): 201–244.

Shklar, Judith. *Montesquieu*. Oxford University Press, 1987.

Men and Citizens. Cambridge University Press, 1969.

Shklar, Judith N. *Legalism: Law, Morals and Political Trials*. Cambridge, MA: Harvard University Press, 1964.

Shleifer, Andrei, and Robert W. Vishny. 'Corruption'. *The Quarterly Journal of Economics* 108 (1993): 599–617.

Shuaib, Farid S. 'The Islamic Legal System in Malaysia'. *Pacific Rim Law and Policy Journal* 21 (2012): 85–113.

Sidak, J. Gregory, and David Teece. 'Favouring Dynamic Competition over Static Competition in Antitrust Law'. In R. Ian McEwin (ed.), *Intellectual Property, Competition Law and Economics in Asia*. Oxford: Hart Publishing, 2011. 53–94.

Siddique, Osama, and Zahra Hayat. 'Unholy Speech and Holy Laws: Blasphemy Laws in Pakistan – Controversial Origins, Design Defects, and Free Speech Implications'. *Minnesota Journal of International Law* 17 (2008): 303–385.

Sieyès, Emmanuel-Joseph. *What Is the Third Estate?* Translated by M. Blondel. London: Pall Mall Press, 1963.

Silberman, Bernard S. *Cages of Reason: The Rise of the Rational State in France, Japan, the United States and Great Britain*. University of Chicago Press, 1993.

Skinner, Quentin. *Liberty before Liberalism*. Cambridge University Press, 1998.

Skowronek, Stephen. *Building a New American State: The Expansion of National Administrative Capacities, 1877–1920*. Cambridge University Press, 1982.

Smilova, Ruzha. 'The General Will Constitution: Rousseau as a Constitutionalist'. In Denis Galligan (ed.), *Constitutions and the Classics*. Oxford University Press, 2014. 265–289.

Smith, Wilfred Cantwell. *Modern Islam in India: A Social Analysis*. London: V. Gollancz, 1946.

Somek, Alexander. *The Cosmopolitan Constitution*. Oxford University Press, 2014.

Spector, Céline. 'Rousseau et la critique de l'économie politique'. In Bruno Bernardi (ed.), *Rousseau et les sciences*. Paris: L'Harmattan, 2003. 237–256.

'Speech by Jacques Delors (Luxembourg, Sept. 9, 1985)', *CVCE.eu*. Available at http://www.cvce.eu/obj/speech_by_jacques_delors_luxembourg_9_september_1985-en-423d6913-b4e2-4395-9157-fe70b3ca8521.html.

Spitz, Richard, with Matthew Chaskalson. *The Politics of Transition: A Hidden History of South Africa's Negotiated Settlement*. Johannesburg: Wits University Press, 2000.

Statistics South Africa. *Poverty Trends in South Africa: An Examination of Absolute Poverty between 2006 and 2011*. Report No. 03-10-06 2014. Pretoria: Statistics South Africa, 2014. Available at http://beta2.statssa.gov.za/publications/Report-03-10-06/Report-03-10-06March2014.pdf.

Stern, Fritz. 'The New Democracies in Crisis in Interwar Europe'. In Axel Hadenius (ed.), *Democracy's Victory and Crisis*. Cambridge University Press, 1997. 15–25.

Streeck, Wolfgang. *Buying Time*. London: Verso, 2014.

'Markets and Peoples: Democratic Capitialism and European Integration'. *New Left Review* 73 (2013): 63–71.

Sullivan, Kathleen. 'Unconstitutional Conditions'. *Harvard Law Review* 102 (1989): 1413–1506.

Sun Shangwu. 'Rally Marks 50th Anniversary of NPC'. *China Daily*, Sept. 15, 2004. Available at http://www.chinadaily.com.cn/english/doc/2004-09/15/content_374799.htm.

Sweezy, Paul. 'Is the Marshall Plan an Instrument of Peace?' *Monthly Review* 1 (1949): 80–83.

Talbot, Ian. *Pakistan: A Modern History*. 2nd ed. New York: Palgrave Macmillan, 2010.

Talmon, Jacob. *The Origins of Totalitarian Democracy*. London: Secker and Warburg, 1950.

Tan, Poh-ling Tan, 'Prime Suspect or Potential Witness? Paying the Price for Religious Freedom: A Non-Muslim Perspective'. In Wu Min Aun (ed.), *Public*

Law in Contemporary Malaysia. Petaling Jaya: Longman Malaysia, 1999. 137–177.

Teachout, Zephyr. 'The Anti-Corruption Principle'. *Cornell Law Review* 94 (2009): 341–413.

Teles, Patrícia Galvão. 'EU Presidency Statement – United Nations 6th Committee: Rule of Law at National and International Levels'. New York: European Union Delegation to the United Nations, PRES07-320EN, Oct. 25, 2007. Available at http://eu-un.europa.eu/articles/en/article_7569_en.htm. Accessed June 6, 2015.

Teschke, Benno. 'Fatal Attraction: A Critique of Carl Schmitt's International Legal and Political Theory'. *International Theory* 3 (2011): 179–227.

Teubner, Gunther. *Constitutional Fragments: Societal Constitutionalism and Globalization*. Oxford University Press, 2012.

Financial Crisis in Constitutional Perspective: The Dark Side of Functional Differentiation. Oxford: Hart Publishing, 2011.

'Idiosyncratic Production Regimes: Co-Evolution of Economic and Legal Institutions in the Varieties of Capitalism'. In John Ziman (ed.), *The Evolution of Cultural Entities: Proceedings of the British Academy*. Oxford University Press, 2002. 161–181.

'Juridification: Concepts, Aspects, Limits, Solutions'. In Robert Baldwin, Colin Scott, and Christopher Hood (eds.), *A Reader on Regulation*. Oxford University Press, 1998. 389–440.

Thapa, Manjushree. 'Nepal's Slippery Fast-Track,' *The Wire*, June 13, 2015. Available at http://thewire.in/2015/06/13/nepals-slippery-fast-track/.

The Nehru Report: An Anti-Separatist Manifesto. New Delhi: Michiko and Panjathan, 1975.

Thio, Li-ann. 'Jurisdictional Imbroglio: Civil and Religious Courts, Turf Wars and Article 121 (1A) of the Federal Constitution'. In Andrew Harding and H. P. Lee (eds.), *Constitutional Landmarks in Malaysia: The First 50 Years, 1957–2007*. Singapore: LexisNexis, 2007. 197–226.

Thiru, Steven, and Ben Dawson. 'The Lina Joy Case and the Future of Religious Freedom in Malaysia'. *Lawasia Journal* (2007): 151–162.

Thomas, Tommy. 'Is Malaysia an Islamic State'. *Malayan Law Journal* 14 (2006): 15–46.

Thompson, E. P. *The Making of the English Working Class*. Rev. ed. London: Penguin Books, 1991.

Thompson, Helen. 'Austerity as Ideology: The Bait and Switch of the Banking Crisis'. *Comparative European Politics* 11 (2013): 729–736.

Thompson, L. M. 'Constitutionalism in the South African Republics'. *Butterworths South African Law Review* (1954): 49–73.

Thornhill, Chris. *A Sociology of Constitutions: Constitutions and State Legitimacy in Historical-Sociological Perspective*. Cambridge University Press, 2011.

'Towards a Historical Sociology of Constitutional Legitimacy'. In *Theory and Society* 37 (2008): 161–197.

Tocqueville, Alexis de. *The Old Regime and the Revolution*. Edited by François Furet and Françoise Mélonio, translated by Alan S. Kahan. University of Chicago Press, 1998.

Democracy in America. Translated by H. Reeve. New York: Vintage Books, 1990.

Tomkin, Jonathan. 'Contradiction, Circumvention, and Conceptual Gymnastics: The Impact of the Adoption of the ESM Treaty on the State of European Democracy'. *German Law Journal* 14 (2013): 169–189.

Tomkins, Adam. 'On Republican Constitutionalism in the Age of Commerce'. In Samantha Besson and José Marttí (eds.), *Legal Republicanism*. Oxford University Press, 2009. 316–336.

Our Republican Constitution. Oxford: Hart Publishing, 2005.

Tong Zhiwei. 'The Core Value of Constitutional Socialism Is to the Rule of Law', *Xianzheng Shehui Zhuyi Luncong* [Constitutional Socialism Forum] 2 (2011): 478–481.

Torres, Jose Arsenio. 'The Political Ideology of Guided Democracy'. *The Review of Politics* 25 (1963): 34–63.

Trapido, Stanley. 'Imperialism, Settler Identities, and Colonial Capitalism: The Hundred-Year Origins of the 1899 South African War'. In Robert Ross, Anne Kelk Mager, and Bill Nasson (eds.), *The Cambridge History of South Africa*. Vol. 2, *1885–1994*. Cambridge University Press, 2014. 66–101.

Tribe, Keith. *Strategies of Economic Order: German Economic Discourse 1750–1950*. Cambridge University Press, 1995.

Tribe, Laurence H. *American Constitutional Law*. 2nd ed. St. Paul, MN: Foundation Press, 1988.

Trincia, Francesco. 'Marx lettore di Rousseau'. *Critica marxista* 31 (1985): 97–127.

Trubek, David. 'The "Rule of Law" in Development Assistance: Past, Present, and Future'. In David M. Trubek and Alvaro Santos (eds.), *The New Law and Economic Development: A Critical Appraisal*. Cambridge University Press, 2006. 74–95.

Tuck, Richard. 'The "Modern" School of Natural Law'. In Anthony Pagden (ed.), *The Languages of Political Theory in Early-Modern Europe*. Cambridge University Press, 1987. 99–122.

Tully, James. 'Middle East Legal and Governmental Pluralism: A View of the Field from the Demos'. *Middle East Law and Governance* 4 (2012): 225–263.

'The Imperialism of Modern Constitutional Democracy'. In Martin Loughlin and Neil Walker (eds.), *The Paradox of Constitutionalism: Constituent Power and Constitutional Form*. Oxford University Press, 2007. 315–337.

Strange Multiplicity: Constitutionalism in an Age of Diversity. Cambridge University Press, 1995.

Tuori, Karlo. 'The Many Constitutions of Europe'. In Kaarlo Tuori and Sankari Suvi (eds.), *The Many Constitutions of Europe*. Farnham, UK: Ashgate, 2010. 3–30.

Tuori, Karlo, and Klaus Tuori. *The Euro-Crisis: A Constitutional Analysis*. Cambridge University Press, 2014.

Tussman, Joseph, and Jacobus ten Broek. 'The Equal Protection of the Laws'. *California Law Review* 37 (1949): 341–381.

Tyler, Tom R. *Why People Obey the Law*. New Haven, CT: Yale University Press, 1990.

Ufena, Andreas. 'The Transformation of Political Party Opposition in Malaysia and Its Implications for the Electoral Authoritarian Regime'. *Democratization* 16 (2009): 604–627.

Unger, Roberto Mangabeira. *The Critical Legal Studies Movement*. Cambridge, MA: Harvard University Press, 1986.

Van Miert, Karel. 'A Pragmatic Approach to Europe's Competition Policy'. *Frontier-Free EUROPE Monthly Newsletter* (April 5, 1993).

Vargas, Yves. 'Marx et Engels, lecteurs de Rousseau'. In Guglielmo Forni Rosa and Frédréric Lefevbre (eds.), *Rousseau dans le XIXe siècle*. Montmorency: Musée Jean-Jacques Rousseau, 2007.

Vauchez, Antoine. 'The Transnational Politics of Judicialisation: *Van Gend en Loos* and the Making of the EU Polity'. *European Law Journal* 16 (2010): 1–12

Vincenti, Luc. *Jean-Jacques Rousseau. L'individu et la république*. Paris: Kimé, 2001.

Viroli, Maurizio. *Jean-Jacques Rousseau and the 'Well-Ordered Society'*. Cambridge University Press, 2003.

Vorster, M. P., M. Wiechers, and D.J. van Vuuren. *The Constitutions of Transkei, Bophuthatswana, Venda and Ciskei*. Durban: Butterworth, 1985.

Vorys, Karl von. *Democracy without Consensus: Communalism and Political Stability in Malaysia*. Princeton University Press, 1975.

Waldron, Jeremy. 'Accountability: Fundamental to Democracy'. NYU School of Law, Public Law Research Paper No. 14-13 (New York, 2014). Available at http://papers.ssrn.com/sol3/papers.cfm?abstract_id=2410812.

'Can There Be a Democratic Jurisprudence?' *Emory Law Journal* 58 (2009): 675–712.

'Precommitment and Disagreement', in Larry Alexander (ed.), *Constitutionalism: Philosophical Foundations*. Cambridge University Press, 1998. 271–301.

Liberal Rights. Cambridge University Press, 1993.

The Right to Private Property. Oxford University Press, 1988.

Walker, Neil. 'Our Constitutional Unsettlement'. *Public Law* (2014): 529–548.

'Europe's Unresolved Constitution'. In Michel Rosenfeld and Andras Sajo (eds.), *The Oxford Handbook of Comparative Constitutional Law*. Oxford University Press, 2012. 1185–1208.

'The Place of European Law'. In Gráinne de Búrca and J. H. H. Weiler (eds.), *The Worlds of European Constitutionalism*. Oxford University Press, 2011. 57–105.

'EU Constitutionalism and New Governance'. In Grainne de Burca and Joanne Scott (eds.), *Law and New Governance in the EU and the US*. Oxford: Hart Publishing, 2006. 15–37.

(ed.). *Sovereignty in Transition*. Oxford: Hart Publishing, 2003.

Wan, Tina. 'Unnecessary Evil of Plea Bargaining: An Unconstitutional Conditions Problem and Not-So-Least Restrictive Alternative'. *The Southern California Review of Law and Social Justice* 17 (2007): 33–61.

Wang Zhanyang. 'Reflections on the Concept of Constitutional Socialism'. *Xianzheng Shehui Zhuyi Luncong* [Constitutional Socialism Forum] 3–4 (2012): 590–600.

'What Is Constitutional Socialism?' *Xianzheng Shehui Zhuyi Luncong* [Constitutional Socialism Forum] 2 (2011): 470–472.

Webber, Gregoire, and Grahame Gee. 'What Is a Political Constitution?' *Oxford Journal of Legal Studies* 30 (2010): 273–299.

Weil, Simone. *The Need for Roots: Prelude to a Declaration of Duties towards Mankind*. London: Routledge, 2003.

Weiler, J. H. H. 'On the Power of the Word: Europe's Constitutional Iconography'. *International Journal of Constitutional Law* 3 (2005): 173–190.

'In Defence of the Status Quo: Europe's Constitutional *Sonderweg*'. In J. H. H. Weiler and Marlene Wind (eds.), *European Constitutionalism beyond the State*. Cambridge University Press, 2003. 7–25.

Weiler, Joseph H. H. 'Editorial: Integration through Fear'. *European Journal of International Law* 23 (2012): 1–5.

'The Case against the Case for Statehood'. *European Law Journal* 4 (1998): 43–62.

'The Transformation of Europe'. *Yale Law Journal* 100 (1992): 2403–2483.

'The Community System: The Dual Character of Supranationalism'. *Yearbook of European Law* (1981): 267–306.

Wertheimer, Alan. *Coercion*. Princeton University Press, 1987.

Whitaker, Gordon P., Lydian Altman-Sauer, and Margaret Henderson. 'Mutual Accountability between Governments and Nonprofits: Moving beyond "Surveillance" to "Service"'. *American Review of Public Administration* 34 (2004): 115–133.

White, Jonathan. 'Emergency Europe'. *Political Studies* 62 (2015): 300–318.

Wiebe, Robert H. *The Search for Order*. New York: Hill and Wang, 1967.

Wilbur, Donald N. *Pakistan: Yesterday and Today*. New York: Holt Rinehart Winston, 1964.

Wilkinson, Michael. 'Economic Messianism and Constitutional Power in a German Europe: All Courts Are Equal but Some Courts Are More Equal Than Others'. LSE Legal Studies Working Paper No. 26/2014. London: London School of Economics, 2014. Available at http://papers.ssrn.com/sol3/papers.cfm?abstract_id=2522919.

Wilkinson, Michael A. 'Authoritarian Liberalism in the European Constitutional Imagination'. *European Law Journal* 21 (2015): 313–340.

'Political Constitutionalism and the European Union'. *Modern Law Review* 76 (2013): 191–222.

'The Spectre of Authoritarian Liberalism: Reflections on the Constitutional Crisis of the European Union'. *German Law Journal* 14 (2013): 527–560.

Wilkinson, Stella, Cass Wilkinson, and Gil Wilkinson. *Growing Up*. Edited by Michele Wilkinson and Michael A. Wilkinson. In press.

Williamson, Oliver E. *The Economic Institutions of Capitalism*. New York: The Free Press, 1985.

Willoughby, Westel. *The Fundamental Concepts of Public Law*. New York: Macmillan, 1924.

Wilsher, Daniel. 'Law and the Financial Crisis: Searching for Europe's New Gold Standard'. *European Law Journal* 20 (2014): 241–283.

Wilson, Edward O. *Consilience: The Unity of Knowledge*. New York: Alfred A. Knopf, 1998.

Wilson, Neil L. 'Substances without Substrata'. *Review of Metaphysics* 12 (1959): 521–539.

Wilson, Woodrow. *Constitutional Government in the United States*. New York: Columbia University Press, 1908.

Wokler, Robert. 'Rousseau and Marx'. In David Miller and Larry Siedentop (eds.), *The Nature of Political Theory*. Oxford University Press, 1983. 219–246.

Wolin, Seldon. *The Presence of the Past: Essays on the State and the Constitution*. Baltimore, MD: The John Hopkins University Press, 1989.

Wollenschlager, Ferdinand. 'A New Fundamental Freedom beyond Market Integration'. *European Law Journal* 17 (2011): 1–34.

Wood, Ellen Meiksins. *Liberty and Property*. London: Verso, 2012.

Wood, Gordon S. *The Creation of the American Republic, 1776–1787*. Chapel Hill: University of North Carolina Press 1998.

The Radicalism of the American Revolution. New York: Vintage Books, 1993.

Wright, John. 'Turbulent Times: Political Transformations in the North and East, 1760s–1830s'. Carolyn Hamilton, Bernard K. Mbenga, and Robert Ross (eds.), *The Cambridge History of South Africa, Vol. 1, From Early Times to 1885*. Cambridge University Press, 2014. 211–252.

Xenos, Nicholas. *Scarcity and Modernity*. London: Routledge, 1989.

Xu Yaotong. 'The Issues Concerning Intra-Party Democracy Need to Be Explored'. *Xianzheng Shehui Zhuyi Luncong* [Constitutional Socialism Forum] 3–4 (2012): 345–349.

Yang Lai Fong, and Md. Sidin Ahmad Ishak. 'Framing Religious Disputes: A Comparative Analysis of the Lina Joy Controversy Reported by Malaysian Newspapers'. *The Journal of the South East Asia Research Centre for Communication and Humanities* 3.2 (2011): 21–37.

'Yang Xiaoqing'. 'A Comparative Study of Constitutionalism and People's Democratic System'. *Hongqiwengao* [Red Papers] No. 10 (2013): 4–10.

Yatim, Rais. 'The Road to Mardeka'. In Andrew J. Harding and H. P. Lee (eds.), *Constitutional Landmarks in Malaysia: The First 50 Years, 1957–2007*. Singapore: LexisNexis, 2007. 1–24.

Yeung, Karen. 'Government by Publicity Management: Sunlight or Spin?' *Public Law* 2005: 360–383.

Yu, Harlan, and David G. Robinson. 'The New Ambiguity of "Open Government"'. *UCLA Law Review Discourse* (2012): 178–208.

Zagor, Matthew. 'England and the Rediscovery of Constitutional Faith'. ANU College of Law Working Paper. Canberra: Australian National University, July 30, 2009. Available at http://papers.ssrn.com/sol3/papers.cfm?abstract_id=1445138.

Zhang Zhixin. 'An Overview of the Socialist Constitutionalism Study'. *Xianzheng Shehui Zhuyi Luncong* [Constitutional Socialism Forum] 2 (2011): 148–149.

Zhao Tao. 'Department of Propaganda and Other Departments Hold a Study Meeting on the Constitution'. *People Daily*, March 26, 2004, at 4.

Zhen Zhixue. 'Understanding the Essence of "Constitutionalism"'. *Dangjian* [Party Construction] No. 6 (2013): 29–31.

Zhou Shuzhi. 'On the Origin of Constitutional Socialism School in China'. *Xianzheng Shehui Zhuyi Luncong* [Constitutional Socialism Forum] 3–4 (2012).

Zhu, Suli. '"Judicial Politics" as State-building'. In Stéphanie Balme and Michael W. Dowdle (eds.), *Building Constitutionalism in China*. New York: Palgrave Macmillan, 2009. 23–36.

Ziadeh, Farhat J. *Lawyers, the Rule of Law and Liberalism in Modern Egypt*. Palo Alto, CA: Hoover Institution on War, Revolution, and Peace, 1968.

Zweig, Egon. *Die Lehre vom Pouvoir Constituant*. Tübingen, Germany: Mohr, 1909.

INDEX

Lightning Source UK Ltd.
Milton Keynes UK
UKHW020407060321
379883UK00005B/84

9 781107 112759